PENGUIN BOOKS

JFK'S LAST HUNDRED DAYS

'A real page-turner . . . deftly weaves together the private, personal, and
te with the public, the political, and the-then-secret public and political,
ikes one want to keep reading to find out even more of the scoop'
Harvey J. Kaye, *Daily Beast*

thusiasm is infectious . . . he entertains and illuminates, writing gracefully,
d with a fine sense of irony . . . He's funny and he's fair and he swims well
gainst powerful cultural cross-currents' *The New York Times Book Review*

'Earnestly exuberant . . . Clarke is an intrepid researcher' *New Yorker*

Clarke does an interesting and in many ways persuasive job of what he
oposes at the beginning: "to view John F. Kennedy through every prism
earch through all his compartments during the crucial last hundred days
ife – days that saw him finally beginning to realize his potential as a man
a president – in order to solve the most tantalizing mystery of all: not who
killed him, but who he *was* when he was killed, and where he would have
led us."' Jonathan Yardley, *Washington Post*

Thurston Clarke's *JFK's Last Hundred Days* manages to surprise and . . . to
delight' *Associated Press*

'Clarke is a good storyteller . . . [He] offers an enjoyable snapshot of the
day-to-day workings of the presidency' *Economist*

'Brilliantly captures Kennedy's entire life through the prism of his final
onths. Deliberately thrusting his crotch for an official portrait, musing about
sassination (he even acts it out in a game of charades, covered in ketchup),
folding his monogrammed handkerchiefs to hide the initials because he
disliked ostentatious wealth, putting a black marine at the centre of a
ceremonial line-up . . . the hero, like the devil, is in the detail'
Mark Mason, Spectator, Books of the Year

[A] compelling portrait of one of the towering figures of twentieth-century
America' *Christian Science Monitor*

'Certainly demonstrates that three often painful years in office had
taught Kennedy valuable lessons . . . Clarke delivers a thoroughly
delightful portrait' *Kirkus Reviews*

'A fascinating analysis of what was . . . and what might have been' *Booklist*

'A graceful, bittersweet chronicle . . . Clarke clearly admires Kennedy but does
not

D1412935

ABOUT THE AUTHOR

Thurston Clarke has written eleven widely acclaimed works of fiction and non-fiction on travel and modern history including *Ask Not: The Inauguration of John F. Kennedy and the Speech That Changed America*. His articles have appeared in *Vanity Fair*, the *New York Times*, the *Washington Post* and many other publications.

JFK's Last Hundred Days

An Intimate Portrait of a Great President

THURSTON CLARKE

973. 922092

PENGUIN BOOKS

PENGUIN BOOKS

Published by the Penguin Group
Penguin Books Ltd, 80 Strand, London WC2R 0RL, England
Penguin Group (USA) Inc., 375 Hudson Street, New York, New York 10014, USA
Penguin Group (Canada), 90 Eglinton Avenue East, Suite 700, Toronto, Ontario, Canada M4P 2Y3
(a division of Pearson Penguin Canada Inc.)
Penguin Ireland, 25 St Stephen's Green, Dublin 2, Ireland (a division of Penguin Books Ltd)
Penguin Group (Australia), 707 Collins Street, Melbourne, Victoria 3008, Australia
(a division of Pearson Australia Group Pty Ltd)
Penguin Books India Pvt Ltd, 11 Community Centre, Panchsheel Park, New Delhi – 110 017, India
Penguin Group (NZ), 67 Apollo Drive, Rosedale, Auckland 0632, New Zealand
(a division of Pearson New Zealand Ltd)
Penguin Books (South Africa) (Pty) Ltd, Block D, Rosebank Office Park,
181 Jan Smuts Avenue, Parktown North, Gauteng 2193, South Africa

Penguin Books Ltd, Registered Offices: 80 Strand, London WC2R 0RL, England

www.penguin.com

First published in the United States of America by The Penguin Press,
part of Penguin Group (USA) Inc. 2013
First published in Great Britain by Allen Lane 2013
Published in Penguin Books 2014
001

ISBN: 978–0–141–04807–9

www.greenpenguin.co.uk

For Kathy Robbins and David Halpern

December 31, 1962

THE PORTRAIT

What makes journalism so fascinating, and biography so interesting [is] the struggle to answer that single question: "What's he like."

—*John F. Kennedy*

Elaine de Kooning, a garrulous, promiscuous, hard-drinking Greenwich Village bohemian who had flirted with communism and championed the death-row inmate Caryl Chessman, came to the Kennedy estate in Palm Beach on the morning of December 31, 1962, to paint a portrait of President John F. Kennedy for the Truman Library in Independence, Missouri. The artist William Walton, a close friend of the president and First Lady, had recommended her because he knew that Kennedy was too restless to tolerate a formal sitting and expected that de Kooning, who was known as "The Fastest Brush in the East," could finish a portrait after a single session. After years of working in the shadow of her estranged husband, the famous abstract artist Willem de Kooning, she had earned a reputation as a figurative expressionist who could capture the essence of a subject in the vivid colors and bold brushstrokes of abstract art, and Walton and the Truman Library trustees were undoubtedly expecting a portrait like her celebrated take on the painter Robert De Niro, Sr. (father of the actor Robert De Niro), praised by one dealer as "a stunning resemblance that expresses so much character in a nearly abstract painting."

She arrived to find Kennedy huddled on the patio with reporters and had trouble picking him out. She had expected, she said, the "gray, sculptural" man of the newspaper photographs. Instead, he was "incandescent, golden" and "bigger than life," no taller than the other men, but inhabiting "a different dimension." She had planned on making some quick sketches and finishing the portrait in the temporary studio she had established in an abandoned West Palm Beach theater. But after a morning with him, she decided he was too intriguing and changeable a subject for a single sitting to suffice and stayed four days. She perched on a ladder above him, sat on a stool opposite him, or stood at an easel, watching as he nervously riffled through papers, patted his hair, and crossed and uncrossed his legs. Phones rang; aides hurried across the flagstone patio; his son, John Jr., tossed pebbles into the swimming pool; and his daughter, Caroline, appeared and stood next to de Kooning with her own easel, sketching him until he came over and drew a cat on her pad.

De Kooning drew him sitting and standing, full face and in profile, arms akimbo or folded over his chest, wearing dark glasses or squinting into the sun. She was a handsome and lively woman whose wit was as quick as her brush. They joked, flirted, and he threw a leg over the arm of a chair, putting his crotch at the center of her sketch and asking, "Is this pose all right?"

"Well, it's supposed to be an official portrait," she said.

He smiled and held the pose.

She thought, *I'll take what I get,* and kept working.

She papered the theater with sketches, charcoals, and watercolors, and worked late into the night. The more she drew him, the more he fascinated her, and frustrated her attempts to capture his essence in a single portrait. She began working on several canvases at once. She was intrigued by his "transparent ruddiness," how his smile and frown both appeared "built-in to the bone," "the curious faceted structure of light over his face and hair," and the way this contributed to his "extraordinary variety of expressions." She was mesmerized by his eyes—"incredible eyes with large violet irises half veiled by the jutting bone beneath his eyebrows"—and liked the way he instinctively assumed "the graceful positions of a college athlete." She told friends she was "in love with his mind" and captivated "by the idea of such a gallant, intelligent, handsome man leading the country and the world." She also admitted falling "a teeny little bit in love with him."

She returned to New York with dozens of sketches and uncompleted portraits. Soon there were more. She realized that she had seen only one facet of him while his staff saw another, as did a public that saw him only on a two-dimensional television screen or in a photograph. She began sketching him when he appeared on television, and clipping his photographs from newspapers and magazines, tacking them to her walls and using them as models for more drawings and oils. Soon she was painting only him.

Walton visited her studio in early November 1963 to find photographs and sketches of Kennedy scattered across the floor, and the walls covered with so many of her studies that she had to climb a ladder to reach them all. Thirty-eight oils between two and eleven feet high and in various stages of completion leaned against walls and sat on easels. He was larger than life and smaller, youthful and athletic, mature and reserved, wearing a two-button suit or polo shirt, standing or sitting in the eye of a hurricane of vibrant colors. After running out of space, she had papered her living quarters with more sketches and photographs so that whenever she cooked, ate, took a bath, used the toilet, or made love, she saw him. A photograph shows her surrounded by photographs, drawings, and oils, as if trapped in a maze of mirrors reflecting and re-reflecting his image. It was testimony to the difficulty and vastness of the task she had assumed: capturing the essence of one of the most complicated and enigmatic men ever to occupy the White House.

The playwright Robert Sherwood once spoke of Franklin D. Roosevelt's "heavily forested interior." Kennedy's was, by comparison, the heart of the Amazon. His friend and groomsman Edmund Gullion spoke of "a shrinking from ostentation or display or for revealing himself or letting go with his emotions that doesn't give the chronicler much to go on." Laura Bergquist of *Look,* who understood him better than any other female reporter, believed that no one "knew the total of him" and called him the "prismatic president" because of the way he cultivated people to serve different needs and play different roles. When she asked, "What does it feel like to be president?" he had nervously rubbed his ankles, fingered his tie, jumped up from his rocking chair, and paced around the room before saying, "Let's go on to another question. I'm not very good at that couch talk."

Ted Sorensen, who had been his principal aide and speechwriter for ten years but seldom socialized with him, decided that "different parts of his life, works, and thoughts were seen by many people—but no one saw it all," adding, "He sometimes obscured his motives and almost always shielded his emotions."

After observing him during the 1960 campaign, the author Norman Mailer concluded that his most characteristic quality was "the remote and private air of a man who has traversed some lonely terrain of experience, of loss and gain, of nearness to death, which leaves him isolated from the mass of others." The journalist Charlie Bartlett, who had introduced him to Jackie, said flatly, "No one ever knew John Kennedy, not all of him."

Because he compartmentalized his friends and family, parts of him remained hidden even to those who thought they knew him best. His brother Bobby was his attorney general and de facto assistant president, but when he and the former cabinet member Abraham Ribicoff went sailing off Palm Beach after Dallas, Ribicoff was shocked to find that he knew things about Jack that Bobby did not. The experience confirmed his sense that Kennedy was a "very introverted man" who had "kept a lot of things to himself," and had "only exposed different facets of himself to different people." He even bewildered Jackie, who called him "a simple man, yet so complex that he would frustrate anyone trying to understand him," and "a romantic, although he didn't like people to know that." She concluded that "to reveal yourself is difficult and almost dangerous for people like that [the Kennedys]—I'd say Jack didn't want to reveal himself at all."

His fondness for secrecy contributed to his elusiveness. He took French lessons and swore his teacher to silence because he wanted to "surprise the world." He sent a friend abroad as a clandestine emissary without informing the State Department, and asked a neighbor in Hyannis Port to run a parallel campaign organization, telling him to communicate via a post office box and coded address so that his secretary Evelyn Lincoln could give it to him directly, and "nobody else's eyes will get to see it."

His contradictory qualities were another barrier. He was a brass-knuckles politician and an idealist whose rhetoric encouraged nobility and sacrifice; a reckless driver but a cautious politician; a man who disliked close physical contact, even with his best friends, but who had a voracious sexual appetite. He was known for his wit and humanity, and for being chilly and remote. He gave the impression of being comfortable in his own skin, but he abhorred solitude. More than most presidents—more than most middle-aged men—he was a work in progress, a moving target for anyone trying to capture him on a canvas or in prose. The literary critic Alfred Kazin decided his most essential quality was "that of the man who is always making and remaking himself," and called him "the final product of a fanatical job of self-remodeling."

When Kennedy was a young man his father frequently told him, "Can't you get it into your head that it's not important what you really are? The only important thing is what people *think* you are!" He took this advice to heart, perhaps too much. Mailer wondered if his "elusive detachment" signified "the fortitude of a superior sensitivity or the detachment of a man who was not quite real to himself." Bergquist detected a vulnerability and insecurity, "not simply because he was part of the upward-mobile Irish, but because I think he recognized himself as an image that had been manufactured. And the question came up: 'Who loves me and wants me for myself, and who loves me for what they think I am, and what I can do?'" While attempting to seduce a young Pulitzer Prize–winning historian in 1953 he had leaped up from a sofa, grabbed her by the shoulders, and exclaimed, "I'm sad; I'm gay; I'm melancholy; I'm gloomy—I'm all mixed up, and don't know how I am!"

De Kooning's obsession may have bordered on madness, but her approach was sound. She understood that to discover the essence of a man who compartmentalized his life, you had to look into all his compartments, and to paint a portrait of a prismatic president, you had to view him through every prism. The following attempts to do with words what she was attempting with paints: to view John F. Kennedy through every prism and search through all his compartments during the crucial last hundred days of his life—days that saw him finally beginning to realize his potential as a man and a president—in order to solve the most tantalizing mystery of all: not who killed him, but who he *was* when he was killed, and where he would have led us.

PART ONE

August 7–14, 1963

PROLOGUE TO THE
LAST HUNDRED DAYS

Even though people may be well known, they still hold in their hearts the emotions of a simple person for the moments that are the most important of those we know on earth—birth, marriage, and death.

—Jacqueline Kennedy

Wednesday, August 7–Saturday, August 10

WASHINGTON, CAPE COD,
AND BOSTON

J ohn F. Kennedy's second son was born twenty years to the day after the
Navy rescued Kennedy from the group of Pacific islands where he had
been marooned for five days after a Japanese destroyer rammed his torpedo boat, *PT 109*, slamming him against the cockpit wall and killing two
crewmen. The medal that he won for "courage, endurance, and excellent leadership" and "extremely heroic conduct" during these five days, and John Hersey's
account of his heroics in *The New Yorker*, became the early engines of his political career. He answered questions about his exploits with a self-deprecating "It
was involuntary, they sank my boat," but he arranged things so that seldom a
moment passed without his eyes resting on some reminder of *PT 109*. When he
looked across the Oval Office he saw a scale model of the boat on a shelf, and
when he looked up from his papers he saw on his desk the coconut shell onto
which he had carved his SOS: "Nauro Isl Commander—Native knows Pos'it—
He can pilot 11 alive—Need small boat—Kennedy." When he emerged from his
helicopter at the family compound in Hyannis Port he heard his nieces
and nephews chanting, "In 'forty-three, they went to sea! / Thirteen men and
Kennedy! / To seek the blazing enemy!" and saw on the beach the dinghy he had
christened *PT 109½*. Twice a day he swam the breaststroke in the White House
pool, the same stroke he had used while towing a badly burned crewman through
shark-infested waters for five hours, gripping the strap of his life preserver in his
teeth. Every morning he fastened his tie with a metal clasp shaped like a torpedo
boat with "PT 109" stamped on its bow, and because he had given copies of this

clasp to his friends and aides, he saw it whenever they walked into his office. All of which may explain why Kennedy's friend and fellow World War II naval veteran Ben Bradlee is certain that when Evelyn Lincoln hurried into the Oval Office at 11:43 a.m. on August 7, 1963, to report that Jackie had gone into premature labor on Cape Cod, there was "no way on God's earth" that he did not think, *My child is being born twenty years to the day after I was rescued,* a coincidence providing an additional emotional dimension to a day that would be among his most traumatic.

Jackie had been scheduled for a cesarean section at Washington's Walter Reed Army Hospital in September, but because John Kennedy, Jr., had arrived prematurely almost three years earlier, the Air Force had prepared a suite for her at the Otis Air Force Base Hospital. Kennedy had asked her obstetrician, John Walsh, and her White House physician, Janet Travell, to vacation on the Cape that summer. He called Travell before flying to Otis, and she reported that Walsh had taken Jackie to the hospital and was preparing to perform an emergency cesarean. Jackie would be fine, she said, but a baby born six weeks prematurely had only a fifty/fifty chance of surviving.

If there was ever a time when Kennedy could imagine beating these odds, it was the summer of 1963, a splendid season that his brother Bobby recalled being "the happiest time of his administration." On June 28 he had given his *Ich bin ein Berliner* oration, a stirring summation of the difference between democratic and totalitarian states (and probably the finest speech delivered by an American president on foreign soil), to a quarter of a million Germans filling the future John F. Kennedy Platz. After Air Force One took off for Dublin he told Ted Sorensen, "We'll never have another day like this one as long as we live," but he was soon describing his visit to his ancestral villages in Ireland as the three happiest days of his life. The day after returning from Europe he went to Hyannis Port for a Fourth of July he called "the greatest weekend of my life." After disembarking from his helicopter he had embraced Jackie, surprising reporters who had never seen them hug or walk arm in arm. The weather had been superb, three sparkling summer days. He felt healthier than he had in years, "bursting with vigor," according to Dr. Travell. He took long swims, flew kites with John off the back of the *Honey Fitz,* the presidential cabin cruiser, and because his chronic back pain had largely vanished, played golf for the first time since 1961. He screened a film of his Irish trip on three straight evenings, and when he could not persuade anyone but his brother Ted to sit through it again they watched it alone, prompting his former Navy buddy Paul ("Red") Fay to complain, "All we are getting here still is his Irish visit. . . . Jack brings the conversation back round to it and invariably shows the film which I have now seen for the sixth time."

He had been a detached father when John and Caroline were infants, telling Fay, "I don't understand how you can get such a big kick out of your children. . . . Certainly nothing they are going to say is going to stimulate you." But once Caroline began talking, they forged a closer relationship, and by the summer of 1963 John had become a rambunctious and personable little boy. When Kennedy arrived at Hyannis Port he would shout, "It's time for Father and Son to get to know each other." John would dash into his arms and they would fall onto the lawn so he could hold the boy in the air, tickling him and saying, "John, aren't you lucky to have a dad who plays with you like this?" His newfound rapport with his children had increased his excitement for his next one, and as he passed Lincoln's desk he often told her, "Soon you'll have three coming over to get candy from your candy dish."

There had been rocky periods in his marriage, but Jackie's pregnancy had brought them closer. Fay and his wife, Anita, had been their houseguests the weekend before Jackie went into labor. When Kennedy failed to appear for an excursion, Fay went upstairs and found them lying in bed, arms wrapped around each other, more intimate than he had ever seen them. Later that weekend Kennedy told Fay, "I'd known a lot of attractive women in my lifetime before I got married, but of all of them there was only one I could have married—and I married her."

After returning to Washington from these summer weekends, he told his friend Dave Powers how much he was enjoying his children and how great everything was. Powers was a puckish, middle-aged Irish American who had been with him since his first campaign. His principal duties involved ushering distinguished visitors into the Oval Office (he had once famously told the Shah of Iran, "You're my kind of shah"), entertaining the president with jokes, reminiscing about earlier campaigns, swimming alongside him in the White House pool, and keeping him company when his family was away, because he was a man, Powers said, who "could not bear to be alone, ever." During the summer of 1963 they often sat together on the Truman Balcony, eating dinner off trays and listening to songs from Kennedy's youth, such as "Stormy Weather" and "The Very Thought of You." The spotlights came on, illuminating the White House fountain and the

Washington Monument, and Kennedy invariably said, "It gets better every night" or "This is the best White House I've ever lived in." When he became sleepy, Powers went upstairs with him, sitting by his bed and talking until he mumbled, "Good night, pal," the signal that Powers could extinguish his light and return to his own family.

The summer of 1963 was also a high point in Kennedy's presidency, "a remarkably intensive but productive period," according to Sorensen. The *Wall Street Journal* reported in its front-page "Washington Wire" on August 9 that "White House optimism grows, little restrained by Washington's summer doldrums. The Kennedy team feels the tide of events runs his way, at home and abroad. The President sees a chance for new accords to ease the cold war. The nation's civil rights crisis seems to come under control. . . . Republican squabbling on issues and candidates pleases him as an omen for 1964."

The chairman of the Joint Chiefs of Staff, General Maxwell Taylor, had known what he called "many President Kennedys." They included the masterful leader of the 1962 Cuban missile crisis, the "supremely confident" man who emerged during the summer of 1963, and the president shaken by the "Bay of Pigs," shorthand for the bungled attempt of CIA-trained Cuban exiles to overthrow the Communist regime of President Fidel Castro in April 1961. The Eisenhower administration had planned the operation, Kennedy's civilian and military advisers had endorsed it, and he had approved what amounted to an amphibious landing on a hostile shore attempted by amateur Cuban soldiers overseen by American amateurs. He shouldered the blame but was furious with the Pentagon and CIA for a fiasco that he feared had mortally wounded his presidency.

As he and a friend drove out of the White House a few weeks after the catastrophe, he smiled and waved at a group of cheering supporters while muttering, "If they think they're going to get me to run for this job again, they're out of their minds." He told his best friend and former prep school roommate Lem Billings that the presidency was "the most unpleasant job in existence," and that he doubted anyone would want to build a library for what was promising to be "a rather tragic administration." He remained pessimistic well into the fall. When the NBC correspondent Elie Abel asked him to cooperate on a book about his first term, he said, "Why would anyone write a book about an administration that has nothing to show for itself but a string of disasters?" But by the summer of 1963, following his successful resolution of the Cuban missile crisis, a strong showing by Democrats in the 1962 elections, and healthy economic growth, he had become almost as happy and confident as President Franklin D. Roosevelt. Like Roosevelt, who had faced the Depression and the Second World War, he was contending with two grave threats to the nation's survival, a nuclear war and a racial conflict. On two successive days in June 1963 he delivered speeches addressing each one that represented a sharp departure from the caution marking his first two years in office.

Contrary to his public image as a dashing and decisive chief executive, Kennedy was, in fact, in the words of his economic adviser Paul Samuelson, "an extremely hesitant person who checked the ice in front of him all the time." Winning the White House by about 113,000 votes out of the 69 million cast, the narrowest margin in almost a century, had encouraged his caution and pragmatism. There had been much ice checking during his first two years in office, leading the columnist Joseph Kraft to say that his motto could have been "no enemies to the right."

At first, Kennedy had avoided challenging the hard-line cold warriors in either party and resisted engaging the Soviet Union in serious disarmament talks. He changed his mind after the Cuban missile crisis demonstrated how easily a misjudgment by either side could start a nuclear war. The crisis had started in October 1962, when Kennedy learned that the Soviet Union was installing missiles armed with nuclear warheads in Cuba capable of attacking the U.S. mainland. He ordered a naval blockade of the island to prevent the arrival of more Soviet arms, and demanded that the Soviets remove the missiles and bases. For almost a week the two nations teetered on the brink of a nuclear war. The crisis was averted by a deal in which the Soviets agreed to dismantle the missiles and close the bases in exchange for a secret undertaking by Kennedy to do the same with U.S. missiles in Turkey. Kennedy's friend David Ormsby-Gore, who was serving as Britain's ambassador, observed that after the crisis, "he finally realized that the decision for a nuclear holocaust was his. And he saw it in terms of children—his children and everybody else's children. And then that's where his passion came in, that's when his emotions came in." The risk of radioactive fallout had worried him since 1961, when the Soviet Union unilaterally decided to resume atmospheric nuclear tests, forcing him to do the same. When he asked his science adviser Jerome Wiesner how fallout returned to the earth from the upper atmosphere, Wiesner explained that it came down in the rain. Staring at the rain falling in the Rose Garden, Kennedy said, "You mean there might be radioactive contamination in that rain out there right now?"

He used a June 10, 1963, commencement address at American University to announce his own unilateral suspension of atmospheric nuclear tests and to propose negotiations in Moscow aimed at drafting a treaty banning nuclear testing in the atmosphere, underground, underneath the oceans, and in outer space. The speech was a dramatic break from eighteen years of cold war rhetoric by Presidents Truman and Eisenhower, and himself. He blamed both sides for the arms race, called on Americans to "reexamine our own attitude—as individuals and as a Nation," acknowledged Russia's wartime sacrifices, declared that "no government or social system is so evil that its people must be considered as lacking in virtue," and reminded Americans that they and the Soviet people "breathe the same air," "cherish our children's future," and "are all mortal," expressing these truths so eloquently that one British newspaper called the address "one of the greatest state papers of American history." Soviet newspapers reprinted its entire text and Soviet leader Nikita Khrushchev praised it as the best speech by any American president since Roosevelt.

The next day Kennedy delivered a nationally televised address on civil rights that James Farmer of the Congress of Racial Equality (CORE) lauded as the "strongest civil rights speech made by any president, Lincoln included." After saying that "race has no place in American life or law," he announced that he was sending Congress a comprehensive civil rights bill guaranteeing all citizens the right to be served in hotels, restaurants, retail stores, and other public facilities. If passed, it would represent the most dramatic advance in civil rights since the Supreme Court's 1954 decision in *Brown v. Board of Education* declared separate public schools for black and white students to be unconstitutional. As in his American University speech, he asked Americans to exercise their moral imaginations. After reminding whites that black citizens could not eat in public restaurants, send their children to the best public schools, or vote for their representatives, he asked, "Who among us would be content to have the color of his skin changed and stand in his place?" When he finished, Dr. Martin Luther King, Jr., told a companion, "Can you believe that white man not only stepped up to the plate, he hit it over the fence!" The next day King sent him a telegram praising the speech as "eloquent, passionate and unequivocal . . . a hallmark in the annals of American history." King and Farmer would have been even more impressed had they known that all of Kennedy's senior advisers except his brother Bobby had opposed him delivering a speech framing the issue in moral terms, and submitting a civil rights bill to Congress.

In *Profiles in Courage,* his Pulitzer Prize–winning biography of eight U.S. senators who had chosen principle over political expediency, he had written about men who, much like himself until 1963, had "sailed with the wind until the decisive moment when their conscience, and events, propelled them into the center of the storm." His two June speeches represented just that moment, and some of the remarks he made after delivering them sounded as if he were nominating himself for a chapter in his own book. After the test ban treaty was initialed in Moscow, he told Sorensen he would "gladly" forfeit reelection to win the sixty-seven votes needed to ratify it in the Senate. After a Gallup poll reported that 50 percent of Americans believed he was moving "too fast" on civil rights, he told a reporter at a press conference, "Great historical events cannot be judged by taking the national temperature every few weeks. . . . I think we will stand after a period of time has gone by," and said to his secretary of commerce, Luther Hodges, a former Southern governor, "There comes a time when a man has to take a stand and history will record that he has to meet these tough situations and ultimately make a decision." During a White House meeting with civil rights leaders he pulled a scrap of paper from his pocket containing the results of a poll showing his approval ratings falling from 60 to 47 percent since his speech and said grandiloquently, "I may lose the next election because of this. I don't care."

His June speeches had been a decisive break from the past: one offered the first concrete proposals for limiting the spread and testing of atomic weapons since the beginning of the cold war; the other represented the first time an American president had identified civil rights as a moral issue. They condemned racial discrimination and nuclear war as immoral, stressed the common humanity of whites and blacks, and Americans and Russians, and were profoundly optimistic. At American University he had said, "Our problems are man-made; therefore they can be solved by man. And man can be as big as he wants. No problem of human destiny is beyond human beings." The following evening, he declared that passage of his civil rights bill would enable America "to fulfill its promise." The author and peace activist Norman Cousins, who had been serving as a clandestine intermediary between Kennedy and Khrushchev, spoke of "a new spirit of hopefulness" abroad in the world that summer, writing, "Nothing is more powerful than an individual acting out of his conscience, thus helping to bring the collective conscience to life."

The political scientist James MacGregor Burns had concluded his 1960 biography of Kennedy by writing, "Kennedy could bring bravery and wisdom [to the presidency]; whether he would bring passion and power would depend on his making a commitment not only of mind, but of heart, that until now he has never been required to make." Kennedy's two speeches answered Burns's criticism and honored a pledge he had made to the poet Robert Frost. During a visit to the White House two days after the inauguration, Frost had presented him with a signed and handwritten copy of the poem that he had composed for the ceremony but could not read because of the glare from a dazzling winter sun. As Frost watched, Kennedy read the poem, which amounted to a challenge to display the kind of courage that he had celebrated in *Profiles in Courage* and concluded by predicting,

A golden age of poetry and power
Of which this noonday's the beginning hour.

"Be more Irish than Harvard," Frost said as they parted. "Poetry and power is the formula for another Augustan age. Don't be afraid of power." At the bottom of a typed thank-you note to Frost, Kennedy scrawled, "It's poetry and power all the way!"

There had been poetry in his early speeches. In November 1961, he warned students at the University of Washington that "the United States is neither omnipotent nor omniscient. . . . We cannot right every wrong or reverse each adversity." During the Cuban missile crisis he spoke of a nuclear war "in which even the fruits of victory would be ashes in our mouths," and said, "Our goal is not the victory of might, but the vindication of right." But it was not until June 1963 that he finally began to be more Irish than Harvard, governing from the heart as well as the head, harnessing poetry to the power of the presidency without checking the thickness of the political ice, promising in his American University speech, "Not the peace of the grave or the security of the slave . . . not merely peace for Americans, but peace for all men and women—not merely peace in our time but peace in all time," and the next day calling civil rights a moral issue "as old as the scriptures and . . . as clear as the American Constitution."

JACKIE GAVE BIRTH to their son while Kennedy was in the air. He sat silently during the flight, staring out a window. Another passenger remembered seeing the same stricken expression on his face on November 25, 1960, when he had flown back to Washington from Palm Beach after learning that Jackie had gone into premature labor with John. He had been tense and perspiring then, and was overheard muttering, "I'm never there when she needs me."

Jackie had suffered a miscarriage in 1955 and had become pregnant again the following year. Her physician had urged her to skip the 1956 Democratic Convention, but she felt obliged to attend because her husband was a candidate for the vice presidency. She went to her mother and stepfather's estate in Newport afterward while he flew to Europe for a holiday. While he was cruising off Capri with what one newspaper called "several young women," she went into labor and gave birth to a stillborn baby girl they planned to name Arabella, after the tiny ship that had accompanied the *Mayflower*. He did not hear about the tragedy until three days later and decided to continue the cruise, leaving Bobby to comfort Jackie and bury Arabella. He flew home after one of his best friends in the Senate, George Smathers of Florida, told him during a transatlantic call, "You'd better haul your ass back to your wife if you want to run for president."

Jackie spent most of the autumn of 1956 in Newport and London, avoiding Hyannis Port and telling her sister, Lee Radziwill, that her marriage was probably over. But when she gave birth to Caroline a year later he arrived at the hospital carrying a bouquet of her favorite flowers, periwinkle-blue irises, and was the first to lay their daughter in her arms. He boasted of her being the prettiest baby in the nursery, and his voice broke when he described her to Lem Billings, who had never seen him happier or more emotional. Caroline had repaired some of the post-Arabella damage, and John's birth would also bring them closer, but neither ended his philandering.

Before flying to Otis he had called Larry Newman, a journalist and friend who lived across the street from the Kennedy compound in Hyannis Port, and asked him to drive to the base hospital and wait for him in the lobby. When he arrived, he began to throw an arm over Newman's shoulder but stopped in midair and shook his hand instead. "Thanks for being here," he said in a voice so choked with emotion that Newman almost burst into tears.

Dr. Walsh reported that his son, whom he and Jackie had decided to name Patrick, was suffering from "hyaline membrane disease" (now known as respiratory distress syndrome), a common ailment among premature infants in which a film covering the air sacs of the lungs hinders their ability to supply oxygen to the bloodstream. The chances that a five-and-a-half-week-premature infant weighing 4 pounds 10½ ounces with this ailment would survive in 1963 were, as Travell had warned, only fifty/fifty. (The chances have since improved dramatically.) Kennedy flew in a pediatric specialist who recommended sending Patrick to Children's Hospital in Boston, the premier medical center in the world for childhood diseases. Before an ambulance took the infant away he wheeled him into Jackie's room in an isolette, a pressurized incubator simulating the oxygen and temperature conditions of the womb. The boy lay motionless on his back, a name band hanging loosely around his tiny wrist. Hospital personnel described him as "beautifully formed" and "a cute little monkey with light brown hair." Jackie was not permitted to hold him and became upset after learning that he was going to Boston.

She had suffered months of postpartum depression following John's birth, and Kennedy feared it might happen again. He pulled aside an Air Force medic, Richard Petrie, and asked what he knew about television. Puzzled by the question, Petrie said, "Well, I can turn one on and off." Kennedy explained that if Patrick died he did not want Jackie hearing the news on television, and to prevent this happening he wanted Petrie to disable her set. The medic slipped back into her room, pried off the back of her television, and smashed a tube.

"Nothing must happen to Patrick," Kennedy told his mother-in-law, Janet Auchincloss, before flying to Boston, "because I just can't bear to think of the effect it might have on Jackie."

A jubilant crowd at Logan Airport, either unaware of Patrick's condition or unable to believe that anything bad could happen to such a charmed family, greeted him with cheers and applause. Flashbulbs popped and girls screamed and held out autograph books. He offered a tight smile and a halfhearted wave.

There was no cure for hyaline membrane disease in 1963, and an infant survived only if its normal bodily functions dissolved the membrane coating the lungs within forty-eight hours. Kennedy had consulted the best physicians and sent his son to the best hospital. Now all he could do was wait. He spent the night at his family's apartment in the Ritz Hotel. Before returning to Children's Hospital the next morning, he called Ted Sorensen to review his formal statement accompanying the presentation of the test ban treaty to Congress. It called the agreement "the finest concrete result of eighteen years of effort by the United States to impose limits on the nuclear arms race" and said it embodied "the hopes of the world." Sorensen remembered him reading these sentences out loud in "a downcast but factual manner."

Patrick's breathing stabilized, and Kennedy returned to Otis to deliver the news to Jackie. She was so encouraged that she spent the afternoon choosing lipsticks and arranging for a ballet company to entertain Emperor Haile Selassie during his state visit in October. Kennedy returned to their rented house on Squaw Island—a spit of land connected to Hyannis Port by a causeway—and lunched on the terrace with Janet Auchincloss and her eighteen-year-old daughter, also named Janet. Young Janet was supposed to have her society debut in Newport the next weekend but wanted to cancel it because of Patrick. Hearing this, Kennedy said, "This is the kind of thing that has to go on. You can't let all those people down." Knowing she was self-conscious about her weight, he added, "You know, Janet, you really are a very beautiful girl." Her face lit up and she said, "Oh, Mr. President, I don't know what you mean." Her mother believed that this last-minute flattery gave her the confidence to have the party.

Patrick's condition suddenly deteriorated, and Kennedy rushed back to Children's Hospital by helicopter, landing on the grass of a nearby stadium. The boy's physicians had decided to force oxygen into his lungs by placing him in a hyperbaric chamber, a thirty-one-foot-long steel cylinder resembling a small submarine, with portholes and air locks between its compartments. It was the only one in the country and had been used for infants undergoing cardiac surgery and victims of carbon monoxide poisoning. Patrick would be the first hyaline membrane baby placed inside it.

Upon returning to the Ritz, Kennedy asked Evelyn Lincoln to bring him some White House stationery. She found him sitting on his bed, staring into space. After a full minute of silence he wrote on a sheet of paper, "Please find enclosed a contribution to the O'Leary fund. I hope it is a success." He enclosed a check for $250 (worth about $1,800 today), sealed the envelope, and told her to have the Secret Service deliver it. Weeks later, an accountant handling his personal finances informed Lincoln that a bank was questioning the validity of his signature on an August 8 check to the James B. O'Leary Fund. She recalled reading about a Boston policeman named O'Leary who had been killed in the line of duty. Kennedy had been so distraught about Patrick that his handwriting on the check was even more indecipherable than usual.

KENNEDY HAD ALMOST DIED from scarlet fever when he was two years old. His temperature rose to 105, blisters covered his body, and he was quarantined in a Boston hospital. His father attended Mass every morning for three weeks and promised God to donate half his wealth to charity if his son survived. He kept his word, up to a point, sending a check for $3,750 to the Guild of Apollonia, an organization of Catholic dentists providing free dental care to needy children. It was a generous sum for the time but could have represented only half the money in his personal bank account, not half his net worth. It would be surprising if Kennedy, like his father and most other parents in his situation, had not bargained with God. Perhaps the O'Leary check was part of the deal. If it was, and the Almighty was keeping score, He could have added it to a long list of acts of thoughtfulness and compassion on Kennedy's part, some trivial but nevertheless part of a pattern.

While serving in the Pacific he had torn the *PT 109* patch off his shirt and mailed it to a cousin who was homesick at boarding school along with a note saying, "I'm not so crazy about where I'm at either, kiddo. Be brave. Wear my patch, and we'll get through this." While staying with Paul Fay in California during leave from the Navy he was so charmed by Margaret ("Miggie") McMahon, the Irish nursemaid who had raised Fay, that he began calling her every year on her birthday, a tradition he continued throughout his life, making his last call from the White House in 1963. While rushing to grab a quick lunch, he had noticed a group of spastic children touring the White House grounds in wheelchairs and insisted on engaging each child in a lengthy conversation. When a boy mentioned that his father had also served in a PT boat squadron, he darted back into his office, found his PT boat skipper's hat, and placed it on the boy's head. "His father was in PT boats, too," he explained to a Secret Service agent who was wiping away tears. "His father is dead." He studied photographs of the agents so he could address each by his first name. One brutally cold winter evening, he asked the agent on duty outside the French doors leading to the garden to come inside. After the man explained that he could not leave his post, he returned with his own fleece-lined coat and insisted he wear it, then reappeared with two mugs of hot chocolate that they drank while sitting on the icy steps.

His practice of moving those who disappointed him to other jobs rather than dismissing them led Undersecretary of State George Ball to conclude that he was "deeply concerned with other people's feelings and sensitivities to the point of being almost physically upset by having to fire anyone." David Ormsby-Gore, who made his acquaintance in London when he was a young man, was struck by his "beautiful manners" and courtesy to the elderly. These attributes had helped him win over Eleanor Roosevelt, who nursed a long-standing grudge against the Kennedy family and had criticized him for failing to censure Senator Joseph McCarthy, declaring that she was reluctant to support "someone who understands what courage is and admires it, but has not quite the independence to have it." After he won the nomination, they had scheduled a meeting during which he hoped to persuade her to campaign for him. Her favorite granddaughter had died in a riding accident the day before, but she insisted on proceeding anyway. Several weeks later, she told the staff of Citizens for Kennedy in Cleveland, "That young man behaved with such sensitivity and compassion throughout that whole day, he gave me more comfort than almost anyone around me: the manner in which he treated me . . . won me as did many things he told me he believed in."

Sorensen described Kennedy as "a good and decent man with a conscience that told him what was right and a heart that cared about the well-being of those around him." But he was unaware of Kennedy's compulsive womanizing. A friend who knew the truth offered a more realistic assessment, saying, "For a man who was very kind to people, and was very concerned about how he treated people, Jack was not very conscious about how much he hurt his wife."

After writing his check to the O'Leary fund, Kennedy went to Children's Hospital and stood outside the hyperbaric chamber, watching through a porthole as physicians labored over Patrick. At 6:30 p.m., Salinger told reporters that the boy's "downward spiral" had stopped but his condition remained serious. Kennedy returned to the Ritz, but an hour later Patrick was struggling and he rushed back to the hospital. Bobby Kennedy and Dave Powers flew up from Washington and joined him outside the chamber. Patrick's breathing improved and his physicians urged Kennedy to get some sleep. Reluctant as ever to be alone, he asked Powers to share his hospital room. Powers lay down on a spare cot in his suit while Kennedy changed into his pajamas and knelt by the bed, hands clasped in prayer. Powers and Lem Billings had probably watched Kennedy fall asleep more often than anyone except Jackie. Neither could recall him ever retiring without first praying on his knees. No one can know what he prayed that evening, but it is unlikely that a man who prayed every day, attended Mass every Sunday, and had turned to religion at other emotional moments in his life would not have beseeched God to spare his son, and in the coming weeks and months there would be clues as to what he may have offered Him in return.

Few presidents have been as religiously observant as Kennedy yet reluctant to discuss their faith. He never raised the subject with Sorensen, leaving him wondering if his attendance at Mass was motivated by "political necessity." But he would banter about religion with Jackie's dressmaker Oleg Cassini, telling him, "I'd better keep my nose clean, just in case He's up there," and scolding him for questioning papal infallibility, saying, "The weakness of man should not weaken the image of God." Jackie insisted that he had not been an atheist or an agnostic, and "did believe in God," but sometimes wondered if his bedtime prayers and faithful attendance at Mass were ways of hedging his bets. "If it [the afterlife] was that way," she said, "he wanted to have that [his adherence to Catholic ritual] on his side."

Sometimes one could glimpse his faith. During his first congressional campaign he had astonished his aide Mark Dalton by impulsively ducking back into a church where they had just attended Mass so he could light a candle for his deceased brother. He was sensitive about being the first Catholic president and avoided public displays of piety, but when he attended Mass at the Basilica of the Virgin of Guadalupe during a 1962 visit to Mexico City his emotions trumped his political caution. As Jackie brought a bouquet of red roses to the altar he was so overcome that he crossed himself, causing the congregation to burst into applause. While recuperating in Palm Beach from a 1955 back operation that had almost killed him, he jotted down some ideas for *Profiles in Courage,* including this passage from Job: "Oh that one would hear me! Behold, my desire is that the Almighty would answer me." A tense 1961 summit with Premier Nikita Khrushchev in Vienna left him so shaken that on the plane returning to Washington he scribbled, "I know there is a God—and I see a storm coming; If He has a place for me, I believe I am ready," a quotation he often used in campaign speeches and attributed to Abraham Lincoln. (Evelyn Lincoln found the paper on the floor of Air Force One and squirreled it away with the other notes and doodles that she was constantly rescuing from wastebaskets.) That fall, after the Berlin crisis had cooled, he had slipped out of the White House on National Prayer Day and sat alone in a rear pew at Washington's St. Matthew's Cathedral, leading Hugh Sidey of *Time* to note, "To many who had watched him [Kennedy] through nine months of crisis, it seemed that his church attendance and the reference in his talks to prayer had become less mechanical and more meaningful."

A Secret Service agent woke him at 2:00 a.m. to report that Patrick was struggling. As he hurried to the elevators the nurses in the corridor looked away. He saw a severely burned infant in one of the wards and stopped to ask a nurse for the name of the child's mother so he could send her a note. Holding a piece of paper against the ward window, he wrote, "Keep up your courage. John F. Kennedy."

For several hours he sat on a wooden chair outside the hyperbaric chamber, wearing a surgical cap and gown and communicating with the medical team by speakerphone. Near the end they wheeled Patrick into the corridor so he could be with his father. When the boy died at 4:19 a.m. Kennedy was clutching his little fingers. After saying in a quiet voice, "He put up quite a fight. He was a beautiful baby," he ducked into a boiler room and wept loudly for ten minutes. After returning to his room he sent Powers on an errand so he could cry some more. He broke down outside the hospital and asked an aide to beg a photographer who had captured his grief not to publish the picture.

His eyes were red and his face swollen when he arrived at Otis that morning. As he described Patrick's death to Jackie, he fell to his knees and sobbed.

"There's just one thing I couldn't stand," she said in a faint voice. "If I ever lost you . . ."

"I know . . . I know . . . ," he whispered.

Lincoln called Patrick's death "one of the hardest blows" he had ever experienced. Sorensen thought he was "even more broken" than his wife. Jackie said, "He felt the loss of the baby in the house as much as I did," and noticed him tearing up when he held John. His tears were all the more astonishing given that Joe Kennedy had frequently told his children, "There'll be no crying in this house." They shortened it to "Kennedys don't cry," repeated it to their children, and according to Ted Kennedy, "All of us absorbed its impact and molded our behavior to honor it. We have wept only rarely in public."

Kennedy's friends believed that he grappled with such powerful feelings that he was afraid of having them surface. Laura Bergquist sensed "a reservoir of emotion" under his "cool cat exterior." Ormsby-Gore detected "deep emotions and strong passions underneath," adding that "when his friends were hurt or a tragedy occurred or his child died, I think he felt it very deeply. But somehow public display was anathema to him." Ormsby-Gore compared him to Raymond Asquith, the brilliant son of Prime Minister Herbert Asquith who was killed in the First World War. In *Pilgrim's Way*, one of Kennedy's favorite books, John Buchan wrote about Asquith, "He disliked emotion, not because he felt lightly but because he felt deeply."

Children, family, and heroism could unlock his emotions. His first words to the crew of the PT boat rescuing him in the Pacific had been "Where the hell have you been?" And when someone shouted, "We've got some food for you," he shot back, "Thanks. I've just had a coconut." But the bravado ended at the base, where a friend found him sitting on his cot, tears streaming down his face, saying between sobs, "If only they'd come over to help me, maybe I might have been able to save those other two." While delivering a Veterans Day address in Boston several years after the war, he broke down after saying, "No greater love has a man than he who gives up his life for his brother." (He was probably thinking of his older brother, Joe, who had been killed in the war.) At a Memorial Day event in Brookline he choked up after proclaiming, "The memory of these young men will abide as long as men are found who will set honor and country above all else." Moments after his inauguration Jackie gently touched his cheek and said, "Oh, Jack—what a day!" and saw his eyes fill with tears. After John's birth, Ireland's ambassador, Thomas Kiernan, had recited an Irish poem in the boy's honor that began, "We wish to a new child / a heart that can be beguiled by a flower." Kennedy was so moved that he remained silent for several minutes, not trusting himself to speak without crying. He finally said in a soft voice, "I wish it had been written for me." During the Cuban missile crisis he wept in front of Bobby while speaking about the millions of children who would perish in a nuclear war, and after the Bay of Pigs invasion Jackie saw him put his head in his hands and cry upon learning that hundreds of Cuban exiles had died on the beach. He cried again while discussing the Bay of Pigs casualties with Cardinal Cushing, who would be presiding at Patrick's funeral.

Kennedy asked Judge Francis Morrissey, a close family friend, to arrange the service. Morrissey chose a white gown for Patrick and a small white casket. He ordered it closed because he recalled Kennedy telling him, "Frank, I want you to make sure they close the coffin when I die."

Cushing celebrated the Mass in the chapel of his Boston residence on the morning of August 10. There were thirteen mourners, all members of the Kennedy and Auchincloss families except for Morrissey, Cushing, and Cardinal Spellman of New York. According to Catholic doctrine, baptized children who die before the age of reason go directly to heaven (Patrick had been baptized at the hospital), and the Mass of Angels is designed to be a comforting ceremony emphasizing their purity and eternal life. Kennedy wept throughout. When it ended, he took the money clip fashioned from a gold St. Christopher medal that Jackie had given him at their wedding and slipped it into Patrick's coffin. Then he threw his arms around the coffin, as if planning to carry it away. "Come on, dear Jack, Let's go . . . Let's go," Cushing murmured. "God is good. Nothing more can be done. Death is not the end of it all, but the beginning."

Joseph Kennedy had recently purchased a family plot at Holyhood Cemetery, and Patrick would be the first Kennedy interred there. As Cushing spoke at the grave, John Kennedy's shoulders began heaving. Putting a hand on the coffin, the president said, "Good-bye," then touched the ground and whispered, "It's awfully lonely here." Seeing him bent over the grave, alone and vulnerable, a Secret Service agent asked Cushing, "How do you protect this man?"

Back at Otis, he wept in Jackie's arms while describing the funeral. After recovering his composure he said, "You know, Jackie, we must not create an atmosphere of sadness in the White House, because this would not be good for anyone—not for the country and not for the work we have to do." His reference to "the work we have to do" stressed their partnership in a way that Jackie had to find gratifying, and promising. According to her mother, it made a "profound impression" on her.

Monday, August 12

CAPE COD AND WASHINGTON

Monday was the nineteenth anniversary of the day that Joseph P. Kennedy, Jr., had been killed in action while participating in Operation Aphrodite, a harebrained and ultimately unsuccessful scheme that involved Navy pilots flying B-17 bombers packed with explosives toward German missile sites and U-boat pens on the French coast before bailing out at the last minute into the English Channel. On Monday morning all of the Kennedy siblings except Rosemary, who had been institutionalized in 1944 after a botched lobotomy, and Jack attended a requiem Mass for Joe at St. Francis Xavier Church in Hyannis Port. The White House announced that the president was missing the service because he was visiting Jackie, but it took only twelve minutes to fly by helicopter from Otis to Hyannis Port, so he could have easily done both, and he later found time to take an excursion on the family speedboat.

He did not skip Joe's Mass because he had been any less devastated by his older brother's death than his siblings. Joe had been more athletic and popular in school, and sometimes teased and bullied him, but they had been competitors, not enemies, and he had mourned him deeply, telling Lem Billings that Joe's death had left him "shadowboxing in a match the shadow is always going to win." The headmaster of Choate, the boarding school both had attended, wrote his mother that he would now have to live Joe's life as well as his own. He ended up living Joe's life *instead* of his own, having the brilliant political career that his father had always imagined for Joe.

It was difficult for a Kennedy to be in Hyannis Port and not be reminded of Joe or his sister Kathleen, who had died in a 1948 plane crash. Ted Kennedy called his family's rambling clapboard house "an oasis of stability and family love," and it was the only real home the Kennedy children had known while shuttling between their parents' winter residences in Palm Beach and suburban New York. JFK had lived in dormitories at two boarding schools and three colleges, then in houses and apartments in Washington, but every summer he returned to Hyannis Port. It had been the backdrop for the iconic 1953 photograph on the cover of *Life* showing him and Jackie on a sailboat, barefoot, tanned, and flashing radiant smiles, and the 1962 photograph on the cover of *Look* in which he was driving a golf cart packed with his nieces and nephews, hair flying and mouths open, screaming in delight. It was where he had devised his strategy for the 1960 election and learned that he had won it when Caroline jumped on his bed and said, "Good morning, Mr. President"; and where he and Bobby had acquired houses adjoining their parents' home, so they could play flashlight tag and touch football on the same lawn, swim off the same beach, and sail in the same waters as they had in their youth, glimpsing the ghosts of their younger selves, and those of Kathleen and Joe.

Hyannis Port was also where the family had donated an altar to St. Francis Xavier Church commemorating Joe. To the left of the crucifix a painted image of St. George represented England, from which Joe had taken off on his final mission; to its right was St. Joan of Arc, representing France, his destination. Above them floated the badge of a naval aviator, a pair of wings against a blue background. It was impossible for a Kennedy to attend Mass here and *not* be reminded of Joe's suicidal mission, one for which he had volunteered, hoping to match his younger brother's *PT 109* heroics. Kennedy never mentioned Joe by name in his speeches, perhaps because he feared he might break down, so it is possible that he skipped the Mass on the nineteenth anniversary of Joe's death because he was afraid he would look at this altar and begin weeping, and after Patrick's death he could not bear any more tears.

HE ARRIVED AT THE WHITE HOUSE at 4:00 p.m. on Monday and immediately resumed what he had been doing before his hurried departure on August 7, trying to find sixty-seven senators willing to ratify his test ban treaty.

An hour before Jackie went into labor, he had been chairing a meeting in the Cabinet Room, called to organize the Citizens Committee for a Nuclear Test Ban. Attending were senior aides; cabinet members; James Wadsworth, a former U.S. ambassador to the United Nations; and Norman Cousins, whose conversations with Khrushchev had led to the treaty. Kennedy had been pessimistic about its ratification, complaining that most senators had yet to announce their support, and mail to Congress and the White House had been overwhelmingly negative. Persuading two thirds of the senators to support anything would be difficult enough, he said; persuading them to ratify a treaty this controversial would be a miracle. Fifteen would vote against anything he supported, and if the vote were held that day he thought the treaty would fail, a catastrophe he compared to America's failure to ratify the League of Nations following World War I.

Cousins provided a list of forty-eight prominent individuals who had agreed to serve on a pro-treaty Citizens Committee. Wadsworth warned that retired military officers and Dr. Edwin Teller, the developer of the hydrogen bomb and a lifelong conservative who was an implacable foe of limiting nuclear testing, would argue that fallout was not dangerous and the Soviets were likely to violate the treaty. Kennedy admitted that he was unsure he could even hold his own administration in line, and assumed some in the military and on the Atomic Energy Commission would work behind the scenes to persuade Congress and the press that the treaty threatened national security. The generals opposing it, he said, believed the best solution to a crisis was "to start dropping the big bombs."

While flying to Otis after this meeting he had scribbled "Fullbright" [sic] and "Senate Preparedness Subcommittee" on a slip of paper. Senator William Fulbright of Arkansas, a Democrat, chaired the Foreign Relations Committee, which would hold open hearings on the treaty beginning August 12. The Senate Preparedness Subcommittee was dominated by cold war hawks like Barry Goldwater, Henry Jackson, and Strom Thurmond, and chaired by Senator John Stennis of Mississippi, a treaty opponent who was insisting on closed hearings. After checking into the Ritz that evening, he had written "Joint Chiefs" on another scrap of paper. He believed the treaty could be ratified only if the Joint Chiefs of Staff supported it, and if enough Senate Republicans voted for it to compensate for the defection of Southern Democrats. He had lobbied the chiefs individually at the end of July, and they had agreed to support it in their testimony before the

Senate Foreign Relations Committee in exchange for his endorsement of what became known as the "four safeguards": a robust program of underground testing, the maintenance of modern nuclear laboratories and programs, the capability to resume atmospheric testing promptly if the Soviets withdrew from the treaty or cheated, and an improved capacity to detect violations.

Senator Stennis had summoned the chiefs to closed hearings, and Kennedy feared that if they testified there first, they might voice reservations about the treaty that would be leaked to the press before they could support it openly before Fulbright's committee. To prevent this happening, he telephoned Senate Majority Leader Mike Mansfield when he returned to the White House on Monday to stress the importance of having the chiefs testify before his committee first. He was making "such a big thing" about it, he said, "because, in my opinion, the chiefs are the key and what they will say in public would be more pro-treaty than what they will say under interrogation by Scoop Jackson."

He addressed the second threat to the treaty's ratification, the opposition of Senate Republicans, during an hour-long off-the-record meeting with Senate Minority Leader Everett Dirksen that began at six that evening. His appointment book does not indicate where they met, but since the weather was fine and the matter under discussion so sensitive that Dirksen had insisted on going into the Rose Garden when they first spoke about it during the winter of 1961, they probably went outside, where there was less risk of having their conversation overheard or intercepted by whatever bugs the CIA, FBI, or other government agencies might have installed in the White House without Kennedy's knowledge, a possibility he did not consider all that far-fetched. Secretary of State Dean Rusk had made a point of telling J. Edgar Hoover, the director of the FBI, in front of Kennedy, that if he discovered a hidden microphone or phone taps in his office he would resign and expose him. Bobby Kennedy often looked up at a chandelier in his office and shouted, "You bugging, Hoover? Well, listen to this, you old son of a bitch. . . ." And having bugged the Oval Office himself and kept it a secret from almost everyone in his family and staff, Kennedy had to entertain the possibility that someone might be doing the same thing to him.

In the summer of 1962, he had ordered the Secret Service agent Robert Bouck to install microphones in the Oval Office, the Cabinet Room, and his upstairs study. Bouck had hidden two microphones in the wall sconces of the Cabinet Room. In the Oval Office, he had placed one underneath the coffee table and another in Kennedy's desk. Wires connected them to tape recorders in a locked basement room. Unlike President Nixon's taping system, which ran continuously and recorded everything, Kennedy's was engineered so he could record only the conversations that he wanted to preserve. In the Cabinet Room, he could press a button disguised as a buzzer to activate the system; in the Oval Office, he pressed one on the coffee table or another concealed in the kneehole of his desk. At first, only Bouck, his assistant Chester Miller, and Lincoln knew about the microphones. Bobby Kennedy and Ken O'Donnell learned about the system later, and Dave Powers figured it out after Kennedy cautioned him to watch his language, saying, "I don't want to hear your bad words coming back at me." None of his other senior advisers and members of his cabinet—not even his press secretary, Pierre Salinger; his aides Arthur Schlesinger, Jr., and Ted Sorensen; Secretary of Defense Robert McNamara; or Secretary of State Dean Rusk—knew that he was recording them. His principal motive for taping selected conversations and meetings was probably to provide accurate and irrefutable material for his presidential memoirs. He had been disturbed that soon after the Bay of Pigs fiasco some of his advisers who had endorsed the operation began claiming that they had actually opposed it. His recordings would prevent a recurrence of this type of revisionism.

Secret Service agents swept through the Oval Office several times a week, looking for bugs in his telephones and unscrewing their mouthpieces to search for transistors that could pick up conversations before the scramblers made them unintelligible. Because assassins had attempted to poison foreign political figures with radioactive material hidden in their watches and rings, they swept the room with a Geiger counter and passed a wand over Kennedy's wristwatch. But even these precautions had not persuaded him that his office was safe. Minutes before civil rights leaders gathered in the Oval Office on June 22, 1963, he had taken Martin Luther King, Jr., into the Rose Garden and prefaced his remarks by saying, "I assume you know you're under very close surveillance." King concluded that he was referring to the FBI, and wondered if he was insisting on speaking outdoors because he feared its surveillance might extend into the White House, and that the Oval Office might be bugged. As they walked, he warned King that the government had evidence that two of his close associates were Communist agents, said their presence in his inner circle might imperil passage of the civil rights bill, and urged him to break off contact with them. By warning him of this surveillance he was in effect thwarting an FBI operation and obstructing justice, reason enough to be sure he was not overheard.

Dirksen had seemed concerned about listening devices when he arrived in the winter of 1961 for a hurriedly arranged meeting. "I would like for you to surrender your title for a few minutes and join me for a stroll in the Rose Garden to discuss a very personal and private matter," he had said. "It simply must be two friends—Jack and Ev—talking on a personal basis."

Once they were outside, Dirksen told him that President Eisenhower wanted Kennedy to persuade his brother Attorney General Robert Kennedy to cancel an impending indictment of the former New Hampshire governor Sherman Adams for tax fraud. Adams was a close friend of Eisenhower and had served as his chief of staff before resigning following allegations that he had received an expensive Oriental rug and fur coat from Bernard Goldfine, a Boston businessman under investigation for violating federal trade regulations. Goldfine had now supplied federal agents with documentary evidence indicating that he had also given Adams more than $150,000 in cash during a five-year period. The Justice Department had presented the case to a grand jury and was preparing to indict Adams for failing to pay taxes on the bribes. Adams's wife had told Mamie Eisenhower that she was afraid he would commit suicide if he was indicted, and Eisenhower had told Dirksen, "I was president for eight years, and I think I have the respect of the American people and I want to retain it. I believe the day will come when President Kennedy will need the public assistance of a former president whose name has prestige and who's beyond partisan arrows. I'd like you to ask President Kennedy, as a personal favor to me, to put the Adams indictment in the deep freeze. You have the authority to advise him he'll have a blank check in my bank if he will grant me this favor."

Dirksen sweetened Ike's offer by also promising a blank check on his bank. It was a tempting deal. Eisenhower remained popular, and his support for a bill could influence public opinion and Republican congressmen. (During a 1962 interview with the television networks' White House correspondents, Kennedy had said that Eisenhower had "great influence today in the Republican party, and therefore in the country.") Dirksen's check was even more valuable. Although Democrats controlled both houses of Congress, Southern Democrats opposed much of Kennedy's domestic agenda, making it difficult for him to pass legislation without Republican support.

Kennedy told Dirksen that he was unaware of any case against Adams. They returned to the Oval Office and he called Bobby, who confirmed that an indictment was imminent. "Cancel it, and do it now," he said. "Don't sign the indictment. Place it in the deep freeze." Bobby argued that showing favoritism to a tax cheat could "destroy us politically." As Dirksen listened, their conversation became increasingly heated until he reminded Bobby who was president and said that if he could not comply "your resignation will be accepted."

He did not mention Eisenhower's "blank check" to Bobby, and anyone overhearing (or taping) their conversation would have concluded that he was extending a professional courtesy to a former president, sparing him the embarrassment of having a close associate indicted. Viewed that way, it was not unlike President Ford's decision to pardon Richard Nixon. But it was one thing to pardon Nixon to end the Watergate nightmare; it would have been another had Nixon or his agents offered Ford something in return. Similarly, once Kennedy cashed Eisenhower's and Dirksen's blank checks he would be transforming an act of presidential discretion and mercy into an unethical bargain, one in which he had obstructed justice to reap a future reward.

Dirksen wrote Eisenhower a carefully worded letter afterward. Referring to "one of your former staff members," he said, "I believe everything is in proper order." Eisenhower's reply was equally opaque: "I am particularly indebted to you for following through the matter mentioned in your second paragraph."

Many politicians would have viewed cashing Eisenhower's blank check as business as usual. For Kennedy, it was a departure from the ethical standards that had guided him throughout his career. He had expounded on the importance of public integrity in his January 1961 farewell speech to Massachusetts legislators, telling them history would not judge them "merely on the basis of color or creed or even party affiliation," nor would their "competence and loyalty and stature . . . suffice at times such as these." Instead, "the high court of history" would measure them by the answers to four questions: were they "men of courage," "men of judgment," "men of dedication," and "men of integrity." A man of integrity, he added, would permit neither "financial gain nor political ambition" to divert him from fulfilling the public's "sacred trust."

Kennedy was in many respects a hard-nosed politician, fond of saying, "Forgive your enemies but never forget their names," and able to drive down a street in his former congressional district and recall which stores had displayed his campaign posters fifteen years earlier. The journalist Fletcher Knebel (who was married to Laura Bergquist) considered him "a very real, a very earthy, a very . . . cynical politician," and noticed that whenever he mentioned someone who had crossed him, "his voice would get sharp, rough, his eyes would narrow and you could tell that the big time grudge was still on," and at moments like these, Knebel said, his blond eyebrows gave him "the eyes of a snake."

Although he demanded loyalty and held grudges against those who withheld it, he often failed to reward it with favors and patronage, an omission leading one Boston politician to complain, "Kennedy doesn't pay for anybody's funeral and seldom goes to wakes and he never seems to get anyone a job. Now what kind of a politician is that?" He was so averse to the patronage politics of his maternal grandfather, John ("Honey Fitz") Fitzgerald, the baby-kissing, saloon-visiting, favor-swapping former mayor of Boston, that he slighted his own family. While he was serving in the U.S. Senate, his maternal uncle Thomas Fitzgerald had continued working as a uniformed toll taker on the Mystic River Bridge, and an unemployed cousin was so certain that Kennedy would refuse to help him get a government job that he approached Governor Foster Furcolo. He had resisted his father's demand that he make Bobby attorney general, giving his personal attorney, Clark Clifford, the bizarre assignment of persuading his own father that it was a bad idea. His other major appointments had been remarkable for their lack of political calculation. National Security Adviser McGeorge Bundy, Secretary of the Treasury Douglas Dillon, and Secretary of Defense Robert McNamara were all Republicans, and he had not met McNamara and Rusk before asking them to join his cabinet. The greatest challenge to his "Ministry of Talent" philosophy came when his father pushed him to appoint Francis Morrissey to a vacant seat on the federal district court in Massachusetts. Morrissey was unqualified for the position, and after much agonizing Kennedy left the seat vacant rather than give it to him.

His distaste for patronage was part of a moral architecture buttressed by *Profiles in Courage,* since after celebrating the bravery and ethics of eight exemplary U.S. senators he could hardly hold himself to a lower standard. Before winning the presidency, he had written in a notebook that if a politician wanted to be "a positive force for public good," he needed to possess "a solid moral code covering his public actions." The phrase "public actions" implied that a politician's moral code as it pertained to his *private* actions was irrelevant—a distinction not lost on Jackie, who once told a guest at a Georgetown dinner party who had praised her husband for being a fine politician, "He may be a fine politician, but do we know if he's a fine person?"

Until now he had allowed Eisenhower's and Dirksen's checks to remain blank. Either he was reluctant to transform his favor to Ike into a quid pro quo or he was waiting for an issue important enough to warrant filling them in. He did not cash them when Republican senators, led by Dirksen, defeated or delayed many of his major domestic initiatives. Nor did he cash them after Dirksen criticized his policies for increasing deficit spending and the size of the federal bureaucracy and called his New Frontier "nothing more than a bright ribbon wrapped around the oldest and most discredited political package on earth—the centralization of power," a centralization that was "the essence of socialism."

He and Dirksen were political adversaries but personal friends. They were an unlikely pair. Dirksen's flamboyant mannerisms, ornate vocabulary, and mellifluous voice had led to nicknames such as "Wizard of Ooze" and "Liberace of the Senate," while Kennedy refused to throw his arms into the air and his speeches were templates of restraint. Dirksen had crossed the aisle to support his foreign policy initiatives, incurring the wrath of other Republicans. Kennedy repaid him by offering tepid support to his Democratic opponent in the 1962 midterm election. This had not prevented Dirksen from raising objections to the test ban treaty and civil rights bill. Like the treaty, which required sixty-seven votes for ratification, the civil rights bill needed sixty-seven senators willing to vote for cloture and end a filibuster. In both instances, Kennedy needed the support of liberal and moderate Republicans, who looked to Dirksen for leadership.

Dirksen, who by the standards of the time could be considered a moderate Republican, was prepared to support all of the provisions of Kennedy's civil rights bill except its most symbolic and important one, the article outlawing discrimination in public facilities and accommodations. Without it, the bill was no longer a historic measure—the twentieth century's Emancipation Proclamation.

While the test ban treaty was being negotiated in Moscow, Dirksen had issued a statement warning that it might amount to the "virtual surrender" of the United States to the Soviet Union. After it was initialed, he had recommended "extreme caution and a little bit of suspicion," and refused an invitation to travel to Moscow with the U.S. delegation to witness its signing. Eisenhower had also been critical. Before boarding the *Queen Elizabeth* for a nostalgic return to

England and Normandy he had told reporters that the Soviet Union's decision to resume atmospheric testing in 1961, breaking an informal moratorium that had lasted since 1958, was reason enough to view the treaty with suspicion.

Although many in the administration and Congress believed the treaty would be ratified, Kennedy remained pessimistic. Several influential Democratic senators were threatening to propose reservations to its text that would make it unacceptable to the Soviet Union. J. Edgar Hoover was secretly lobbying against it, Edward Teller was condemning it as a Soviet victory, and the dean of Notre Dame Law School had declared that any treaty with "militant activated atheism" was inherently evil. Bobby Baker, the secretary to the Democratic majority leader and a legendary Capitol Hill fixer and prognosticator about whom the *Washington Post* had said "His nose counts were regarded by press gallery admirers as close to infallible," told Kennedy that his count showed a majority of senators voting for it, but not necessarily two thirds. When Baker said the treaty might be a lost cause, Kennedy replied, "Maybe not."

Kennedy faced two decisions on August 12: whether to fill in his blank checks with Ike and Dirksen, and if he did, whether to ask them to support the civil rights bill or test ban treaty. History might judge him harshly for calling in his markers from the Sherman Adams deal, but it might judge his first term a failure if neither measure passed Congress. He had concluded his inaugural address by saying, "With a good conscience our only sure reward, with history the final judge of our deeds, let us go forth to lead the land we love." But what if a favorable judgment from history conflicted with the sure reward of a good conscience?

By August 12, it would have been impossible for him *not* to recognize that he had thwarted justice in the Adams case in the expectation of reaping a future reward. The month before, he had refused to intervene in a far less serious case of tax fraud in which the potential defendant had been James Landis, a former dean of Harvard Law School and a close friend of the Kennedy family for more than thirty years. Due to a combination of negligence and psychological problems, Landis had failed to file returns between 1956 and 1960. He submitted delinquent returns in 1961 and 1962, paying back taxes and fines. Had he not been so close to the Kennedys, the IRS might have closed the case, but to avoid any appearance of favoritism it referred him to the Justice Department for possible prosecution. Bobby Kennedy recused himself, leaving the decision to Assistant Attorney General Nicholas Katzenbach.

During a telephone call on July 25, Kennedy told Katzenbach that he had consulted his attorney Clark Clifford, who had concluded that Landis would have to be indicted. "I guess we have to proceed," he said, his reluctance evident in his voice. "Is that your judgment?"

"More damage not to go ahead," Katzenbach replied.

"Five years [of not filing returns] is so serious that if anyone ever gets the idea that the President's friends can get away with it, Christ, I think it would be an awful moral cracker to the Internal revenue, to taxpayers. The next time anybody got arrested, they'd say, 'What the hell about Landis?'"

Landis pled guilty on August 2, and it could not have escaped Kennedy's notice that he had helped Eisenhower's friend Sherman Adams escape jail but had not saved his own friend from indictment for a less venal offense.

While walking in the Rose Garden with Dirksen on Monday, he finally filled in his blank checks. Faced with choosing between his ethics and history, he chose history; with choosing between a historic bill that began redressing centuries of wrongs and a treaty reducing the threat of a nuclear war, he chose the treaty.

He had told Sorensen that he would "gladly forfeit his reelection, if necessary for the sake of the test ban treaty," and his ambassador to France, Charles ("Chip") Bohlen, believed that he was "emotionally more wrapped up in the test ban than almost any other effort." Glenn Seaborg, who headed the Atomic Energy Commission and met with him often that summer, thought he felt more passionately about it than any other measure sponsored by his administration, and called his determination to halt atmospheric testing and the spread of nuclear weapons "like a religion" to him. The treaty was neither perfect nor comprehensive, but it was a start. On July 31, he had told Seaborg and other senior government scientists that he believed the treaty would give the United States as much as eighteen months "to explore the possibility of détente with the Soviet Union—which may not come to anything but which quite possibly could come to something." Because the United States and Soviet Union were unable to agree on protocols for policing a ban on underground testing, its official title was "The Limited Nuclear Test Ban Treaty," but it was still more important to him than the civil rights bill. His decision proved that he had meant it when he said, "Domestic policy can only defeat us; foreign policy can kill us."

He told Dirksen, "Ike said I had coin in his bank, and you say I have coin in yours. Ev, I must write a check on you and Ike."

Dirksen agreed that they "owed him one."

"Ev, I want you to reverse yourself and come out for the treaty. I also want Ike's public endorsement of the treaty before the Senate votes. We'll call it square on that other matter."

"Mr. President, you're a hell of a horse trader," Dirksen said. "But I'll honor my commitment, and I'm sure that General Eisenhower will."

Both men kept their word. For Dirksen it was probably just another deal. But it left such a sour taste in Eisenhower's mouth that during his first conversation with President Johnson on November 23 he complained, somewhat boorishly under the circumstances, about the "tactics" of the IRS and Kennedy's Justice Department.

After Dirksen left, Kennedy swam in the White House pool and went upstairs to the family quarters. Sometime that evening, before or after drinking four Bloody Marys, he called an attractive Hungarian émigrée whom he had met at a dinner party. He had included her in White House events, but she knew about his womanizing and had resisted his attempts to seduce her. When he persuaded her to come to the White House in June, on the pretext of helping him pronounce some German phrases he wanted to use in Berlin, they had met alone in the family quarters and he had behaved impeccably, saying as she left, "See, I've been good." Perhaps he simply wanted companionship again. He sounded depressed when he called, and after she refused his invitation to the White House they had a lengthy conversation during which he asked why God would let a child die.

That evening (or possibly the next day) he sat on the second-floor White House balcony with Mimi Beardsley, a young intern who had become his lover the year before. He picked up one condolence letter after another from a stack on the floor and read them out loud as tears rolled down his cheeks. He did not have sexual relations with Beardsley then, or ever again following Patrick's death, although she continued seeing him and accompanying him on trips. She believed, she wrote later, that Patrick's death had "filled him not only with grief but with an aggrieved sense of responsibility to his wife and family," and that afterward, he began "obeying some private code that trumped his reckless desire for sex—at least with me."

Tuesday, August 13

WASHINGTON

On Tuesday morning Kennedy complained to his chief White House physician, Rear Admiral George Burkley, about some discomfort in his right eye and a bout of abdominal cramps and loose stools. He blamed his distress on "an emotional factor," admitting that drinking four Bloody Marys had probably "not helped." Burkley found his eye normal. After he returned several hours later to say it felt "itchy," Burkley referred him to an ophthalmologist, who also found nothing wrong. He reported the president's abdominal problems to a gastroenterologist, writing in a note, "We should stress the fact that emotional tension rather than food could be the cause of the distress and that no actual organic change was taking place."

None of Kennedy's illnesses had proved more persistent and resistant to treatment, or led to as many lengthy hospitalizations, as those involving his digestive system. He had first experienced severe cramping at the age of thirteen, and between 1934 and 1940 had undergone months of invasive tests and hospitalizations. He complained to Lem Billings from one hospital that he was "suffering terribly," had "a gut ache all the time," and had endured eighteen enemas in three days. Few teenagers suffering his symptoms in Depression-era America would have been subjected to so much expensive and ultimately futile medical attention. His physicians diagnosed spastic colitis (now known as irritable bowel syndrome) and recommended stress reduction and antispasmodics. A gastroenterologist at the Leahy Clinic in Boston put him on a dietary regimen that he would follow for the rest of his life, calling for small meals and bland, milky foods. He devoured ice cream, sometimes drank glasses of heavy cream instead of milk, and loved fish chowder made with large quantities of butter and milk. It was a calamitous diet for anyone suffering from lactose intolerance, as he probably was, and raised his cholesterol to stratospheric levels.

The public saw a vigorous and youthful man who suffered recurrent backaches, an affliction bedeviling millions of middle-aged men, but his close friends and advisers knew a man who had seemingly suffered years of illness and pain without complaint. The diplomat George Ball praised him for bearing his ailments "with gallantry and with no perceptible loss of alertness," Arthur Schlesinger was impressed that he never uttered "a word of self-pity or complaint," and Ted Sorensen wrote, "In retrospect, it is amazing that, in all those years, he never complained about his ailments." He certainly considered himself a stoic. When asked at a news conference to comment on the complaints of army reservists recalled to active duty, he said, "There is always inequity in life. Some men are killed in a war, and some men are wounded, and some men never leave the country. . . . It's very hard in military or in personal life to assure complete equality. Life is unfair. Some people are sick and others are well."

His physicians, however, knew a man who was preoccupied with his health and intent on micromanaging his treatment, who demanded remedies for every tickle in his throat, itch in his eye, grumble in his stomach, sleepless night, aching knee, and throbbing muscle—the kinds of complaints most people treat with aspirin, ice packs, and Pepto-Bismol. He was not a hypochondriac, merely someone who after a lifetime of illnesses and pains had become accustomed to seeking treatment for minor complaints. His principal health problems were real and painful. He frequently woke with cramping and diarrhea, and urinary tract infections had plagued him for decades, sometimes causing a burning sensation when he urinated or ejaculated. He was allergic to dust, animals, and certain foods, and afflicted by gum disease, deafness in one ear, and rapidly worsening vision. Athletic injuries, *PT 109*, and risky surgeries had aggravated a chronic back condition stemming from one leg being shorter than the other, and during much of his first years in office, he could not sit for any length of time, touch his toes, or put on his socks, and often used crutches in private. He also suffered from Addison's disease, a debilitating and potentially life-threatening malfunctioning of the adrenal glands that had weakened his immune system to such an extent that a routine illness could turn serious, a factor undoubtedly contributing to his tendency to fuss over minor ailments.

He spent several hours every day attempting to alleviate his discomfort and pain. He wore hot mustard packs, soaked in hot baths, and swam twice daily in a White House pool that he kept heated to 90 degrees. Every morning he strapped himself into a canvas corset, anchoring it with Ace bandages looped around his chest and thighs; every afternoon he took a long nap, changing into pajamas, darkening the room, and lying under the covers on a heating pad. He spent a half hour daily in a small White House gym, following a regimen of back-strengthening exercises. He swallowed a pharmacopoeia of capsules and pills—steroids for his Addison's, Lomotil and antispasmodics for his diarrhea and spastic colon, antibiotics for his urinary tract infections, vitamin B supplements, salt tablets, Choloxin for his high cholesterol, and antihistamines for his allergies. He cloaked his health under a carapace of secrecy. When he hired Dr. Travell he told her, "It's best if you don't go into any [of my] medical problems with Jackie. I don't want her to think she's married either an old man or a cripple," adding, "Ted Sorensen is the only person here [in his Senate office] who is fully informed about my health. Discuss it with no one else."

During a taped January 5, 1960, interview with Ben Bradlee and Jim Cannon for a book they were writing about contemporary politics, he essentially confirmed that he had Addison's and was willing to lie to keep it secret. After Bradlee mentioned how green and sickly he had looked while running for Congress, he admitted suffering from "malaria and some adrenal deficiency." When Bradlee asked if that meant Addison's, he said, "Jack Anderson [who then worked for the influential political columnist Drew Pearson] asked me today if I had it. . . . I said, 'No. God, a guy with Addison's disease looks brown and everything. Christ, that's the sun." At this, everyone in the room had a good laugh.

When supporters of Senator Lyndon Johnson, Kennedy's principal rival for the nomination in 1960, spread rumors about his health, he responded with a misleading letter drafted by Travell and signed by her and his endocrinologist, Eugene Cohen. It called his health "excellent" and said, "Your vitality, endurance and resistance to infection is [sic] above average. Your ability to handle an exhausting workload is unquestionably superior." It skirted the Addison's issue by stating that "your adrenal glands do function," side-stepping the question of how *well* they functioned. He told reporters at his first postelection press conference that he had never had Addison's disease, his back had been fine since his operation in 1955, and his health was "excellent." None of these statements was even remotely true.

His robust physical appearance made it easier to dismiss the rumors about his poor health. When the journalist Hugh Sidey joined him for a swim in the White House pool, Sidey was impressed by his strong and handsome physique, calling his body "graceful and well-proportioned: broad shoulders, narrow hips and well-muscled legs," yet scarred from his war injuries and back operation. Senator Fulbright, who saw him naked in a locker room after a round of golf, described him as "a very strongly built fellow" who had "tremendously strong arms and legs," adding that, "surprisingly enough he looked much stronger and better built naked."

Of the two secrets that could have ended his political career—his health and his womanizing—his health posed a greater threat because there were medical files that could confirm his illnesses. A month after Cohen and Travell released their letter, intruders broke into their offices on the same weekend. At Travell's office they were thwarted by a steel door with hardened locks that protected the room containing her patients' records. Cohen arrived Monday morning to find his cabinets open and the files of patients whose last names began with a "K" scattered across the floor. Luckily, he had given Kennedy a pseudonym beginning with another letter.*

KENNEDY'S FABLED DETACHMENT failed him when it came to his health. Otherwise, he might have recognized the harmful effects of the rivalries between his physicians, and of his addiction to questionable treatments promising rapid but temporary relief. His search for a quick fix had led him to Dr. Max Jacobson, a New York physician who injected his wealthy and famous patients with "vitamin shots" laced with amphetamines. On multiple occasions between 1960 and 1962 Jacobson gave him a cocktail of vitamins and speed. Dr. Burkley

---

* In 1973, Cohen noticed the similarities between his burglary and a break-in at the office of a psychiatrist treating Daniel Ellsberg, who had leaked the Pentagon Papers to the *New York Times,* and wondered if Richard Nixon had ordered both.

became so alarmed that he wrote a stern letter cautioning, "You cannot be permitted to receive therapy from irresponsible doctors like M.J., who by form of stimulating injections offer some temporary help." He added that Jacobson's injections should not be taken by "responsible individuals who at any split second may have to decide the fate of the universe."

Janet Travell's expertise was in pharmacology and skeletal muscle pain. She had placed lifts in Kennedy's shoes to equalize the disparity between his legs, recommended a hard mattress, tinkered with the height and pitch of his chairs, and suggested a rocking chair. She treated his back pain with anesthetics, temporarily alleviating his pain without addressing the underlying condition. Dr. Cohen had recommended her, but by November 1961 he had become so alarmed by her behavior that he told Kennedy he believed that she posed "a potential threat to your well-being" and urged him to dismiss her. In February 1964, Cohen unburdened himself to Dr. Burkley in a single-spaced four-page letter that could have been describing intrigues at the Russian imperial court. He said he was writing because he was horrified that Travell was being retained by the Johnson administration, and he wanted to record some facts about the White House tenure of a woman he called "a deceiving, incompetent, publicity-mad physician."

He wrote that during the transition he had suggested another doctor for the post of White House physician. Travell, however, had accompanied Kennedy to Palm Beach, where she "wormed her way into having him agree that she be his physician," despite being unqualified for the position because she was not an internist. Several days later, the president reversed himself and asked Cohen to choose a physician. He had arranged for a Dr. Donnally to attend to him during the inauguration, but Travell continued lobbying for the position, informing Cohen that Mrs. Kennedy disliked Donnally. Cohen succumbed and endorsed Travell because, given the secrecy surrounding the president's medical background, there was no time to find another physician who could be trusted. He told himself that since Admiral Burkley, an internist who had treated Eisenhower, was on the White House medical staff, Kennedy would receive adequate care.

Within days he regretted his decision. Travell immediately called in reporters, providing them with material for several articles and leading Cohen to conclude that she was obsessed with publicity, a dangerous situation given the president's medical history. After Kennedy injured his back during a tree-planting ceremony in Ottawa in May 1961 and Travell's injections failed to alleviate his pain, Cohen recommended that he consult Dr. Hans Kraus, a renowned New York orthopedic surgeon and legendary mountaineer, medical contrarian, and fierce advocate for the medical benefits of physical fitness. (Kraus's pioneering studies on the connection between exercise and muscular health had so impressed President Eisenhower that he had instituted the President's Council on Youth Fitness and made Kraus a founding member.) Kraus had also developed a series of exercises to strengthen the back muscles that had proved effective in cases like Kennedy's. Travell resisted summoning him to Washington and capitulated only in the fall of 1961 after Burkley and Cohen threatened to go to the president and charge her with incompetence.

When Kraus examined Kennedy in October 1961, he noted that his leg muscles were "as taut as piano wires," he could not perform a single sit-up, and his fingertips dangled above his knees when he tried touching his toes. "You will be a cripple soon if you don't start exercising," he told him. "Five days a week. And you need to start now."

Kraus flew to Washington three times a week to supervise his exercises and train White House therapists to handle additional daily sessions. He insisted on complete cooperation from the president and his medical staff as a condition of his employment. There were to be no second opinions, interference from other physicians, or interruptions during his exercise sessions. He prescribed a daily routine of breathing exercises, leg raises, stretches, knee bends, and toe touches, later adding weights, sit-ups, and leg spreads. After a month Kennedy was more mobile, his pain had diminished, and Kraus noticed, "a definite increase of strength and flexibility. . . . Patient is now able to do knee bends all the way down and get up without difficulty. He can walk well without shoes and without brace while he used to support his left hip and limp." He reduced the frequency of his visits and told Kennedy his back brace was an unnecessary psychological crutch. He noted that he hoped to persuade him to discard it, "in a not too distant future," writing in Kennedy's file that when he did, "a very long step will have been taken toward the ultimate goal, namely, having a healthy person with occasional discomfort rather than an invalid."

In November 1961, Kennedy asked Ken O'Donnell to fire Travell. O'Donnell delegated the task to Cohen, who wrote Kennedy on November 12 that he regretted he had been "burdened with initiating a housecleaning in your medical staff." Speaking of Travell, he said, "In spite of repeated advice against her personal publicity . . . her own interests were placed above yours." Cohen flew to Washington and was flabbergasted when Travell demanded several years' worth of severance pay. On Christmas Day, a Washington newspaper reported that she was leaving and Salinger informed Cohen that he was about to issue a statement announcing her resignation. He called back an hour later to say that Travell had just met with the president and would not be resigning. Furthermore, the White House would be denying the newspaper story. "I hate to use the word blackmail," Cohen wrote in his 1964 letter to Burkley, "but essentially this is how she has kept her tentacles stuck to the White House."*

Just as Kennedy's womanizing made it risky for him to fire J. Edgar Hoover, the perilous state of his health made it too dangerous to dismiss Travell. Unlike Hoover, she kept her title but not her power. Burkley became Kennedy's White House physician in all but name, Kraus assumed sole responsibility for his back, and Travell was relegated to treating Jackie and the children.

Kennedy's back improved throughout the winter of 1962, and he told Kraus, "I wish I could have known you ten years ago." By April, Kraus had reduced his visits to several times a month and their relationship had ripened into a friendship. Kennedy admired mental and physical courage, and Kraus had demonstrated both, becoming the first climber to pioneer difficult climbing routes in the Shawangunks and Dolomites. (Kennedy was probably also impressed that James Joyce had taught Kraus English in Vienna, a fact Kraus was not shy about sharing.) Kraus was impressed that during the Cuban missile crisis Kennedy had come to the White House dispensary, where he was waiting for his scheduled exercise session, and had taken his hand and said, "I know, Doctor, you've come a long way to take care of me, but please forgive me. Tonight, I simply have no time." He was floored that on the most important day of his presidency, he had taken the time to apologize to him personally. "You know I really liked Kennedy before that incident," he said. "But after that, I liked him even more."

---

* Cohen closed his letter by saying, "I was taken in by this psychopathic, dishonest, incompetent doctor. I am responsible for her being where she is. . . . Fortunately, you were there to take over completely. No one can ever realize the strain it is to have this venomous creature always there as a potential threat to the well being of anyone she contacts. As mentioned in the beginning of this letter, it would require a book to record just what Doctor Travell did and just what she is. I feel like a shower now. Cordially . . ."

Kraus returned to his office from a weekend in 1962 to find his cabinets open and his files scattered across the floor. Because he had labeled Kennedy's file "K" and kept it in a separate drawer, the burglars had left empty-handed. Many in the White House suspected the FBI, the Soviets, or the GOP, in order of probability. Kennedy had scrambler phones installed in Kraus's office, apartment, and country home, and whenever Kraus needed to consult Cohen and Burkley about the president's condition he left his office and used a pay phone.

By the summer of 1963, Kraus considered Kennedy cured. He was playing golf, had not experienced any back pain during his strenuous European tour, and could toss his son in the air. Kraus remained on call for emergencies and saw Kennedy sporadically, but had he been a regular patient he would have discontinued their appointments. Kennedy had once told Jackie plaintively, "I wish I had more good times," meaning more healthy times. By that standard, the summer of 1963 was a very good time. The gap between his robust physical appearance and the actual state of his health had narrowed to the point that he felt almost as well as he looked. Desensitization shots had reduced his allergies to animals and dust, making him less susceptible to sinusitis and other respiratory infections, his Addison's was being managed with cortisone, and he boasted of feeling better than at any time in his adult life. All that remained was to discard his back brace, a device that made him sit bolt upright in chairs and in the backseats of limousines.

Wednesday, August 14

CAPE COD

When Kennedy arrived in Jackie's room at Otis to bring her home to Squaw Island, he found her upset that she could not persuade her private nurse, Luella Hennessey, to spend the rest of the year with her at the White House. Hennessey was a cheerful and confident fifty-seven-year-old spinster who had been caring for Kennedys since 1937, when she nursed thirteen-year-old Patricia following an emergency appendectomy. After Bobby was admitted to the same hospital several days later with pneumonia, Joe and Rose asked her to come to Cape Cod and see both Patricia and Bobby through their convalescence. She soon became a family fixture, summoned when anyone became ill and often serving as a surrogate mother while Rose was away on her frequent shopping trips abroad. Once the Kennedy children began having their own children, she called every year to see who was expecting so she could plan her vacations around their delivery dates. Since the birth of Robert Kennedy's daughter Kathleen in 1951 she had been present at the births of eighteen Kennedy children, including Caroline and John. She did not deliver or nurse the babies but looked after their mothers, sitting in their hospital rooms, reassuring them, and attending to their needs.

During all her years of nursing Kennedys only Jack had imagined that Hennessey might have greater ambitions and talents, and he was paying her tuition for a course at Boston College that would prepare her to open a school for mentally challenged children. She had arrived at Otis hours after Patrick was born and had been at Jackie's side ever since. She had refused her invitation to come to the White

House only because it would have meant postponing her studies at Boston College. Forced to choose between Hennessey's education and his wife's recovery, Kennedy chose his wife. "There are ninety-six thousand R.N.s [registered nurses] in this country," he told Hennessey. "And I think ninety-five thousand nine hundred and ninety-nine would jump at the chance to go to the White House for the winter!"

"But you see, Jack, that's the difference between the other nurses and me, and that's why you want me," she said. She proposed staying with Jackie through August. If Jackie still felt she needed her after that (it turned out that she did not), she would postpone her studies. "But I'm sure after having my company for a whole month she will be so fine I won't be needed."

Jackie presented the hospital staff with framed and signed lithographs of the White House and said gamely, "You've been so wonderful to me that I'm coming back here next year to have another baby. So you better be ready for me."

Kennedy gave an impromptu speech thanking the nurses and airmen gathered in her suite. Given the ruckus that he had raised the previous month about the renovations to these rooms, he should have felt sheepish when he saw Jackie's standard-issue hospital bed, wooden nightstand, and gooseneck lamps. The improvements had been as modest as the furniture. Walls had been washed instead of repainted, a portable dishwasher rolled into a small kitchen, a room converted into a nursery, some carpeting replaced, and a couch and chairs sent to be refurbished at Jordan Marsh, the venerable Boston department store. The Secret Service had demanded the most expensive changes, insisting that an open corridor be glassed in, bulletproof steel mesh installed over the windows, and air conditioners rented, since the windows would have to remain shut whenever the president visited.

He had hit the roof when he read about the renovations in the *Washington Post*. He telephoned General Godfrey McHugh, his Air Force attaché, called them a "fuck-up," and thundered, "Are they crazy up there? I want to find out what we paid for that furniture and I want it to go back to Jordan Marsh!" He was particularly incensed by a photograph of the Otis public information officer standing next to Jackie's bed. He was a "silly bastard," he said, adding, "I wouldn't have him running a cat house."

His tantrums usually exploded suddenly and disappeared just as quickly. This time he stayed mad. Later that morning he called Assistant Secretary of Defense Arthur Sylvester and raged, "I'd like to send that goddamned

furniture . . . right back to Jordan Marsh on an Air Force truck this afternoon
with that captain on it. What about transferring his ass out of here. . . . And that
silly fellow who had his picture taken next to the bed, I'd have him go up to
Alaska, too." He said he was afraid that Congress would seize on the renovations
as an excuse for cutting his defense budget, but that was unlikely, and insufficient to explain his fury.

A month earlier he had become furious while visiting his second cousin Mary
Ryan in Ireland. After discovering that Ambassador Matthew McCloskey had
used embassy funds to pave her yard, he told Fay, "To think that big blockhead [McCloskey] could insult this wonderful woman by thinking that her yard
wasn't good enough to receive me." He threatened a punishment similar to making the Air Force officer ride on the truck returning the furniture, saying, "I'll
tell you what, McCloskey will pay for that concrete going in and he'll pay for that
concrete coming out, out of his own pocket." This never happened, but like the
furniture, Mary Ryan's yard had struck a nerve.

The Kennedys were probably the richest Irish American family in the country. Although their money was new, earned by Joe Kennedy on Wall Street and
in Hollywood, he and Rose had raised their children in the style of old-money
Boston Brahmins. He knew that those whom Rose called "the nice people of
Boston" might never accept him, but they might accept his children if he instilled
the proper old-money values in them, raising them on the Yankee principle that
living simply was evidence of a virtuous life. Rose reinforced the message, telling
them, "Money is never to be squandered or spent ostentatiously. Some of the
greatest people in history have lived lives of the greatest simplicity," and repeating St. Luke's admonition "Of those to whom much has been given, much will
be required."

After Joe Kennedy was blackballed from joining the country club in Cohas-
set, a WASP summer resort, he bought a rambling house with a broad lawn
running down to the water in Hyannis Port. It was comfortable but simply furnished, and after years of use by his large and rambunctious family, many of the
sofas and chairs could have used a trip to Jordan Marsh. He did not give his
children bicycles until their friends had them, and enforced the same rule about
cars. After Ted acquired a loud horn that blasted the sound of a mooing cow as
he drove around Harvard, he wrote him, "It's all right to struggle to get ahead of
the masses by good works, by good reputation and hard work, but it certainly

isn't by doing things that [could lead people to say] 'Who the hell does he think he is?'"

Kennedy inherited his parents' dislike of ostentation. When he and Lem Billings (who was on a tight budget) traveled across Europe, they picnicked and ate in cheap cafes, and either camped or slept in hostels and flophouses. After visiting the Duke of Devonshire, whose late son had been married to his sister Kathleen, Kennedy noted approvingly in his diary that the duke "does have great integrity and lives simply with simple pleasures." When he came to Washington as a young congressman, he rented a small house in Georgetown, seldom entertained, wore old chinos and sneakers to the office, and threw on a food-stained tie before appearing on the House floor. His legal residence in Boston was a small apartment on Bowdoin Street with wobbly tables, broken chairs, and an ancient Victrola. Visitors were shocked that someone of his wealth and background would live in such a dump. But since Rose had moved the Kennedy children around like hotel guests, never giving them their own permanent rooms, Bowdoin Street, in a way, really *was* his home, where he kept his yearbooks and Navy sword.

After Jackie taught him to appreciate fine clothes and furniture, he began offering fashion tips to friends, warning them away from button-down collars and brown shoes with dark suits. The day after his inauguration, he toured the White House with the economist John Kenneth Galbraith and delivered a caustic commentary on the low quality of the furnishings, telling him, "I hope to make this house the repository of the best." When Galbraith related this to Kay Halle, a friend of the Kennedy family, she imagined the president marching upstairs and saying to Jackie, "You've got great taste. I know the job for you." He later gave his friend Joe Alsop, a newspaper columnist, a similar tour, taking him into Ike's former bedroom and pointing out that the only decent piece was a huge highboy that, he added with a wicked grin, blocked the door to Mamie's bedroom.

Despite his newfound connoisseurship, he never lost his aversion to displaying his wealth. He bought monogrammed handkerchiefs but folded them so the initials were hidden, and he banned photographers from taking pictures of his private cabin on Air Force One because he thought it looked too much "like a rich man's plane." Jackie's lavish spending was a constant irritant, as was the weekend house she had bullied him into building in Virginia hunt country. While it was under construction they gave Paul Fay a tour. Fay thought they had skimped too much and encouraged Jackie to increase the size of the living room windows. Kennedy pulled him aside and said, "Are you out of your mind? Can you imagine what's going to happen if I come in with a house that costs over sixty thousand? . . . You were down in West Virginia [where he had run in the 1960 Democratic primary]. You know what the conditions were like down there. Can you see what those people in West Virginia are going to think when here I am building myself a house? I've got a White House already. I've got the one on the Cape—my family's house—and we've been down in Florida, and now I'm building this one out in Middleburg, Virginia." He had agreed to build a modest ranch house costing under $60,000, but as the costs mounted during construction, he hired an accountant to shadow the contractor and make sure he bought the cheapest materials.

Many politicians affect a bogus egalitarianism, but Kennedy's was genuine. It predated his political career and was evident in his choice of friends. In the Navy, he had preferred the enlisted men and junior officers to the brass, and unlike many PT boat commanders, he worked alongside his crew, scraping and painting. Sam Elfand, a poor farm boy from Tennessee who was under his command during the war and remained a lifelong friend, remembered him as being "not a stuck-up individual" who was "receptive to everybody." One of Kennedy's complaints about Eisenhower was that he had ditched his old friends when he became famous. "He is a terribly cold man," he told his White House aide Arthur Schlesinger. "All his golfing pals are rich men he has met since 1945." He also criticized Eisenhower for attacking his proposal for providing medical care to the aged as socialized medicine, "and then getting into his government limousine and heading out to Walter Reed [the army hospital]," and was horrified when, speaking about the Cuban refugees in the United States, Eisenhower told him, "Of course, they'd be so great if you could just ship a lot of them in trucks from Miami and use 'em as servants for twenty dollars a month."

U. E. Baughman, who headed the Secret Service when Kennedy took office, thought that his egalitarian spirit surpassed even President Truman's, a surprising observation to make about a man who had a million-dollar trust fund, had been dressed by a valet for much of his adult life, and had rarely if ever cooked his own breakfast, cleaned his own house, or washed his own clothes. But like Truman, he had maintained close friendships with people of modest means, such as Dave Powers and his driver Muggsy O'Leary. Deirdre Henderson, who served as his informal liaison with the New England academic community, was struck by how people like Muggsy—the real people, the cops, the staff in the kitchen—instinctively felt that he liked them, and returned his affection. After spending a summer weekend in 1959 at the Newport estate of Jackie's mother and stepfather while she was traveling in Italy, he wrote to Jackie, "I was taken into the kitchen and introduced to all the help, who were just over from Ireland, and found them much more attractive than the guests." During his first congressional campaign, he looked down at an audience of stevedores and truckers and said to himself softly, "These are the kind of people I want to represent," which may explain why Larry O'Brien, Ken O'Donnell, and Dave Powers, the triumvirate of Irishmen who had worked on so many of his campaigns and knew him so well, were certain he would have wanted what O'Brien called "a plain, inexpensive casket . . . one any average American might have."

Photographs of him and Jackie walking arm-in-arm or holding hands are rare. When she kissed him during a campaign appearance in New York, he maneuvered her so that photographers missed it, ignoring their shouts of "Kiss her again, Senator," and "Hug him, Jackie." But when they descended the steps of the Otis base hospital on August 14, he was gripping her hand, and a photographer remarked that they walked to their car hand-in-hand, "like a couple of kids." An old friend who saw the resulting photograph was stunned, realizing that in all the years she had known them she had never seen them hold hands, even in private.

After helping her climb inside the convertible, he rushed around to the other side and reached across the seat to grab her hand again. Jackie's Secret Service agent Clint Hill called it "a small gesture but quite significant to those of us who were around them all the time," adding that after Patrick's death, he and other agents "noticed a distinctly closer relationship, openly expressed, between the President and Mrs. Kennedy." Their hand-holding was not the only sign that their relationship had changed. Between August 14 and September 24, when she returned to Washington, he spent twenty-three nights with her at Cape Cod and Newport, sometimes flying up midweek, something he had never done before. Arthur Schlesinger sensed their reluctance to reveal their feelings falling away as they became, he said, "extremely close and affectionate."

PART TWO

August 15–31, 1963

DAYS 100–84

Thursday, August 15

WASHINGTON

Eisenhower began honoring his part of the Sherman Adams bargain while Kennedy was flying back to Washington. After the *United States* docked in New York, he announced at a press conference that although he would not reach a final conclusion about the test ban treaty before studying its full text, "Unless there is . . . some rather hard evidence that the Soviets are way ahead of us in something, or that the security of the United States would be endangered, then I would certainly be on the favorable side." A front-page headline in the *New York Times* the next day declared, "Eisenhower Hints He Backs Treaty," and it was later reported that he had sent Senator Fulbright a letter formally announcing his support for the treaty.

Minutes after arriving at the White House, Kennedy met with Henry Cabot Lodge, Jr., the former political rival he had appointed ambassador to South Vietnam. Lodge's decision to accept the post struck many as just as inexplicable as Kennedy's decision to offer it to him. It was not a first-rank embassy, certainly not for a distinguished sixty-one-year-old former U.S. senator, ambassador to the United Nations, and vice presidential candidate. Soon after the inauguration, Lodge had told Secretary of State Rusk that he had "one more tour of public duty in his system" and would accept a "challenging" position in the administration. Two years later, Kennedy ran into Lodge at a dinner and afterward instructed his military attaché, Major General Chester Clifton, to ask him if he was interested in an embassy. Lodge told Clifton that although he was not looking for a job, he would consider something "challenging and difficult." Clifton relayed this to Secretary of State Dean Rusk, who recommended Saigon.

After Lodge accepted the post, he received a condescending letter from the Republican congresswoman Frances Bolton, a prominent member of the House Foreign Affairs Committee, informing him that she and many Republicans were "deeply disturbed" by his decision. If South Vietnam fell to the Communists during his tenure, she wrote, the GOP would share the blame, and she believed that Kennedy was "perfectly capable of using a possible defeat in Southeast Asia to ruin the Republican Party." Was Lodge certain he understood "the complexities of these countries," she asked, and certain of his "capacity for patience, understanding, and really infinite wisdom?" Lodge replied, "American security must always be considered from a totally unpartisan viewpoint, without regard to party politics, important though party politics are." South Vietnam was vital to U.S. security, the commander in chief had asked him to serve, and under these circumstances, "service is a patriotic duty as well as an honor"—a stirring defense all the more impressive for being voiced in a private communication.

Kennedy's motives for sending Lodge to Saigon were less estimable. His first choice had been Edmund Gullion, the current ambassador to Ghana and a friend and usher at his wedding who had frequently advised him about foreign affairs. Rusk argued that the post called for someone with more experience and seniority and pushed for Lodge. Kennedy's other advisers opposed sending a Republican of his stature to Saigon on the grounds that he might resist taking orders from a Democratic administration and prove difficult to fire. Bobby warned him that in about six months they might find him causing a lot of trouble. (In fact, he began causing trouble in less than a week.) Sorensen thought Lodge "lacked the qualities of prudence which were necessary in this kind of area," and joked that he hoped he was being sent to North Vietnam. O'Donnell was shocked because Kennedy had often disparaged his political skills and dismissed him as lazy. Schlesinger suggested that appointing him might have appealed to the president's "instinct for magnanimity." But had he really wanted to be magnanimous he could have offered him a more prestigious post, and Schlesinger conceded that "involving a leading Republican in the Vietnam mess appealed to his instinct for politics." O'Donnell and Jackie arrived at a similar conclusion, with O'Donnell saying, "The idea of getting Lodge mixed up in such a hopeless mess as the one in Vietnam was irresistible," and Jackie remarking later that he believed sending a Republican to Saigon "might be such a brilliant thing to do because Vietnam was rather hopeless."

Kennedy certainly had reason to be magnanimous. His victories over Lodge in the Massachusetts Senate race in 1952 and in the 1960 general election, when Lodge had run for vice president, had capped a family rivalry spanning generations. It had started when Lodge's grandfather Henry Cabot Lodge, Sr., had introduced a bill in Congress in 1895 aimed at curbing immigration from southern and eastern Europe by requiring immigrants to be literate in their national languages. When his bill reached the House, Kennedy's maternal grandfather, who was then a congressman, had fiercely opposed it. According to a story that Fitzgerald told for years and his grandson surely knew by heart, when he and Lodge met in the Senate chamber, Lodge had called him an "impudent young man" and asked, "Do you think the Jews or the Italians have any right in this country?" Fitzgerald had shot back, "As much right as your father or mine. It was only a difference of a few ships." Fitzgerald ran against Lodge for the Senate in 1916 and lost. In 1952, his grandson challenged Lodge's grandson for the same seat and won. Lodge served as Eisenhower's ambassador to the United Nations until he resigned to run for vice president in 1960, and lost to Kennedy again. Two years later, Ted Kennedy beat Lodge's son in an election to fill the president's former Senate seat.

The reporter Joe McCarthy had interviewed Kennedy and his father as they cruised off Hyannis Port in 1959. As Jack listened, his father thundered that he had moved his family out of Boston because the anti-Catholic, anti-Irish prejudice of the Yankee elite made it no place to raise Irish-Catholic children. "I didn't want them to go through what I had to go through when I was growing up there," he told McCarthy, adding, "They wouldn't have asked my daughters to join their deb clubs; not that the girls would have joined anyway—they never gave two cents for that society stuff. But the point is they wouldn't have been asked in Boston." Kennedy had enjoyed more social success than his father, attending Choate, an elite prep school, and becoming the first Irish Catholic to join Harvard's Spee Club. But he remained convinced that the WASP elite was determined to exclude him from its private clubs. While playing golf at the Newport Country Club before his wedding, he had been reprimanded because his foursome did not include a member. "I'm afraid that they feel their worst fears are being realized," he told his friends, "the invasion by the Irish-Catholic hordes into one of the last strongholds of America's socially elite."

The presidency did not knock the chip off his shoulder. The Irish ambassador to Washington, Thomas Kiernan, was surprised by his frequent references to the legendary (and perhaps imaginary) "No Irish Need Apply" signs in Boston, and he once told Paul Fay, "Do you know it is impossible for an Irish Catholic to get into the Somerset Club in Boston? If I moved back to Boston even after being President, it would make no difference." He told the columnist Betty Beale that his family was the only Gentile one in the Palm Beach Country Club because it was the only club they could join, and Beale noticed that he seemed upset because he remained on the waiting list to join Washington's Cosmos Club, although it customarily admitted presidents upon their election. After reading a critical letter in the *New York Times* signed by a man with a Protestant name and a Westchester County address, he remarked to an aide that WASPs seemed to think that "the world should be made in their image." After it came out that Ted Kennedy had cheated on a Harvard examination, he said, "It won't go over with the WASPs. They take a very dim view of looking over your shoulder at someone else's exam paper. They go in more for stealing from stockholders and banks."

How, then, could he look at Lodge and *not* see the kind of Brahmin who had driven his father from Boston, and would have blackballed an Irish American president from the Somerset Club? Ken O'Donnell, an expert on the dimensions of the Kennedy chip, believed that he "nursed an Irish distaste for the aloof North Shore Republican [Lodge]," and remembered that after seeing him join Nixon on the dais at the 1960 GOP convention, he had said, "That's the last Nixon will see of Lodge. If Nixon ever tries to visit the Lodges in Beverly, they won't let him in the door," a comment raising the question of how warm a welcome *he* would have received on the Lodge doorstep. When Bobby Kennedy was asked if his brother had held Lodge in "high regard," he replied carefully, "I think a fair regard."

THE OFFICIAL PHOTOGRAPH OF the August 15 meeting between Kennedy and Lodge shows Kennedy leaning back in his rocking chair while Lodge sits perched on the edge of a couch, hands clasped between his knees like a schoolboy summoned to the principal's office. Here they were, then, inches apart, the last Yankee Brahmin to have a distinguished political career, and the first Irish Brahmin to become president. Ignore for a moment that when Kennedy was a boy his family had moved to New York to escape the snobbery of Brahmins like the Lodges, and that when Lodge was of a similar age he moved with his widowed mother to Paris, where the novelist Edith Wharton ("a most loyal and devoted friend to both my father and mother," according to Lodge) took them under her wing. And ignore that Lodge's father had been a poet and a favorite of President Theodore Roosevelt, who described him in a letter that Lodge quoted as "the only man I have ever met who, I feel, was a genius," and that after an acrimonious meeting with Joe Kennedy, President Franklin D. Roosevelt had told his wife, "I never want to see that man again as long as I live." Ignore all the differences of religion, class, and upbringing, and you have two men with more in common than either suspected or cared to acknowledge.

Lodge had lost his father when he was seven, an event leaving him absorbed with his health and, like Kennedy, a careful eater, devotee of bland soups, and afternoon napper. Both had followed mediocre prep school careers with success at Harvard. Lodge had been thirty-four when he won his Senate seat, Kennedy thirty-five, and both were criticized for being young men in a hurry. Both won medals for valor and ran on their war records—Kennedy for the House, and Lodge to regain the Senate seat he had resigned to fight in the war. Kennedy had dabbled in journalism and considered making it a career; Lodge had spent nine years at newspapers in Boston and New York. Both were appalled by baby-kissing, arms-in-the-air politics. When David Halberstam of the *New York Times* wrote about Lodge, "He is a total politician in the best sense. That is, he is attuned to the needs, ambitions, and motivations of others. Yet his background, coolness, and reserve mark him as essentially different from other, more genial and back-slapping politicians," he could have been describing Kennedy. Both were also considered liberals, although Kennedy was uncomfortable with the label and Lodge the more progressive of the two. Lodge had written in the *Atlantic Monthly* in 1953, "In becoming a Republican, I thought I was joining something affirmative, evolutionary, and idealistic—which demanded sacrifice and generosity—not a party which said no to all proposals for change." He had introduced a bill in the Senate requiring public funding of presidential campaigns "to the exclusion of all other methods of financing," accused the GOP of becoming a "rich man's club" and a "haven for reactionaries," and blindsided Nixon during the campaign by announcing that a Nixon-Lodge administration would appoint the first Negro to a cabinet post. Despite all this, the aristocratic Lodge never connected with ordinary voters, while Kennedy, in the words of one friend, could "loft a pass, swap a joke, hoist a beer, hurt his back and hug his kids like millions of other Americans."

The button activating the secret Oval Office microphone was concealed somewhere on the round mahogany coffee table. The August 15 photograph shows wires running from the base of this table into the floor. One led from the microphone to the basement tape recorder, although a visitor would assume that they were all telephone wires. In fact, Kennedy was concealing more than a hidden microphone from Lodge. Had Lodge known that he doubted that the government of President Ngo Dinh Diem could defeat the Communist insurgency, and was considering how and when to extricate the more than sixteen thousand U.S. military advisers currently serving in South Vietnam, he might have paid more attention to Congresswoman Bolton's warning.

KENNEDY AND HIS BROTHER BOBBY had stopped in Vietnam in 1951 during a private fact-finding tour of the Middle East and Asia. They arrived at a violent juncture in the struggle between the French colonial authorities and Viet Minh guerrillas led by Ho Chi Minh. A suicide bomber had killed a French general, antigrenade nets covered government ministries, and artillery flashes lit the horizon as they dined at a rooftop restaurant in Saigon with Edmund Gullion, then serving as the political counselor at the embassy. Kennedy asked Gullion what he had learned. "That in twenty years there will be no more colonies," Gullion said. "We're going nowhere out here. The French have lost. If we come in here and do the same thing we will lose, too, for the same reason. There's no will or support for this kind of war back in Paris. The home front is lost. The same thing would happen to us." Gullion believed that the only way to defeat the Viet Minh was by encouraging a strong and countervailing nationalism among the South Vietnamese, an impossible strategy for a colonial power.

Jack and Bobby also visited Hanoi and the Mekong Delta. A colonel at a frontier post told them France would win, but it might not happen in his lifetime.

General de Lattre rolled out maps and declared that if France lost the rich delta, the Communists would seize all of Southeast Asia—the domino theory. Jack spent several hours with the *New York Times* correspondent Seymour Topping at his apartment in Saigon. Topping told him the French were doomed as long as the Chinese could supply the Viet Minh through mountain passes, and that many Vietnamese detested Americans because they were assisting the French. By the time Kennedy left his apartment, Topping believed that he had been persuaded "that only a truly independent Vietnamese government had any prospect of attracting popular support."

Bobby wrote in his diary that Vietnam had made "a very, very major impression" on his brother, and had taught them "the importance of associating ourselves with the people rather than just the governments." Jack added his own entry to the diary, writing, "We must do what we can as our contribution gets bigger to force the French to liberalize political conditions," "We are not here to help French maintain colonies," and "Reason for spread of communism is failure of those who believe in democracy to explain this theory in terms intelligible to the ordinary man and to make its ameliorating effect in life apparent."

After returning to Washington he went on *Meet the Press*, accused the Eisenhower administration of supporting "the desperate attempt of a French regime to hang on to the remnants of empire," and warned that attempting to defeat the Communist insurgency without recognizing the nationalism of the Vietnamese people "spells foredoomed failure." While running for the Senate against Lodge the following year he stood in front of a map of Vietnam with a pointer and criticized the conflict as "a white man's war against the natives."

During a fifty-seven-day siege in 1954 that would end in the humiliating surrender of the French garrison at Dien Bien Phu, Kennedy rose in the Senate to oppose a French request for additional military assistance. Change the dates, substitute the United States for France, and his speech could have been delivered by an antiwar politician in 1968. He said, "To pour money, materiel, and men into the jungles of Indochina without at least a remote prospect of victory would be dangerously futile and self-destructive." After recalling Secretary of State Dean Acheson's 1952 statement that "the tide is now moving in our favor," and Secretary of State John Foster Dulles's insistence that American aid would "reduce this Communist pressure to manageable proportions," he concluded, "I am frankly of the belief that no amount of American military assistance in

Indochina can conquer an enemy which is everywhere and at the same time nowhere, 'an enemy of the people,' which has the sympathy and covert support of the people."

The French surrendered two weeks later, and negotiations at Geneva led to an agreement to divide Vietnam at the seventeenth parallel. The Communists under Ho Chi Minh ruled the North, and Emperor Bao Dai appointed Ngo Dinh Diem head of state in the South. The division was meant to be temporary, and the Geneva Accords called for elections in 1956 to unify the country under a single government. Diem refused to participate, arguing that the Communists would never permit free elections in the North. After the Viet Minh attacked government offices and assassinated officials in the South, Eisenhower increased U.S. economic and military assistance to the Diem government.

Kennedy's reputation as a zealous cold warrior rests partly on his 1960 campaign speeches, in which he charged the Eisenhower-Nixon administration with allowing the United States to fall behind the Soviet Union militarily, and on the famous passage in his inaugural address in which he pledged to "pay any price, bear any burden, meet any hardship, support any friend, oppose any foe to assure the survival and the success of liberty." His cold war rhetoric was not an act. He subscribed to the domino theory and believed that the charge that his party had "lost" China meant that no Democratic politician could become president without being tough on communism. After taking office, he continued ornamenting his speeches with cold war rhetoric, even after it became apparent to his advisers that if he *was* a cold warrior, he was a fairly nonviolent one, ready to talk tough, call up reserves, impose blockades, deploy aircraft carriers off coasts, and order convoys up autobahns, but unwilling to "pay any price" if the price was nuclear war, or "bear any burden" if the burden included sending combat troops to Vietnam.

He had hinted at this in his inaugural address. After his "pay any price" passage he had warned, "Man holds in his mortal hands the power to abolish . . . all forms of human life," and spoke of "that uncertain balance of terror that stays the hand of mankind's final war." He followed this with a call for negotiations, saying, "Let both sides begin anew the quest for peace," "Let us never negotiate out of fear. But let us never fear to negotiate," and "Let both sides, for the first time, formulate serious and precise proposals for the inspection and control of arms—and bring the absolute power to destroy other nations under the absolute control of all nations." The newspapers got it right. Headlines in San Francisco, New York, Philadelphia, and Washington proclaimed, "Kennedy Is Sworn In— Asks Grand Alliance for Peace," "Kennedy Takes Oath as President, Proclaims a 'New Quest for Peace,'" "Kennedy Asks World Peace Quest," and "Kennedy Sworn In, Bids for Peace."

At a White House meeting a day before Kennedy's inauguration, Eisenhower warned that the most immediate and important foreign challenge would be the small, landlocked Southeast Asian nation of Laos, where an insurgency by the Communist Pathet Lao was threatening a pro-Western regime. "If we permit Laos to fall, then we will have to write off the whole area," Eisenhower said, adding that the only solution might be a unilateral military intervention. After leaving the meeting, Kennedy remarked caustically, "There he sat, telling me to get ready to put ground forces into Asia, the thing he himself had been carefully avoiding for the last eight years."

Laos monopolized his attention that winter. The Joint Chiefs of Staff and Secretary of Defense McNamara recommended sending in U.S. ground forces and bombing North Vietnam. The chiefs warned that if the Chinese Communists intervened, the United States might have to retaliate with nuclear weapons. In March, the chiefs recommended an expeditionary force of 60,000 troops, with an additional 140,000 readied and armed with tactical nuclear weapons. Their chairman, Lyman Lemnitzer, promised victory if Kennedy approved the use of nuclear weapons.

The president was appalled, telling an aide after the meeting, "Since he couldn't think of any further escalation, he would have to promise us victory." Instead, he ordered a show of force in Thailand and in waters off Vietnam, and asked the veteran diplomat W. Averell Harriman to negotiate the neutralization of Laos. Secretary of State Dean Rusk and National Security Adviser McGeorge Bundy both opposed a neutral Laos, arguing that it could hand South Vietnam to the Communists. He ignored them and told Harriman during an overseas phone call, "Do you understand? I want a negotiated settlement in Laos. I don't want to put troops in." General Maxwell Taylor, who succeeded Lemnitzer as chairman of the Joint Chiefs a year later, believed Kennedy had resisted escalation in Laos because of "his knowledge of the French problem in Vietnam." His refusal to intervene in

Laos to prevent it falling to the Communists also indicated that, his rhetoric notwithstanding, he did not believe that its loss would imperil neighboring Southeast Asian nations, and represented a de facto rejection of the domino theory.

He also refused the Joint Chiefs' request to provide air cover and marines to save the Cuban exiles pinned down at the Bay of Pigs, a decision leading to a strained relationship between himself and the chiefs. He was furious at himself for approving the invasion, and furious at the CIA, the military, and his advisers for endorsing it. While dining with family and friends at Hyannis Port that summer, he could still work himself up into a fury over it. "When I sat there and looked at that fat ass [Admiral] Arleigh Burke and fat ass [General] George Decker," he said, "I looked at their four stars and that wide gold braid, and . . . I figured the selection process that they had to go through in order to achieve that pinnacle in the military—having been in the military myself—I just figured these fellows have got to know what they're doing." Later that evening, he resumed his rant while playing dominoes with Fay. "Nobody is going to force me to do anything I don't think is in the best interest of the country," he said. "I will never compromise the principles on which this country is built, but we're not going to plunge into an irresponsible action just because a fanatical fringe in this country puts so-called national pride above national reason. Do you think I'm going to carry on my conscience the responsibility for the wanton maiming and killing of children like our children we saw here this evening? Do you think I'm going to cause a nuclear exchange—for what? Because I was forced into doing something that I didn't think was proper and right? Well, if you or anybody else thinks I am, he's crazy." He picked up his crutches, announced he was going to bed, then swiveled around and added, "I'll tell you I don't care who it is, nobody is going to force me to do anything irrational just because they feel that it is going to save the image or the name of the country."

When Khrushchev threatened to cut off access to Berlin in August 1961, and the East Germans erected a wall separating East from West Berlin, the Pentagon recommended that Kennedy consider using nuclear tactical weapons to maintain Western rights in the divided city. Instead, he increased military spending on conventional forces, called up reserves, doubled draft calls, and put American forces on alert. During the crisis he arrived two hours late for a small White House dinner party. His hands shook as he said, "God, I hope you've been enjoying yourselves over here because I've been over there in that office, not knowing whether the decisions I made were going to start a war and send the missiles flying."

In the fall of 1962, he learned that the Soviet Union was installing missiles in Cuba. His civilian and military advisers urged him to bomb the missile sites and invade the island, measures that would have probably precipitated a nuclear exchange. Air Force Chief of Staff Curtis LeMay recommended surrounding Cuba with warships and sending Strategic Air Command bombers to bomb it with nuclear weapons. Kennedy told John Kenneth Galbraith, the Harvard economist who was serving as his ambassador to India, that he never had the slightest intention of doing this, and that the worst advice always seemed to come "from those who feared that to be sensible made them seem soft and unheroic." Instead of bombing Cuba he imposed a naval blockade, demanded that the Soviets dismantle the missiles, and during secret exchanges with Khrushchev agreed to remove U.S. missiles from Turkey in exchange for the Soviet Union doing the same in Cuba. He told Rusk that if the blockade and Turkish deal failed to persuade the Soviets to remove the missiles, he would bring the dispute to the United Nations Security Council instead of attacking Cuba.

He had prefaced his 1954 Senate speech on Vietnam by declaring that American citizens had a right "to inquire in detail into the nature of the struggle in which we may become engaged," before traveling "the long and torturous road to war—particularly a war which we now realize would threaten the survival of civilization." After making his own inquiry, he concluded that the United States should not send combat units to save the French. This conclusion guided his own Vietnam policy throughout his presidency, repeatedly putting him at odds with the Joint Chiefs and his civilian advisers.

In the spring of 1961, the chiefs urged him to send 3,600 combat troops to assist Diem's beleaguered forces. He sent 500 military advisers.

During a visit to South Vietnam in May 1961, Vice President Johnson hailed President Diem as the "Winston Churchill of Southeast Asia" and recommended increasing U.S. economic and military assistance. Kennedy listened instead to General Douglas MacArthur, who had commanded American forces in Asia during World War II and the Korean conflict. The two men got along so famously when they dined in New York in the spring of 1961 that Kennedy invited him to the White House for lunch. Before he arrived he read aloud to Bobby and Powers the citation for the decoration that he had won in the First World War. He prefaced it by asking Powers, "Dave, how would you like this to be said about you"—by which he meant that he wished it had been said about him—and read, "On a field where Courage was the rule, his courage was the dominant feature." In a quiet voice, Bobby, who had never been in combat, said shyly, "I would love to have that said about me." With this as an introduction, he naturally hit it off with MacArthur again.

MacArthur told him, "What has happened after eight years of Eisenhower is that the chickens have come home to roost. And you live in the chicken house." He said that anyone who advocated putting American ground troops in Asia should have his head examined. He dismissed the domino theory, saying it would be a mistake to fight the Communists in Vietnam, and recommended drawing a defensive line around Japan, Formosa, and the Philippines. He further endeared himself to Kennedy by saying, "If I was in combat and I commanded an army, I would hope that someone like General Eisenhower was commanding the opposing army." General Taylor believed that MacArthur's advice made "a hell of an impression" on Kennedy. Whenever Taylor or others urged him to increase the U.S. military commitment to Vietnam, he would tell them, "Well, now, you gentlemen, you go back and convince General MacArthur, then I'll be convinced."

After returning from a fact-finding mission to Vietnam in the fall of 1961, Taylor and Deputy National Security Adviser Walt Rostow recommended sending 8,000 combat engineers to South Vietnam and making preparations to dispatch an additional 205,000 combat troops if North Vietnamese forces launched an invasion. They concluded their report by urging that the United States commit itself to preventing the fall of South Vietnam "by the necessary military actions." Taylor and McNamara followed this with a memorandum warning, "The chances are against preventing [the fall of South Vietnam] by any measures short of the introduction of U.S. forces on a substantial scale."

Kennedy told Taylor that he was "instinctively against the introduction of U.S. forces." Bundy tried to change his mind, reminding him that his advisers had unanimously recommended sending combat units, and suggesting cabling Ambassador Frederick Nolting, Jr., that combat troops would be sent "when and if the U.S. military recommend it on persuasive military grounds." Kennedy refused. He did, however, approve Taylor and Rostow's recommendation that the United States increase economic aid and the number of military advisers. He may have done this to placate the Joint Chiefs, who were becoming increasingly mutinous after his responses to Cuba, Berlin, and Laos, and in the hope that the advisers might stabilize the situation sufficiently for Diem to survive until the 1964 U.S. election, or succeed in training enough South Vietnamese forces to wage the kind of successful anti-insurgency operations that the British had mounted against Communist guerrillas in Malaya. What *is* certain is that he repeatedly and categorically refused to send U.S. combat units to Vietnam, a position leading Taylor to conclude, "I don't recall anyone who was strongly against [sending combat troops], except one man and that was the President." Kennedy may have had this in mind when he told reporters at a 1962 press conference, "Well, you know that old story about Abraham Lincoln and the Cabinet. He says, 'All in favor say "aye,"' and the whole Cabinet voted 'aye,' and then, 'All opposed no,' and Lincoln voted 'no,' and he said, 'the vote is no.'"

He realized that sending armed American advisers on patrol with South Vietnamese forces risked drawing the United States deeper into the conflict. To minimize this happening, he insisted that they participate only in combat-training missions. In the summer of 1962, he was cruising off Newport with Fay when he received a call from the Pentagon reporting that a contingent of U.S. Marine advisers was requesting permission to assist a unit of South Vietnamese troops who were preparing to ambush a Viet Cong detachment. He had the call transferred to the forward cabin, where he and Fay could be alone. "I want you to hear this," he told Fay. "We've got twenty advisors out there who want to attack the Viet Cong. They think they can kill at least over 100 or 150." While Fay listened, he forbade the marines to engage in combat, adding, "For every one of those advisors that gets involved in it, I'm going to pull them out and an equal number to that." After hanging up he turned to Fay and said, "We're going to settle this thing diplomatically."

Throughout 1962 Kennedy received cables from Ambassador Nolting and General Paul Harkins, commander of the U.S. advisory mission, stating that the counterinsurgency strategy of gathering South Vietnamese peasants in "strategic hamlets" was succeeding. Majority Leader Mike Mansfield, the Senate's leading expert on Asia, was the first major dissenter. He had been among Diem's earliest supporters, praising him in a 1959 speech as a man of "vision, strength, and selflessness," but while visiting Saigon in November 1962, he was dismayed to find that he was becoming a recluse and had fallen under the influence of his sinister brother, Vice President Ngo Dinh Nhu, and Nhu's wife. Nhu was an unsavory paranoid who commanded a private army of shock troops trained by U.S. advisers. Because Diem was a celibate bachelor, Madame Nhu had become South Vietnam's de facto first lady. She was a tangle of contradictions: a dragon lady with long fingernails and tight dresses split from ankle to waist, and a militant Catholic and sexually voracious puritan who had sponsored legislation outlawing contraceptives, abortion, prostitution, and taxi dancing.

Ambassador Nolting told Mansfield, "We can see the light at the end of the tunnel," a comment unlikely to impress him since he had first heard it from the lips of the commander of the French forces in 1953. He wrote in a private memorandum that he had left Vietnam "with a feeling of depression and with the belief that our chances may be little better than 50-50." After returning to Washington he sent Kennedy a confidential report that ranks among the most prescient and depressing documents ever written about that conflict. "Seven years and billions of dollars later . . . it would be well to face the fact that we are at the beginning of the beginning," he wrote. Success was theoretically possible, but only if both the Vietnamese and Americans pursued the current strategy with "great vigor and self-dedication," a possibility he considered unlikely. The only alternative was "a truly massive commitment of American military personnel and other resources—in short going to war fully ourselves against the guerrillas—and the establishment of some sort of neo-colonial rule in South Vietnam." He concluded that Kennedy must stress that the primary responsibility for the war rested with the South Vietnamese. Failure to do this could "not only be immensely costly in terms of American lives and resources but it may also draw us into some variation of the unenviable position in Vietnam which was formerly occupied by the French."

Kennedy invited Mansfield to Palm Beach over the Christmas holidays to discuss Vietnam. As they cruised on the *Honey Fitz* he became furious as he reread his memorandum, and exclaimed, "This is not what my advisors are telling me!" Mansfield said he was courting disaster unless he stopped increasing the advisers and began withdrawing the ones already there. "I got angry at Mike for disagreeing with our policy so completely," he told O'Donnell afterward, "and I got angry at myself because I found myself agreeing with him."

At the end of December he sent Michael V. Forrestal of his National Security

Council and the State Department's director of intelligence and research, Roger Hilsman, to Vietnam to assess the state of the war. Forrestal was close to Averell Harriman, who had become his mentor after the suicide of his father, former secretary of the Navy James Forrestal. Hilsman was a West Point graduate whose experience fighting behind Japanese lines with Merrill's Marauders during the Second World War had made him an early expert in counterinsurgency warfare. In a special "eyes only" annex to their report for President Kennedy, they described the situation as "fragile," and pointed out serious problems in the conduct of the counterinsurgency efforts of the South Vietnam army. As Kennedy was digesting this, the Joint Chiefs made another pitch for combat units, writing in a memorandum to McNamara that if the Diem government could not bring the Vietcong under control, there was "no alternative to the introduction of U.S. military combat forces."

Kennedy made Hilsman assistant secretary of state for Far Eastern affairs, summoned him to the White House to discuss Vietnam, and told him that he had received an assessment from Edmund Gullion that had shaken his confidence in Diem. He had decided to continue supporting Diem for the moment, but would not send U.S. troops into battle or bomb North Vietnam. He wanted Hilsman to do everything possible to help the South Vietnamese win without getting the United States dragged into the fighting. Hilsman summarized his position as "Keep it down, no more advisors, we're going downhill. We've reached the peak. From now on we're going to cut the advisors back. If the Vietnamese win it, okay, great. But if they don't, we're going to go to Geneva and do what we did with Laos."

ON MAY 8, South Vietnamese police fired into a procession of Buddhists who had gathered in the formal imperial capital of Hue to celebrate the Buddha's birthday and were flying religious banners in defiance of a law banning them. Although Buddhists constituted almost 90 percent of the population, Diem had given his fellow Catholics easier access to education and government jobs, and demonstrations against the Hue massacre turned into nationwide protests against religious discrimination. On June 12, an elderly monk sat down in a Saigon intersection, doused himself with gasoline, and burned himself alive.

Kennedy saw a wire service photograph of the man engulfed in flames, shouted "Jesus Christ!" and bolted from the room. He waved the photograph at Lodge when he asked him to go to Saigon.

That spring he complained to his friend Charlie Bartlett, a newspaper reporter and columnist, "We don't have a prayer of prevailing there. Those people hate us. They are going to throw our tails out of there at almost any point. But I can't give up a piece of territory like that to the Communists and then get the American people to reelect me."

He asked Undersecretary of State for Political Affairs Averell Harriman to be ready "to seize upon any favorable moment to reduce our involvement, recognizing that the moment might yet be some time away."

He had told Deputy Secretary of Defense Roswell Gilpatric at the end of 1962 that he believed the United States had been "sucked into Vietnam little by little," and by the fall of 1963, Gilpatric came to believe that he had become "sick" of Vietnam, and noticed him frequently asking how to extricate America from the conflict.

In the spring of 1963, he told Mansfield that he had made a mistake in increasing the number of advisers, agreed with Mansfield's recommendation for a complete withdrawal, and said he would begin bringing troops home at the beginning of 1964 but would not remove them all until he was reelected. If he made his intentions known earlier, conservatives would pillory him and he might lose the election. After Mansfield left, he turned to O'Donnell and said, "In 1965, I'll become one of the most unpopular Presidents in history. I'll be damned everywhere as a Communist appeaser. But I don't care. If I tried to pull out completely now from Vietnam, we would have another Joe McCarthy red scare on our hands, but I can do it after I'm reelected. So we better make damn sure I *am* reelected."*

Kennedy could point to the Pentagon's optimistic reports about the progress of the war as an argument for reducing the U.S. commitment. A prime example was a MACV (Military Assistance Command Vietnam) memorandum in the spring of 1963 reporting, "Barring greatly increased resupply and reinforcements of the Viet Cong by infiltration, the military phase of the war can be virtually

---

* Mansfield confirmed O'Donnell's recollection of this conversation in a letter to the author Francis Winters, in which he put the meeting in March and wrote, "I can tell you with great confidence that in March 1963 the President told me he was going to leave Vietnam after he was reelected, but not before, and that he would withdraw some troops in advance."

won by 1963." The military's assessments became more cautious after the Buddhist revolt, and on the morning of August 15, the *New York Times* carried a front-page article by David Halberstam that Lodge and Kennedy had probably read before they met. Headlined "Vietnamese Reds Gain in Key Areas," it began, "South Vietnam's military situation in the vital Mekong Delta has deteriorated in the last year and informed officials are warning of ominous signs."

KENNEDY ACTIVATED the hidden Oval Office microphone as Lodge was in midsentence. He may have waited until he was distracted, or made a spur-of-the-moment decision to record his former rival. Lodge was describing his dinner with Madame Nhu's parents, Mr. and Mrs. Tran Van Chuong. Although Mr. Chuong owed his position as South Vietnam's ambassador to the United States to nepotism, as did his wife, who represented South Vietnam at the United Nations, they had become estranged from Diem, Nhu, and their increasingly erratic and terrifying daughter. Lodge told Kennedy that Madame Chuong believed that the Diem regime was responsible for mass executions, that a coup was inevitable, and that unless her daughter and husband fled, they would be assassinated. She also thought that her daughter's bizarre and inflammatory comments—she had celebrated the Buddhist immolations as "barbecues," and had said, "Let them burn, and we shall all clap our hands"—reflected the thinking of her husband and Diem.

As Lodge delivered his dinner-party aperçus about the dysfunctional Chuong family (in 1984 Madame Nhu's brother would strangle his parents in their bed), Kennedy said, "Uh-huh, uh-huh . . . yeah . . . yeah . . . yeah." Like his tooth-tapping, finger-drumming, and doodle-drawing, it was a sign that he was bored. Those who knew Kennedy well knew that boring him was a cardinal sin. His former girlfriend Nancy Dickerson, who would become NBC's first female correspondent, noticed that "when he was bored, a hood would come down over his eyes and his nervous system would start churning. You could do anything to him—steal his wallet, insult him, argue with him—but to bore him was unpardonable."

During his thirty-five-minute meeting with Lodge he filled a page with doodles, writing in a column down one side, "Saigon / Lodge / No press comment / Cabot Lodge / Henry Cabot Lodge / Ambassador Lodge / Governor / Senator," and on the other, "No press comment / USOM [United States Operations Mission]," with an arrow pointing downward. "No press comment" was a reminder to ask Lodge not to comment to the press after the meeting, an instruction that, presaging things to come, Lodge would immediately ignore. To be fair, it was not only Lodge's insights into the Chuong family that Kennedy found tiresome, it was the whole Vietnam mess, a sideshow compared with civil rights, the test ban treaty, and U.S.-Soviet relations.

When he and Lodge met on June 12 he had held up the photograph of the Buddhist monk engulfed in flames. After saying, "I suppose these are the worst press relations to be found in the world today," he had told Lodge that he expected him to take charge of relations with U.S. journalists in Saigon. Mindful of that exchange, Lodge now offered him a preview of how he planned to handle his first Saigon press conference, saying, "Suppose I am asked, 'Do you think we can win with Diem?'"

Kennedy, who persisted in viewing Vietnam as primarily a public relations problem needing better management, suddenly showed more interest in the conversation. "You have to think of a rough one for that," he suggested. Referring to the American press corps, he added, "You're going to have a difficult time having a satisfactory relationship with them."

"The very first day I'm going to invite them to lunch with me and my wife and ask their advice. I'll be too fresh for them to get anything out of me . . . and at least [I can] try to get them into a human frame of mind."

"The time may come when we're going to have to do something about this war." Referring to the possibility of a coup, Kennedy added, "I don't know who we would sort of support. . . . They [Diem and the Nhus] ought to go but there's the question of how skillfully that's done and if we get the right fellow. . . . I just want to be sure that it would be someone better." Wearying of the conversation, he concluded, "I think [we] have to leave it almost completely in your hands."

Realizing he had just given a carte blanche to a proud man who had been famously resistant to following orders at the UN, he pulled back slightly, saying, "I don't know whether we'd be better off with the alternative maybe . . . we'll have to move more in that direction, but I'll have to take a look at it before I come to that conclusion."

"That's helpful, very helpful. I'll certainly give it my best. But if they all get assassinated, then you're really going to have to get on top of it."

"What about Madame Nhu?" Kennedy asked. But instead of inquiring if Lodge thought she might also be assassinated, he said, "Is she a lesbian, or what? She looks awfully masculine." (A recent *Time* cover story had called her "a fragile exciting beauty" known for her "flaming feminism.")

Lodge could not have anticipated this line of inquiry, but he smoothly shifted gears. "I think she is," he agreed. "I think she also was very promiscuous, sort of a nymphomaniac." Realizing he had found a subject that interested the president, he described her campaign to curb vice by shutting down Saigon's dance halls.

Kennedy declared that promiscuity and Puritanism were "a dangerous combination," prompting this descendent of Massachusetts Puritans to exclaim, "Very well put!"

The sex lives of heads of state, congressmen, Hollywood stars, and, for that matter, almost anyone crossing his path fascinated Kennedy. Nancy Dickerson recalled a foreign ambassador being shocked when he leaned close to him in a receiving line and asked, "Are you getting any lately?" A young female reporter told Dickerson that while she was interviewing him he had suddenly asked, "How's your romance going?" After learning that Laura Bergquist had interviewed Fidel Castro in 1961, he asked her, "Who does he sleep with? . . . I've heard he doesn't even take his boots off." Bergquist said she had no idea, but he persisted. "He runs around making these long speeches," he said, "but where are the dames?" Bergquist went to Hyannis Port a year later, hoping to persuade him to let *Look* run some candid photographs of Caroline. While flipping through the pictures of his daughter he asked her about Che Guevara. She had just met him in Havana and had described him as "cool, brainy, blunt, witty, and sensible"—a pragmatic man who could inspire the young, in fact a man not unlike Kennedy. After peppering her with more questions he gave her an appraising look and said, "Something gives me the feeling you've got the hots for the 'Che.'" She spluttered that it was an "odd remark" and reminded him that a photograph of her and Guevara showed they had been two wary antagonists. "Yeah, but you know what psychiatrists say . . . that kind of hostility often leads to an opposite emotion." She left convinced that he was "a very swinging sexual animal and saw others in his own light."

He ended his meeting with Lodge soon after discussing Madame Nhu's sex life. A week later, the proud and imperious Lodge arrived in Saigon believing that the president had left things "almost completely" in his hands.

CAPE COD

As Kennedy's helicopter landed on the lawn of his family compound, his nieces and nephews came running. They surrounded him, and Caroline shouted, "It's my daddy's turn! It's my daddy's turn!"—meaning it was his turn to treat at the candy store. They clambered aboard his golf cart, sitting on his lap and clinging to the front and rear bumpers as he sped across the lawn and into the village.

"What's the limit? What's the limit?" he demanded as they trooped into the store.

"Everyone gets five cents' worth," Caroline explained.

"Anybody got a buck?" he asked his Secret Service agents.

"Daddy, did you take us to the store with no money?"

"Oh, Caroline," he said, "I've goofed again."

Before his inauguration *Look* had published an article by Fletcher Knebel titled "What You Don't Know About Kennedy." It portrayed him as appealingly human and forbiddingly smart, as well as a notorious moocher who seldom carried cash. Knebel's opening sentence set the tone: "John Kennedy can quote from the classics, poke fun at himself, be as aloof as Charles de Gaulle or as convivial as an Irish baritone, eat gallons of fish chowder, fume like dry ice, drive a car like a fugitive from justice, go weeks without wearing a hat, read esoteric French philosophy, take three showers a day, face physical hazards without a ripple of nerves, lead others with assurance, be casually gracious." Readers learned that he seldom exploded in anger, was repelled by anything "corny," demanded privacy, possessed "not a sliver of snobbishness," could be "thin-skinned," used profanity "with the unconcern of a sailor," was "an avid reader," and was widely regarded as "the most intellectually curious and self-possessed man to win the Presidency in our era."

"A friend describes the life of the President-elect and his wife as rather like an iceberg," Knebel wrote, "one part fully exposed to public view and most of it quietly submerged." He did not reveal that the "friend" was Jackie, or that she had referred to two icebergs in her letter to him, writing, "I would describe Jack as rather like me in that his life is an iceberg. The public life is above the water—& the private life—is submerged." It was an arresting and disturbing metaphor. There are few things colder and more forbidding than an iceberg, and Knebel had tinkered with her words to make them more compatible with the article's lighthearted tone. His most telling change was to turn her twin icebergs into a shared one. Two icebergs implied that their submerged lives remained separate and mysterious, even to each other, which was probably what Jackie had meant by her comment "I'd say Jack didn't want to reveal himself at all."

She struck others as equally unfathomable. Her secretary Mary Gallagher described Jackie's life in the White House as "strangely remote," and claimed she had no really close female friends. Norman Mailer detected "something quite remote in her . . . distant, detached as the psychologists say, moody and abstracted the novelists used to say." *Newsweek* described "the subtle smile of a self-restrained pixie," but the author Marya Mannes had a more perceptive take, calling it "a smile that had nothing public about it, that spoke of things withheld and guarded," and possessed a quality of "serene removal" found in Greek statuary. Ethel Kennedy thought her brother-in-law would "have a hard time getting to the bottom of *that* barrel, which is great for Jack, who's so inquisitive." When Jackie sat silently during one of the countless Kennedy family celebrations in Hyannis Port, he had said, "A penny for your thoughts," only to have her reply, "If I told them to you, they wouldn't be mine, would they, Jack?"

Her intelligence and ambitions lay in the submerged regions of her iceberg. When she graduated from boarding school at eighteen, she wrote in her class yearbook under Ambition in Life, "Not to be a housewife." The editor of the *Washington Star,* where she worked in the early fifties, recalled "a bright young woman" who could "see around corners," and her professor of advanced composition at George Washington University had praised her "brilliant imagination" and ability to "write like a million." Her greatest literary accomplishment had been beating twelve hundred other applicants to win *Vogue*'s Prix de Paris in 1951. In her winning essay she speculated on what she would do if she became what she called "a sort of overall art director of the twentieth century."

Her breathless voice masked an iron will, and a mean streak. She loathed Frank Sinatra, and when he made small talk while escorting her into the Washington armory for the pre-inauguration gala, she elbowed him in the ribs and said with a frozen smile, "Look, Frank. Just smile. That's all you have to do, okay?" Schlesinger believed that a "tremendous awareness, an all-seeing eye and a ruthless judgment," lay "underneath a veil of lovely inconsequence." She sometimes turned this judgment on her husband. When he sent Major General Clifton to her table during a state dinner to request that the marine band play some livelier tunes, she told Clifton, "I chose the music myself. But if he insists, have them play 'Hail to the Chief' over and over. That should amuse him." When Kennedy chided her for not caring what people thought about her, she said, "The trouble with you, Jack, is that you care too much what people think of you." A reporter overheard her saying, "Where is this great Irish wit you're supposed to have, this celebrated wit? You don't show much of it when you're home." During the 1956 convention he had asked one of his staff, within her hearing, "Jackie is superb in her personal life, but do you think she'll ever amount to anything in her political life?" She turned the question on him, asking the staffer, "Jack is superb in his political life, but do you think he'll ever amount to anything in his personal life?" Yet she still slipped notes to the newsmen preparing to grill him on *Face the Nation* that said, "Don't ask Jack mean questions."

His iceberg was a Greenland-sized mass of secrets and subterfuge that included his frantic philandering, the White House taping system, and his perilous health. His attorney Clark Clifford saw a man who was adept at "never allowing intimacies to go beyond a certain point," and kept "a very tight rein on his personal emotions." Jackie had the best grasp of the contours of his iceberg's submerged terrain. Before their wedding she had asked the wife of a known womanizer how to manage an unfaithful husband, only to be told, "You have to believe that he loves only you. But I didn't think I was marrying an unfaithful husband going into my marriage."

"Well, I think I am," she replied.

Their icebergs also concealed various physical imperfections and vanities.

She wore custom-made glasses to accommodate her widely spaced eyes, white gloves to hide her nicotine-stained fingers and huge hands, and extra-wide shoes to accommodate her enormous feet. He wore a back brace, sometimes hobbled around on crutches, used a sun lamp, and disliked carrying cash because he thought that a wallet marred the drape of his suits. He was so sensitive about his "Fitzgerald breasts" that he avoided swimming in public, so concerned with his weight that he traveled with a bathroom scale, and so vain about his thick chestnut hair that he kept a brush in his desk drawer. When he traveled by convertible he waited for an underpass or tunnel before whipping out his comb.

During a campaign trip to Oregon in 1960, Jacques Lowe took a photograph that captured their iceberg-like isolation. It resembled *Nighthawks*, Edward Hopper's painting of a man and a woman sitting in a nearly empty urban diner, eyes averted, silent, bored, and alone. In Lowe's photograph they are sitting side by side in the corner booth of a diner. She is holding a mug of coffee to her mouth and looking down at a magazine. He is resting his elbows on the table, has clasped his hands together in front of his mouth, and is staring across the table at his brother-in-law Stephen Smith, whose back is to the camera. Sunlight streams through some venetian blinds, throwing stripes of sun and shadow across his face. The perfect caption would have been the observation of his friend Chuck Spalding that Jack and Jackie were "the two most isolated, most *alone* people I ever met."

Chuck and Betty Spalding were their guests at Brambletyde, their Squaw Island house, the first weekend after Patrick's death. Both sensed that the loss had drawn them closer. Pointing to Jackie, Jack told Chuck, "See that smile on her face? I put it there." Jackie told Betty she had been stunned when he wept in her arms. She had never seen anything like it before, and it had left her thinking, "Maybe now I'm getting through to him," and hoping they might have a different kind of marriage.

There are no photographs of the August 17–18 weekend, but when Jackie returned from Otis on August 14, the White House photographer Cecil Stoughton took some color pictures that are the antithesis of Lowe's "two icebergs at the diner" shot. Stoughton's photographs show them sitting in blue lounge chairs on Brambletyde's flagstone terrace. She is wearing a bright pink shift; he is in a blue polo shirt and long trousers. Everyone in the family except John is barefoot and they are surrounded by their dogs: Charlie the Welsh terrier; Shannon the cocker spaniel; Clipper the German shepherd; an Irish wolfhound named

Pushinka, a Russian space dog that had been a gift from Premier Khrushchev; and Pushinka's two mongrel puppies. Many of the dogs had already been on the Cape, but Kennedy had brought the others up from Washington to distract the family from its grief. In some photographs Caroline rests her head on Charlie, John hugs Shannon, and Jackie holds the puppies in her lap. In others, the president is talking on a white telephone or leaning back and smiling, a proud father admiring his family.

Saturday, August 17, was the kind of pleasant summer day that Kennedy usually liked to spend on the water and at the golf course. Instead, he stayed with his family at Brambletyde until five o'clock, when he played a quick round of golf. Sunday was overcast, and except for attending Mass in Hyannis Port he was at home until four thirty, when he played more golf before taking Jackie and the children on a cruise. His phone logs show a few telephone calls on Saturday and Sunday; otherwise he devoted the weekend to the Spaldings and his family, and to reading a book that Jackie had given him.

He and Jackie were voracious readers. For her, books had been an escape from her parents' troubled marriage; for him, an escape during his many illnesses and hospitalizations. His reading had a determined and remorseless quality, and he read at meals, in the bathtub, and even propped a book up on his bureau as he dressed. He had told his friend Larry Newman, "I feel better when there are books around. That's really where my education comes from." Exchanging books had become a form of communication for them—a way of expressing feelings they had difficulty voicing. As a homecoming present from Otis, he had given her *Letters from Vatican City* by Xavier Ryne, the *New Yorker* correspondent who covered the Vatican, and a biography of Catherine de' Medici, a flattering reminder of her contribution to "the work" they had to do together. When he returned that weekend, she reciprocated with Jon Manchip White's *Marshal of France: The Life and Times of Maurice de Saxe*.* During their 1961 state visit to Paris she had held a long conversation in idiomatic French with President Charles de Gaulle about eighteenth-century French history, making it unlikely that she did not know that in addition to being the foremost military genius of his time, Maurice de Saxe had also been a legendary lover and philanderer.

---

* She had read the book earlier that summer, and he thought it sounded so interesting that he had leafed through it. Now he had his own copy.

Kennedy was a fast reader and could have finished the biography that weekend. At the very least he would have read in White's concise foreword that the count had been "the brilliant adornment of a brilliant age, one of the most renowned and admired men in the Europe of his day," and "the lover of many celebrated women" who had "won the lifelong friendship of men the stature of Voltaire." He had also been "among the wittiest and most elegant" military heroes of all time, "a dreamer and an idealist," and "a deeply interesting person in his own right" who "loved noise, excitement, rewards, women, wine, and glory—especially glory," and had become a great man "in spite of sickness ... and the most bitter and ruthless opposition."

White's early chapters revealed more similarities. Like Rose Kennedy, who sometimes scooted through her houses in Hyannis Port and Palm Beach with reminder notes pinned to her cardigan and Scotch tape plastered across her forehead to smooth her wrinkles, the count's mother was "growing increasingly eccentric as the years passed." His father, Frederick Augustus I, the king of Poland and elector of Saxony, had been a notorious satyr, "an ogre of self-indulgence who regarded the debauching of his brilliant son's character with positive complacency." Nevertheless, White wrote, "He was unable wholly to corrupt his son, and many of the princely qualities of Maurice's nature survive," including "the energy, magnanimity, and gusto that made him so attractive a person."

When Jackie lost Arabella, Kennedy had been on a yacht in the Mediterranean; when Maurice de Saxe's wife had their first child, who would live only a few days, "the father was not at his wife's side but was rollicking with a sledging party on the frozen Elbe." Kennedy may have had an affair with Marilyn Monroe; while living in Paris in 1720, Maurice de Saxe "soon became notorious among the ladies of Paris, taking as a lover the glamorous young actress Adrienne Lecouvreur, who discerned in him a real-life hero with the soul of an artist." Like Jackie, who had taught her husband to care about clothes, food, and furnishings, Lecouvreur found her lover "a promising subject for any woman who had a taste for polishing rough diamonds." Their romance was troubled, with her complaining, "You were not made to love me in the way that I want to be loved." After his death, the editor of his memoirs called him a man who "preferred to command love rather than merit it."

Jack and Jackie had a running argument about whether French or British history was more interesting. Her gift may have been meant as another salvo in that good-natured quarrel, chosen because of his interest in heroism and great men. But because so much of it dwelled on the count's extraordinary sexual exploits, it would have been difficult for him to ignore that she might have also intended it as a cautionary tale, a warning that this could happen to him: a biography exposing *his* scandalous philandering.

Monday, August 19 – Tuesday, August 20

WASHINGTON

During Kennedy's weekly Tuesday breakfast with Democratic congressional leaders, Senator Mansfield handed him a three-page memorandum titled "Observations on Viet Nam" that suggested the change in American ambassadors presented him with an opportunity to reexamine "the fundamental premise" behind U.S. involvement in the war: the conviction that its outcome was as important to the United States as it was to the South Vietnamese. If it was, Mansfield wrote, "We are stuck with it and must stay with it whatever it may take in the end in the way of American lives and money and time to hold South Vietnam." He argued that it was not, although Americans had talked themselves into believing that it was by describing Vietnam as vital to U.S. security and giving it "a highly inflated importance." The crucial question, he said, was "Have we, as in Laos, first over-extended ourselves in words and in agency programs and then, in search of a rationalization for the erroneous over-extension, moved what may be essentially a peripheral situation to the core of our policy considerations?"

He contended that South Vietnam was peripheral to U.S. interests because it offered no great economic or commercial advantages, and any policy requiring the commitment of hundreds of thousands of U.S. troops to the Asian mainland, where U.S. naval and air superiority was less effective, was clearly irrational. Given this, he urged Kennedy to consider "the point at which the cost in men and money to the United States of essentially unilateral action to achieve the objective outweighs any possible advantage which it might provide to the security and welfare of this nation," and to declare that although the United States was concerned with the freedom of Vietnam, "in the absence of responsive indigenous leadership or adequate international cooperation . . . the essential interests of the United States do not compel this nation to become unilaterally engaged in any nation in Southeast Asia." He also recommended toning down the rhetoric, stressing the relatively limited importance of the area in terms of specific U.S. interests, referring the problem to the United Nations, and considering "withdrawing abruptly and in a matter-of-fact fashion a percentage—say, 10 percent—of the military advisors which we have in Vietnam, as a symbolic gesture."

Hours after Kennedy read Mansfield's memorandum, South Vietnamese police and Special Forces units trained by U.S. advisers invaded Buddhist pagodas across South Vietnam. They vandalized shrines, and arrested and beat more than a thousand priests and nuns, killing an unspecified number. Diem declared martial law, imposed a curfew, and cut phone lines to the U.S. embassy. The crackdown violated his promise to Ambassador Nolting not to take any further repressive measures against the Buddhists, and was a calculated insult to the United States, timed to occur between Nolting's departure and Lodge's arrival.

At 4:00 p.m., before knowing the full extent of what was happening, Kennedy took the stage at the State Department auditorium for his sixtieth live televised press conference. The conferences played to his strengths. He looked younger in black and white, had a quick wit, a good memory for facts and statistics, and was a superb extemporaneous speaker. Like his debates with Richard Nixon, they were unequal contests in which he came off as more intelligent, charming, confident, better-looking, better-dressed, and more amusing and thoughtful than his opponents—in this instance, the White House press corps. He held one about every sixteen days, calling them when Salinger warned that reporters were getting restless, or when he wanted to pressure Congress into passing a piece of legislation. The main purpose of his August 20 press conference was to scold House members for making draconian cuts to his foreign aid bill. It was a typical Kennedy performance: fluent responses that read as well as they sounded, and an impressive marshaling of facts and logic leavened by humor. When asked if he was "seeking a man with a business background or a political background" to serve as his next postmaster general, he drew laughs by replying, "There are other fields that are still to be considered, including even a postal background."

There was more laughter when he answered a question about Senator Barry Goldwater of Arizona, his probable opponent in 1964, becoming a captive of the radical right by saying, "I don't know who has captured who."

Sometimes his cool-cat façade fell away and he turned testy, reflective, or passionate, offering a glimpse of his deeply forested interior. This happened on August 20—after calling his foreign aid bill "essential to the continued strength of the free world," and insisting that with unemployment at 5.6 percent "the state of the economy is good," and replying to a question on whether black Americans deserved "special dispensation" for having suffered years of second-class citizenship by saying we should "make sure we are giving everyone a fair chance, but not [through] hard and fast quotas"—when, after delivering these replies in a calm and reasoned manner, he was asked to comment on Dr. Edwin Teller's testimony on the test ban treaty before the Senate Foreign Relations Committee. Teller had called the treaty a "tragic mistake" that would weaken American defenses and invite a Soviet attack. When Fulbright reported to Kennedy that Teller had impressed some members of the committee, the president had replied, "There's no doubt that any man with complete conviction, particularly who's an expert, is bound to shake anybody who's got an open mind. That's the advantage of having a closed mind."

When Kennedy was asked at his press conference to rebut Teller's charges, his voice hardened and he said, "I understand Dr. Teller is opposed to it. Every day he is opposed to it. I recognize he is going to continue being opposed to it." He reminded reporters that the United States had needed only a single test to develop the first atom bomb, and now its bombs were "many, many, many times stronger than the weapon that flattened Hiroshima and Nagasaki." Pounding on the podium, he asked, "How many weapons do you need and how many megatons do you need to destroy? . . . What we now have on hand, without any further testing, will kill three hundred million people in one hour," adding sarcastically, "I suppose they could even improve on that if it's necessary."

Wednesday, August 21–Friday, August 23

WASHINGTON AND CAPE COD

While Kennedy was upstairs in the family quarters, he received an early morning call from Undersecretary of State George Ball, reporting that Diem's government had ended the raids but imprisoned thousands of Buddhists, closed airports, and occupied telegraph offices. Nhu's shock troops, trained by U.S. advisers to fight the Viet Cong, had acted with appalling brutality. Ball thought that Lodge, who was in Japan and planning to arrive in South Vietnam several days later, should wait before flying to Saigon, since if he arrived now he could not present his credentials.

Kennedy disagreed. "I think this is going to be a big thing. Cabot can't be sitting on his butt. . . . He may be helpless, but he oughta be out there. I think it's going to make us look bad if he's not."

Ball said that several journalists, including David Halberstam of the *New York Times*, were claiming to have proof that the U.S. embassy had engineered the crackdown, and suggested preempting their stories by issuing a statement denying U.S. involvement. He read Kennedy a draft statement that condemned the repression as a direct violation of the South Vietnamese government's assurances that it would seek reconciliation with the Buddhists, and concluded, "The United States deplores repressive actions of this nature. We shall continue to assist Vietnam to resist Communist aggression and maintain its independence."

"I don't know about that last sentence," Kennedy said. "Why don't you leave the last sentence out?"

Ball admitted that it had been "an afterthought."

Kennedy criticized it as "sort of almost [a] non sequitur." It was also precisely the kind of rhetorical flourish that Mansfield's memorandum had cautioned him against using.

Several hours later, Lodge boarded a special military flight for Saigon and was probably airborne about the same time as Kennedy, who was flying to the Cape for another midweek visit with Jackie. And while they were both in the air, or slightly later, an Air Force transport left Andrews Air Force Base for West Germany carrying Ellen Rometsch, a statuesque twenty-seven-year-old former East German refugee who had become one of the president's sexual partners. Also aboard was La Verne Duffy, a former investigative aide to Robert Kennedy who had fallen in love with Rometsch and had been given the assignment of escorting her out of the country.

Bobby Baker, the secretary to the Senate majority leader, had often introduced women like Rometsch—whom he described as "eager young ladies who'd let it be known they were out for a good time"—to congressmen, Capitol Hill staffers, lobbyists, and government officials. She had come to the attention of the FBI after boasting to a former Bureau informant about her activities at the Quorum Club, a warren of rooms that Baker had leased at a Capitol Hill hotel, and her frequent visits to the White House. Her FBI file described her having a "rough complexion" and being fond of heavy makeup; photographs showed a voluptuous woman with a towering beehive hairdo. On July 3, 1963, J. Edgar Hoover sent Special Agent Courtney Evans to inform Robert Kennedy that Rometsch was claiming to have had "illicit relations with highly placed government officials," including the president. Evans also told Bobby that she had been raised in East Germany, where she had belonged to several Communist youth groups before fleeing to the West in 1955 at the age of nineteen. According to Evans's memorandum of their meeting, the attorney general "was appreciative of the Director's sending this information to him on a confidential basis," and "made particular note of Rometsch's name." When they parted, he "again expressed his appreciation for the discreet manner in which this information was handled."

Bobby had long been concerned about his brother's failure to ascertain even the most rudimentary information about some of his sexual partners, once warning him, "You've got to be careful about these girls. A couple of them might be spies." Britain's recent Profumo scandal had made Kennedy's behavior seem even more reckless. The British press had revealed in March that the secretary of state for war, John Profumo, had been patronizing the prostitute Christine Keeler at the same time that she was seeing a Soviet military attaché. Keeler was English and had not passed any government secrets to the Soviet attaché, but Profumo had resigned and the scandal was threatening to topple the Macmillan government.

The FBI agents who interviewed and investigated Rometsch could not substantiate the allegations that she had enjoyed "high-level sex contacts" or that she was a Communist agent. Because she was married to a West German airman stationed at the embassy, the FBI report recommended informing the State Department of the investigation, while cautioning, "Of course, no mention will be made of the President and the AG [attorney general]." The report did not quiet Bobby's fears. The Bureau had found no evidence that Rometsch was a spy, but it had confirmed that she had belonged to Communist youth groups, had known the East German leader Walter Ulbricht, still had relatives living in the East, and had enjoyed a liaison with a Soviet embassy official while living in Washington. If her relationship with the president became public, there would be a congressional investigation that would inevitably call into question all of the administration's dealings with the Soviet Union, including the test ban treaty. It was also possible that a more thorough investigation might reveal contacts between Rometsch and Soviet bloc intelligence agencies.*

KENNEDY HAD BEEN IGNORANT of Rometsch's background, but his inordinate interest in the Profumo case indicated that he appreciated the danger of becoming ensnared in a similar scandal. He had badgered the London embassy for updates on Profumo, and knowing of his interest in the case, his friends offered him frequent reports. After returning from Britain, Schlesinger

---

* After the fall of the Berlin Wall, an author conducting research for a book about the Stasi, the East German secret police, learned from former West and East German intelligence operatives that there were "strong indications" that Rometsch had been an agent for the Stasi's foreign espionage bureau, only marrying her husband after he was posted to Washington. She had been turned over to the KGB by the Stasi because the Soviets had jurisdiction over espionage activities in North America. When asked about her, a former KGB intelligence officer who had served at the Washington embassy said enigmatically, "Yes, I know of such a woman." (Rometsch lives in Germany and routinely refuses to be interviewed.)

told him, "It is hard to overstate the atmosphere of political squalor in London today," and said the scandal had served "to reinforce the impression that the Government is frivolous and decadent." Profumo remained on Kennedy's mind all summer. While editing a draft of his July 26 speech on the test ban treaty, he objected to using the word "proliferation," telling Ball that he feared some people might think it had something to do with Christine Keeler. If someone disparaged Profumo, he leaped to his defense, saying how easy it would be for a fellow to make that kind of a mistake, and that such extreme criticism was unjustified. During a small White House dinner the year before, honoring the British philosopher Isaiah Berlin, he had become testy when Berlin mentioned that a historian had recently published an article about a sexual affair between Lenin and a woman that predated the Russian Revolution. "He thought this was not at all the way to treat a great man," Berlin said later. "I had the feeling that he felt one mustn't talk about the private affairs of great heads of state in quite that tone of voice. I felt put in my place."

Bobby decided it was too dangerous for Rometsch to stay in Washington, where she might talk to someone who would tip off the press, and could be subpoenaed to appear before Congress or a grand jury. He ordered her deported, instructed the State Department to deny her a visa if she attempted to return, and asked Duffy to chaperone her on the flight back to West Germany. But if he and the president had imagined that this would end the threat, they would be proved wrong two months later, when they would open the *New York Times* to see her photograph underneath a headline reading, "Baker Inquiry Is Asked If German Woman's Ouster by U.S. Involved Security."

Kennedy's affair with Rometsch was one of the most egregious instances of a womanizing so compulsive and careless that even those who believed they knew him well would struggle for decades to fathom it, falling back on words such as "inexplicable" and "incomprehensible." His defense of Lenin and Profumo showed that he appreciated the risks to his presidency and his place in history. Then why did he do it? How could a man who cared so much about the judgment of history engage in behavior that as a student of history he must have known would surely come to light? How could a man who had shown such integrity in his public life show so little in private, risking his reputation for hurried and, according to several of his partners, unsatisfying couplings with call girls, strippers, interns, and secretaries?

One of his mistresses suggested that his need for a secret life was a greater motivation than the sex. His friends have speculated that his wartime brush with death had left him addicted to risk, and that aside from driving like a madman, this was the riskiest thing he could do. It has been said he did it because he could not tolerate being bored and illicit sex was a pleasant antidote to boredom, because the steroids he took to control his Addison's had supercharged his libido (although he had been sexually promiscuous before taking the medicine), and because he believed he would die young, and sex was at the top of his bucket list. He told Senator Smathers, who sometimes supplied him with women, "You've got to live every day like it's your last on earth," and said to Joe Alsop, "I've got this slow-motion cancer [he was referring to his Addison's], which they say gets you when you're forty." It is also possible that abstinence really did give him, as he claimed, insomnia and migraines. He confided in Clare Boothe Luce that he "went all to pieces" unless he had sex every day, and told Harold Macmillan that if he went without sex for a day he suffered punishing headaches. According to the more questionable theories, he was promiscuous because being circumcised at the age of twenty-one for tight foreskin problems had left him desperate to prove his manhood, or because he had been traumatized as a boy by finding his father in flagrante with the film star Gloria Swanson, although there are doubts whether this occurred. The most widely accepted theory blames his father, a notorious philanderer who, according to Kennedy, encouraged him and his brothers "to get laid as often as possible."

The fact that Kennedy's sexuality remained so unchanged over the years suggests that it was fixed during his adolescence and youth, and that his father was responsible. One member of his staff called him "an adolescent in terms of his sexual relationships," adding, "All this stuff was casual—as if he were in high school—hijinks." Lem Billings, who was a closeted homosexual, believed that he had "an immature relationship with girls—that is, while he was terribly interested in going out and having fun with them at night, I don't think he was really terribly excited about girls as friends." Bobby Baker observed that he "seemed to relish sharing the details of his conquests" and "came off as some-thing of the boyish braggart"; the White House intern Mimi Beardsley thought that "part of him still seemed to be an adolescent teenager at Choate"; and the stripper Tempest Storm described him as "a little boy who wouldn't grow up," although in other respects, she found him "one of the most mature men" she had ever known.

His affair with Tempest Storm showed how widely he cast his sexual net. His partners included Jackie's press secretary Pamela Turnure, the White House secretaries Priscilla Wear and Jill Cowan—two spunky twenty-somethings nicknamed "Fiddle" and "Faddle"—and Ben Bradlee's sister-in-law Mary Meyer. Prior to Rometsch, his most risky relationship had been with Judith Campbell, a two-year affair beginning in 1960 when Frank Sinatra introduced them in Las Vegas, and ended with him sharing Campbell with the Mafia boss Sam Giancana.

Whatever demons lay behind his voracious womanizing, he seemed incapable of taming them. Betty Spalding described it as "a real compulsion . . . something so deep in that man." Charlie Bartlett, who had introduced him to Jackie, believed he never should have married, because "he had this thing about him, which was not under control." During a Washington dinner party in the late fifties, he told Priscilla McMillan, who had formerly worked in his Senate office, that he had married Jackie "because I was thirty-seven years old, and people would think I was queer if I wasn't married." Encouraged by his candor, she asked, "Jack, when you're straining every gasket to be president, why do you endanger yourself by going out with women?" After a long pause he shrugged and a sad expression crossed his face that reminded McMillan of a little boy preparing to cry. "I guess it's because I just can't help it," he said.

Jackie's sister, Lee Radziwill, believed that Kennedy had "absolutely no guilty conscience," but if that was true, why would he say "I just can't help it," or tell Charlie Bartlett that he intended "to keep the White House white," or look for precedents to justify his philandering, showing a keen interest in polygamy during a discussion of the Kama Sutra and the sexual morals of the ancient world with Jackie's couturier Oleg Cassini. He sometimes justified his womanizing as the mark of a great man. When his friend Marie Ridder asked during the 1960 campaign if he planned to continue having affairs while living in the White House, he replied breezily, "Oh, it'll be much easier, because the Secret Service will protect me. Anyway all great men have this failing. Wilson stopped the conference at Versailles to have his 'nooner,' and Alexander the Great had so many sexual appetites he never knew next what gender would appeal to him." He went on at great length, listing other great leaders who had been unfaithful and viewing his sexual morals, as he did so many things, in the context of the sweep of history and great men.

The most perceptive take on his sexual pathology can be found in the letters, diary, and testimony of Margaret Coit, a Pulitzer Prize–winning biographer who was perhaps the smartest and most sensitive woman whom he ever attempted to seduce. After she won a Pulitzer in 1951 at the age of thirty-one for her biography of Senator John C. Calhoun, the eminent financier and presidential adviser Bernard Baruch asked her to write his biography. Before traveling to Washington in the spring of 1953 to conduct research at the Library of Congress and speak with senators who had known Baruch, she manufactured a pretext to interview Kennedy, writing him that since her book encompassed Baruch's times, she hoped he could provide her with some background about his prewar years in London. "I had designs on John F. Kennedy," she admitted. "He was the golden boy, the most eligible bachelor in New England."

Despite her literary fame, Coit was a country girl and a virgin who admitted knowing "very, very, very little" about the outside world. She dressed for their interview in a gray silk suit, pink lace gloves, and a gray bonnet with a pink lace veil, an outfit more suited to a date. ("He got the idea right away," she said.) His Senate office was spartan. There was a small sofa, some straight-backed chairs, and bookcases crammed with works on history, economics, and politics. She was encouraged that none of his secretaries were "very young, chic, or pretty," but shocked by his appearance. His eyes, hair, and lips looked gray, and under his tan even his skin had a grayish tinge. After several minutes of desultory conversation he admitted knowing little about Baruch. Then he gave her a long, searching look and said, "You're the smartest thing to come into this office since the election," and invited her to a party at his house.

She was disappointed that he spent most of the evening in a corner with Senator Symington. As she was leaving he suddenly threw an arm around her waist and announced, "Isn't she the darlingest thing to come into this house for a long time?" He tracked her down at the Library of Congress manuscript room several days later and asked her out. "I just glowed," she told her diary. "And as I bathed and dressed for the big date, I felt—this is the biggest day of my life. Dreamed of him as the fairy prince . . . grey and ethereal."

She arrived at his office to find him in shirtsleeves, signing photographs for his constituents while chewing a wad of Juicy Fruit gum, snapping it so forcefully that his head shook. "My brother told me that you won the Pulitzer Prize," he said, adding that he was impressed that she had not mentioned it. He noticed her examining his history books and said, "Try me on them. I've read them all." She did, and was amazed that he really *had* read and digested them. He fired questions. Was she married? Had Bernard Baruch made a pass at her? Was there any passion left in the relationship between Baruch and Clare Boothe Luce? He took a call from Jackie and spoke to her in a cold and offhanded manner, even though he would propose to her a month later. After hanging up, he plopped down on the sofa, threw back his head, and closed his eyes, and the remaining color drained from his face.

Coit said he seemed too exhausted to take her out and suggested postponing their date. He agreed but insisted on driving her back to her rooming house. He hobbled down the office building corridor on crutches, but the fresh air revived him and he bit a stick of Juicy Fruit in half and popped some into her mouth. Once they were seated in his battered blue sedan he leaned across her to shut the passenger-side door tightly, grinning as he pressed his arm against her breasts. Thinking he might want to rest before driving home, she invited him to her rooms. He immediately threw himself onto her couch and tried dragging her down. "Wait a minute," she said, struggling to escape. "I made up my mind that I was not going to kiss you on the first date."

"We've been making eyes at one another three times now," he said, lunging again. She asked if he would want his sisters to give in on the first date. "I don't care what they do," he said.

She struggled up from the sofa and he grabbed her shoulders and exclaimed, "I'm sad; I'm gay; I'm melancholy; I'm gloomy—I'm all mixed up, and I don't know how I am!"

As they began grappling again, she said, "Don't be so grabby. This is only our first date. We've got plenty of time."

He stared deeply into her eyes and said, "But I can't wait, you see. I'm going to grab everything I want. You see, I haven't any time."

She finally kissed him. After he murmured, "Darling," she said, "That's the first gentle word you have ever said to me."

"How would you like a husband who was harsh to you first and gentle to you afterwards?" he asked. "How would you like a husband who beat you every morning?"

After she accused him of being "a spoiled Irish Mick on the make," and he called her "a spoiled Irish bastard," they both broke down laughing and he promised not to bother her anymore. She agreed to ride back with him to his house in Georgetown on condition that he send her home in a taxi.

As they were driving she asked if he was disappointed. "Of course I'm disappointed," he admitted. He had wanted to sleep with her and learn how Bernard Baruch made his money. "I want to make millions," he said. "I am going to outdo my father." A few minutes later he told her, "I would rather win a Pulitzer Prize than be president of the United States," and asked, "Why don't you write a book about me? What I am interested in is me." As they passed the White House he announced in a hard voice, "I am going to go there."

She asked if he had the drive to be president. He conceded that he was unsure, adding, "I often wonder—do I have the brains to be president?"

He put her in a cab and promised to call her.

"You won't see me again," she promised. He was the most driven person she had ever met, and he frightened her. What scared her most was the effortless, machine-like way that he had shifted between the intellectual and the carnal. "We had been talking about books and ideas and . . . he had seen me as one kind of person. He had seen me as a mind; and now he saw me as just something female," she recalled. "He couldn't fit the two together, and it was if he were two parts. He was like a fourteen-year-old high school football player on the make; and he was like an elder statesman of sixty in his intellectual process."

Before they parted he urged her to read *The Young Melbourne,* a biography of Queen Victoria's first prime minister, as a way of understanding him. Like the Kennedy family, Lord Melbourne's had been new-money arrivistes, and like him, Melbourne had been a second-oldest son and a political realist with what his biographer called "a mocking wit," who had assumed family leadership after the death of his older brother. After finishing the book she sent him a long and thoughtful letter. "As for you, I believe you do have the drive to be President—and the dignity, on occasion—and the brains and these will provide the momentum," she wrote, "but who knows where the wild horse will run. . . . There is more in luck and fate than we think, and we can do no more than turn it loose." She wrote again to congratulate him when he won his own Pulitzer Prize. He scrawled at the bottom of his reply, "When are we going to meet again?"

On August 21, he was still shifting gears. On the same day that he had told

Ball not to pledge that America would continue resisting Communist aggression in Vietnam, and had returned to Cape Cod to comfort Jackie, the plane carrying Ellen Rometsch could have flown over Squaw Island, perhaps while he was writing a reminder on White House stationery to investigate a new cure for cancer or sketching an emblem for a new naval medal, an eagle holding two branches, as Caroline sat on his lap, happily adding her own scribbles to his.

The day after Ellen Rometsch returned to Germany, a column by the Pulitzer Prize–winning journalist Richard Wilson titled "Personal Conduct in High Office—President Lauded for Highest Standard in Both Public and Family Life" appeared in the Washington *Evening Star*. Wilson wrote, "One need not agree with all, or any, of his [Kennedy's] policies to recognize that in his behavior, attitude, and demeanor he provides the needed example that the troubled or misguided may turn to with respect and admiration."

When Kennedy read the column the next day, as he surely did, he found himself praised as "a man of intellectual attainment and with wide and varied interests . . . ranging into areas of mind *and* spirit which define the ultimate values of life" and "a cultivated modern man of vigorous spirit and wit and pleasing habits, manners, and appearance" who "publicly and privately" was "setting a national tone of responsibility." Wilson contrasted his "sense of responsibility [for] . . . how he behaves in his exalted office publicly and privately" with Profumo and politicians like Nelson Rockefeller, who had just divorced his wife of thirty years. He concluded, "High officials must surely recognize, as President Kennedy recognizes, that the probity of their lives should at least match the level of their responsibility."

CAPE COD

Jackie loved their rented house on Squaw Island so much that she had ordered its sixteen rooms measured and photographed so she could build a replica on an adjoining lot. Everything she liked about Brambletyde—the isolation, privacy, and spectacular position on a promontory facing the sea—made it gloomy on stormy days like this one, when you heard only the wind, crashing surf, and a lanyard clanging against a giant flagpole. The White House press office announced that the president would spend the day reading reports on the deteriorating situation in South Vietnam, and released a letter from Dr. Albert Schweitzer, the renowned humanitarian physician. Writing in longhand from his clinic in equatorial Africa, Schweitzer had congratulated Kennedy for "having had the foresight and the courage to inaugurate a world policy toward peace," and called the test ban treaty "one of the greatest events, perhaps the greatest, in the history of the world," praise that did not seem so excessive ten months after several hundred million human beings had narrowly escaped being incinerated during the Cuban missile crisis.

The press office narrative of a busy president using the inclement weather to catch up on his work did not match the mood inside Brambletyde. Bill Walton, the only guest that weekend, spoke of the house being "full of sadness." Caroline remained upset by Patrick's death, and only her father could calm her. When she was not in his lap, he read and reread the condolence letters, passing them to Walton with comments such as "Look at what the Pope said." He was keeping score and had already complained to Schlesinger that Adlai Stevenson had neglected to write Jackie. "I wish you would tell him to send her a letter," he said. "Don't mention that it came from me, but I have spent most of my life in the midst of people getting hurt because someone doesn't write a letter or attend a funeral, and I want to avoid that thing as much as possible."*

Walton, who was equally close to both of them, remembered the weekend as the most intimate he had ever spent with them, saying later, "She hung on to him and he held her in his arms." Each took him aside during the weekend: Jack to unburden himself about the pressures of dealing with Khrushchev over access to Berlin; Jackie to confide that she knew Jack had badly wanted a second boy and was the kind of man who needed a large family.

A telegram arrived from Lee Radziwill inviting Jackie to join her on a cruise through the Greek islands in October with the shipping magnate Aristotle Onassis. The Kennedys had met Onassis while traveling through Europe in 1955, and he had asked them to dinner with Winston Churchill aboard the *Christina,* his opulent 325-foot yacht. Thrilled by the opportunity to meet the man whose speeches he had memorized, Kennedy had arrived overdressed in a white dinner jacket. The aging Churchill ignored him, and Jackie teased him afterward, saying, "Maybe he thought you were a waiter, Jack." He dined with Onassis again in Washington in 1959, and a few months later Onassis arranged a more satisfying meeting between him and Churchill.

The prospect of Jackie cruising with Onassis appalled Walton, but Kennedy seemed torn. She had already canceled her official engagements until the end of the year, and the trip might head off another lengthy bout of postpartum depression like the one she had experienced following John's birth. But he also understood the political risks. When she had traveled to Italy the previous year, she had been criticized for vacationing outside the country without her husband. And rumors of an affair between Lee and Onassis had prompted the columnist Drew Pearson to ask, even though Lee was married, "Does the ambitious Greek tycoon hope to become the brother-in-law of the President?" The troubled relationship between Onassis and the U.S. government was another concern. Onassis had paid a fine to avoid a criminal trial on charges of violating Maritime

---

* Stevenson sent a graceful note that concluded, "I *know* there is much joy and peace and fulfillment for *you*—for, as Fra Giovanni said, there is radiance and glory in the darkness, could we but see. And you, dear Jackie, *can* see."

Commission regulations, leading Kennedy to refer to him in private as a pirate and crook, and to tell Clint Hill, the Secret Service agent accompanying Jackie on her visit to Greece in 1961, "Whatever you do in Greece, do not let Mrs. Kennedy cross paths with Aristotle Onassis."

On Saturday afternoon, Deputy National Security Adviser Michael Forrestal called to ask Kennedy to approve a cable to Ambassador Lodge that Forrestal had drafted in consultation with Averell Harriman and Roger Hilsman. Forrestal read him a draft of Cable 243, their proposed reply to an earlier cable from Lodge requesting guidance on how he should respond to a group of South Vietnamese generals wanting to know the U.S. position if they deposed Diem. The crucial passage in 243 said, "US Government cannot tolerate situation in which power lies in Nhu's hands. Diem must be given chance to rid himself of Nhu and his coterie and replace them with best military and political personalities available. If, in spite of your efforts, Diem remains obdurate and refuses, then we must face the possibility that Diem himself cannot be preserved." If Diem refused to remove Nhu, the cable instructed, "You may also tell appropriate military commanders we will give them direct support in any interim period of breakdown central government mechanism." Since Diem was unlikely to cashier his brother, this represented a green light to stage a coup.

At the end of an emotional day when he and his family were still mourning Patrick, Kennedy was being asked to approve a cable that would involve the United States even more deeply in South Vietnam's political shenanigans, and risked complicating any future attempts to reduce American involvement in the conflict. His senior foreign policy advisers were out of Washington. Secretary of Defense McNamara was in Aspen; the CIA director, John McCone, was sailing in Puget Sound; National Security Adviser McGeorge Bundy was at his house on Cape Ann; and Secretary of State Dean Rusk was in New York, preparing for the fall meeting of the United Nations General Assembly.

Kennedy asked if he could delay making a decision until Monday, when everyone would be back in town.

Forrestal replied that the Buddhist crisis was spiraling out of control, and Harriman and Hilsman wanted to send an immediate response.

"Well, go and see what you can do to get it cleared," he said.

Hilsman and Harriman found Undersecretary Ball, the senior State Department official in Washington, on a golf course and asked him to approve the cable. Realizing its importance, Ball called Kennedy and read him the critical passages. The president struck him as favorable to sending it, despite recognizing the danger that Diem's replacement might be no better, and asked Ball for his opinion. Ball was an old-school diplomat who leavened his realpolitik with a belief in American exceptionalism. He believed that encouraging coups "ran counter to the grain of American principles," but he also thought that the Nhus had undermined "what little moral justification remained for our position in Vietnam." He told Kennedy that he supported sending the cable. Kennedy replied that he would approve it as long as Rusk and Roswell Gilpatric, the senior Defense Department official in McNamara's absence, also signed off.

Ball called Rusk, who sounded cautious but finally agreed to approve the cable provided the president understood its implications.

Forrestal reached Gilpatric at his Virginia farm. He viewed the cable as a matter between State and the White House, and since Rusk and Kennedy apparently wanted to send it, he considered his approval a formality.

Forrestal reported back to Kennedy that everyone was on board. If he thought that some had signed on because they believed that Kennedy had already approved the cable, he did not voice this suspicion. And so, believing the matter was urgent and that everyone had weighed the consequences, Kennedy told Forrestal to send the cable, at a stroke violating the two most hard-won lessons of his presidency. From the Bay of Pigs he had learned not to accept the unanimous recommendations of his civilian and military advisers without subjecting them to a rigorous interrogation; from the Cuban missile crisis he had learned the value of gathering a select group of advisers in a room, listening as they debated policy options, then having the courage to make a contradictory decision.

Sunday remained chilly and blustery, but the rain had stopped. Kennedy asked the White House photographer, Cecil Stoughton, to take an 8-millimeter film of him playing golf so he could send it to Arnold Palmer and have him critique his swing, an example of following his father's advice always to seek the opinion of the top expert in any field. In the afternoon, he and Jackie and the children, accompanied by Walton and Stoughton, went out on the *Honey Fitz*. They sat on lounge chairs in the stern, wearing thick sweaters and wrapped in gray blankets. The sea was dotted with whitecaps as he watched a sailing race through binoculars. One of Stoughton's photographs shows Caroline holding a stuffed animal and leaning her head on his shoulder as he stares into the distance. His skin is deeply lined and weathered from a lifetime of tanning in Hyannis Port and Palm Beach, his eyes are puffy, his hair frosted with gray.

Upon returning to Squaw Island he received Lodge's response to Cable 243. Lodge had been instructed to give Diem the "chance to rid himself of Nhu and his coterie" and to approach the "appropriate military commanders" only if Diem remained "obdurate." Although he had been in Vietnam only four days, he was already insisting on fast-tracking the coup. "Believe that chances of Diem's meeting our demands are virtually nil," he cabled. "At the same time, by making them we give Nhu chance to forestall or block action by military. Risk, we believe, is not worth taking. . . . Therefore, propose we go straight to Generals with our demands, without informing Diem. Would tell them we prepared to have Diem without Nhus but it is in effect up to them whether to keep him." Here, already, was the result of leaving things "almost completely" in Lodge's hands.

WASHINGTON

During a meeting on Monday, the Soviet ambassador, Anatoly Dobrynin, presented Kennedy with a letter from Soviet leader Nikita Khrushchev representing the latest installment in the secret correspondence between them that had led to the test ban treaty and an agreement to install a "hotline" between Washington and Moscow that would begin functioning on August 30 and transmit its first operational message on November 22.

They had started exchanging letters after the Cuban missile crisis made them the first men in history forced to make decisions that could lead to the instant death of millions of human beings. Kennedy had initiated the correspondence by writing to Khrushchev on October 28, 1962, a day after the most perilous moment in the crisis, "I think we should give priority to questions relating to the proliferation of nuclear weapons, on earth and in outer space, and to the great effort for a nuclear test ban." When Norman Cousins, who served as an intermediary between them during the spring of 1963, met with Kennedy before leaving for Moscow in April, Kennedy predicted that Khrushchev would say that he wanted to reduce tensions but could see no reciprocal interest in Washington. "It is important that he be corrected on this score," he said. "I'm not sure Khrushchev knows this, but I don't think there's any man in American politics who's more eager than I am to put Cold War animosities behind us and get down to the hard business of building friendly relations."

Cousins would make several observations about Khrushchev that also applied to Kennedy, among them his description of the Soviet leader as "a lonesome figure who gave the impression of being gregarious," and a man who "never attempted to conceal his peasant background" yet "didn't hesitate to wear expensive silk shirts and gold cufflinks." Their correspondence also shows them sharing concerns about the health risks of nuclear fallout and proliferation, and understanding that the other faced similar pressures from hard-liners within his own government and military. Kennedy referred to this in his April 11, 1963, letter to Khrushchev, writing, "In closing, I want again to send my warm personal wishes to you and your family. These are difficult and dangerous times in which we live, and both you and I have grave responsibilities to our families and to all of mankind. The pressures from those who have a less patient and peaceful outlook are very great—but I assure you of my own determination to work to strengthen world peace." Two weeks later, Kennedy told Cousins, who was briefing him on his conversations with Khrushchev, "One of the ironic things about this entire situation is that Mr. Khrushchev and I occupy approximately the same political positions inside our governments. He would like to prevent a nuclear war but is under severe pressure from his hard-line crowd, which interprets every move in that direction as appeasement. I've got similar problems. Meanwhile the lack of progress in reaching agreements between our two countries gives strength to the hard-line boys in both, with the result that the hard-liners in the Soviet Union and in the United States feed on one another, each using the actions of the other to justify its own position."

Kennedy had witnessed this when Khrushchev sent him two contradictory communications on successive days during the Cuban crisis. The first was a conciliatory letter, the second a brusque ultimatum. The former U.S. ambassador to Moscow Llewellyn Thompson advised him that Khrushchev might have sent the second message to placate hard-liners and recommended ignoring it and responding to the first message.

The crisis afforded Khrushchev a similar understanding of the pressures on Kennedy. He wrote in his 1970 memoirs that during a secret meeting between Robert Kennedy and Ambassador Dobrynin, Robert Kennedy had said, "The President is in a grave situation, and he does not know how to get out of it. We are under very severe stress. In fact we are under pressure from our military to use force against Cuba." Considering this, he said, the president "implores Chairman Khrushchev to accept his offer." He also warned that although the president was "very much against starting a war over Cuba, an irreversible chain of events could occur against his will. If the situation continues much longer, the President is not sure that the military will not overthrow him and seize power. The American army could get out of control."

The American editor of Khrushchev's memoirs wrote in a footnote, "Obviously, this is Khrushchev's own version of what was reported to him. There is no evidence that the President was acting out of fear of a military take-over." Dobrynin gave an account of his conversation with Robert Kennedy in his memoirs that was based on a report he had written in 1962 that supported Khrushchev's version. He wrote that during his pivotal late-night meeting with Robert Kennedy on Saturday, October 27, the president's brother "remarked almost in passing that a lot of unreasonable people among American generals—and not only generals—were 'spoiling for a fight.'"

It is possible that Bobby told Dobrynin that his brother feared a military coup, hoping to frighten the Soviets into removing their missiles from Cuba. But what *is* certain is that by the fall of 1962 the president not only believed a coup was possible, but had repeatedly discussed its likelihood. That fall, Harper and Row published *Seven Days in May,* a thriller by Fletcher Knebel and Charles V. Bailey II about a coup against a U.S. president instigated by his decision to sign a controversial nuclear arms pact with the Soviet Union. Knebel got the idea from an interview with Air Force Chief of Staff Curtis LeMay shortly after the Bay of Pigs. LeMay was still furious with Kennedy for refusing to provide air support for the Cuban rebels, and after going off the record he accused him of cowardice. Knebel also found inspiration in a 1962 conversation with Secretary of the Navy John Connally. With LeMay's remarks fresh in his mind, Knebel had turned the conversation to the military's unhappiness with the president. Connally acknowledged that some of his admirals disliked taking orders from the New Frontiersman, and felt they could not express themselves politically. Later in the conversation, Connally mused that the atomic bomb had created conditions in which "the U.S. might unwittingly be laying the groundwork for a military dictatorship."

On March 13, 1962, six months before the publication of Knebel's book, the Joint Chiefs of Staff had sent Secretary of Defense McNamara a top-secret memorandum proposing Operation Northwoods, a program of clandestine actions designed to provide what the chiefs called "adequate justification" for the United

States to invade Cuba. It resembled the incursions by German troops dressed in Polish uniforms that Hitler used as a pretext for invading Poland. The chiefs recommended a "logical build-up of incidents" that would "camouflage the ultimate objective and create the necessary impression of Cuban rashness and irresponsibility of a large scale," and "place the United States in the apparent position of suffering defensible grievances from a rash and irresponsible government of Cuba." To accomplish this, they suggested "well-coordinated incidents" at the U.S. Navy base at Guantánamo Bay, in the airspace over Cuba, and on the U.S. mainland. At Guantánamo, anti-Castro Cubans dressed in Cuban Army uniforms would be "captured" by U.S. forces after pretending to attack the base. "Blow up ammunition inside the base," the Northwoods memorandum recommended. "Burn aircraft on air base (sabotage). . . . Lob mortar shells from outside of base into base. . . . Sink ship near harbor entrance. Conduct funerals for mock victims." The chiefs also proposed what they called a "Remember the *Maine*" incident that involved blowing up a U.S. ship in Guantánamo Bay or destroying an unmanned drone vessel in waters off Havana, and blaming Castro. "The U.S. could follow up with an air/sea rescue operation . . . to 'evacuate' remaining members of the non-existent crew," they suggested. "Casualty lists in U.S. newspapers would cause a helpful wave of national indignation." The memorandum's most disturbing paragraph began, "We could develop a Communist Cuban terror campaign in the Miami area, in other Florida cities and even in Washington," which might entail "exploding a few plastic bombs in carefully chosen spots." It continued, "The terror campaign could be pointed at Cuban refugees seeking haven in the United States. We could sink a boatload of Cubans en route to Florida (real or simulated). We could foster attempts on lives of Cuban refugees in the United States even to the extent of wounding in instances to be widely publicized."

After receiving a summary of the memorandum, Kennedy told Chairman of the Joint Chiefs Lyman Lemnitzer that he could not imagine a set of events "that would justify and make desirable the use of American Forces for overt military action" against Castro's Cuba. Three months later, he transferred him to Europe to serve as supreme allied commander of NATO, replacing him with Maxwell Taylor. Kennedy was too smart, and too suspicious of the brass, not to recall Operation Northwoods when he read *Seven Days in May* in galleys a few months later, and not to reason that if the chiefs were prepared to recommend deceptive, violent, and illegal actions on the U.S. mainland that risked harming civilians, it was not preposterous to imagine them cooking up a similar scheme to justify overthrowing a president whose policies they viewed as threatening national security. After finishing the book, he told Laura Bergquist that he had been pondering the possibility of a military coup, and then named some generals at the Pentagon whom he thought "might hanker to duplicate fiction."

During a discussion of *Seven Days in May*, Fay asked Kennedy if he really believed a coup was possible. He said it was, and believed it would require three confrontations between a president and the military similar to the one between himself and the Joint Chiefs during the Bay of Pigs. "The conditions would have to be just right," he said. "If the country had a young President, and he had a Bay of Pigs, there would be certain uneasiness, and maybe the military would criticize him behind his back [as LeMay had done during the Knebel interview] but this would be written off as the usual military dissatisfaction with civilian control. Then if there was another Bay of Pigs, the reaction of the country would be, 'Is he too young and inexperienced.' The military would almost feel that it was their patriotic obligation to stand ready to preserve the integrity of the nation, and only God knows just what segment of democracy they would be defending if they overthrew the elected establishment."

This second Bay of Pigs scenario bore a resemblance to how some of the chiefs would react several months after his conversation with Fay, when he rejected their recommendation to bomb Soviet missile sites in Cuba and instead imposed a naval blockade. At a meeting in the Cabinet Room during the crisis, LeMay told him, "I just don't see any other solution except military intervention *right now*," and condemned a blockade as "almost as bad as the appeasement at Munich." A few minutes later, LeMay said bluntly, "I think that a blockade and political talk would be considered by a lot of our friends and neutrals as being a pretty weak response to this. And I'm sure a lot of our own citizens would feel that way, too. In other words, you're in a pretty bad fix at the present time."

"What did you say?" Kennedy asked, forcing LeMay to repeat himself.

"You're in a pretty bad fix."

"You're in there with me." After a pause, he added, "Personally."

"Can you imagine LeMay saying a thing like that?" he asked O'Donnell afterward. "These brass hats have one great advantage in their favor. If we listen to them, and do what they want us to do, none of us will be alive later to tell them that they were wrong."

LeMay's comment bordered on insubordination and may have contributed to Bobby's remark to Dobrynin that "the President is not sure that the military will not overthrow him and seize power." LeMay would call the peaceful outcome of the Cuban missile crisis "the greatest defeat in our history." If he really believed that, why not consider extralegal means to remove the man responsible?

After the crisis ended, Kennedy told Schlesinger, "The military are mad. They wanted to do this [invade Cuba]. It's lucky for us that we have Mac [Robert McNamara] over there." He told Bradlee, "The first advice I'm going to give my successor is to watch the generals and to avoid feeling that just because they were military men their opinions on military matters were worth a damn." A year later McNamara informed Kennedy that according to Admiral Hyman Rickover, Chief of Naval Operations Admiral George Anderson had been "absolutely insubordinate" during the missile crisis and had "consciously acted contrary to the President's instructions." Kennedy asked what Rickover had meant by this. McNamara answered, "Rickover said enough to let me know that Anderson was objecting to the instructions that you and I were giving relating to the quarantine and the limiting of action in relation to stopping the Russian ships." Kennedy asked if this meant Anderson wanted to sink a ship. "That's right," McNamara said.

The actor Kirk Douglas was serving himself in a buffet dinner line in the White House in January 1963 when Kennedy came up behind him and asked, "Do you intend to make a movie out of *Seven Days in May*?" Douglas confirmed that he was producing and starring in a film version of the book being directed by John Frankenheimer. Kennedy said, "Good!" and as their meals cooled spent twenty minutes explaining why Knebel's book would make a great movie.

Pierre Salinger told Frankenheimer that the president wanted the film made "as a warning to the Republic." Schlesinger thought he hoped it would "raise the consciousness about the problems involved if the generals got out of control," and might also serve "as a warning to the generals." After the Defense Department denied Frankenheimer permission to film at the Pentagon, Kennedy took a long weekend in Hyannis Port so the director could shoot crowd scenes outside the White House.

Kennedy concluded his 1962 conversation with Fay about a *Seven Days in*

May–style coup by saying flatly, "Then, if there were a third Bay of Pigs, it [a coup] could happen." He paused to emphasize the significance of his comment before concluding with an old Navy phrase, "But it won't happen on my watch."

By August 1963, some opponents of the test ban treaty were calling it a betrayal of America's strategic interests. An ad hoc organization calling itself the Committee Against the Treaty of Moscow ran a full-page advertisement in U.S. newspapers that quoted General LeMay as saying that he would have opposed the treaty had it not been signed in Moscow before he learned about it. The advertisement also repeated Edwin Teller's warning to senators that by ratifying the treaty, "You will have given away the future safety of our country." Referring to the forthcoming ratification vote, it declared, "In September 1963, we shall be asked to repeat the reckless venture in appeasement that culminated in the 'Peace in Our Time' agreement signed in Munich on September 30, 1938."

A *New Republic* article in September titled "Rebellion in the Air Force?" began, "The Air Force's ruling hierarchy is in open defiance of its Constitutional Commander-in-Chief, and in some ways the situation bears a growing resemblance to the fictional story line of last year's best-seller *Seven Days in May,* the account of a nearly successful military coup by an Air Force general in protest against a nuclear arms treaty just concluded with the Russians." The article's author, Raymond Senter, reported that during its recent convention, the Air Force Association (AFA), an organization of retired and active-duty Air Force personnel, aerospace contractors, and lobbyists, had issued a blistering statement opposing the test ban treaty. Active-duty AFA members were prohibited from participating in drafting AFA statements, but Senter argued that the prohibition was meaningless since they seldom deviated from official Air Force views. Secretary of the Air Force Eugene Zuckert, usually a strong AFA supporter, condemned the AFA statement as "immoderate" and "alarmist," and canceled his appearance at its convention.

The test ban treaty may have pushed the most extreme elements in the military-industrial complex to the brink of mutiny, but it was not—at least not yet—the "third Bay of Pigs" that Kennedy had mentioned to Fay. But there were two others on the horizon: Vietnam and Ellen Rometsch. Kennedy had told O'Donnell that he expected to be "damned everywhere as a Communist appeaser" when he removed U.S. advisers from South Vietnam, and the revelation that he had bedded a former member of the East German Communist Party months before negotiating the test ban treaty might have tempted his opponents in the military to circumvent a drawn-out impeachment process with an Operation Northwoods–style action.

Khrushchev had also run afoul of his military establishment in the months preceding the treaty. He had told a February 1963 meeting of the Soviet Defense Council, "The time has come when he who is successful in preventing war wins, not he who counts on military victory." According to his son Sergei, his father followed this with "some absolutely unusual things—things that seemed to me not only seditious, but improbable as well." These included a plan to stop increasing the Soviet nuclear arsenal because, as Khrushchev told Marshal Zakharov, who headed his general staff, "You plan hundreds of targets, but even a dozen missiles with thermonuclear warheads are enough to make the very thought of war senseless." (At his August 20 news conference Kennedy had said, "How many weapons do you need and how many megatons do you need to destroy?") Khrushchev also recommended scaling back the conventional army on the theory that if nuclear missiles had made war between the great powers senseless, it was equally senseless to spend money to maintain a large conventional army.

Khrushchev believed that more agreements like the test ban treaty might reduce cold war tensions to the point that a large standing army and growing nuclear arsenal might become unnecessary. This was the reasoning behind the letter that Dobrynin handed Kennedy at their August 26 meeting. As Dobrynin watched, Kennedy opened it and read, "Availing myself of the return of our Ambassador A. Dobrynin to Washington I would like to express some of my thoughts in connection with the state of things shaping up now after the Treaty on banning nuclear weapons has been signed in Moscow." These "thoughts" were so similar to the points Kennedy had made in his nationally televised July 26 speech that Khrushchev could have been plagiarizing them.

On July 26, Kennedy had praised the treaty as "a shaft of light cut into the darkness" and the first agreement to seek control over "the forces of nuclear destruction," and had said that although it did not "mean an end to the threat of nuclear war" it would "radically reduce the nuclear testing" that might otherwise occur. "This treaty is not the millennium," he continued. "It will not resolve all conflicts . . . or eliminate the dangers of war. . . . But it is an important first step—a step towards peace—a step towards reason—a step away from war." He stressed that although "no one can predict with certainty, therefore, what further agreements, if any, can be built on the foundations of this one. . . . The important point is that efforts to seek new agreements will go forward." He warned against assuming that the new atmosphere between the United States and the Soviet Union would last forever, saying, "We have learned in times past that the spirit of one moment or place can be gone in the next." After declaring, "for the first time in many years, the path of peace may be open," he evoked the Chinese proverb "A journey of a thousand miles must begin with a single step" and concluded, "My fellow Americans, let us take that first step. Let us . . . step back from the shadows of war and seek out the way of peace. And if that journey is a thousand miles, or even more, let history record that we, in this land, at this time, took that first step."

Khrushchev reiterated these points in his letter, writing that it was important to follow the treaty quickly with more agreements that would demonstrate to critics that its economic and political benefits outweighed any security risks. He called the treaty a "good beginning" and said it "strengthens the hopes of the peoples [of the world] for a further relaxation of tension, [and] gives a prospect of solution of other unsettled questions." He agreed that "it is important now not to stop at what has been achieved but to make further steps from the good start taken by us" and urged that "there should be no slowing down the pace," and that the problems separating them "should rather be solved now when a more calm and consequently more favorable atmosphere has been created."

Dobrynin was a glib and charming man who had served in Washington and at the United Nations during the fifties. He spoke excellent English, so he and Kennedy conversed without interpreters. Ambassador-at-Large Llewellyn Thompson, the only other person in the room, took notes, and Kennedy secretly recorded the meeting. Thompson's official memorandum is lengthy and detailed. It corresponds closely to the tape but omits some of Kennedy's playful banter with Dobrynin, and several of the president's statements that would have been deeply embarrassing had they become public. For example, speaking of the fierce attacks on the treaty during the Senate hearings, Kennedy had asked rhetorically, "What can I do with people like Teller or Senator Goldwater?" Like General de Gaulle, they were, he said, "impervious to reason and raised absurd arguments."

He told Dobrynin that he hoped the treaty would lead to further agreements, and said that once the Senate ratified it he was prepared to discuss ways to prevent surprise attacks, a declaration prohibiting the introduction of weapons into outer space, and a civil aviation agreement, and would raise all this with Foreign Minister Gromyko when he visited the United States the next month. Kennedy assured Dobrynin that America would not allow West Germany to "carry us into an adventure which we would have to finish," and, speaking of a possible escalation of tensions in Southeast Asia, said, "I wish one of us never got into Laos." After Dobrynin confirmed that Khrushchev would soon be visiting Cuba, he said that when the chairman spoke there, he hoped he would remember how sensitive Cuba was in the United States, particularly for a president facing reelection.

Dobrynin pressed him to promise that there would be more agreements and "no slowing down the pace." He countered that they would have to find "the right time" to sign a civil aviation agreement. Dobrynin pushed back, suggesting they sign it immediately and have it take effect later.

After bemoaning the cost of the space program, Kennedy suggested that the United States and Soviet Union consider coordinating their activities in outer space. Since neither was exploring space for military purposes, it was largely a matter of "scientific prestige," he said, and even then, the prestige turned out to be fleeting "three-day wonders." He proposed that they "come to some understanding as to what our space schedules might be." That way, they might each save "a good deal of money." He added, "If we're both going to the moon, we ought to both go to the moon on some arrangement where we don't use so many resources for something that is, in the final analysis, not that important."

This was not the first time that Kennedy had proposed that the two nations cooperate in space, even to the point of mounting a joint moon expedition. During the campaign, he had told the *Bulletin of the Atomic Scientists* that "certain aspects of the exploration of space might be handled by joint efforts, for the cost of space efforts will mount radically as we move ambitiously outward." He had proclaimed in his inaugural address, "Let both sides seek to invoke the wonders of science instead of its terrors. Together let us explore the stars," and had expanded on this in his 1961 State of the Union address, saying that although the United States was ahead in "the science and technology of space," the Soviet Union led in the capacity to place large vehicles in orbit, and that both should consider "removing these endeavors from the bitter and wasteful competition of the Cold War."

He had abandoned these noble sentiments after the Soviet Union launched the first human into orbit on April 12, 1961. The flight by Yuri Gagarin was a

Sputnik-like shock to American self-esteem, and within weeks Secretary of Defense McNamara and NASA's administrator James Webb had given him a report recommending a program aimed at landing a man on the moon before the Soviet Union. They argued, "Dramatic achievements in space . . . symbolize the technological power and organizing capacity of a nation." Such achievements might be "economically unjustified," but America should nevertheless decide to "pursue space projects aimed at enhancing national prestige," not least because the competition in space was "part of the battle along the fluid front of the Cold War." Putting a man on the moon first would represent a decisive victory on this battlefront. With the memory of Gagarin's triumph fresh, they told Kennedy, "The orbiting of machines is not the same as the orbiting or landing of a man. . . . It is a man, not merely machines, that captures the imagination of the world."

After accepting the nomination Kennedy had promised Americans a "New Frontier," of "unknown opportunities and perils" beyond which lay "the uncharted areas of science and space." In his nationally televised address to a joint session of Congress on May 25, 1961, he compared the space race to the exploits of explorers like Lewis and Clark, and declared, "I believe that this nation should commit itself to achieving the goal, before this decade is out, of landing a man on the moon and returning him safely to earth. No single space project in this period will be more impressive to mankind. . . . None will be so difficult or expensive to accomplish."

For a competitor like Kennedy, a race to the moon was the ultimate competition. For a man who loved the sea, space was "the new ocean," and in September 1962 he told students at Rice University, "We set sail on this new sea because there is knowledge to be gained, and new rights to be won and used for the progress for all people." But he still harbored doubts about the cost and value of a lunar mission. Soon after announcing the program, he suggested a joint expedition to Khrushchev during their summit in Vienna. After initially dismissing the idea, Khrushchev returned to it later, saying, "All right—why not?" But when Kennedy raised it again, he insisted it could only follow a general disarmament.

He remained conflicted about a moon landing throughout 1961 and 1962. The romantic and visionary Kennedy liked its daring and challenge; the practical Kennedy fretted about its expense and wondered if it was simply a cold war stunt. At an August 1962 news conference he said that the United States remained behind the Soviet Union in long-range booster rockets but would soon surpass it. Achieving this, however, was requiring expenditure that he called "a very heavy burden upon us all."

During a November 1962 meeting he and Webb argued about the relative importance of winning the race to the moon compared with NASA's other projects. Webb believed that the lunar program was part of the goal of making America preeminent in space, calling it "one of the top-priority programs."

"Jim, I think it is *the* top priority," he said. "I think we ought to have that very clear. Some of these programs can slip six months, or nine months, and nothing strategic is going to happen. . . . But this is important for political reasons, international political reasons. This is, whether we like it or not, in a sense a race. If we get second to the moon, it's nice, but it's like being second any time." When Webb suggested linking the lunar program to a broader one of making the United States preeminent in space, Kennedy became exasperated, and said, "I'm not that interested in space. I think it's good, I think we ought to know about it, we're ready to spend reasonable amounts of money. But we're talking about these fantastic expenditures that wreck our budget and all these other domestic programs, and the only justification for it . . . is because we hope to beat them [the Soviets] and demonstrate that starting behind, as we did by a couple of years, by God, we passed them."

At his July 20, 1963, press conference a reporter asked about rumors that the Russians were abandoning the race to the moon, and wanted to know whether, if this proved to be correct, the United States would still continue its lunar program, or perhaps consider a joint moon mission. Kennedy replied that the United States should push on with its own program in light of "any evidence that they [the Soviets] are carrying out a major campaign," and called a moon flight important not only for its own sake, but because it would demonstrate "the capacity to dominate space." He was skeptical about the possibility of a joint flight, saying it would require "a breaking down of a good many barriers of suspicion and hostility."

Either he was being less than candid or he had changed his mind by the time he and Dobrynin met a month later. When he announced the lunar program in 1961, it had seemed a necessary response to a series of Soviet space triumphs, but if the test ban treaty led to more agreements and a reduction of cold war tensions, then beating the Soviets to the moon suddenly seemed less important, and a joint moon program could both symbolize and further the emerging détente between the two nations. His willingness to dismiss the program as "not that important" also suggests that he trusted Dobrynin and Khrushchev to keep his comments confidential, and that he never intended the recordings of meetings like this one to become public, at least during his lifetime.

After the meeting ended, Kennedy asked Thompson for his impressions. Thompson said that Dobrynin, and by extension Khrushchev, "appeared to be looking for an agreement on almost anything." Two days later, the Moscow correspondent of the *New York Times* reported that "Soviet propaganda has shown unusual restraint toward the United States for the last two and a half months." Articles about the U.S. racial situation had also suddenly disappeared from the Soviet press, and the Soviets had stopped jamming the Russian-language broadcasts of the Voice of America.

Minutes after reading Khrushchev's letter and discussing initiatives to further his spirit of détente with the Soviet Union, Kennedy joined McNamara, Rusk, Harriman, Ball, Hilsman, Forrestal, Taylor, and others in the Cabinet Room to discuss whether a coup in Vietnam might harm or further U.S. interests. The meeting was among the most contentious of his presidency and involved him in a detailed discussion of the loyalties of individual South Vietnamese generals. It quickly became obvious that his advisers had only the vaguest notion of who these generals were. When McNamara asked who belonged to this "general officers group," Hilsman replied that U.S. officials in Saigon had contacted only three, and that they had declined to name their colleagues.

Kennedy asked what forces they commanded, only to be told that they included staff officers who did not command any combat units and generals who were stationed in the countryside. The preponderance of military forces in Saigon would probably remain loyal to Diem.

Cable 243 had committed the United States to offering the generals "direct support." McNamara wondered what this meant. Hilsman said it meant assistance that would not be channeled through Saigon. Marine Corps General Victor Krulak, the Joint Chiefs' expert on counterinsurgency warfare, thought this might prove "extremely difficult."

Kennedy asked Chairman of the Joint Chiefs Taylor to estimate the chances that the generals could mount a successful coup, taking into consideration his own experience at the Pentagon. Taylor replied tartly that in Washington they did not turn over the problem of changing a head of state to the military.

During this and four subsequent meetings held over the next three days,

Kennedy persistently posed two questions: Was a coup likely to succeed? And could he call it off if he changed his mind?

When the Bay of Pigs invasion had been under consideration, the military and the CIA had argued that because the Eisenhower administration had signed off on the operation and the rebels had been trained, canceling it would be difficult and risky. Now he was being told the same thing about a possible coup in South Vietnam. His military and civilian advisers had unanimously approved the Bay of Pigs, but on August 26 they were sharply divided over the wisdom of encouraging a coup. McNamara, Taylor, and the CIA had serious reservations and believed that Lodge, Hilsman, Forrestal, and Harriman had stampeded him into approving the cable. Taylor would call it "an egregious 'end run,'" writing, "The anti-Diem group centered in State had taken advantage of the absence of the principal officials to get out instructions which would never have been approved as written under normal circumstances."

There were two factions at these meetings: a State Department one consisting of Harriman, Hilsman, and Ball, joined by Forrestal of the National Security Council, who viewed Vietnam as a crucial cold war conflict that the United States could win only if Diem was deposed; and a Pentagon faction of McNamara, Taylor, and Krulak, who also viewed it as a critical conflict, but one that Diem was more likely to win than were the generals plotting against him. There was also a third, less obvious faction in the Cabinet Room that week, which doubted that Vietnam really *was* a crucial cold war battleground. It consisted of one person, the president. Forrestal had an inkling of this. He later observed that "we began to lose our Presidential support in the summer of 1963," and that after the Buddhist crisis, the president was "beginning to resist his staffs' insistence, and the State Department's insistence, and the Defense Department's insistence on increasing the effort," and "beginning to dig in his heels."

Wednesday, August 28

WASHINGTON

Hours before Kennedy delivered his June 11 civil rights speech, a spokesman for Dr. King's Southern Christian Leadership Conference (SCLC) announced that the organization would sponsor a "massive, militant, and monumental sit-in demonstration" in Washington coinciding with nationwide acts of civil disobedience. Eleven days later, Kennedy implored a delegation of civil rights leaders that included King, Roy Wilkins of the NAACP, and A. Philip Randolph, the president of the Brotherhood of Sleeping Car Porters, to cancel their march, telling them, "We want success in Congress, not just a big show at the Capitol. Some of these people are looking for an excuse to oppose us. I don't want to give them the chance to say, 'Yes, I'm for the bill—but not at the point of a gun.'"

Once he realized that he could not stop them, he tried to control them. "They're going to come down here and shit all over the [Washington] Monument," he told a Justice Department official. "I've got a civil rights bill to get through. We'll run it." Following consultations with the Justice Department, the leaders agreed to cancel acts of civil disobedience planned for the Capitol, stage a shorter march between the Washington and Lincoln Memorials, hold the event on a Wednesday to discourage participants from remaining in the city over the weekend, limit speeches to seven minutes, and advance the schedule so that most participants would leave by nightfall. Kennedy gave the demonstration his blessing at a press conference, saying, "They [the marchers] are going to express their strong views. I think it is in the great tradition [of our democracy]." Having decided to support the march, he now feared that a low turnout would enable opponents of his civil rights bill to argue that he had exaggerated the demand for it, and so he added, "I look forward to being there."

He later changed his mind about attending, probably because he feared his presence might inflame the South and connect him to any violence occurring during the demonstration. So instead of joining the 150 members of Congress at the Lincoln Memorial rally and witnessing the largest mass protest in American history, he asked one of the black White House employees, a doorman, Preston Bruce, to accompany him to the third-floor solarium, where they stood at an open window, too far away to see the crowd of a quarter million over the treetops, but close enough to hear the strains of the civil rights anthem, "We Shall Overcome." Gripping the windowsill so hard that his knuckles turned white, Kennedy said in a choked voice, "Oh, Bruce, I wish I were out there with them!"

He returned downstairs in time to see Dr. King deliver the only speech that a panel of distinguished historians would rank above his inaugural address when asked to choose the finest orations of the twentieth century. He watched King on the First Family's only television set, a thirteen-inch black-and-white portable with rabbit ears. Blair Clark, a CBS executive who had roomed with Kennedy at Harvard, thought he had a natural "instinct" for the medium, and "never forgot that he was an actor in a public drama." He was so telegenic that his appearance more than his words had accounted for his victory in his debates with Nixon. After seeing a replay of them, he had remarked, "We wouldn't have had a prayer without that gadget," a comment perfectly expressing his conflicted emotions toward television: a respect for its power, and a disdain for a "gadget" that bored him so much that except for watching football games, he seldom tuned it on. One of its black marks was that Eisenhower had loved it so much that he and Mamie had installed sets throughout the White House, including two in their sitting room so they could watch different programs while eating dinner off trays. Kennedy had ordered the White House electrician to remove all of Ike's sets, but after Caroline protested that she would miss *Lassie,* he left the small portable in the West Hall so that it could be moved out of sight when guests arrived.

Today was the first time he had heard King deliver an entire speech. After listening to his "I Have a Dream" litany, Kennedy turned to his aide Lee White and said, "Jesus Christ, that's a terrific speech. He's damn good, isn't he?" An hour later he welcomed the organizers of the march to the White House, telling King as he shook his hand, "I have a dream." King had dreamed of Mississippi "transformed into the oasis of freedom and justice," and America becoming a "beautiful symphony of brotherhood" where children were judged "by the content of their character." Kennedy was dreaming of sixty-seven U.S. senators prepared to override a filibuster of his civil rights bill, and would support whatever furthered that dream, and oppose whatever threatened it.

By the time the leaders arrived at the White House, it was evident that their march had been an epic success. They had promised to bring 100,000 demonstrators to Washington, and more than twice that number had come. Although Kennedy had ordered the largest peacetime mobilization of armed forces in U.S. history, there had been no violence, the troops had stayed in their barracks, and Americans had witnessed an inspiring television spectacle that had advanced his bill more than weeks of backroom arm-twisting.

Roy Wilkins saw "relief written all over his face" as he praised the leaders for doing "a superb job of making your case," overlooking that his civil rights bill had made it his case as well.

Wilkins and King had the best understanding of the journey that Kennedy had traveled since his inauguration, and why a man whose cautious approach to equal rights had once left them so frustrated had at last become, in their opinion, a greater champion of black Americans than any president in U.S. history, Lincoln included. Wilkins called his transformation "the education of JFK on the race question," and credited his willingness to learn and be moved by events for finally awakening him "to the poison and venom that had been the daily lot of the Negro." King had a similar take on his evolution. When they first met in 1960 he had sensed that Kennedy had an intellectual commitment to civil rights but not an emotional one, and blamed the fact that like most white men of his age and class, he had simply not known many black people. There had been no black students at Choate and only a few at Harvard in the 1930s, and the Navy remained segregated throughout the war. During his six years in the House there had been just two black representatives, and during his eight in the Senate, not a single black senator. In the 1940s and 1950s, Washington had been a segregated city, the first Jim Crow metropolis south of the Mason-Dixon Line. Black passengers moved into the Colored Only coaches at Union Station before continuing south, classified advertisements specified race, and black employees at the Capitol were prohibited from swimming in its pool or eating in its restaurants, so it is hardly surprising that Kennedy had never attended a black wedding, funeral, or church service, and had no way of understanding what Wilkins called the "joys and hardships" of being black in America.

During his first congressional race he had courted his district's small black vote by praising the wartime heroism of black servicemen and recruiting black college students to work as volunteers in his campaign headquarters. His black valet George Taylor protested after noticing that only the white volunteers were being invited upstairs to share lunch with his sisters. "Jack, I think that's bullshit," he said. "They're all giving their time. They're all human beings. Why segregate in this way?" Kennedy called him "thin-skinned," and justified excluding the black students as "one of the things of the time." But at his inauguration fifteen years later he had immediately noticed that there were no black cadets in the Coast Guard Academy unit marching in his parade and told his aide Richard Goodwin, "That's not acceptable. Something ought to be done about it." Goodwin called Secretary of the Treasury Douglas Dillon, who oversaw the Coast Guard, and within the year the Coast Guard academy was integrated.

During his first year in office Kennedy appointed more blacks to high-level positions in the federal government than any of his predecessors, yet he remained emotionally detached from the civil rights struggle. He persisted in viewing racial discrimination through the lens of the anti-Irish prejudice that had humiliated his parents, and so when a party leader urged him to seek the vice presidency instead of the presidency in 1960, he had said caustically, "Oh, I see, the back of the bus for Catholics."

The 1960 Democratic platform had a strong civil rights plank, and his speeches and gestures raised the hopes of African Americans that he would submit civil rights legislation to Congress and enforce the desegregation of Southern schools. A turning point came near the end of his campaign when King was imprisoned in a county jail in rural Georgia, and Kennedy's brother-in-law Sargent Shriver suggested that he telephone Mrs. King to offer his sympathy and support. "What the hell. That's a decent thing to do," he told Shriver. "Why not? Get her on the phone." Shriver had expected the call to pay political dividends, but Kennedy's decision to make it had been spontaneous, motivated more by his good manners and humanity than political calculation. "The decent thing to do" won him 70 percent of the black vote, a crucial difference in some closely contested states.

Because he had won the presidency by such a narrow margin, and opinion polls showed equal rights being a low priority for white Americans, he took office believing that it was an inopportune time to submit sweeping civil rights legislation to Congress. Instead, he used his executive powers to enforce the court-ordered integration of Southern universities and to pursue voting rights cases. He remained reluctant to use federal powers to protect civil rights workers and enforce school desegregation, arguing that submitting a civil rights bill would be a pointless exercise because Southern Democrats would stall it in the House, filibuster it in the Senate, and retaliate by sabotaging the rest of his legislative program. "I'm not going to just play at this business," he told a journalist. "We can't get any civil rights legislation through at this point, we don't have any political muscle over there [in Congress] and until [then] . . . I'm not going to engage in just token show business."

Roy Wilkins called his decision to pursue executive action instead of legislation "an offering of a cactus bouquet to Negro parents and their children." King criticized him for vacillating, and later spoke of "two Kennedys: a Kennedy [of] the first two years and another Kennedy emerging in 1963 with . . . a great understanding of the moral issues."

King believed that events had changed him. The transformation began in April 1961, when white mobs attacked interracial groups of Freedom Riders attempting to desegregate bus stations and interstate buses in Alabama and Mississippi, firebombing one bus and pummeling one of Robert Kennedy's aides. It continued in September 1962, when the registration of James Meredith at the University of Mississippi led to riots and two deaths, forcing him to send troops. The turning point came in May 1963, when police and firemen in Birmingham attacked civil rights demonstrators. Kennedy said that photographs and news footage of firemen blasting schoolchildren with high-pressure hoses and policemen loosing German shepherds on black teenagers and pummeling demonstrators with nightsticks had made him "sick." King believed that Birmingham had convinced him that segregation was morally wrong. "Lincoln had real agonizing moments over this question of signing the emancipation proclamation," King said. "He vacillated a great deal. But finally the events caused him to see that he had to do this and he came to the moral conclusion that he had to do it no matter what it meant." Birmingham had also convinced Kennedy that segregation might lead to black violence that could threaten national security, and that civil rights had become the great domestic issue of his presidency, one he needed to tackle as courageously as FDR had the Depression.

In a June 10, 1963, television interview that was reported the next day on the front page of the *New York Times,* King compared Kennedy's civil rights record with Eisenhower's, criticized him for substituting "an inadequate approach for a miserable one," and urged him to discuss integration in moral terms. The following evening, Kennedy told Americans, "We are confronted primarily with a moral issue. It is as old as the Scriptures, and is as clear as the American constitution." He warned that America faced a "moral crisis as a country and a people," and insisted that the crisis could not be solved (as he had previously tried to do) "by token moves or talk." After delivering the speech he told a friend, "Sometimes you look at what you've done and the only thing you ask yourself is—what took you so long to do it?"

King praised him for addressing the "morality of integration," and later called his speech "the most eloquent, passionate, and unequivocal plea for civil rights, for justice toward the Negro ever made by any President." That same evening in Jackson, Mississippi, a white supremacist shot and killed the NAACP official Medgar Evers as he was walking to his front door. Kennedy invited his widow and children to the White House. Evelyn Lincoln told them that if you made a wish while sitting in the president's chair it would come true. Evers's eldest son climbed into the chair, bowed his head, and said he wished his father had not died in vain. The meeting left Kennedy so moved that he told Schlesinger, "I don't understand the South. I'm coming to believe that Thaddeus Stevens [the firebrand abolitionist who wanted to punish and humiliate the South after the Civil War] was right. I had always been taught to regard him as a man of vicious bias. But, when I see this sort of thing [the Evers assassination], I begin to wonder how else you can treat them." On June 19, the same day that Evers was being buried at Arlington with military honors, Kennedy submitted his civil rights bill and asked congressmen "to look into your hearts . . . for the one plain, proud, and priceless quality that unites us all as Americans: a sense of justice."

He reaped the whirlwind. Southern Democrats voted against other administration legislation, including a bill to establish VISTA, a domestic version of the

Peace Corps that had been expected to pass easily but barely survived. Senator James Eastland of Mississippi condemned the civil rights bill as "a complete blueprint for a totalitarian state." The retiring president of the American Bar Association, the Mississippian James Satterfield, said its passage would mean "the destruction of the United States of America as we have known it," which was of course the point. Kennedy's approval rating fell, and a Gallup poll taken in late June found that 36 percent of Americans thought he was pushing integration "too fast," a number climbing to 50 percent by late August. After reviewing the polls with Bobby, he looked up and said, "Well, if we're going down, let's go down on a matter of principle."

Although liberals in the North wanted a civil rights bill passed, many did not want blacks moving into their neighborhoods. When the speechwriter John Bartlow Martin visited his former hometown of Oak Park, Illinois, he reported finding "considerable anxiety over the President's civil rights speech" in the predominantly Jewish and liberal suburb, and people "alarmed over the pace of the integration movement." James Lanigan, a New York reform politician, spoke to Schlesinger about "widespread and intense panic in the suburbs," and said that "even good Democrats were appalled by the nightmare of an inundation of their neighborhoods and their schools by Negroes." A survey of non-Southern whites by the pollster Oliver Quayle and the journalist Stewart Alsop, taken over the summer and reported in the *Saturday Evening Post* (which undoubtedly ended up on Kennedy's desk), supported the anecdotal evidence that even Northern liberals who supported Kennedy's civil rights bill had reservations about sharing their schools and neighborhoods with black Americans. A startling 42 percent said they would prefer that their children attend all-white schools, and 77 percent believed that whites should have the right to refuse to sell a house to a black on the basis of race. Quayle and Alsop concluded, "It is remarkable that any politician who has favored anti-discrimination statutes in housing survives in office."

As soon as Kennedy learned that the leaders of the march had not eaten since breakfast, he ordered sandwiches and beverages from the White House canteen. The food arrived, an official photograph was taken, and pleasantries exchanged. Minutes later, he and the leaders were at odds. Both sides wanted a civil rights bill passed, but he remained convinced that expanding its scope would doom it. He had submitted the most radical civil rights legislation since the Civil War, risking his reputation, presidency, and reelection. He had met with more than sixteen hundred governors, religious leaders, executives, attorneys, labor officials, and editors, urging them to lobby congressmen, energize their constituencies, write letters, and sign petitions, and having done all this, he was determined to win. The last two years had educated him about civil rights, and Birmingham and the Evers assassination had sickened him, but he still prized success and was unwilling to back a bill that stood little chance of being passed. But this appeared to be what the leaders wanted him to do. They had called their demonstration "The March on Washington for Jobs and Freedom." His civil rights bill had addressed the freedom issue by prohibiting discrimination in places of public accommodation, but did nothing about jobs. Emboldened by their successful march, they pressed him to expand his bill to include a Fair Employment Practices Commission (FEPC), which would prohibit racial discrimination in hiring.

Speaking first, Wilkins said, "You made the difference. You gave us your blessings. It was one of the prime factors in turning it [the march] into an orderly protest to help our government rather than a protest against our government." The compliments finished, Wilkins made his pitch: "It fell to my lot, sir, in this afternoon of superlative oratory to be the one to deal rather pedantically and pedestrianly with the hard business of legislation. . . . We would like to see included in your package . . . an FEPC bill for the reasons all of us outlined in our speeches." Such a provision would not imperil the bill, he said, "if the right words could go to the right people."

Randolph said, "We feel it needs to have presidential backing, the presidential imprimatur for it to receive the recognition it deserves," and he launched into a monologue about unemployment among young black men who were "running out of hope."

Kennedy cut in to say, "I thought we might go into a little discussion of the legislation, of how we stand—"

Walter Reuther interrupted to praise him for submitting the bill, but to add that he considered an FEPC provision "a very critical element." He rambled on for several minutes, promising that everyone would mobilize their constituencies to persuade Congress to pass such legislation. As he and the others droned on, Kennedy appeared to be taking notes, but his doodles showed that his mind was wandering. He wrote "Afghanistan" at the top of one page, and according to

Evelyn Lincoln, who later deciphered his writing, he was thinking about his September 6 state dinner to honor King Zaher. He scribbled "Hanoi," scratched a line through it and added, "Education," "voting," "progress," and "Birmingham," subjects he wanted to raise when the civil rights leaders yielded the floor.

When Reuther paused, he interjected, "Very fine, but let me just say a word about the legislation." But before doing that, he delivered a lecture about how black families should emulate the Jews by concentrating on education. "Isn't it possible for the Negro community to take the lead in committing major emphasis on the responsibility of these families, even if they're split and all the other problems they have, on the education of their children?" he asked. The Jewish community had suffered discrimination, but had found its salvation through education. Midway through this spiel he stopped and said, "This has nothing to do with what you've been talking about," but resumed it anyway. But why was he asking these men, just hours after their historic march, why they could not be more like Jews? For someone who was usually so sensitive, it was a remarkably insensitive performance, an indication that his civil rights education remained incomplete.

As he was saying "If we can get the Negro community to regard the education of their children as really the best way out . . . making education the same way that it's in the Jewish community and to a degree in—" one of the leaders, whose identity is not apparent on the tape, interrupted to say that black college graduates were driving garbage trucks in California. Floyd McKissick of CORE chimed in that his organization had trained two hundred young people in North Carolina only to have them rejected for jobs for which they were clearly qualified.

Kennedy responded with a lengthy tutorial on the political hurdles facing the bill, enumerating state by state how many Democratic members of the House were what he called "right," "doubtful," and "wrong" on the bill. Because there were roughly 160 Democrats "right" and 100 "wrong," he needed 60 Republicans to pass the bill. Their votes would be hard enough to get for the bill as written, he said, but with an FEPC provision the bill would never attract enough Republicans. He ran through the Senate state by state. He could have summarized the results, but must have thought that a detailed recitation would be more sobering. There were 48 senators "right," 44 "wrong," and 6 to 8 "possible," he said, and even if all the possibles supported the bill, there would still not be enough votes to stop a filibuster. Again, the key was attracting moderate Republicans. His point was obvious: instead of lobbying him to expand the bill, they should be lobbying the Republicans to pass it.

A. Philip Randolph, the eldest and most experienced member of the delegation, resorted to flattery. "Mr. President, from the description you have made of the state of affairs in the House and Senate, it's obvious that it's going to take nothing less than a crusade to win approval for these civil rights measures," he said. "And if it's going to be a crusade, I think that nobody can lead this crusade but you." He suggested appealing to the American people "over the heads of the congressmen and senators."

It would be "helpful," Kennedy said delicately, if Randolph and the other leaders told the wavering Republicans that they "anticipated their support." Knowing that reporters were waiting to interview them, he suggested they say it was their "strong judgment" that both parties should support the bill, and concluded, "Keep in touch, particularly in this question of a head count."

Thursday, August 29–Saturday, August 31

WASHINGTON AND CAPE COD

Kennedy spent the last week in August attempting to regain control of his administration's Vietnam policy and to distance his administration from a coup that was sounding more and more like a potential second Bay of Pigs.

On Monday, he worried that David Halberstam's negative articles about Diem were having an undue influence on administration policy. "When we move to eliminate a government," he told his advisers, "we want to be sure we're not doing it because the *New York Times* is excited about it." He scolded Forrestal for the slipshod way he had cleared Cable 243. When Forrestal offered to resign, he turned on him and said, "You're not worth firing. You owe me something, so you stick around."

On Tuesday, he suggested asking Lodge and General Harkins, the commander of the U.S. military assistance program in Vietnam, "what they feel their prospects are for success and do they recommend continuing it [support for the coup] or do they recommend now waiting." Minutes later, he worried about the consequences of rescinding his approval for the coup, asking, "Ah, do we cut our losses in such a way where we don't endanger those who we've been in contact [with]?" He added bleakly, "The response that we've gotten on the coup at this point does not give us assurances that it's going to be successful."

The cables from Saigon were contradictory and confusing. On Wednesday, the CIA station chief reported that according to the chief plotter, a General Khiem, a committee of unnamed generals had decided to mount a coup within a week. The same day, Ambassador Lodge cabled, "As of now there are no signs, apart from Khiem's receptiveness to initial approach, that these or any other generals are really prepared to act against the government." Lodge continued to support a coup, cabling the next day that he believed its members were the "best group that could be assembled in terms of ability and orientation," although "our knowledge of composition of coup group and their plans is derived from a single source." He warned that "chances of success would be diminished by delay," and said he was "concerned over possibility attempt by Nhu to preempt the coup by arresting its leaders." The CIA station chief agreed, cabling, "Situation here has reached point of no return. . . . It is our considered estimate that General officers cannot retreat now."

At the Wednesday meeting on Vietnam, Kennedy was even more pessimistic, musing aloud about calling off the generals. "I don't think we ought to take the view that this has gone beyond our control," he said, "'cause I think that would be the worst reason to do it." When Bundy responded that both Lodge and Harkins favored the operation as currently planned, he said, "Well, I don't see any reason to go ahead unless we think we have a good chance of success."

The former ambassador to South Vietnam Richard Nolting was at the Wednesday meeting and argued that only Diem had "a reasonably good prospect of holding this fragmented, divided country together." Harriman interjected, "Needless to say I don't agree with this." When Nolting attacked Cable 243 as improvident, Harriman yelled, "Shut up!"

At one point during the meeting Kennedy said, "This shit has got to stop!" and he told Bobby afterward, "My God! My government's coming apart."

Before attending Thursday's Vietnam meeting, he received a cable from Lodge that began, "We are launched on a course from which there is no respectable turning back: The overthrow of the Diem government." There was no turning back, he said, "because U.S. prestige is already publicly committed to this end . . . and will become more so as facts leak out," and because "there is no possibility . . . that the war can be won under a Diem administration." After reminding Kennedy that this was the policy Cable 243 had instructed him to carry out, he recommended making an "all-out effort to get Generals to move promptly." He explained that he had decided to ignore the instructions in an earlier cable directing him to ask Diem to rid himself of the Nhus before giving the generals his final approval, because the generals were already concerned about American indecision and delay.

Lodge's vaguely insubordinate cable prompted Kennedy to shoot back a top-secret cable. Soon after arriving at Squaw Island on Thursday evening, he called McGeorge Bundy and dictated a cable flagged "Personal for the Ambassador from the President" and "No Department or other distribution whatever." He told Lodge, "We will do all that we can to help you conclude the operation successfully. Nevertheless, there is one point on my own constitutional responsibilities as President and Commander in Chief which I wish to state to you in this entirely private message, which is not being circulated here beyond the Secretary of State." With the Bay of Pigs obviously in mind, he continued, "Until the very moment of the go signal for the operation by the Generals, I must reserve a contingent right to change course and reverse previous instructions. While fully aware of your assessment of the consequences of such a reversal, I know from experience that failure is more destructive than an appearance of indecision. I would, of course, accept full responsibility for any such change as I must bear also full responsibility for this operation and its consequences." He added, "When we go, we must go to win, but it will be better to change our minds than fail. And if our national interest should require a change of mind, we must not be afraid of it."

Had the nationally syndicated columnist George Dixon known about any of this he might not have written in his weekend column, one Kennedy must have read because it appeared in the *Washington Post,* "I wouldn't be surprised if John Fitzgerald Kennedy looks back upon the week of Aug 25 to 31, 1963 as the most gratifying week of his life." During these seven days, Dixon said, "a nuclear test ban treaty grew almost certain of passage, not a single incident marred the civil rights march," and the president was "more popular than the day he took office." He concluded, "No matter what reversals may be in store for him in the years ahead, the President can assuage his woes by looking back upon last week."

KENNEDY RETURNED FROM a cruise on the *Honey Fitz* on Friday afternoon to find that Lincoln had left a message on his bed reporting that a federal judge had just sentenced James Landis to thirty days in jail for tax fraud, a reminder that his own deal with Dirksen had spared Sherman Adams from a similar fate.

He was having second thoughts about Jackie's cruise, perhaps because he had been aboard the *Christina* and could imagine how the press would play up the First Lady's presence on a ship boasting a liveried crew, gold-plated faucets, El Greco paintings, and bar stools upholstered with the skin of whale testicles—the kind of vulgar wealth-flaunting he had been raised to disdain. On Labor Day she proposed bringing Undersecretary of Commerce Franklin D. Roosevelt, Jr., and his wife as chaperones. He gave in, calling Roosevelt at his farm in upstate New York and telling him, "Lee wants Jackie to be her beard [to disguise her affair with Onassis]. You are the only one she has agreed to have come along." The Roosevelts understood their role. "I don't think Jack wanted Jackie to go," Susan Roosevelt said later. "I think he was appalled by it, so he arranged for us to make it look less like the jet set."

He had reinjured his back by stepping into a hole on the Hyannis Golf Course at the beginning of August and aggravated it by playing more golf two weeks later. X-rays were taken, diagrams drawn, hot packs prescribed, bandages wound around his back and groin, and a misleading story concocted for the press to explain why he appeared to be limping. "I don't want to read anything in the papers about my groin," he told Salinger. "We can attribute it all to the back. . . . I don't want the American public thinking that their president is falling apart: 'Now he's got a bad back, now his groin is going.'"

Dr. Kraus was on a climbing holiday in Italy so his associate, Dr. Willibrand Nagler, examined Kennedy on August 22 and 27. He diagnosed a muscle sprain, recommended continuing with the hot packs and bandages, and told him to avoid walking or climbing stairs. When the pain persisted, Kennedy insisted on seeing Kraus in person. Kraus and the famed mountaineer Gino Solda had just climbed Cima Kennedy, a mountain in the Dolomites that Solda had arranged to have named for Kennedy despite the custom of naming alpine peaks posthumously. Burkley called Kraus in the middle of the night and said that an Air Force jet was being sent to fly him to Cape Cod.

Kraus arrived on August 31, examined Kennedy, and confirmed Nagler's diagnosis, a strain of the hip flexor muscle, and not a very serious one. He advised him to continue the hot packs and bandages for two or three days, and then resume exercising. Kennedy pretended not to know that Kraus had cut his holiday short, although it is unlikely that Nagler and Burkley would not have told him that Kraus was abroad. The next day he telegrammed Kraus, "I have just learned that you cut your vacation to come up here. I am extremely sorry that this was permitted although I am grateful to you for your kindness in coming." It was a gracious gesture, but it might have been more gracious to have borne the pain a few days longer.

Sometime that weekend, most likely on Saturday, Clifton handed Kennedy a sealed envelope from Bundy containing Lodge's reply to his eyes-only cable as well as a copy of the initial cable. Bundy had instructed Clifton in an accompanying memorandum that "the enclosed envelope should be opened by the President only, and when he has read the messages it contains you should destroy them. The reason for this extraordinary procedure is that these messages are not in the normal series and their existence is not known except to the President and to the Secretary of State, so I do not want them in a message file that may be seen by others who believe themselves privy to most classified material."

Lodge's reply was curt and to the point: "1. I fully understand that you have the right and responsibility to change course at any time. Of course I will always respect that right. 2. To be successful, this operation must essentially be a Vietnamese affair with a momentum of its own. Should this happen you may not be able to control it, i.e. the 'go signal' may be given by the Generals." In other words, it was too late to for the president to countermand Cable 243. He could order Lodge around, but he could control neither the Vietnamese officers nor the timing or success of their coup. It was the reply he deserved. He had appointed Lodge for frivolous and political reasons, cavalierly told him that he would leave the planning of a coup in his hands, and approved Cable 243, ignoring the lessons of the Bay of Pigs and the Cuban missile crisis. The only good news was that leaks to the press and mixed signals from the embassy in Saigon had so unsettled the generals that they had suspended their plotting.

PART THREE

September 1–30, 1963

DAYS 83–54

Sunday, September 1

CAPE COD AND MARTHA'S VINEYARD

Kennedy had met the author William Styron at a 1962 White House dinner honoring Nobel Prize winners. Styron's first novel, *Lie Down in Darkness,* had won critical acclaim and prestigious awards, making him the kind of intellectual celebrity Kennedy liked to cultivate, and so on Sunday he and Jackie cruised to Martha's Vineyard to collect Styron and his wife, Rose, and give them lunch aboard the *Honey Fitz.* Styron was anticipating an afternoon with a man he considered "the glamorous and gorgeous avatar of American power at the magic moment of its absolute twentieth-century ascendancy."* He was not disappointed and would describe Kennedy as "lethally glamorous," and possessing a "beguiling and self-effacing modesty." The food on the *Honey Fitz* was another matter: stone-cold hot dogs in soggy buns, frozen beer, and runny or rock-hard *oeufs gelés,* with a pitcher of stiff Bloody Marys the only saving grace.

They discussed Massachusetts politics, race, and whether Alger Hiss was guilty (Kennedy thought he was). He asked Styron if he had read "The President and Other Intellectuals," an essay by the New York literary critic and all-purpose

---

* In a 1983 article in *Esquire,* Styron wrote that he cruised with Kennedy in late August 1963. Thirteen years later in *Vanity Fair,* he put the cruise the year before, in August 1962. If the cruise occurred in 1963, it would have happened on September 1, when the Secret Service records show Kennedy motoring to Martha's Vineyard. It is also possible that Styron cruised with Kennedy in both 1962 and 1963, explaining his confusion. In any case, Kennedy's obsession with Kazin's article and the verdict of history would have been the same in either year.

intellectual Alfred Kazin that had appeared in the October 1961 issue of *The American Scholar*. Kazin had conceded that Kennedy possessed "the sex appeal of a movie hero" and "as much savvy as a Harvard professor," but then dismissed him as a poseur and "would-be intellectual." He peppered his essay with snide comments about his "restless ambition" and "determination to succeed," and criticized *Profiles in Courage* as devoid of "any significant ideas" and resembling "those little anecdotes from the lives of great men that are found in *Reader's Digest*." He concluded that his most essential quality was "that of the man who is always making and remaking himself," belittling him as "the final product of a fanatical job of self-remodeling."

Schlesinger heard prepublication rumors about the article and persuaded Kazin to come to the White House for lunch, hoping that meeting Kennedy might change his mind. Afterward, Kazin added a few grace notes and praised Kennedy's "freshness of curiosity." He kept the most wounding passages, however, and told Schlesinger that most New York intellectuals agreed with him that the president was "slick, cool, and empty, devoid of vision." Kennedy tried making light of it, telling Schlesinger, "We wined him and dined him, and talked about Hemingway and Dreiser with him. . . . Then he went away and wrote that piece." Kazin was unrepentant, and in his 1978 autobiography he spoke of Kennedy's "wistful need for more confident learning than he possessed" and his "need to charm," and called him "a personality under construction," as if that were a crippling flaw.

Carefully keeping his voice neutral, Styron admitted to having read Kazin's article.

"Well, what did you think?" Kennedy demanded.

Styron felt as if he had been passed a conversational hot coal. He had found the article tough and caustic, but thought Kazin had made a case that Kennedy lacked the intellectual voltage usually ascribed to him. As he was struggling to formulate a diplomatic response, Kennedy posed a question that showed how deeply the article had wounded him, asking, "What qualifies a critic [i.e., Kazin] to make an assessment of a work if he himself has never created one?" Styron thought, "Boy, Alfred's really got Kennedy's goat," and told him that the critical and creative faculties were different talents, and not necessarily interdependent.

Styron had stumbled upon something more complicated than a New York intellectual getting the goat of a thin-skinned president, although Kennedy was certainly that. In 1961, he had become so exercised over the *New York Herald Tribune*'s biased reporting that he had canceled the White House subscriptions. After some one-sided articles appeared in *Time,* he had ordered an aide to compare how the magazine had covered his first year in office with how it had treated Eisenhower's first year.* He and Ben Bradlee had been friends for almost a decade, but after an August 1962 article in *Look* quoted Bradlee as saying, "It's almost impossible to write a story they [the Kennedys] like. Even if a story is quite favorable to their side, they'll find one paragraph to quibble with," he refused to speak to him for several months. Making his reaction to negative press articles so puzzling was the fact that in other respects he was a tough-skinned political warrior capable of shrugging off brutal ad hominem attacks. Presidents Johnson and Nixon would also be sensitive about criticism, but they were concerned about its short-term political consequences. Kennedy had his eye on history, and he understood that articles in newspapers like the *Herald Tribune* were its rough draft and that future historians might weigh the opinions of critics like Kazin.

He had meant his warning to Massachusetts state legislators that "at some future date, the high court of history sits on judgment on each of us," and he imagined himself surrounded by current and future historians constantly taking his measure, telling Bradlee, "Those bastards, they're always there with their pencils out." In *Profiles in Courage,* he had been the one delivering the verdict, praising eight senators for possessing "the breath-taking talents of the orator, the brilliance of the scholar, the breadth of the man above party and section, and, above all, a deep-seated belief in themselves, their integrity and the rightness of their cause"—all qualities that he was cultivating in himself. By calling his scholarly brilliance a sham, Kazin was threatening what he cared about most: a favorable judgment from history's high court.

All presidents govern with an eye on history, but not all care equally. If

---

* The aide concluded that *Time* had put the two administrations "in very different lights," and that while Eisenhower "was given every benefit of the doubt . . . [and] dealt with in only glowing terms and heroic prose," the Kennedy administration "was nary given a chance and criticism was never spared."

historians ranked presidents by ambition instead of achievement, Kennedy would be near the top of most lists. He was swinging for the fences from his first day in office, determined to be ranked alongside or above Lincoln and FDR. Even joining the pantheon of great presidents was not enough; he wanted to be celebrated as a great man who had shaped his times. For this he looked for inspiration to de Gaulle and Churchill, men who had worked at becoming heroic figures ("making and remaking themselves") and had proved that greatness can be fashioned from a convergence of willpower and historical circumstance. When the French statesman Jean Monnet told Schlesinger that one of de Gaulle's most remarkable features was "his precise and persistent concern with the figure he will cut in history," and that whenever he considered a decision "he wonders how it will look in the history books thirty years from now," he could have been describing Kennedy.

Jackie knew how much he valued history's judgment, and her famous post-Dallas "Camelot interview" with the journalist Theodore White was an attempt to preempt the historians. Referring to a journalist who had written some unflattering lines about her husband, she told White, "Men are such a combination of bad and good . . . and what is history going to see in this except what Merriman Smith wrote, that bitter man." White decided that she had agreed to the interview because she did not want her husband "left to the historians." After recounting the events in Dallas, she likened his presidency to King Arthur's mythical Camelot. Most of Kennedy's knights would dismiss the comparison as the kind of sentimental claptrap he would have hated, but they overlooked the rest of her interview, during which she delivered a passionate exegesis of his love of history. In a stream-of-consciousness monologue, she told White, "But Jack loved history so. But history to me was about Jack. But history made him what he was . . . this lonely sick boy . . . he sat and read history . . . scarlet fever . . . this little boy in bed for so much of the time . . . all the time he was in bed this little boy was reading Marlborough, he devours the Knights of the Round Table . . . history made Jack that way, made him see heroes." Returning to her memories of Dallas, she punctuated them with "history," the one-word refrain that explained him: "*History* . . . everybody kept saying to me to put a cold towel around my head . . . my whole face splattered with blood and hair . . . I wiped it off with Kleenex. *History.*"

Kennedy was not shy about his ambitions. He told Billings that his goal was "greatness." He advised Sidey to "go for the top. If you aim for second you will end up there," leading Sidey to conclude that he was gripped by "the romantic conviction that he was astride history." The diplomat Charles ("Chip") Bohlen, who had known many of the century's great leaders, was impressed by Kennedy's fierce determination to be numbered among them and sensed an "unknown quality" that "gave you infinite hope that somehow or other he was going to change the course of history."

During a White House dinner on the eve of the Cuban missile crisis, Isaiah Berlin had noticed that whenever Kennedy spoke about Churchill, Stalin, Lenin, and Napoléon, "his eyes shone with a particular glitter, and it was quite clear that he thought in terms of great men and what they were able to do." When Berlin returned a few weeks later, Kennedy admitted that he had worried that the Bay of Pigs "would always be this fearful stigma which historians would always note." Berlin decided that he had never known anyone "who listened to every single word that was uttered more attentively," and his "remorseless attention" reminded him of Lenin, another man who could "exhaust people simply by listening to them." Like Lenin, Kennedy was "on the job all the time," Berlin said, and spoke "like a man with a mission or some kind of calling . . . [and] as if there was not much time and great things had to be done." He decided that his ambition was "terrifying but rather marvelous."

His terrifying ambition to be judged a great man was an obsession that, with the possible exception of sex, trumped all else. He ran for Congress and the presidency at a young age, and fussed about his health so much because he feared dying before he could leave his mark on history. When he discovered that Bradlee had been keeping a diary, he made him promise not to publish anything without his permission until five years after the end of his administration, to prevent him scooping his own memoirs. He made Arthur Schlesinger a special assistant because he had written acclaimed books about Andrew Jackson and FDR, and he hoped he would write a more sympathetic account of his presidency if he co-opted him.* He kept a watchful eye on Schlesinger, and after he appeared to be claiming in a newspaper article that he was responsible for giving him crucial

---

* Jackie also assumed that Schlesinger would write something. She forwarded a document to McGeorge Bundy accompanied by a memorandum saying, "I thought you might find this a valuable addition to your state papers—if you don't—I am sure Arthur Schlesinger can use it in the trilogy I dread to think he will write about the present administration."

advice during the Cuban missile crisis, he swore and told Fay, "Look at that damn interview. Schlesinger sounding off that it was his advice that got the President to change his position he previously held and accept Artie's advice. I'll tell you what Artie can advise on. He can devote all his mental capacity to advising Jackie on the historical significance of the furniture she puts in the White House." It was another idle threat.

His ambition explained why he had read a compendium of presidential wisdom, *Sayings of Great Presidents,* the day after he won the election; kept the current issue of *History Today* on his night table; and pressed historians to explain what made a president great. When he heard that the Princeton historian and Abraham Lincoln expert David Herbert Donald was scheduled to speak at Bobby's house, he moved the event to the White House and asked Donald: Where would he rank various presidents? What separated a great president from a mediocre one? How did a president acquire greatness? And what about Lincoln? Would he have been regarded as a great president if he hadn't been assassinated? He argued that Lincoln's assassination had saved him from the problem of Reconstruction, and Donald agreed that Lincoln may have been lucky in his reputation to die when he did. Donald left a private meeting with him unimpressed by his understanding of American history but fascinated by his determination to become a great man, writing a friend, "This is a man determined to go down in our history books as a great President, and he wants to know the secret."

Every month brought another hundred-year anniversary of a crucial Civil War battle or Lincoln milestone, making it impossible for him *not* to keep a competitive eye on Lincoln. He asked Sorensen to study the Gettysburg Address and determine its "secret" before writing a first draft of his inaugural address. He invited the poet and Lincoln scholar Carl Sandburg to the White House for a private tutorial, and must have been pleased when Sandberg said, "There has never been a more formidable set of historical conditions for a president to face since Lincoln."

He made Churchill his template, borrowing or emulating his phrases and constructions. He titled his first book *Why England Slept,* an homage to Churchill's *While England Slept.* Churchill had opened his 1922 study of world leaders, *Great Contemporaries,* "Courage is rightly esteemed the first of human qualities." He opened *Profiles in Courage,* "This is a book about the most admirable of human virtues—courage." Kay Halle never forgot visiting him in a hospital room when he was twelve to see him hidden behind stacks of books, immersed in Churchill's *The World Crisis.* When he was a young congressman, his legislative aide Mark Dalton found him sitting up in bed in Hyannis Port, reading one of Churchill's early books. "Just listen to this," he said in an excited voice. "This is one of the most interesting things I have ever read." Referring to a leader in the Middle Ages who had to make a fateful decision, Churchill had written, "At that moment, all history stood still." After repeating the passage out loud, he asked Dalton, "Did you ever read anything like that in your life?"

While he was in Florida in 1955, recovering from a risky operation that had not only failed to alleviate his chronic back condition but had almost killed him, he had spent hours rereading Churchill's books, copying and memorizing passages. He was channeling Churchill when he told an audience at the National Press Club that America needed a president "who is willing and able to summon his national constituency to its *finest hour.*" The call in his inaugural address for the United States and Soviet Union to renew the search for peace "before the dark powers of destruction unleashed by science engulf us all in ruin" was a wordier version of Churchill's warning about a world "made darker by the dark lights of perverted science." His summons to "pay any price, bear any burden, meet any hardship, support any friend" replicated the cadences of "We shall fight on the beaches, we shall fight on the landing grounds, we shall fight in the fields." His warning to the newly independent nations of Asia and Africa that "in the past, those who foolishly sought power by riding the back of the tiger ended up inside" was an homage to Churchill's remark that "dictators ride to and fro upon tigers which they dare not dismount. And the tigers are getting hungry."

He opened a 1961 speech to a gathering of historians in Washington by quoting Churchill's statement that history would judge his role in World War II favorably because he intended to write it. Behind his decision to tape certain White House meetings lay his determination to write the definitive account of his administration. He was selective about what he recorded, choosing meetings and conversations that promised to be historically significant. The tapes would give him a huge advantage over Schlesinger and other historians, and because he was the only one in the room who knew a meeting was being recorded, he could also engage in some historical stage-managing.*

Because he viewed history as a competitive enterprise, Kennedy approached the task of becoming a great president with the same spirit that he and his siblings had brought to swimming contests, sailboat races, and touch football. When Bradlee and Cannon asked during their 1960 interview if he had a lot of "super competitive" spirit, he replied, "I think I do have a lot of it. I don't know if it is out of my family or what it is," and praised ambition as "what moves the world." He was concerned about being compared with FDR, once telling Schlesinger, who had praised FDR effusively in his New Deal trilogy, "That's the trouble, Arthur, with all you historians! That's what you did to Roosevelt and his crowd. You made all those New Dealers seven feet tall. They weren't that good. They were just a bunch of guys like us."

He understood that presidents are always compared closely with their predecessors and was fascinated by how historians were already judging Eisenhower. In the summer of 1962, the Sunday *New York Times Magazine* carried a long article by Schlesinger's father reporting on how seventy-five distinguished historians had ranked the presidents. The article included a photograph of Kennedy, hunched over a table with his back to the camera, captioned, "President Kennedy in his White House office—How will he be rated by historians." The article was encouraging. The historians had picked Lincoln, Washington, Franklin D. Roosevelt, Wilson, and Jefferson as the five greats, in that order. Arthur Schlesinger, Sr., summarized the eight crucial qualities of a great president this way: (1) "Each held stage at a critical moment in American history and by timely action attained timeless results." (2) "Each took the side of liberalism and the general welfare against the status quo." (3) "[Each] acted masterfully and far-sightedly in foreign affairs. All cared profoundly about keeping the country out of war." (4) They were "not only constructive statesmen but realistic politicians." (5) [Each] "left the Executive Branch stronger and more influential than he found it." (6) They "offended vested economic interests and long-standing popular

---

* He had been guilty of this after dictating many of his most important contributions to his inaugural address to Evelyn Lincoln ten days before the inauguration. To establish his authorship of these passages, and to persuade future historians that he had written them, he copied them down from memory on a yellow legal pad a week later, and invited the reporter Hugh Sidey into his private compartment on the *Caroline* to witness the performance.

prejudices." (7) They "were more deeply loved than they were hated. The rank and file of Americans re-elected every one of them to a second term." (8) They "possessed a profound sense of history. . . . Essential as it was to win approval at the polls, they looked as well to the regard of posterity."

Kennedy possessed all eight qualities. He prided himself on being a realistic politician, and had offended "vested economic interests" during his handling of the 1962 steel crisis. He had a "profound sense of history," was "loved more than he was hated," and was governing during a "critical moment" in the cold war and struggle for civil rights. He had kept the country out of war during the missile crisis, taken the side of liberalism as opposed to the status quo of the Eisenhower years, and made the Executive Branch more influential and powerful. Judged by these criteria, he needed only to win reelection and attain "timeless results" by ending the cold war and passing his civil rights bill.

He told Schlesinger that he was surprised his father had ranked Woodrow Wilson so high, ahead of Truman and Polk, but delighted that Eisenhower was twenty-second out of thirty-four.* "At first I thought it was too bad that Ike was in Europe and would miss the article," he said, "but then I decided that some conscientious friend in the United States would probably send him a copy." After Eisenhower criticized him for his handling of the Cuban missile crisis he speculated that the historians' poll was behind his attacks. "For years Eisenhower has gone along, basking in the glow of the applause which he has always had," he told Schlesinger. "Then he saw that poll and realized how he stood before the cold eye of history—way below Truman; even below Hoover. That is what is eating him now. He hates me because I am his successor; but his real quarrel is [with] what he now fears may be the judgment of history. That is why he is going around the country trying to defend his administration and to blacken us."

During a 1960 campaign stop in Philadelphia he had proclaimed that when historians assessed the next decade he wanted them to cry out, "These were the great years of the American life, the nineteen sixties. Give me those years!" He had taken office at a time when America was prosperous, the civil rights movement in its infancy, and his biggest campaign issue, a supposed "missile gap"

---

* After their conversation Schlesinger wrote in his diary, "It is clear that his [Kennedy's] measure is concrete achievement, and people who educate the nation without necessarily achieving their goals, like Wilson and Teddy Roosevelt, rate below those, like Truman and Polk, who do things without bringing the nation along with them."

between the United States and the Soviet Union, was a fallacy, leaving him a prospective great man in search of great challenges. The Cuban missile crisis finally provided his Churchillian moment—"when all history stood still"—and convinced him that in the atomic age, great men avoided war rather than leading their nations into it. The Birmingham demonstrations gave him his great domestic cause, and by Labor Day his "romantic conviction" that he was astride history and that historians might someday cry, "These were the great years of the American Republic!" seemed within grasp.

After lunch, he handed Styron an expensive Havana cigar encased in a silver tube. (Before ordering a ban on Cuban imports he had told Pierre Salinger to cruise through Washington and buy up every top-grade Cuban cigar.) As he put it in his pocket, Styron thought of Castro and decided, "Of all the world's leaders, the Harvard man and the Marxist from Havana were temperamentally and intellectually most alike."

Styron had heard that Kennedy hated being bored, so he offered only the briefest summary of his work-in-progress, a novel about the Nat Turner slave revolt in Virginia. But Kennedy was fascinated and pressed him for details, mounting what Styron called a "bright and persistent interrogation."

As they steamed into harbor at Martha's Vineyard, Kennedy noticed that they were heading straight for the Edgartown Yacht Club. He quickly ordered his captain to reverse engines and steer away from that WASP bastion to the public pier, "My God! They'd have my hide if they learned I'd just barged in there without permission," he said. Running a hand through his hair, he added, "I'll bet there's not a Democrat within five miles of here."

Monday, September 2

CAPE COD

The fifteen-minute television news broadcasts were Radio Age relics. By 1963, network executives had decided that a medium that broadcast both images and words needed more time and therefore expanded the evening news to thirty minutes. To inaugurate the longer format, CBS sent its anchorman Walter Cronkite to Cape Cod to interview the president on Labor Day. He was checking into a motel the night before when another journalist alerted him to an AP story predicting that Kennedy was planning to make "a major statement on Vietnam" during their interview. Cronkite was furious that the president was intending, as he put it, "to plant a statement to suit his purposes"—an odd complaint considering that CBS was using him to launch its new program. He lit into Pierre Salinger in the motel bar, threatening not to pose a single question about Vietnam. Salinger spent the rest of the evening and their ride to Squaw Island the next morning trying to change his mind, arguing that if he failed to raise the subject, the president would make his statement to another journalist and Cronkite would look stupid for missing the scoop.

Cronkite was still smarting from two acrimonious encounters with Kennedy during the campaign. On the eve of the Wisconsin primary he had angered Kennedy by raising the issue of his religion. Kennedy complained to CBS's president, Frank Stanton, pointedly reminding him that as president, he would be naming members of the Federal Communications Commission. After the conventions, Cronkite had conducted a half-hour interview with each candidate. He did Nixon first, then Kennedy at his home in Georgetown. He asked both the same concluding question: "What single quality do you think will be the most important that you take into the White House?" Nixon gave a smooth reply. Kennedy responded with an incoherent statement (much like the one his brother Ted would give to the CBS correspondent Roger Mudd in 1980), saying, "Well, I think it's . . . well, I think you would find probably . . . well, I think you'd probably find my sense of history. It's my sense of history. I have a sense of history." Realizing he had blown it, he asked to do a second interview. Cronkite refused on the grounds that Nixon had not been offered a similar deal. When he persisted, Cronkite threatened to announce on air that he had redone his interview. He claimed not to care, and Cronkite capitulated. As Cronkite was walking to the door he told Kennedy, "I think this is the lousiest bit of sportsmanship I've ever seen in my life." Shamed by this accusation, Kennedy shouted, "Wait a minute! Wait a minute! Go ahead and use it."

Cronkite held the Labor Day interview on the lawn outside Brambletyde. Once he had settled into a wicker chair facing the president, he changed his mind, reasoning that since the interview would be edited for time he might as well let Kennedy make his statement. He began by asking about the economy. Kennedy acknowledged that the current unemployment rate of 5.5 percent was too high, but said it would drop if Congress passed his tax cut. Asked if he would probably lose most of the South, he replied, "I am not sure that I am the most popular political figure in the country today in the South."

When Cronkite finally mentioned Vietnam, he delivered a response calculated to increase the pressure on Diem and prepare Americans for the possibility that the war might be unwinnable. "I don't think that unless a greater effort is made by the government to win popular support that the war can be won out there," he said. "In the final analysis, it is their war. They are the ones who have to win or lose it. We can help them, we can give them equipment, we can send our men out there as advisors, but they have to win it. . . . We are prepared to continue to assist them, but I don't think the war can be won unless the people support the effort and, in my opinion, in the last two months, the government has gotten out of touch with the people."

He called Diem's repression of the Buddhists "very unwise," and when Cronkite asked if he thought Diem's government could regain the support of the people, he said, "With changes in policy and perhaps in personnel [i.e., Nhu], I think it can. If it doesn't make those changes, I would think that the chances of winning it [the war] would not be very good."

"Hasn't every indication from Saigon been that Diem has no intention of changing his pattern?" Cronkite asked.

"Our best judgment is that he can't be successful on this basis. We hope that he comes to see that, but in the final analysis it is the people and the government itself who have to win and lose this struggle. All we can do is help, and we are making it very clear, but I don't agree with those who say we should withdraw. That would be a great mistake."

It is inconceivable that Kennedy's major statement on Vietnam was that the United States would not withdraw. Instead, the news dominating front pages the next day would be his warning that Diem would lose the war if he continued repressing the Buddhist majority and keeping his brother in the government. His pledge not to withdraw was hard to square with the rest of the interview. James Reston pointed out the contradiction in the *New York Times,* writing, "He both threatened and reassured Diem. He said: Change or we'll string along with you anyway." The two statements made no logical sense because his remark about not withdrawing was a smokescreen meant to conceal his real agenda and to avoid being "damned everywhere as a Communist appeaser." It contradicted what he had told Mansfield, Hilsman, Harriman, O'Donnell, and others, and what he would soon announce: the withdrawal of a thousand U.S. advisers. Like his statement that he did not suffer from Addison's disease, it was simply not true.

He closed the interview by vehemently denying Cronkite's assertion that he had sent Lodge to Saigon to keep the conflict from becoming a partisan issue in 1964. Speaking of Lodge, he said, "If he were as careful as some politicians are, of course, he would not have wanted to go there. He would have maybe liked to have some safe job, but he is energetic and has strong feelings about the United States and, surprising as it seems, he put this ahead of his political career. Sometimes politicians do those things, Walter."

Cronkite's assessment of the interview was that the president had "effectively pulled the rug out from under Diem and changed the course of events in Vietnam."

———

DURING THE AFTERNOON, KENNEDY cruised to Nantucket and back with his family and played nine holes of golf. (His hip flexor muscles had apparently undergone a miraculous recovery since Dr. Kraus's flying visit.) His last appointment was a conference with Vice President Lyndon Johnson, who was planning to fly back to Andrews after their meeting and embark on a five-nation goodwill tour of Scandinavia. For days Johnson had been lobbying for a briefing with the president to boost the status of his trip. After O'Donnell rebuffed him, General Clifton had done an end run and arranged this last-minute meeting.

Like most White House aides, O'Donnell disliked Johnson and had either forgotten or chosen to ignore Kennedy's warning, delivered at the beginning of his term, that Johnson was "a very insecure, sensitive man with a huge ego," and Kennedy's request to "literally kiss his ass from one end of Washington to the other."

Kennedy had struggled to follow his own advice. He had made Johnson chairman of the National Aeronautics and Space Commission, and chairman of his Presidential Commission of Equal Opportunity, but the other members griped that he showed little leadership and contributed almost nothing, leading Kennedy to complain, "That man can't run this committee. Can you think of anything more deplorable than him trying to run the United States? That's why he can't ever be President of the United States." He had told State Department Chief of Protocol Angier Biddle Duke to "look out" for Johnson and include him in official functions, explaining, "We're all going to forget. We've got too much to do around here." He had invited Johnson to opening day of the baseball season, but he talked so much that he ruined the game, and the next time, Kennedy sat Dave Powers between them. He sent him a birthday telegram but complained that Johnson's sensitivity made composing it "worse than drafting a state document." He accepted Johnson's invitation to visit his ranch, but Johnson presented him with a ten-gallon cowboy hat and sulked when Kennedy refused to wear it. He disliked hunting, but Johnson insisted that he shoot a deer (leading him to complain to a friend, "That will never be a sport until they give the deer a gun"), and then had the head mounted and sent to the White House. When it arrived, he told Jackie, "The three most overrated things in the world are the State of Texas, the FBI, and mounted deer's heads." He joked about repaying Johnson by taking him sailing during a hurricane.

Kennedy could not make himself like the man. "LBJ's simple presence seems to bug him," Bradlee observed. "It's not very noble to watch, and yet there it is." They had nothing in common. He was a cool and restrained campaigner; Johnson was a cornball like Kennedy's grandfather Honey Fitz. (He had told Bradlee and Cannon during their 1960 interview, "I think I'm the antithesis of my grandfather. . . . I'd rather read a book on a plane than talk to the person next to me, and my grandfather [would have] wanted to talk to him and probably everyone else on the plane." Johnson would also have talked to every passenger.) He golfed, sailed, and swam; Johnson lived, breathed, and talked politics, and never relaxed. He could not stand people feeling sorry for themselves; since becoming vice president, Johnson had done little else, bitching to Fay during a reception honoring the astronaut John Glenn, "Nobody cares whether I come or I don't come. I don't even know why I'm here." He could not bear being around unhappy people; Johnson was a world-class sulker. "I cannot stand Johnson's damn long face," he told Smathers. "He comes in, sits at the Cabinet meetings with his face all screwed up, never says anything. He looks so sad." Johnson was a bullshitter; Kennedy was so impatient with bombast and verbosity that he would abruptly leave a meeting to avoid it. He was secretive; Johnson reveled in exposing himself. He was thoughtful to his staff; Johnson was "an insufferable bastard," according to his aide George Reedy, who had accompanied him to the Labor Day meeting on Squaw Island. Their only shared ground was that they both were energetic philanderers with inferiority complexes. Kennedy felt inferior to the WASPs, while Johnson felt inferior to the Kennedys, complaining to reporters that instead of Harvard, he had attended a "little crappy Texas college." All in all, it was an unpromising terrain for a friendship.

By the summer of 1963, Johnson was miserable. He spoke of withdrawing from the ticket in 1964 and going back to Texas to run for his old Senate seat or to become the president of his alma mater, Southwest Texas State Teachers College. He claimed that the Kennedy inner circle had convened a secret meeting and decided to ditch him, and that Jackie had cast the only dissenting vote. He sat at White House meetings gray-faced, sullen, and silent, an "almost spectral" presence, according to Schlesinger. His aide Harry C. McPherson, Jr., was appalled when he saw him in a swimsuit. His stomach was enormous, his face blotchy and flushed, and he had obviously been eating and drinking too much. He spent hours in bed, staring at the ceiling and growling at anyone who disturbed him. George Reedy spoke of his "obvious depression," and given Kennedy's keen interest in White House gossip and the eagerness of his staff to relate anything reflecting poorly on "Uncle Cornpone," it is unlikely that Johnson's downward spiral had escaped his notice.

The only vice presidential duties Johnson relished were goodwill trips like the one he was preparing to take to Scandinavia. He had resisted them at first, suspecting a Bobby Kennedy plot to get him out of town, but discovered that he liked escaping the White House, playing the statesman, and being cheered by friendly foreign crowds. Kennedy probably viewed the Hyannis Port meeting as an opportunity to massage his ego and send him to Scandinavia in a good mood, but Johnson had a different agenda. After reviewing his schedule with Kennedy he said, "I think it would be a good idea to expand my itinerary to include a visit to Poland." Kennedy remained silent, forcing him to add, "It would be a dramatic sign of our desire to be friendly with the countries behind the Iron Curtain, particularly those that have shown a desire for freedom."

Taken by surprise, Kennedy remained silent as Johnson argued his case. The prospect of the loosest cannon in his administration making a last-minute excursion to a Soviet satellite at one of the most delicate and promising moments of the cold war had to be an appalling one. Intemperate remarks and impulsive gestures had marked his earlier trips, and his talk of making a "dramatic sign" in Poland suggested off-the-cuff speeches that might damage the fragile détente. He had to forbid him to go, but do it without hurting his feelings. After Johnson finished he played for time, asking if the State Department had approved adding Poland to his itinerary. Johnson admitted it had not. "I didn't want to start any planning until I knew your reaction," he said.

Kennedy finally weighed in, telling him, "I don't think such a trip is a good idea at this time. Maybe some time later." After a strained moment, he said, "What do you plan to talk about on your trip? If you have a prepared speech, I'd like to see it."

He took a pencil to Johnson's speech, crossing out sentences and whole paragraphs, explaining that he was removing a few sections that were "better unsaid."

Although Kennedy had gutted his speech and vetoed Poland, Johnson was pathetically grateful that he had agreed to meet with him at all. After boarding his helicopter he stepped out again and said to Clifton, "I want you to tell that young man that he did a very great and generous thing today."

"What was the pitch about wanting to go to Poland?" Fay asked after Johnson left.

"The poor guy's got the worst job in the government, and just wants to make a significant contribution. Unfortunately the timing isn't right," Kennedy said, adding condescendingly, "Otherwise I'd love to see him go and have a little fun."

The Scandinavian trip would be the most calamitous of Johnson's vice presidency. He was boorish and cranky, plagued by kidney stones, and unable to connect with the middle-class audiences. In Finland, he walked across the graves of the honored dead in a cemetery commemorating a famous massacre. In Norway, he interrupted the food service at a state dinner by having a long conversation with an aide, standing in the aisle and blocking the waitresses. He infuriated the Danes by ordering all the furniture designed by a famous craftsman removed from his hotel room. There is no telling what this miserable and impulsive man might have done in Poland.

Tuesday, September 3–Friday, September 6

WASHINGTON

The official diary of Kennedy's engagements kept by Ken O'Donnell shows the short week following Labor Day as among the least eventful of his presidency. He did not return from Cape Cod until Tuesday morning, and spent most of Thursday and Friday entertaining King Zaher of Afghanistan. On Tuesday afternoon, during a discussion of French atomic tests and the peaceful uses of nuclear power, he filled two pages with doodles, scribbling "test," "biological," "megaton," "peaceful uses," and, evidence that his mind was wandering, "Panama" (five times), "1964," "discrimination," and "Cuba." He covered the bottom of the second sheet with an eighteenth-century man-of-war in full sail.

Many of his doodles were composed of words taken from meetings and conversations, written several times, underlined, crossed out, and placed in boxes piled into towers or connected in chains. On rare occasions he would doodle his thoughts, once writing during a briefing, "I don't understand all this." When he drew something, it was usually a boat, perhaps because he would rather have been on it. In one of his more inventive doodles, he turned a U.S. flag into a treble clef, in another he drew the pillar of a canopy bed. He doodled when he was bored or wanted to release tension and frustration. "Vietnam" appeared frequently in his doodles that summer and fall, written down a page, put in boxes, crossed out, and underlined again and again.

The political situation there remained stalemated. The generals had suspended their plotting, and Diem was refusing to dismiss his brother. The

Pentagon insisted the war was being won and recommended supporting Diem; the State Department and U.S. press corps in Saigon believed it would be lost if he remained in power. The pro-Diem English-language *Times of Vietnam* condemned Kennedy's statements to Cronkite and accused the CIA of plotting to overthrow Diem. The State Department dismissed the charge as "something out of Ian Fleming."

Roger Hilsman attended a meeting of the Far East Subcommittee of the Senate Foreign Relations Committee on Wednesday. He reported to Lodge, and presumably to Kennedy as well, that its members had "far-reaching doubts regarding not only Diem-Nhu leadership but also advisability of continued US participation in Viet-Nam war" and were considering introducing a resolution stating, "It is the sense of the Senate that the American people are no longer willing to support a regime in South Viet-Nam that oppresses the people and religious sects. Continued support of such a regime is inconsistent with the basic precepts of American democracy."

Kennedy missed most of Friday's National Security Council meeting because he was entertaining King Zaher. In his absence, Bobby asked "whether we could win the war with Diem and Nhu." When Rusk said we could not if the Nhus remained in power, Bobby replied, "If we have concluded that we are going to lose with Diem, why do we not grasp the nettle now?" Rusk called pulling out "very serious," saying we would be in "real trouble" if the Vietcong took over. Bundy thought we had not yet reached "a moment of decision." General Taylor pointed out that three weeks ago the administration had believed we could win with Diem, and that the Joint Chiefs still shared that view. Bobby wanted to know what they should do if it became apparent that Diem could not win. McNamara said that the Pentagon had insufficient information to answer that question. To remedy that, Bobby proposed sending a mission to solicit the opinions of the U.S. servicemen who were advising and training South Vietnamese military units.

The president joined the meeting at this point and approved his brother's suggestion. McNamara said he would ask General Harkins, who headed the U.S. military mission in Vietnam, to begin canvassing the advisers. Taylor proposed sending Major General Victor Krulak to Vietnam to solicit the views of South Vietnamese officers. It was agreed that Joseph Mendenhall, a State Department official with extensive experience in the country, would join him and that they would leave immediately and spend two days there assessing the situation. The notion that they could fly twenty-four thousand miles in four days, spend forty-eight hours in Vietnam, and return with any worthwhile insights indicated the confused state of the administration's policy. The public affairs officer at the Saigon embassy who briefed them called their assignment "a symptom of the state the U.S. government was in."

Kennedy's appointments usually filled several pages of his official diary. On Wednesday they took up only half a page. Between 10:30 a.m. and 12:52 p.m., he reportedly participated in an "OFF THE RECORD MEETING. (No list and no subject supplied)," an unusual notation since O'Donnell usually included these details. He had in fact spent these hours planning his reelection campaign, studying reports and polls, and conferring by telephone with his brother-in-law Steve Smith, who had agreed to manage his 1964 campaign, and with Bobby, who had managed his last one.

Lincoln affixed a memorandum to the notes that he made that morning, explaining that they had been written as he "was going over some suggestions on campaign strategy for 1964." On one page he had written, "Must win the South" and "We would at this point." This was probably a reference to a recent memorandum from the pollster Louis Harris titled "The South in 1964" that suggested he could win the region by appealing to its more enlightened governors over the heads of its congressional delegation. The most important recent development in the South, Harris wrote, had been an "industrial explosion" accompanied by an "educational awakening" that had been "hidden mostly from view over the surface manifestations of segregation and the pratings about states' rights." He recommended targeting dynamic Southern cities like Atlanta, Houston, and Charlotte. "You can also stick it to the Republicans and the renegade Democrats by saying that . . . the main stream of the new South is not states' rights, not bitter end segregationist, not ultra-conservative," he advised, "and that you are willing to take your chances with this new South."

On the second page of his notes, Kennedy had written, "dismiss him as a second rate figure," a reference to Senator Barry Goldwater, his likely Republican opponent. He was already making moves to counter Goldwater, and Salinger had announced that at the end of September he would be making a five-day conservation trip to ten Midwestern and Western states, visiting national parks, wilderness areas, dams, and power projects. Salinger called the trip nonpolitical, but reporters immediately put quotation marks around the word. His itinerary included states where Goldwater was expected to be strong because of his Western roots, eight states where Democratic senators were running for reelection, and six that had voted for Nixon in 1960 and that Kennedy hoped to win to offset expected losses in the South.

It was probably on Monday that he decided to appoint Wisconsin's commissioner of taxation, John Gronouski, to the vacant position of postmaster general, making him the first Polish American to hold a cabinet position. Although Kennedy needed to solidify his support among Polish Americans, who voted heavily in major Eastern and Midwestern cities, he also had strong personal reasons for making the Gronouski appointment.

His strained flexor muscle continued bothering him, and on Thursday Lincoln noted that he was experiencing "discomfort" and had not been following Kraus's exercise regimen. Despite having flown Kraus back from Italy, Kennedy had disregarded his advice and now wanted a fourth opinion. Unwilling to tolerate the pain of a minor muscle strain any longer, he called Carroll Rosenbloom, a family friend who owned the Baltimore Colts, and asked him to arrange a consultation with the team's orthopedic surgeon. Lincoln reported that on Friday, "Dr. McDonald came & he reassured the President that his leg would snap out of it. He told him to continue the therapy he was getting from Dr. Kraus. The President felt much better from this reassurance."

Kennedy fussed over the trappings of his presidency almost as much as he did over his health. He had designed the sterling-silver calendars that he presented to members of the ExComm (Executive Committee) who had met throughout the Cuban missile crisis, and he had chosen the new colors and interior decoration of Air Force One, ordering that "United States of America" be painted in large letters on its fuselage and U.S. flags added to its tail fin. He was so pleased with the blue-and-white color scheme that he asked Postmaster General Day to hire the same designer to improve the appearance of the nation's mailboxes and the hats worn by its mailmen, and commissioned a New York firm to make recommendations for improving the look of the brochures, logos, and visual footprints of other government agencies. While walking down Pennsylvania Avenue toward the Capitol with Jackie one evening, he was so shocked by its dilapidated shops that he established a commission to improve the thoroughfare's architecture and ambience, and closely monitored its progress. He sampled the wines before

White House dinners and pored over the guest lists, demanding an explanation for anyone he failed to recognize. He supervised the renovation of the White House Rose Garden, a place it was said he loved so fiercely that no one dared leave a heel print in it. He oversaw the placement of the television cameras broadcasting a ceremony bestowing honorary citizenship on Winston Churchill, directing that a fine-looking contingent of marines in dress uniform be framed in the middle of the picture, and a black marine stand in the center. He had a fondness for well-executed rituals and ceremonies (his Catholic upbringing), and understood that the design of his jet, the furniture and paintings in the White House, and a well-executed state dinner contributed to the nation's prestige, and that in the cold war, prestige was a weapon.

Much of what King Zaher and Queen Homaira of Afghanistan experienced during their state visit reflected changes instituted by the president and the First Lady. State visits had formerly been cumbersome three-day affairs, but Kennedy had cut the schedule in half so he could host more foreign leaders. Because he had decided that traveling out to Andrews Air Force Base to greet a visiting head of state was a waste of time and that the Ellipse and the White House South Lawn were more impressive backdrops for an arrival ceremony, King Zaher and his party landed in a helicopter on the Ellipse and drove to the White House by motorcade. Because Kennedy had been impressed by the soldiers in breastplates and plumed helmets lining his route to the Élysée Palace during his state visit to Paris, he decided to replicate the spectacle at the White House, so that when Zaher arrived that evening for his state dinner, marines in dress uniform lined the White House driveway. His first honor guard had represented all four services, but after noticing that the marines looked healthier, had better posture, and wore more elegant uniforms, he eliminated the other services. Guests at state dinners had customarily sat side by side at long tables, unable to converse with anyone except their immediate neighbors. He and Jackie had introduced round tables to facilitate conversation among larger numbers of guests. During Thursday's state dinner he undoubtedly asked Zaher to sign his place card. No other president had entertained as many foreign heads of state in such a short space of time as he had, and he would have added Zaher's card to about sixty others in a collection that Bradlee recalled him boasting about, "as pleased as a small child talking about his bug collection."

The guests trooped outside after dinner to watch a drill team of marines illuminated by crisscrossing searchlights perform on the South Lawn, and to hear the Air Force Drum and Bugle Corps bagpipers play Irish melodies. Kennedy had recently noticed that the Jefferson Memorial was sited directly opposite the South Lawn and had asked General Clifton to find some old searchlights and illuminate it as an experiment. He drove over to inspect the memorial, liked what he saw, and ordered trees on the South Lawn trimmed so that guests would have an unobstructed view. Tonight was the first time it had been lit for a state dinner, and it provided a stunning backdrop to the festivities, "brilliantly lit, like a rounded jewel," one guest reported. Afterward, he ordered it illuminated every evening.

Jackie had read that fireworks were the customary welcome for honored guests in Afghanistan, so the evening concluded with the first display in White House history. Because Kennedy feared that a twenty-minute display might be too long, boring his guests (and himself), he cut it to ten minutes. The organizers shot off twenty minutes' worth of fireworks in ten, and the display was so brilliant and loud that calls from people convinced that the city was under attack jammed police switchboards. The evening concluded with a lone bugler standing in a spotlight, sounding taps.

HYANNIS PORT

Ken O'Donnell and Pam Turnure, Jackie's press secretary, both urged Kennedy to persuade the First Lady to decline the Onassis invitation, arguing that Americans would view taking a vacation so soon after Patrick's death to be unseemly. He told them, "I think it would be good for Jackie, and that's what counts." He was more honest with Charlie and Martha Bartlett, who had introduced him to Jackie. The Bartletts were their guests that weekend, and he made a humorous show of falling to one knee in front of them and begging Jackie not to go. She refused to budge. "When she wanted to do something," Martha Bartlett observed, "she did it."

It was gray and rainy all weekend, but he and Jackie, the Bartletts, and Lem Billings went out on the *Honey Fitz* anyway. The cabin cruiser was ninety-two feet long and had a spacious cabin and open deck, so Jackie may not have overheard him asking Bartlett, "How do you think Lyndon would be if I got killed?" Bartlett knew that an assassination was often on his mind, and had been with him when a speeding car had overtaken them and their Secret Service escort on a country road in Virginia and Kennedy had joked, "He could have shot you, Charlie."

His closest call had come a month after his election, when a retired postal worker, Richard Pavlick, packed his car with dynamite and began tailing him, renting a room in Hyannis Port, cruising past his town house in Georgetown, and following him to Florida. On December 11, Pavlick had parked outside the Kennedy home in Palm Beach, waiting for him to leave for church so he could ram his limousine and ignite the explosives. Pavlick changed his mind when

Jackie and Caroline appeared at the front door. He wanted to kill the president-elect, not his family. The Secret Service apprehended him, and soon afterward Kennedy said to Larry Newman, "Brother, they could have gotten me in Palm Beach. There is no way to keep anyone from killing me." He had been researching presidential assassinations, and told Newman that President Coolidge had once said that any well-dressed man willing to sacrifice his own life could kill a president. He also shared his research with Dr. Travell while they were sitting on the patio at Palm Beach—one suddenly less shady after the Secret Service had lopped off the fronds of surrounding palms to deny cover to an assassin.

He asked Travell, "What do you think of the rule that for the last hundred years every president of the United States elected in a year divisible by twenty [Lincoln, Garfield, McKinley, Harding, and FDR] died in office?"

"You don't *really* believe such a coincidence can continue?" she said. "The odds against it are too great, and anyway, you aren't superstitious."

He raised the subject with her again a few weeks later, saying it was a relief knowing that if anything happened, "My wife will have a pension and my children will be well cared for."

Soon after the inauguration he and Fay had been walking back from the Army and Navy Club to the White House across Lafayette Square when a Secret Service agent jumped between him and a suspicious-looking man. Kennedy admitted to Fay that an assassination was never far from mind, adding, "I guess that is one of the least desirable aspects of the job."

After a radio correspondent burst into his box on the opening day of the baseball season, shoving a microphone into his face and rattling off questions, he asked Powers, "What would you have done if that fellow had a grenade in his hand instead of a mike?"

During a game of charades in Palm Beach he acted out his assassination, collapsing to the floor and going through his death throes as a teammate doused him in ketchup.

While attending Mass in Hyannis Port, he turned to reporters sitting in the pew behind him and said, "Did you ever stop and think, if anyone tried to take a shot at me, they'd get one of you guys first?"

After disembarking at a small airport, he scanned a crowd waiting behind a fence and exclaimed, "Boy! Aren't we targets?"

But he still plunged into crowds and ordered his drivers to slow down so he could reach out and shake hands. A man in Rome kissed him and yanked him over a wooden barricade. When he arrived at the gates of the American ambassador's residence in Dublin a cheering mob surrounded his limousine and forced him to walk. "Crowds don't threaten me," he told the ambassador. "It's that fellow standing on the roof with a gun that I worry about."

But he worried about more than that. While he was being driven through heavy traffic in Virginia, the lead Secret Service car passed a slow-moving sedan going in the same direction and oncoming traffic kept his own car from following it. When a boy in the backseat pointed a motion-picture camera against the rear window, he tensed, took a deep breath, and murmured, "I will not live in fear. What will be, must be."

He often speculated about the best way to die, weighing the relative merits of hanging, strangling, and drowning. His sister Kathleen and brother Joe had died in planes, so he was sensitive to the risks of flying. As his valet George Thomas was packing Kennedy's bags for a short trip to Ohio, the president turned to Ted Sorensen and said, "If this plane goes down, Old Lyin' Down [Vice President Lyndon Johnson] will have this place cleared out from stem to stern in twenty-four hours—and you and George will be the first to go!"

He discussed an interparty feud with Governor William Lawrence of Pennsylvania as they rode to a political event at Washington's Shoreham Hotel. After Lawrence remarked that one of the warring politicians would not be up for reelection until 1968, he said, "Well, probably neither you nor I will be here then." Lawrence said, "Wait a minute, wait a minute, that may apply to me at my age, but not to you."

Minutes before delivering a speech to Congress proposing that the United States land astronauts on the moon, Kennedy told relatives and aides gathered in the Oval Office, "I firmly expect this commitment to be kept. And if I die before it is, all you here now just remember when it happens I will be sitting up there in heaven in a rocking chair just like this one, and I'll have a better view of it than anybody."

After his successful handling of the Cuban missile crisis he told Jackie, "Well, if anyone's going to shoot me, this would be the day they should do it."

Many of the jokes he shared with Powers concerned death and wakes, but when death was real and close, it was no laughing matter. When Caroline brought her dead parakeet into the Oval Office he recoiled in horror and said, "Get it away from here!" A friend who witnessed this said, "He didn't want to see it and he didn't want to know necessarily about the funeral arrangement. He just wanted it out of the way."

His sensitivity to the narrow margins separating life and death, success and failure was understandable. Had the Japanese destroyer hit *PT 109* a few feet nearer to where he was standing, he would have been killed. Had he not encountered the two Solomon Islands natives, he and his men would have died of exposure or been captured. Had cortisone not been discovered as a treatment for Addison's disease, he might have died before turning thirty-five. Paper-thin margins had also marked his political career. He had won the presidency by the smallest popular vote margin in almost a century, and had barely avoided nuclear war during the Cuban missile crisis—narrow escapes that may explain why he could be so full of good humor and optimism one moment, and so morbid the next.

ON SATURDAY EVENING he and five of his six surviving siblings celebrated their father's seventy-fifth birthday in the same way they had before he suffered a massive stroke in December 1961, leaving him paralyzed on one side and confined to a wheelchair, capable of hearing and understanding everything but capable only of grunting and saying "No!" They tied blue and yellow Mickey Mouse balloons to his wheelchair and pushed him into the living room, where they showered him with gifts and entertained him with poems, songs, toasts, and limericks. His daughter Jean Kennedy Smith and son-in-law Sargent Shriver unfurled a flag resembling the presidential one, except that it had a wide-eyed cartoon animal instead of an eagle above the words of a long-standing family joke, "He's Always in the Bushes!"

Stoughton's photographs show Joe Kennedy's children standing in his low-ceilinged living room, singing and applauding. The rugs are worn, the coffee table flimsy, and the upholstered furniture mismatched, with a low dark red couch next to a pale green easy chair, near a chair covered with the same busy and flowery pattern as the curtains. At dinner almost everyone except for Jack and Jackie is wearing a paper birthday hat. The grandchildren have not joined them, but the table is decorated for eight-year-olds, with balloons, a "Happy Birthday" tablecloth, and noisemakers, as if they were still his little boys and girls. No one in the photographs—even the candid ones—looks grumpy or bored. Everyone is laughing and smiling, thin and fit, blessed with brilliant white teeth, dark tans, and glossy hair.

Jackie sat next to her father-in-law at dinner, and during the skits and present-giving she took a seat at the end of the red couch, closer to him than anyone except her husband. One photograph shows her kneeling next to him while the others stand in a semicircle behind his chair. She insisted that she loved him "more than any other man except my husband and my father." But why she would choose to idolize a man who had been such a spectacular womanizer, and whose behavior had probably steered her husband in the same direction, remains a mystery.

Another photograph reveals that the Bartletts and Lem Billings have been relegated to a small table at the side of the dining room reminiscent of the "children's table" at Thanksgiving. Although they are among Jack and Jackie's oldest friends, they remain outsiders. Rita Dallas, the registered nurse who was caring for Joe Kennedy, believed that the Kennedy children were "loyal to the extreme" and saw them as a monolithic unit. In fact, their relationships had altered as they married, had children, changed jobs, and moved. The Palm Beach and Cape Cod houses were a powerful formaldehyde, but Joe's and Kathleen's deaths, Jack's political career, and Joe Sr.'s stroke had shuffled things. Jack had been closest to the high-spirited Kathleen, whose magnetism and charm most closely resembled his own. After she died in 1948, he turned to Eunice, the next-youngest and most driven of the surviving girls, teasing and competing with her as if she were Joe. He often sat with her in the library at Hyannis Port, briefing her on his speeches and seeking her advice. She would tell her father afterward, "He's pretty good, Daddy, but I could do it better."

The eight-year difference between him and Bobby had kept them apart when they were younger, but they became close after traveling to Asia together in 1951. He spoke with Bobby more than anyone in his cabinet, and trusted him and valued his advice more than anyone on his staff, but their relationship was less intimate than many imagined. He did not include him in the last-minute White House dinners, and seldom attended social events at his home in Virginia. Bobby's large and rambunctious family was one barrier; another was a subterranean competition that he was more willing than Bobby to acknowledge. Billings recalled times when Bobby would call and Jack would hold the telephone away from his mouth and say to whoever happened to be in the Oval Office, "I think it is the Second Most Important Man in the capital calling."

No one in the family had influenced Kennedy more or contributed more to his success than his father. Joe Kennedy had raised a family of ferocious competitors, weaning them on maxims such as "We don't want any losers around here. In this family we want winners" and "Don't come in second or third—that doesn't count—but win." When Schlesinger invited Kennedy to speculate as to why his father's children had turned out so much better than FDR's, he said, "It was all due to my father," explaining that although he had not been around as much as some fathers, when he was, "he made his children feel that they were the most important things in the world to him," and "seemed terribly interested in everything we were doing." By 1960, however, Kennedy had stopped paying attention to his advice. After his father criticized him for courting union members in Michigan, he told a friend, "I'm not going to listen to Dad anymore in this campaign because he doesn't understand what a Democrat has to do to get elected. In this country, a Democrat can only win if he excites an awful lot of people to believe their lives are going to be better if he gets into the White House." He tipped his top hat to him during his inaugural parade but seldom invited him to the White House, and he found his advice and criticisms oppressive. But he was gentle and loving after Joe's stroke. During Joe's first post-stroke visit to the Oval Office Kennedy patiently explained the significance of the mementoes on his desk, and as tears of pride streamed down his father's face he wheeled him to another part of the room and said, "This is my rocker, Dad. It looks as though we both need special chairs, doesn't it?"

Joe Kennedy's birthday party continued in the living room after dinner. Teddy's wife, Joan, played "Happy Birthday" on the piano, and as if this birthday was like the others, Teddy sang "When Irish Eyes Are Smiling" so loudly that the veins on his neck bulged. At Joe's seventieth birthday, everyone had sung, to the tune of "Yankee Doodle," "He's the famous bear of Wall Street / Just a grizzly in his house . . . And he's our Happy Birthday boy," and they probably reprised it this night. The evening concluded with Jack singing, from the melancholy "September Song," "O, the days dwindle down to a precious few. . . ."

"He did it so well," Martha Bartlett recalled. "That was a killer, the old man in a wheelchair, the son singing. You almost felt Jack knew he wasn't going to see old age." More likely, he sang it because he liked the song and it *was* September, and if the mood turned sad when he finished, it was probably because everyone was afraid that the days were dwindling down to a precious few for this frail patriarch. Each of his children and their spouses leaned down and kissed him lightly on the forehead before retiring. Jack had started the custom and was the last to kiss him. "Happy Birthday, Dad," he said as he straightened up. "And may you have many, many more."

On Sunday, he and Jackie and the Bartletts went cruising on the *Honey Fitz* and discussed what he would do after the White House. He would be only fifty-one when he left office in 1969, he said, "too young to write my memoirs and too old to start a new career," but he might like being U.S. ambassador to Italy, "because it would be good for Jackie." During an earlier conversation on the subject, he had told Bartlett that he wanted to take the famously efficient White House telephone operators with him when he left office, although "then nobody will want to talk to me, but at least I'll have them."

"What *are* you going to do, Jack?" Jackie asked. "I don't want to be the wife of a headmaster of a girls' school."

"Well, now, let's not worry, Jackie," he said, trying to end a conversation that was beginning to annoy him. "Something will turn up."

He once told Paul Fay, "We could go back to the South Pacific and revisit those waters where we personally turned the tide of war. Then drift through the Greek islands, with our wives administering to our every wish." In a more serious vein, he said he might run for the Senate, pointing out that John Quincy Adams had served in the House after his presidency, but adding, "Of course, when Bobby or Teddy becomes President then I'd probably be most useful as Secretary of State." He was ambivalent about a Bobby Kennedy presidency, worried that it might muddy or detract from his legacy. "I'm just not quite sure that I would ever get adjusted to addressing Bobby or Teddy as 'Mr. President,'" he told Fay. "Let's not dwell too long on the prospect of taking orders from Lovable Bob."*

---

* Charlie Bartlett had also sensed his unease about Bobby succeeding him. While swimming at Camp David that spring, he had suddenly asked Bartlett whether he thought the nominee would be Bobby or Lyndon, adding that he considered Johnson unfit for the presidency. Bartlett said later, "I didn't have the feeling from this conversation and some others that John Kennedy was particularly thrilled by the fact that Bobby had decided that he would try to succeed him." He expressed the same reservations to Chuck Spalding, telling him that he thought Bobby was overly ambitious and "hard-nosing it."

Monday, September 9

WASHINGTON

Kennedy appointed John Gronouski to the cabinet position of postmaster general on Monday even though he lacked a "postal background." An article in the *New York Times* called it a repayment for Gronouski's support in 1960, and a way of bolstering Kennedy's support among Polish Americans. David Broder headlined his column "Kennedy Building for '64" and compared the appointment to that of former Cleveland mayor Anthony Celebrezze as secretary of Health, Education, and Welfare, calling them "pre-election investments the President hopes will pay off in the 1964 election returns." Broder added that by naming the first Italian American and first Polish American to cabinet posts, Kennedy was seeking to blunt white backlash against his civil rights bill. If Gronouski's last name had been Collins or Green, he wrote, and if he had come from Georgia or Colorado, Kennedy would not have chosen him.

What Broder and the other pundits missed was that the Gronouski appointment also reflected Kennedy's determination to make it easier for other ethnic groups to walk through the door that his election had kicked open. Nor did Broder or other commentators connect the appointment to the immigration bill that Kennedy had submitted to Congress in July, one promising the most radical transformation of U.S. immigration laws in almost half a century.

The Immigration Act of 1924, also known as the National Origins Act (NOA), restricted immigration from eastern and southern European nations, and made it virtually impossible for Asians by restricting immigration to approximately

1,000 people a year from the so-called Asian-Pacific Triangle, an imaginary area including all of the countries from Pakistan to Japan as well as Pacific islands north of Australia and New Zealand. It set an annual quota for each nation at 2 percent of the number of its former citizens residing in the United States in 1890, a formula allowing about 156,000 yearly slots. After 1927, the quota was based on the ethnicity of the U.S. population in 1920. The large yearly quotas for nations like Britain, Ireland, Sweden, and Germany were seldom filled, while nations whose citizens were considered less desirable had huge backlogs. By 1963, Greece had an annual quota of only 308 and a backlog of 97,000, and Poland, with a quota of 6,488, had a backlog of 55,000.

The National Origins Act denied other nationalities the opportunity that Kennedy's ancestors had enjoyed, and no single issue troubled him so deeply for so long. While serving in the House, he had submitted numerous private bills to provide permanent resident status to immigrants in his district facing deportation.* In the Senate he fought to repeal the 1952 McCarran-Walter Immigration and Nationality Act, a bill modifying the National Origins Act while preserving its odious racial and ethnic preferences, and in 1957 he sponsored an amendment that chiseled away at the quota system by permitting the spouses, parents, and children of an alien who might have been disqualified for inconsequential reasons to achieve permanent resident status.

Two years after the publication of *Profiles in Courage,* Kennedy had written *A Nation of Immigrants,* a slim volume published by the Anti-Defamation League of B'nai B'rith that received few reviews and little press attention, perhaps luckily for him as it is possibly the most passionate, bitter, and controversial book ever written by a serious presidential candidate. It was only fifty-one pages, more pamphlet than book, and resembled the unsparing accounts of racism and discrimination that would become a feature of left-wing alternative histories a decade later. He was also ahead of his time in his celebration of racial diversity

---

* Typical were his dogged efforts to secure permanent resident status for the Chinese immigrant Toy Lin Chen. He won several temporary extensions of Chen's visa, submitted and resubmitted private bills, and continued championing the case even when Chen moved to another state. After he had lobbied on Chen's behalf more than five years, the Senate finally passed a private bill permitting Chen to remain in the country. A grateful Chen sent him a set of sterling silver dessert spoons.

and multiculturalism, writing, "The idea of the 'melting pot' symbolized the process of blending many different strains into a single nationality, and we have come to realize in modern times that the 'melting pot' need not mean the end of particular ethnic identities or traditions."

The book's thirty-two-page photo insert was a chronicle of the dark side of American history. It included the deck plan of an eighteenth-century slave ship captioned "It took another century for freedom to be transformed into the beginnings of first-class citizenship," a lithograph of a nativist mob in Philadelphia attacking Catholics, and another of an anti-Chinese riot in Denver. The public was not demanding the liberalization of immigration laws in 1958, yet Kennedy advocated increasing yearly quotas and allocating them more fairly, and condemned the current laws for their "strong orientation of an indefensible racial preference" and their favoritism of "so-called Anglo-Saxons." In a caustic conclusion, he wrote, "The famous words of Emma Lazarus on the pedestal of the Statue of Liberty read: 'Give me your tired, your poor, your huddled masses yearning to breathe free.' Until 1921 this was an accurate picture of our society. Under present law it would be appropriate to add: 'as long as they come from Northern Europe, are not too tired or too poor or slightly ill, never stole a loaf of bread, never joined a questionable organization, and can document their activities for the last two years.'"

His immigration bill redressed these injustices. It was blind to race and ethnicity and gave preference to immigrants whose skills and training meant they were likely "to add to the national welfare," then to the relatives of U.S. citizens and residents, and finally to foreign applicants on a first-come, first-served basis. In an accompanying message to Congress he argued that it represented "the principle of equality and human dignity to which our nation subscribes," and would "insure that progress will continue to be made toward our ideals and toward the realization of humanitarian objectives."

WHEN PRESIDENT ROOSEVELT was campaigning for a third term in 1940 he had courted isolationists by saying, "I give you one more assurance. I have said this before, but I shall say it again and again and again: Your boys are not going to be sent into any foreign wars." Kennedy did much the same thing during an interview with the NBC news anchors David Brinkley and Chet Huntley on September 9. When asked if his administration was likely to reduce aid to South Vietnam, he replied, "I don't think that would be helpful at this time," adding that this course of action might weaken the Diem government sufficiently that South Vietnam would fall to the Communists. When asked if he doubted the "Domino Theory," which postulated that if South Vietnam fell the rest of Southeast Asia would go Communist, he said, "I believe it. I believe it," and concluded, "I think we should stay. We should use our influence in as effective a way as we can, but we should not withdraw."

Historians and Kennedy's advisers have struggled to reconcile these statements with those he had made to Cronkite the week before, and with what he had told Mansfield, Hilsman, Harriman, and others. In fact, his statement to Huntley and Brinkley bore no more resemblance to his real intentions than Roosevelt's pledge not to involve America in the Second World War did to his. Kennedy wanted to placate hawks in the Pentagon and Congress just as Roosevelt had wanted to placate the isolationists. He also knew that minutes after NBC aired the interview he would be meeting with Senator Henry ("Scoop") Jackson of Washington, the most implacable and influential cold war hawk in the Democratic Party, and a man whose support for the test ban treaty vote he considered crucial to winning a decisive ratification vote in the Senate. The last thing he needed was to face Jackson moments after telling Huntley and Brinkley that he might withdraw U.S. advisers from South Vietnam.

After reminding Kennedy that former president Harry Truman had recently criticized his tax cut bill, Brinkley asked, "What do you think about cutting taxes while the budget is still in deficit?" He mounted a spirited defense of his bill, saying that a tax cut would reduce unemployment, "give the stimulus to our economy over the next two or three years ... [that would] provide for greater national wealth," and "get our budget in balance quicker." After the interview Kennedy told Evelyn Lincoln, "I think they should shoot everyone over seventy." He was thinking of Truman.

He met with Mansfield and Dirksen on Monday afternoon to discuss the test ban treaty ratification vote. Dirksen confirmed that he would be supporting the treaty but said that some senators were still on the fence because they feared it would leave the United States "disadvantaged by the Soviets in the nuclear field." To allay those senators' fears, Dirksen and Mansfield had drafted a letter for

Kennedy to sign, an action Dirksen admitted being "a little presumptuous." Kennedy read the letter out loud, agreed to sign it, and said he hoped it would be read on the floor of the Senate. Dirksen reminded him that he himself was paying a heavy price for supporting the treaty and mentioned attacks by the right-wing *Chicago Tribune*. Kennedy replied that at least he was fortunate that no one had written a book about him like Victor Lasky's *JFK: The Man and the Myth*. Lasky, a former Nixon campaign aide, had recycled some old stories illustrating his shortcomings while ignoring his successes, making just two brief references to the Peace Corps and devoting a single sentence to his handling of the Cuban missile crisis. The reporter Tom Wicker, no Kennedy idolater, had savaged the book in the *New York Times* as "an exercise in political assassination."

During their meeting, Senator Jackson told him that he remained undecided about the treaty, and then exploited his pivotal role to complain about what he called "nutty characters" in the Arms Control Agency who believed, he said, that "peace is breaking out all over and are ready to make all sorts of proposals." (He was unaware that the president was among these nutty characters and was about to propose a U.S.-Soviet lunar mission.)

Kennedy reminded Jackson that he had appointed a number of hard-liners to key positions—naming McCone, McNamara, and Dillon—and flattered him by implying that he was presidential material, saying, "I think you may learn when you sit here that there's a helluva vested interest in proving any Democratic president to be wrong or soft on communism."

Jackson urged him to send combat units to Vietnam.

"Helluva place to intervene."

Jackson said he did not believe that the question of intervening militarily in Laos was settled.

"I think it is," Kennedy replied.

He urged Jackson to support the test ban treaty out of patriotism, pragmatism, and party loyalty, pointing out that it could be "of some significance" to the Democrats in the 1964 election, adding, "All I want to say, Scoop, is I think you can make a hell of a difference in this debate and, I think, having gone this far and having signed this [the test ban treaty], if we get beaten on it we'll find ourselves in a much worse position than if we hadn't brought it up." It was his "guess," he said, that the Chinese Communists would test an atomic bomb in a few years, forcing the United States to reconsider resuming atmospheric testing. He was telling Jackson what he wanted to hear, pretending the treaty was a strategic political move that could help Democrats in 1964, not a first step toward ending the cold war. In the end, Jackson voted for the treaty and Kennedy gave him nothing in return—no military intervention in Laos, no combat troops in Vietnam.

Kennedy feared that the concessions he had made to placate the Joint Chiefs and cold war hawks like Jackson had so diluted and weakened the treaty that it risked becoming an anomaly rather than a landmark agreement initiating an era of détente. To remedy this he decided to address the United Nations General Assembly on Friday, telling Harriman, Stevenson, and Schlesinger during a Monday meeting, "The treaty is being so chewed up in the Senate, and we've had to make so many concessions to make sure it passes, that we've got to do something to prove to the world that we still mean it. If we have to go to all this trouble over one small treaty, people are likely to think we can't function at all—unless I can dispel some doubts in New York."

His advisers brainstormed all week about what form of cooperation with the Soviet Union he could propose at the United Nations. Rusk suggested an "Alliance for Man," in which the United States, the Soviet Union, and the United Nations would pledge to achieve breakthroughs in health, nutrition, and agriculture. After canvassing government agencies, Schlesinger dismissed Rusk's idea as trivial compared with the dramatic possibilities of a joint space mission. Unaware that Kennedy had already proposed a joint lunar venture to Ambassador Dobrynin, he included it in his first draft of a proposed General Assembly speech.

The next day Kennedy received a personal message from Khrushchev, expressing his hope that the test ban treaty would "lead to a real turning point and the end of the cold war." He replied, "The President wishes Mr. Khrushchev to know that he shares his view that the signing of the test ban treaty and the recent exchange of views with the Soviet government is encouraging and he hopes it will be possible to proceed with the solution of other problems."

WASHINGTON

Tuesday was the first day of school in Alabama. To thwart the court-ordered desegregation of schools in Birmingham, Tuskegee, and Mobile, Governor Wallace had called out the Alabama National Guard and ordered it to prevent black students from entering the buildings. Kennedy thwarted him by federalizing the Guard and sending the troops back to their armories. Black students attended the previously all-white public schools without incident, demonstrating that even in the Deep South, integration could occur without the intervention of U.S. marshals and troops.

At a National Security Council meeting on Tuesday morning, Victor Krulak and Joseph Mendenhall reported on their four-day mission to South Vietnam. Krulak had interviewed members of the U.S. advisory mission and the South Vietnamese military. He told Kennedy that the Buddhist crisis had not harmed the war effort or damaged relations between the American and South Vietnamese military and that the war was being won "irrespective of the grave defects of the ruling regime." Mendenhall had met with Vietnamese nationals in Saigon, Hue, and several provincial towns. He said there had been a breakdown of civil government in Saigon, spoke of "a pervasive atmosphere of fear and hate arising from the police reign of terror," and concluded, "We will lose the war with the Diem government."

After asking if they had visited the same country, Kennedy said bleakly, "This is not a new thing, this is what we've been dealing with for three weeks.

On the one hand you get the military saying that the war is going better, and on the other hand you get the political [opinion]. . . . What is the reason for the difference—I'd like to have an explanation what the reason is for the difference."

Krulak said he was reporting on "national" attitudes to the war while Mendenhall had been concerned with sentiment in the urban areas, a lame explanation that left Kennedy unsatisfied. He decided to reconcile their conflicting reports by saying, "It seems to me after listening to General Krulak and those fellows from State [Mendenhall et al.] that they're probably both right. There hasn't been a real deterioration yet but it could set in. I think maybe two months from now. . . . So my judgment would be that we're probably going to be worse off in two to four months."

McNamara disagreed. It was impossible to forecast so far ahead, he said, and he disputed claims that the Buddhist crisis had weakened the military effort. He supported Rusk's recommendation that they rein in Lodge, whose latest cable had "recommended that we decide today to get rid of Diem and Nhu."

After receiving Krulak and Mendenhall's dispiriting report, Kennedy attended a luncheon meeting of the Business Committee for Tax Reduction in 1963. He told the businessmen that his tax cut bill was "the most important domestic economic measure to come before the Congress in the past fifteen years." Current tax rates hobbled the economy, he said, and his bill would "give a major responsibility and opportunity to American business to meet those needs [for jobs] through private means," provide "recession insurance," and expand "consumption and investment." The result would be "a reduction in our budgetary deficits." He received a standing ovation.

Lincoln noted in her diary, "At 3:45 today Marlene Dietrich came to see the President. She looks mighty good—leggy for 62." He was meeting the famed actress and singer in the Oval Office because he had a 4:15 appointment with the U.S. ambassador to Egypt, making it unlikely that their encounter would be as intimate as it had been the previous September, when she had visited him in the family quarters on a Saturday evening while Jackie was in Virginia. On that occasion he had poured her a glass of her favorite German wine, led her onto the balcony, and launched into a discussion of Abraham Lincoln. After noticing that she seemed impatient, he stopped and said, "I hope you aren't in a hurry." She explained that in half an hour she was due at the Statler Hotel, where Jewish war veterans were holding a dinner to honor her for aiding Jewish refugees. He stared deeply into her eyes and said, "That doesn't give us much time, does it?" Staring straight back, she replied, "No, Jack, I guess it doesn't."

In her recounting of the story to the theater critic Ken Tynan, Kennedy took her glass and led her to a bedroom. In Tynan's hands, their coupling became a scene from an X-rated screwball comedy. As Kennedy unwound the bandages holding his back brace in place, she thought, "I'd like to sleep with the President, sure, but I'll be goddamned if I'm going to be on top!" But he took the superior position and she reported it being over "sweetly and very soon." He fell asleep; she threw on her clothes, shook him awake, and shouted, "Jack—wake up! Two thousand Jews are waiting! For Christ's sake get me out of here!" He wrapped a towel around his waist and led her down the corridor to the elevator. Then, as she told it, "standing right there in his towel, without any embarrassment, as if it were an everyday event—which in his life it probably was," he told the elevator operator to have a car take her to the Statler. Before the door closed he said, "There's just one thing I'd like to know. Did you ever make it with my father?" She insisted she had not and he said, "Well, that's one place I'm in first."

He could have scheduled a repeat performance when she returned to the White House on Wednesday. Jackie was in Newport and he had no official events scheduled that evening. Perhaps he had decided to remove temptation by seeing her in the middle of a busy afternoon, because after Patrick's death he really *was* trying harder to "keep the White House white," and because the next day was his tenth wedding anniversary.

He had already bought Jackie a private anniversary gift, a gold ring decorated with tiny chips of emerald symbolizing Patrick's Irish heritage. Because he planned on giving it to her in private he also needed something she could open in front of their guests. He had left this second gift to the last minute, and on Thursday morning he called John Klejman, an art dealer specializing in Greek, Roman, and Byzantine antiquities who owned a New York gallery opposite the Carlyle Hotel, where the Kennedys had an apartment. He asked Klejman to throw together a collection of his best pieces, ones he thought Jackie might like, and have them flown with a price list to Andrews Air Force Base so he could take them with him to Newport that afternoon. According to Klejman, Kennedy had "fallen in love" with one of his most costly antiques, a life-sized fourth-century B.C. Greek bronze of a handsome athlete. It was too expensive to give Jackie, but he was hoping to persuade the National Gallery to acquire it. In the meantime, Klejman kept it for him on private display in his basement, where it sat on a pedestal surrounded by floodlights. When Kennedy was in New York he would cross Madison Avenue to the gallery and stand in the basement for several minutes, mesmerized by the statue.

He was in high spirits at his pre-press-conference briefing on Thursday morning, leading Walter Heller, his economic adviser, to describe it as "the best humored briefing breakfast we have had at any time." He asked everyone what he should say about Lasky's book, but since no one had read it they could only discuss the reviews. After learning that the columnist Roscoe Drummond had praised it, he said, "Never trust a man who serves only soft drinks," explaining that the only time he had visited Drummond at home he had been offered orange pop. Rusk chimed in that Drummond had served him a soft drink, too, one with artificial rum flavoring. It had been "the supreme indignity."

After saying that he anticipated being challenged on Gronouski's qualifications, Kennedy asked, "Why shouldn't we have a Pole or an Italian in the cabinet? Nobody thinks anything of it when his name is Day." After a pause he added, "I hope I get a question on this."

Heller complained that when the stock market fell it was called the "Kennedy market," but when it rose his opponents called it something else. Recognizing a clever sound bite when he heard it, Kennedy promised to use it. He mentioned that the money American tourists spent abroad was contributing to the balance-of-payments crisis and admitted that his own family bore some responsibility. Heller facetiously suggested a "See America First" trip for the First Lady. He laughed and called it "a good project for next year."

THE NET EVALUATION SUBCOMMITTEE (NES) was an Orwellian title for a committee of military officers and civil servants given the task of providing the president with what was called, in bureaucratese, "integrated evaluations of the net capabilities of the USSR, in the event of a general war, to inflict direct injury on the continental U.S., and to provide a continual watch for change which would significantly alter these net capabilities." In plain language, the NES estimated how many million Americans would die in a nuclear war. Although the NES was supposed to give the president a yearly briefing, Kennedy's last one had come during the 1961 Berlin crisis. According to a declassified summary of that meeting, Chairman of the Joint Chiefs Lyman Lemnitzer had stated that their assumption was "a surprise attack in late 1963 preceded by a period of heightened tensions"—a scenario resulting in the deaths of more than a hundred million Americans. Kennedy asked if an assessment had ever been done of the damage that a preemptive U.S. attack would inflict on the Soviet Union. The CIA director, Allen Dulles, said such a strike would be less effective until the end of 1962, but that his agency and the Pentagon believed that between then and the end of 1963 the United States would enjoy a "window of superiority" in land-based missiles. Kennedy had turned to Rusk afterward and, with a strange look on his face, had said, "And we call ourselves the human race." Rusk believed that the 1961 NES briefing had convinced him that waging a nuclear war was inconceivable, writing, "To see it all laid out vividly confirmed Khrushchev's warning 'In the event of a nuclear war, the living would envy the dead.'"

In their 1993 article "Did the U.S. Military Plan a Nuclear First Strike for 1963?" James K. Galbraith and Heather Purcell stated that the 1961 NES briefing had offered Kennedy a "glimpse of the opportunity that lay ahead in the winter of 1963: U.S. nuclear superiority so complete that a first strike might be successful." It had also alerted him to the danger that American nuclear superiority might be such that "rogue elements from the military and intelligence forces, seeking to precipitate an American first strike, might not feel deterred by fear of Soviet retaliation." They speculated that one reason Kennedy had been so determined to push the test ban treaty and nourish a détente with the Soviet Union in 1963 was to blunt pressure from military hard-liners to mount a first strike before the end of the year, when the window of superiority in land-based missiles would close. McNamara made a similar observation in 2003, saying that Kennedy had been concerned about right-wing hawks who believed that at some point "we were going to face a nuclear war with the Soviet Union" and that we should strike first when we had the greatest advantage. He identified this period of superiority as stretching from the Cuban missile crisis until the end of 1963. "It was the belief of many, including General LeMay. . . . [that] we had to fight the Soviets in a nuclear war," he said, and it would be better to do it when we had a seventeen-to-one advantage in nuclear warheads.

The Net Evaluation Subcommittee report that General Taylor presented to Kennedy on the morning of Thursday, September 12, 1963, is missing from the records. A summary that the Pentagon provided Bundy indicates that it forecast the results of a general war at various intervals between 1963 and 1968, predicting that casualties and damage would "increase over the years." According to the summary, "during the years 1964 through 1968 neither the US nor the USSR can emerge from a full nuclear exchange without suffering very severe damage and high casualties, no matter which side initiates the war." The summary also warned that the U.S. window of nuclear superiority was closing, making it too late to launch a successful preemptive attack.

Seizing on this aspect of the report, Kennedy asked Air Force General Leon Johnson if it was true that "even if we attack the USSR first, the loss to the U.S. would be unacceptable to political leaders [i.e., himself]." Johnson agreed that the Soviets would have enough weapons left to produce an "unacceptable loss" in the United States. Had we, then, reached a period of nuclear stalemate? Kennedy asked. Johnson said we had. Pressed further, he conceded that "there is no way, no matter what we do, to avoid unacceptable damage to the U.S. if nuclear war breaks out."

McNamara reported that he had received the results of a study predicting the fatalities if the United States added $80 billion to the defense budget for blast shelters and more offensive and defensive weapons systems. Even with all these improvements, if the United States struck first and the Soviets were in a low state of alert, the minimum number of U.S. fatalities would still exceed 30 million. According to the Pentagon's summary of the meeting, "The President again said that preemption was not possible for us and that that was a valuable conclusion growing out of an excellent report."

After concluding these grim discussions, Kennedy presided over a press conference notable for what newspapers called "more laughter . . . than most reporters could remember," and "one of his wittiest performances of evasion and rebuttal in months."

The *Boston Globe* headlined its story, "JFK Press Talk: Laughs for All," but the article was mildly critical of his conferences for producing "more laughs than headlines." Unnamed members of the Washington press corps had complained in a *New York Times* article published several days earlier that they had become "more nearly an instrument of Presidential power than a useful tool of the press" that left them "playing minor roles in a bit of show biz that might be called: 'See

Kennedy Run, or A Young President Makes Good.'" Instead of questioning him, one reporter said, they had been reduced to "merely holding him up for the world to admire." Their gripes boiled down to this: he had become so skilled at handling these conferences that he had turned them into a clamoring mob while he stood on the stage in the cavernous State Department auditorium, cool and confident.

He conducted his Thursday briefing as if intent on confirming these flattering cavils. Asked if he would care to comment on recent attacks by Senator Goldwater, he replied, "No. No," and after a well-timed pause added, "Not yet. Not yet." The laughter was audible to the millions of Americans watching the conference.

A reporter attempted to draw him into a debate with Governor Nelson Rockefeller of New York, who had expressed disappointment that he had not stimulated more economic growth. The governor was not alone in expressing his disappointment, he said. "I got I suppose several thousand of letters when the stock market went way down in May and June of 1962, blaming me, and talking about the 'Kennedy Market.' I haven't gotten a single letter in the last few days about the 'Kennedy Market' now that it has broken through the Dow Jones Average. So Governor Rockefeller is not alone in his disappointment."

He was asked to comment on resolutions passed by the California Federation of Young Democrats, urging the recognition of Red China and the withdrawal of U.S. forces from South Vietnam. After saying that he disagreed with their positions, he received the loudest laughs of the afternoon when he added, "I don't know what is happening with the Young Democrats and Young Republicans, but time is on our side."

Asked to comment on Victor Lasky's nasty biography and on a book about him by Hugh Sidey that reviewers were calling a hagiography, he said, "I thought Mr. Sidey was critical, but I have not read all of Mr. Lasky, except I have just gotten the flavor of it. I have seen it is highly praised by Mr. Drummond and Mr. Krock and others, so I am looking forward to reading it . . . because the part that I read was not as brilliant as I gather the rest of it is, from what they say about it."

He also gave a light touch to his response to the complaints about the Gronouski appointment, saying, "I don't know why it causes so much excitement when the name is Gronouski as opposed to when it may be Smith or Brown or

Day [the previous postmaster general]. . . . I think Mr. Gronouski is a fine public servant and I am glad to have him here and I think we just happen to be fortunate that his grandparents came from Poland."

He was in such a good mood that instead of waiting for the senior White House correspondent, Merriman Smith, to close the session with the traditional "Thank you, Mr. President," he offered his own "thank you" and walked off the stage with a broad grin.

While he was flying to Newport, Eunice called Evelyn Lincoln and asked her to relay this message: "I saw your picture in the paper this morning showing you now and ten years ago. Congratulations, we all know God is riding on your shoulder. You always get your wish. You wished that you would look older and God only knows you do today." It was a mischievous tease for someone whose vanity was a family joke, and uncomfortably close to the truth. Television footage of his news conference showed deep lines meeting across the top of his nose, and the start of a double chin.

Thursday, September 12–Sunday, September 15

NEWPORT

After Air Force One landed at Quonset Naval Air Station in Newport, Kennedy warned Ben Bradlee and his wife, Tony, that he needed to spend a few minutes doing what he called "a little toe dance" with Rhode Island's new Republican governor, John Chaffee. He was livid when he rejoined them in the helicopter taking them to Hammersmith Farm, the waterfront estate of Jackie's stepfather, Hugh Auchincloss. Chaffee had given him a cheap silver-plated vase as an anniversary gift, an obvious all-purpose present accompanied by a printed card announcing, "The Governor of Rhode Island." Kennedy, who was scrupulous about writing notes and observing the social graces, was appalled that Chaffee had not bothered to sign the card. Even worse, the official cameraman had failed to capture the welcoming ceremony and Chaffee had grabbed back the vase and insisted on running through everything again, speeches and all. "Boy, he learns fast," Kennedy said. "I didn't have that much brass until I'd been in Congress five years . . . pushing a president around like that." He mentioned the vase all weekend, each time suggesting a new way to get even with Chaffee and "put him in his place"—threats as hollow as posting the Otis officer to Alaska or making Ambassador McCloskey restore Mary Ryan's yard.

He landed at twilight on the lawn in front of Hammersmith Farm. As he disembarked, Jackie came running and greeted him with an embrace that the Bradlees thought was the most affectionate they had ever seen them exchange. As he entered the house, he handed his mother-in-law Chaffee's vase, calling it "a token of my undying affection." Missing his sarcasm, she thanked him profusely but eyed it with dismay, probably wondering for how long she would have to display it. He finally admitted that it had been a present from the people of Rhode Island, and asked, "Don't you think it was a funny thing for the governor to hand it to me this way?"

Twelve hundred guests had attended the Kennedys' wedding reception at Hammersmith Farm in 1953, dining and dancing under a vast white marquee. The *New York Times* reported the event on its front page, describing the guests as "the cream of society and important government officials," and saying that no marriage had elicited such intense public interest since the famous Astor-French nuptials of 1934. Twelve people had gathered to celebrate the Kennedys' tenth anniversary. They included a former bridesmaid, Jackie's mother, stepfather, half brother and sister, the Bradlees, and Senator Claiborne Pell of Rhode Island and his wife. Over cocktails, Jackie gave Kennedy three scrapbooks titled "The White House Before and After," "The President's Park," and "The Making of a Garden." One chronicled the transformation of the Rose Garden and contained well-chosen quotations about gardening written in her hand, accompanied by photographs showing how the garden had looked on a particular day and his schedule for that day. The White House head usher, J. B. West, who had watched her laboring over these scrapbooks for months, compared them to "fine art books."

He reciprocated by reading out loud a letter from Klejman listing the antiquities he had brought from Washington. They included a Greek statue, an ancient Egyptian head, and some bracelets. Nothing cost less than a thousand dollars, and some items cost much more. He omitted the prices and told her to choose what she wanted, but repeatedly said, "Now, you can only keep one; you have to choose." The expression of faint alarm crossing his face as he proceeded down the list made it apparent that he was reading it, and the accompanying prices, for the first time. As he came to the most expensive items he whispered to Bradlee, "Got to steer her away from that one." She chose a gold bracelet resembling a coiled serpent because, she said, "It was the simplest thing of all and I could see how he loved it."

Her gift to him had required months of thought and labor. His had been organized at the last minute with a single phone call and was almost as hurried and impersonal as Chaffee's vase. He redeemed himself when they exchanged their more personal gifts. When he had knelt at her bedside weeping after Patrick's death, she had begged him for something that would remind her of their son. Now he gave her the gold ring with green emerald chips symbolizing that their son had fought like an Irishman to live. She reciprocated with a gold-plated St. Christopher medal fashioned into a money clip that she had ordered from Tiffany's to replace the one he had slipped into Patrick's coffin. After the anniversary she would write Charlie Bartlett an effusive letter, telling him that Jack had helped "re-attach" her to life following Patrick's death, and made her appreciate "all the lucky things" they shared. She believed that he could have lived a "worthwhile life" without being happily married, but without him, hers would have been "a wasteland."

She took Ben and Tony Bradlee aside later that evening and with tears glistening in her eyes said, "You two really are our best friends." It struck Ben Bradlee as a forlorn remark, the kind that "a lost and lonely child desperately in need of any kind of friend" might make. He doubted they were really their best friends, but the comment touched him and he wrote in his diary that because the Kennedys were so remote and independent, those rare occasions when they revealed their emotions were especially moving. The year before, Jackie had made a similarly impetuous declaration to her personal secretary, Mary Gallagher, suddenly embracing her and saying through tears, "You know, you're my only friend in this impersonal White House." Gallagher was taken aback, since they had recently been embroiled in an acrimonious dispute over her salary and civil service rank.

DURING THEIR LONG WEEKEND in Newport the Bradlees and Kennedys followed the same schedule: swimming at Bailey's Beach Club in the morning, lunch and a cruise on the *Honey Fitz*, then golf at the Newport Country Club. Jackie was not a keen golfer but tagged along, riding in the cart with her husband and even playing thirteen holes on Saturday. A home movie taken during one of their *Honey Fitz* outings shows him fingering a cigar, twiddling his sunglasses, and stroking John or Caroline, anything to keep his hands in motion. He gave John a swimming lesson in the pool and sat with him in a beached dinghy, teaching him how to row. He sent a cable to Lyndon Johnson, who had suffered excruciating pain from kidney stones throughout his Scandinavian trip, urging him to "pay more attention to the doctors than you usually do." Johnson's gaffe-filled trip had produced more ill will than good, but Kennedy generously praised him as "the best of our ambassadors."

He decided to split the next summer between rented houses in Hyannis Port and Newport, and asked Senator Pell to persuade the owner of Annandale Farm, the fifteen-acre waterfront estate bordering Hammersmith Farm, to rent it to them for August and September but not to tell Jackie. He knew it would make her happy and wanted to surprise her. She had grown up in Newport during the summers, had friends there, and preferred it to Hyannis Port. He was more conflicted, once complaining to a friend, "All around me I see ponies and horses running around the backyard. What the hell is there for *me* to do?" Still, it had great waters for sailing, and he liked Hammersmith Farm enough that while Jackie was in Italy he had invited himself for the weekend and had asked her mother if he could return again, sleeping next time in Jackie's childhood room, the same one they had shared as newlyweds.

He and Jackie attended Sunday Mass at the same church where they had been married. As they were driving to Bailey's Beach Club he stopped to talk with some nuns standing in a crowd along the road. "Jackie here always wanted to be a nun," he told them mischievously. "She went to a convent school and really planned to take the orders."

It was at about this moment that a box of dynamite hidden near the basement steps of the Sixteenth Street Baptist Church in Birmingham exploded, killing four young black girls on their way to Sunday school. The bombing had been perpetrated by four members of an offshoot of the Ku Klux Klan and was one of the landmark atrocities of the civil rights struggle, but it appears to have had surprisingly little impact on Kennedy, which is doubly curious since anything threatening the lives or happiness of innocent children usually engaged his emotions. Bradlee devoted several pages of his book *Conversations with Kennedy* to recounting their anniversary weekend but made no mention of his reaction to the deaths of the four girls.

After leaving Bailey's Beach Club, Kennedy took his usual luncheon cruise and played golf. His phone logs show that after coming off the links he called

Bobby, probably to discuss the bombing and send Assistant Attorney General Burke Marshall to Birmingham. He also decided to return to Washington that evening instead of the following morning, but the notes he made on the plane showed that his mind was not on the bombing, and included reminders such as "speeches for Western trip."

WASHINGTON, NEW YORK, NEWPORT

O n Monday morning Kennedy expressed "outrage and grief" at the bombing and charged that "public disparagement of law and order"—a reference to Governor Wallace's defiance of the integration of Birmingham schools—had "encouraged violence which has fallen on the innocent." It was a strong statement but not a passionate one, and ignored the demand of civil rights leaders that he send federal troops to the city to protect its black population. He could have read it to reporters himself instead of having Salinger release it, or proclaimed a day of national mourning, attended the funerals, or sent a relative. His muted reaction resembled that of many white Americans. After Medgar Evers's assassination and the bombings of black homes and gathering places in Birmingham, another bombing—even one killing four children—seemed less shocking. He praised "the Negro leaders of Birmingham who are counseling restraint instead of violence" but offered only an FBI investigation and the cold comfort of protection from the all-white Birmingham police force. He may have failed to speak out more forcefully because he would be delivering a nationally televised address urging support for his tax-cut bill on Tuesday and addressing the United Nations General Assembly on Friday, and he believed that giving a high-profile speech on civil rights during the same week would dilute their impact.

On Tuesday, the White House press office released a mendacious statement about the First Lady's trip to Greece. The result was a *New York Times* story headlined "President's Wife Will Stay with Sister Near Athens on Private Island" that reported she would spend the holiday in a house rented by her brother-in-law and sister, Prince and Princess Radziwill. Kennedy presumably hoped to mitigate the damage by keeping Onassis and his yacht under wraps until the last minute, then present the cruise as a spur-of-the-moment decision.

On Tuesday morning he asked the American ambassador to Moscow, Foy Kohler, what he thought about the possibility of U.S.-Soviet cooperation in outer space. Kohler said that his suggestion to Ambassador Dobrynin of a joint lunar mission had left the Soviets "intrigued." Minister of Foreign Affairs Andrei Gromyko had given the idea a cautious welcome but was waiting for some concrete proposals. Kennedy admitted not having considered the details but said he wanted to proceed and believed the United States could save a lot of expense by teaming up with the Russians. "I would like to have an agreement on when we both try to go to the moon," he added. "Then we wouldn't have this intensive race—I don't [even] know whether they are going to the moon."

He did not tell Kohler that he had decided to propose a joint moon mission at the UN on Friday, nor did he tip his hand to the NASA administrator Jim Webb when they met on Wednesday to review the space program. But he did say that he was beginning to question whether beating the Russians to the moon should be a top priority and was concerned that Congress and the public had become concerned about its cost. "If the Russians do some tremendous feat, then it would stimulate interest again," he said. "But right now space has lost a lot of its glamour."

Webb countered that a successful lunar landing would be "one of the most important things that's been done in this nation." Throughout their conversation Kennedy appeared to be thinking out loud and challenging Webb to offer convincing arguments for continuing the space race. He finally asked flatly, "Do you think the . . . manned landing on the moon is a good idea?" When Webb said he did, Kennedy asked, "Could you do the same with instruments much cheaper?" Webb gave a rambling reply about inspiring American youth, searching for extraterrestrial life, and discovering how the universe was formed. He concluded, "And I predict you are not going to be sorry, no sir, that you did this."

Kennedy remained skeptical. He repeated to Webb what he had recently said to McNamara: "This looks like a hell of a lot of dough to go to the moon when you can . . . learn most of that you want scientifically through instruments, and putting a man on the moon really is a stunt and isn't worth that many billions."

After meeting with his foreign policy advisers on Tuesday, Kennedy approved an "eyes-only personal" cable to Lodge outlining an interim plan that amounted to treading water. The cable told Lodge that, given the reluctance of the South Vietnamese generals to move against Diem, there appeared to be "no good opportunity for action to remove present government in immediate future." Lodge should meanwhile "apply such pressures as are available to secure whatever modest improvements . . . may be possible." The cable left open the possibility of a "more drastic effort [a coup] as and when means become available," and gave Lodge permission to delay or reduce or reroute U.S. assistance to Diem, "bearing in mind that it is not our current policy to cut off aid entirely." It enumerated a familiar list of reforms—freedom of press, free elections, and "a real spirit of reconciliation" toward opponents—that Lodge should pressure Diem to enact, adding, "We recognize the strong possibility that . . . pressures may not produce this result, but we are convinced that it is necessary to try." The cable also announced that Kennedy had decided to send McNamara and Taylor on a mission to Vietnam to assess the progress of the war, but promised that they would confine their inquiries to military matters, assuring him that "all political decisions are being handled through you as the President's senior representative."

Lodge was not fooled. He cabled back that distinguishing between the political and military was "quite impossible." McNamara and Taylor would have to call on Diem, he would have to accompany them, Diem would take the meeting as a sign that the administration had decided "to forgive and forget," and it would "put a wet blanket on those working for a change in government," that is, the generals plotting a coup.

The press interpreted the McNamara-Taylor mission as more evidence of Kennedy's indecisiveness. In fact, he was sending McNamara and Taylor to Vietnam not to help him decide what to do, but to make it easier for him to do what he had already decided: begin withdrawing U.S. advisers and reduce assistance to the Diem government. Schlesinger noted in his diary that the president was hoping "that their experiences there and Lodge will convince them that it is harder than they imagined to win with Diem."

He instructed Taylor and McNamara to tell Diem, "Unless you do certain things we have described, we are going to pull out in a relatively short time." Yet if Diem *did* make the requested reforms, according to Taylor, this "would make possible a termination of the situation [the U.S. troop presence] in about two years." In other words, if Taylor and McNamara reported that Diem was instituting reforms and the war was being won, as the Pentagon was claiming, Kennedy would have a rationale for a phased withdrawal of the advisers. If they reported that Diem's intransigence was crippling the war effort, he had reason to withdraw even sooner. Taylor wrote in his memoirs, "If further deterioration of the political situation should occur to invalidate the target date [for withdrawal], we would have to review our attitude toward Diem's government and our national interests in Southeast Asia." In short, Kennedy had made it clear to Taylor and McNamara before they departed that he planned to remove American advisers regardless of the military situation.

MINUTES BEFORE DELIVERING his televised tax-cut address to the nation on Wednesday evening, he became concerned that it did not sufficiently explain how his bill would benefit the average American family. As the network crews prepared the Oval Office for the broadcast, he huddled with Ted Sorensen and Walter Heller, revising the text.

Like most presidents, Kennedy had taken office with little understanding of economics, but unlike most of his predecessors, he had been determined to master the subject. Heller had spent the last two years giving him such a strong grounding in Keynesian economics that by 1963 he felt that Kennedy had become "a good orthodox economist." Director of the Budget Kermit Gordon, who had witnessed their informal tutorials and read many of the hundreds of memoranda flowing between them, believed that Kennedy had become a good-enough economist to teach a respectable college course on the subject. He sensed that Kennedy had immersed himself in the subject not only because he thought it would make him a better president, but because he was naturally curious, "a person who liked playing with ideas," and who "in moments of relaxation . . . would sometimes give an inordinate amount of time to matters that just happened to intrigue him." Kennedy had also become intrigued by nuclear science, and his probing questions during an Atomic Energy Commission (AEC) briefing at a Nevada test site left the AEC's chairman, Glenn Seaborg, convinced that he possessed "a first-rate intellect, a mind of a caliber equal to that of the best scientists I have known." Walt Rostow, who served on Bundy's White House staff and briefed Kennedy on foreign policy issues said flatly that "his mind was capable of grasping any idea," and grasping it so quickly that he would become irritated if someone went on too long, repeatedly saying, "All right, I've got the idea. But what do you want me to do about it today?"

Heller had persuaded Kennedy that a tax cut would stimulate demand, increase growth, lower unemployment, and prevent a recurrence of the mild recessions of 1957 and 1960. Although it would add to the federal deficit in the short term, its simulative effects would eventually produce a surplus. Kennedy had proposed a tax cut in his 1963 State of the Union speech, and then in a special message to Congress during which he made the argument that under certain circumstances a budget deficit could be healthy. Making his proposed tax cut even more extraordinary and controversial was the fact that the economy was growing, the deficit was substantial, unemployment was at 5 percent, and the business community was not demanding tax relief. Another president might have been content with this record, but he was determined to double the growth rate he had inherited from Eisenhower, preside over eight recession-free years, and leave office with the nation enjoying full employment—a record befitting a great president. During a meeting in December 1962 that he recorded, he told his economic team that the 1960 recession had ruined Nixon. "If you're running for reelection in 1964, what is it you worry about most?" he asked. "Recession. That is what I'm worried about. . . . I don't think the country can take another recession. Otherwise we are likely to get all the blame for the deficit and none of the advantage of the stimulus in the economy." And so, motivated by a typical Kennedy mixture of optimism and hubris, ambition and realpolitik, he had proposed his tax cut.

It received a lukewarm reception. Conservatives in both parties and most businessmen viewed a planned deficit as reckless and unnecessary. The bill languished in the House Ways and Means Committee for months, blocked by Southern Democrats extracting revenge for his civil rights policy. After it finally cleared the necessary committees, the House scheduled a vote for September 23. Before then, Kennedy wanted to explain it to a public that seemed neither to want it nor to understand it.

Forty-five seconds before going on air he received a call from Teddy reporting that he had just had lunch in Belgrade with Madame Nhu, who was attending the same conference of parliamentarians. "This woman kicks me in the nuts," he told his younger brother, referring to her recent comment that she did not feel "terribly safe" with him in the White House, "and the next day you have lunch with her." Moments later, he was telling the American people that his tax cut was the most important piece of domestic legislation in fifteen years, a statement certain to unsettle the civil rights movement.

Current tax rates were harmful, he said, because they did not "leave enough money in private hands." His cut would mean "more jobs for American workers," "more buying power for American consumers and investors," "new protection against another tragic recession," and "higher family income and higher business profits and a balanced federal budget." Decades later, Republicans would offer the same arguments to support their own tax cuts. But in 1963, Kennedy was proposing cuts to the extraordinarily high marginal rates that Congress had passed to finance World War II and fight inflation. His bill reduced the top marginal rate from 91 to 70 percent, and the lowest from 20 to 14 percent. Nevertheless, in response to his speech, the chief GOP spokesman on taxes in the House attacked him for taking "an unprecedented gamble" by cutting taxes without reducing expenditures, and for "playing Russian roulette with our destiny."

Kennedy and Heller went to the Cabinet Room afterward so they could speak without being overheard by technicians dismantling the broadcast equipment. Senator Fulbright called to praise the speech as a model for how a president should educate the public. (After the 1960 campaign, Kennedy had told a journalist that he thought Nixon's fatal mistake had been talking down to the American people. "In a presidential campaign," he insisted, "you have to talk 'up,' over their heads.") Treasury Secretary Douglas Dillon and his wife also telephoned to praise him during what Heller described condescendingly as "a touching little call" that led to Kennedy referring to them as "dear Phyllis" and "dear Dougie." Heller did not mention Kennedy's praising *him,* a curious omission for a man priding himself on his sensitivity and social graces, particularly since if anyone deserved plaudits, it was surely Heller, whose ideas and phrases Kennedy had just articulated.

The previous month, Heller had complained to the Washington hostess and Democratic Party stalwart Katie Louchheim that Kennedy seldom praised his staff, finding it difficult, he said, "to give one a boost or a pet." Instead, he had the curious habit of offering praise to a third party. "He said great things about me to my brother, of Kermit Gordon to his child," he told Louchheim, adding that Arthur Goldberg had said that he never would have resigned to accept a seat on the Supreme Court if he had known how much the president valued his services as secretary of Health, Education, and Welfare. Louchheim was sympathetic, saying that she had sometimes noticed a "chilly aloofness" in Kennedy. "How warmly he greets 'pals,'" Heller said bitterly, "leaving the official [presumably Heller] standing there ill at ease." For pals like Powers and O'Donnell there was "the warm handshake and 'let's go swimming' check [that] he never tends the help."

Heller, like many in the administration, had fallen in love with Kennedy. It was a platonic affair, but romantic nonetheless, and his complaints sounded like someone bitching about a callous lover. The White House aide Walt Rostow spoke of an "unspoken but very powerful affection—going both ways" between Kennedy and his staff, and the CIA director, John McCone, a Republican, claimed, "Never in my time in public life have I known a man who drew so much affection from those with whom he closely dealt." Schlesinger was also in love. In the summer of 1960, he had condemned Kennedy's choice of Johnson as a running mate as "evidence of the impressively cool and tough way Jack is going about his affairs," calling him "a devious and, if necessary, ruthless man," and saying, "My affection for him and personal confidence in him have declined." Kennedy invited Schlesinger to Hyannis Port three weeks later and seduced him all over again. After a four-hour cruise complete with Bloody Marys, swimming, and target shooting, Schlesinger was describing him as "warm, funny, quick, intelligent and spontaneous."

AT THE TIME OF THE BIRMINGHAM BOMBING, the civil rights bill had been stalled in the House Judiciary Committee, where liberals led by the chairman, Emmanuel Celler, were threatening to add amendments that would make it unpalatable to moderate Republicans. During a mass meeting in Birmingham on Monday, civil rights leaders had urged the government to send the Army into the city to protect the black community. King had endorsed their request, calling the city "in a state of civil disorder" and accusing Wallace of fomenting "an atmosphere of violence."

If Kennedy refused to send troops to Birmingham, he would embolden the House liberals insisting on a tougher civil rights bill, but occupying it with federal troops would smack of a second Reconstruction, leaving its white population still more embittered and hostile. He believed that the only realistic solution was to facilitate communication and accommodation between leaders of the black community and moderate white businessmen and politicians, presuming they existed. To promote this, he decided to send a two-man committee to the city to mediate between the communities. Bobby's first choice for the assignment had been Earl Blaik, a sixty-six-year-old retired West Point football coach whom he had recruited the previous year to resolve a feud between the NCAA and AAU that was threatening the U.S. Olympic effort. Blaik had persuaded General Douglas MacArthur to join him and they had quickly settled the dispute. Bobby hoped they could perform the same magic in Birmingham, but this time Blaik refused to involve MacArthur on the grounds that the assignment was too taxing for an eighty-year-old man. He suggested General Kenneth Royall, who had supposedly integrated the troops while serving as Truman's secretary of the Army. Bobby called Royall, who agreed to serve if Blaik joined him. Bobby pressed for an immediate commitment, explaining that the White House wanted to make an announcement within the hour, before the president met with a delegation of black leaders. Had he and his brother been in less of a hurry, they might have discovered that instead of presiding over the integration of the Army, Royall had fought it, telling a congressional committee that he did not believe the armed forces should be turned into "an instrument for social evolution." The black journalist Simeon Booker, who would soon expose Royall, would also reveal that in Blaik's eighteen years as head coach at West Point he had never had a single black player on his team. As with Kennedy's other mistakes, his impatience and his preoccupation with public relations lay behind this one.

Dr. King opened the White House meeting by declaring that the Negro community in Birmingham was reaching "a breaking point." He warned that without "a new sense of hope and a sense of protection" there could be "the worst race rioting we've ever seen in this country." Kennedy asked if there was any hope. King said there were "many white people of goodwill," and agreed that troops could not solve the problem. He suggested that the attorney general visit the city and attempt to open lines of communication.

Kennedy announced that he had asked Mayor Albert Boutwell to send a delegation to the White House on Monday, and had appointed Royall and Blaik, "two very good men," as his personal emissaries. If the situation continued to deteriorate despite these measures, he would consider troops. He urged the leaders to consider the larger historical picture. "If you look ... at any of these struggles over a period across the world, it is a very dangerous effort," he said. "So everyone just has to keep their nerve." If they responded with violence, they risked losing the support of whites of goodwill, and once that happened, "we're pretty much down to a racial struggle."

The leaders praised the Blaik-Royall mission at a press conference, with King calling Kennedy's pledge not to allow the property and rights of Negro citizens to be trampled, "the kind of federal concern needed."

Kennedy flew to New York that evening. While he was dining at a friend's apartment, two men in a station wagon hurled a paint bomb at his parked limousine, spattering it and hitting a Secret Service agent. It was not known if they had been targeting the president. He did not leave the Carlyle for the United Nations until late the following morning, allowing time for him to cross Madison Avenue and spend several minutes in the basement of Klejman's gallery, staring at the floodlit statue of the handsome Greek athlete.

He told the UN General Assembly, "Today the clouds have lifted a little so that new rays of hope can break through," and that although "the long shadows of conflict and crisis envelop us still, we meet today in an atmosphere of rising hope, and at a moment of relative calm." Speaking of "a pause in the cold war," he said, "If we can stretch this pause into a new period of cooperation . . . then surely this first small step [the test ban treaty] can be the start of a long and fruitful journey." He proposed "agreements on measures which prevent war by accident or miscalculation," "further measures to curb nuclear arms," and a treaty "to keep weapons of mass destruction out of space."

He waited until the end to spring his surprise. "Finally, in a field where the United States and the Soviet Union have a special capacity—in the field of space—there is room for new cooperation, for further joint efforts in the regulation and exploration of space," he said. "I include among these possibilities a joint expedition to the moon." After asking, "Why . . . should man's first flight to the moon be a matter of national competition? Why should the United States and the Soviet Union . . . become involved in immense duplications of research, construction, expenditure?" he proposed sending to the moon "not the representatives of a single nation, but the representatives of all our countries."

He concluded on a note of grandiloquent optimism that reprised his American University speech: "I believe the problems of human destiny are not beyond the reach of human beings." The test ban treaty might not end war, resolve every conflict, or bring freedom to every nation, he admitted, but it could be a lever, "and Archimedes, in explaining the principles of the lever, was said to have declared to his friends, 'Give me a place where I can stand—and I shall move the world.' My fellow inhabitants of this planet . . . let us see if we, in our own time, can move the world to a just and lasting peace."

The usually dour Soviet foreign minister, Andrei Gromyko, was smiling broadly as he stood in the receiving line. When he reached Kennedy he held up the line for several minutes to deliver a personal message from Khrushchev. When a reporter asked if this new spirit of détente would last, he replied, "It must last."

Kennedy's proposal had caught everyone, including most in his own administration, by surprise. A boldface, front-page headline in the *New York Times* proclaimed, "Kennedy Asks Joint Moon Flight by U.S. and Soviet as Peace Step." The *Washington Post* banner headlines said, "Kennedy Urges Joint Moon Trip" and "Air of Optimism About Cold War Marks U.N. Talk." His proposal was described as "a sudden reversal of the Administration's position on the 'space race'" and "the first step toward pulling out of the costly 'moon race.'" Like his civil rights speech and his American University "Peace Speech," his UN address had been a closely held secret until he delivered it.

Before Kennedy left the United Nations, Adlai Stevenson briefed him on a memorandum he had received from William Attwood, a member of his staff who had recently completed a tour as U.S. ambassador to Guinea. Earlier that week the Guinean ambassador to Cuba had informed Attwood that Castro resented being pushed around by the Russians and might be prepared to reach an accommodation with the United States. After hearing similar comments from other African diplomats, Attwood, who during his career as a journalist had held a groundbreaking interview with Castro, wrote Stevenson a memorandum asking for authorization to contact Cuba's UN delegate, Carlos Lechuga, with a view to determining whether Castro was willing to participate in a secret dialogue.

Attwood had been two years behind Kennedy at Choate and knew him well enough to craft a memorandum that would catch his attention. He opened by saying that he was proposing "a course of action which, if successful, could remove the Cuban issue from the 1964 campaign." Instead of offering Castro a "deal," he recommended "a discrete inquiry into the possibility of neutralizing

Cuba on our terms," and argued that the present policy of isolating Cuba was leaving America "in the unattractive posture of a big country trying to bully a small country," and aggravating Castro's anti-Americanism. Given this, he said, "We have something to gain and nothing to lose by determining whether in fact Castro does want to talk and what concessions he would be prepared to make." He offered to solicit an invitation from Lechuga and travel to Cuba as a private citizen. His diplomatic rank was high enough to guarantee that his conversations with Castro would be serious, yet he was not so well known that reporters would notice his absence. Their meeting would be "purely exploratory" and the president could decide afterward whether to pursue more formal negotiations. "At the moment," Attwood wrote, "all I would like is the authority to make contact with Lechuga. We'll see what happens then."

He handed his memorandum to Stevenson on Thursday. Stevenson liked the idea but said, "Unfortunately, the CIA is still in charge of Cuba." He nevertheless promised to raise it with Kennedy. Averell Harriman, who happened to be at the UN mission at the time, said he was "adventuresome enough" to favor the scheme and suggested running it past Bobby Kennedy because of its political implications. Stevenson briefed the president on it while he was at the UN, and Kennedy approved Attwood's request to arrange a chance social meeting between himself and Lechuga.

After a week that had seen Kennedy proposing to end the space race, sending a high-level delegation to South Vietnam, lobbying a skeptical public to support his tax cut, persuading Dr. King not to demand troops in Birmingham, and authorizing secret negotiations with Cuba, he arrived in Newport in a slaphappy mood.

To mark National Library Week, the White House had just released a list of his twelve favorite books. Ten were nonfiction, and nine of those were biographies, including Margaret Coit's *John C. Calhoun.* (Jackie believed he liked biographies because he was "looking for lessons . . . from history.") The only novels were Stendhal's *The Red and the Black,* an early-nineteenth-century work about the ambitious son of a carpenter whose attempt to crash Parisian society resembled Joe Kennedy's struggle to win the acceptance of Boston, and Ian Fleming's *From Russia with Love,* the best of the James Bond novels. Kennedy liked Fleming's books so much that he was attempting to write his own Bond-style thriller involving a coup d'état masterminded by Vice President Johnson. There are no notes for the book among his personal papers, so he was probably keeping the plot in his head. He called Chuck Spalding periodically to bring him up to date, recounting that in one chapter, "Lyndon has tied up Mrs. Lincoln and Kenny O'Donnell in the White House closet and he's got a plane to take them away."

While cruising on the *Honey Fitz* on Saturday afternoon he persuaded Paul and Anita Fay to act in a Bond homage that would be filmed by Chief Petty Officer Robert Knudsen. He assigned everyone parts before docking at the private pier in front of Hammersmith Farm, not realizing that the reporters Frank Cormier and Merriman Smith were shadowing the *Honey Fitz* in a speedboat and watching some of his amateur dramatics through binoculars. Their article reported that Fay had "stretched prone on the long pier . . . clowning with Mr. Kennedy for the benefit of a government photographer." The president then walked down the pier and "laughingly put his foot on Mr. Fay's stomach."

Jackie persuaded the Secret Service agents to play supporting roles. "We're making a film about the President's murder," she told them, "and we'd like you and the other agents to drive up to the front of the house, then jump out and run toward the door." The agents agreed and followed in their car as the president and his friends drove up from the pier. When they arrived, she said, "Look desperate, like you heard shots and are concerned that the President might be hurt and you need to respond fast."

Luckily for Kennedy, Cormier and Merriman witnessed only his film's tamer scenes. Knudsen recalled that at one point in the filming Kennedy clutched his chest and fell flat onto the pier. While he was down, Knudsen said, Jackie and her friend Countess Vivian Stokes Crespi had "simply stepped over the President's body—as if he were not there." They were followed by Fay, who stumbled and fell on top of the president. At that moment, Kennedy spewed out some red liquid (probably tomato juice) that he had been holding in his mouth. Knudsen shot the scene several times, with Fay taking a turn at playing the corpse, and later wondered if the president had experienced some kind of "premonition." More likely, the skit reflected his high spirits after a successful week, his love of the Bond thrillers, and a rich but carefully concealed fantasy life, a Walter Mitty streak he revealed only to his closest friends.

He was so furious with Cormier and Merriman that he stopped addressing Cormier by his first name. Two weeks later, Cormier dined with Salinger and O'Donnell at a lodge in Jackson Hole during Kennedy's Western tour. Salinger chewed him out for being a "Peeping Tom reporter," and said that writing about what he had seen in Newport had been "in terrible taste." Cormier replied, "Well, if it was in terrible taste for me to write about it, it was in terrible taste for the President to do it." O'Donnell, who seldom criticized the president, said, "I agree with you."

Monday, September 23

WASHINGTON

Monday was one of the busiest days of Kennedy's presidency, packed with so many meetings and ceremonies that he ate lunch at three and missed his swim and nap. He began with a morning conference with Taylor and McNamara, who were preparing to depart for Vietnam, and ended with an evening meeting with Blaik and Royall, who were leaving for Birmingham. In between, he chaired the first cabinet meeting since July, conferred with the Italian foreign minister and the Laotian prime minister, met with his new Marine Corps commandant and with officers of the National Rural Electronic Cooperative Association, and held an hour-long conference with a delegation of white civic leaders from Birmingham.

He had sent McNamara and Taylor a memorandum stating that recent events in Vietnam had "raised serious questions about the present prospects for success against the Viet Cong." When they met, he stressed that they should not threaten Diem with cuts in aid, but let whatever cutbacks occurred "speak for themselves." Taylor, who now understood what he wanted, proposed that they "work out a time schedule within which we expect to get this job done and to say plainly to Diem that we were not going to be able to stay beyond such and such a time with such and such forces, and that the war must be won in this time period." Kennedy suggested that they impress upon Diem "the need for reform and change as a pragmatic necessity and not as a moral judgment." (A week later, Harriman would tell Arthur Schlesinger over dinner, "The only thing that really counts for us in the world is our moral position. Every time we compromise our moral position, we take a loss."*)

A month after Kennedy had worried about his government "coming apart," the split between the Pentagon and the State Department remained bitter and intractable. At the Pentagon, Krulak and Taylor, and to a lesser extent McNamara, believed Diem had the best chance of defeating the Communists. The State Department faction of Harriman, Ball, Hilsman, and Lodge viewed the Taylor-McNamara mission as a threat, evidence that Kennedy was siding with the Pentagon. Harriman told Forrestal that he and Hilsman believed the mission would be "a disaster," because it entailed "sending two men opposed to our [the State Department's] policy." Hilsman wrote a "Top Secret; Personal and Private" letter to Lodge that he asked Forrestal, who was accompanying Taylor and McNamara, to hand deliver. Hilsman made what he called "four rather personal points." These included "More and more of the town is coming around to our point of view and that if you in Saigon and we in the Department stick to our guns the rest will also come around"; "No pressures—even a cut-off in aid—will cause Diem and Nhu to make the changes we desire and that what we must work for is a change in government"; and "You have handled an incredibly difficult task superbly. My very heartiest and most sincere congratulations."

KENNEDY MET WITH BOBBY and Burke Marshall before seeing the delegation of Birmingham's white leaders. Marshall reported that the leaders had not delivered on their promises to hire black department store clerks and form a biracial committee, leading Kennedy to ask why there were no Negro policemen in the city.

"They say it would be bad for morale," Marshall replied.

"Of the white policemen?" he asked incredulously.

He wanted to know what he should say if the whites blamed outside agitators

---

* At another dinner party, Harriman complained that Kennedy was "still trying too hard to get a national consensus before he moved on anything." Turning to Schlesinger, he said, "I told one of you White House fellows the other day that, whatever you do, whatever compromises you make, you are never going to get the support of the [far-right] John Birch Society. Those fellows [at the White House] think too much about passing legislation and too little about mobilizing the country. Tell them that. Tell them I said that."

like Dr. King for stirring up trouble. Marshall said that King had not been in Birmingham since May, and had only returned after the bombing in an effort to calm the situation.

"What do I want people to *do*?" he demanded.

Form a biracial committee, Marshall said. Hire Negro policemen.

William Hamilton, an aide to Mayor Albert Boutwell, opened the meeting by pleading for "a little bit of calm" and "a little bit of time." Kennedy despised this kind of stalling tactic. "I'm just interested in . . . what you can do in Birmingham to ease the situation there," he said.

Hamilton said Birmingham's white leadership had already done "a great many things." Another man blamed "constant agitation" from people "outside the community" for preventing them from making reforms.

"Now tell me why it is you can't get a Negro policeman around there," Kennedy snapped. "Seems to me, if you've got forty percent of the community that's Negro . . . I would think you'd be much better with Negro policemen."

They blamed civil service regulations, an absence of qualified Negro applicants, and the possibility that a third of the Birmingham police force would resign if they hired a Negro. Frank Newton, a telephone company executive who chaired the moribund biracial committee, blamed outside agitators for his city's troubles. Five days after a Birmingham policeman had shot a Negro youth in the back, and four months after the photograph of a white policeman turning a German shepherd loose on a Negro teenager had sickened Kennedy, Newton insisted that charges of police brutality were unwarranted, because "in reality, we have a well-trained police force, and they have acted with admirable restraint."

"Why isn't it possible to do something?" Kennedy asked. "It seems to me that there are two or three things that aren't very difficult to do." He pointed out that the Washington police force was integrated. Why could Birmingham not do the same? His voice hardening, he added, "It isn't any use . . . to say to me to get the agitators out . . . because I didn't put them in—"

Newton interrupted to say, "If I may give you a straightforward answer, but a respectful answer. There's people, though, that think you have given these people encouragement—"

"Let me make it clear that I regard getting on the police force as legitimate, and I regard people working as clerks as legitimate."

Newton argued that the public accommodation section of his civil rights bill was certainly not a limited measure.

Kennedy had had enough. The conference had already run too long. The black delegation from Birmingham had withdrawn its demand for troops and praised him at a press conference. The whites were not only refusing to hire a single black policeman, they were scolding him for encouraging the demonstrations. He seldom spoke at length at meetings like this but now delivered a testy ten-minute monologue about integration. "Oh, public accommodation is nothing. When I think what Harry Truman did in integrating the armed forces—to give you an honest answer and a respectful one—that was really tough," he said, throwing Newton's "respectful answer" comment back in his face. "Imagine . . . taking kids out of Mississippi and all the rest, putting them together in a barracks, putting them under a Negro sergeant? They did that fifteen years ago." Compared with that, permitting Negroes to rent a hotel room was easy, and so was integrating the workplace and universities. The "tough one" was integrating elementary and secondary schools. "I understand Mississippi, where it's forty-five to fifty percent Negro, where half of them, three quarters, haven't gone beyond the sixth grade, what it means to try to integrate those schools," he said, and he could understand "the gut feeling about that," but not the gut feeling about the police force, clerks, and public accommodation or about whether a student goes to a state university. "Now that's my feeling about it," he concluded in a firm voice.

For another thirty minutes, he pleaded with them to do something that could "give everybody outside of Birmingham and all of us up here and other places, a chance to say, well, now they're trying." He begged them to hire a Negro policeman—to do *something*, even if it was "window dressing." They refused to budge. At a press conference following the meeting, Hamilton declared that most of Birmingham's residents, including its Negroes, were "firmly, deeply dedicated to the principle of segregation."

ONCE KENNEDY HAD APPROVED Attwood's request to meet with Lechuga, Attwood moved fast. He asked the ABC correspondent Lisa Howard to throw a cocktail party on Monday evening and invite the Cuban diplomat. As Kennedy was briefing Blaik and Royall before their departure for Birmingham,

Attwood was huddled with Lechuga at Howard's Park Avenue apartment, discussing a possible meeting with Castro.

Howard was a former soap opera actress who had become a correspondent for the Mutual Radio Network and had scored an interview with Nikita Khrushchev during his 1960 visit to the United States. In April 1963, she had held the first television interview with Fidel Castro in four years. Upon her return, she informed the CIA that during their eight hours of private talks Castro had stressed that he wanted negotiations with the United States and was ready to discuss the Soviet military presence in Cuba, compensation for expropriated American investments, and the question of Communist subversion in the hemisphere. She urged that a U.S. official be sent on a quiet mission to Havana to hear him out. Deputy Director Richard Helms wrote in a memorandum based on their conversation, "It appears that Fidel Castro is looking for a way to reach a rapprochement with the United States government, probably because he is aware that Cuba is in a state of economic chaos." He added that Howard believed that "Castro's inner circle was split on the idea of a rapprochement with the U.S. with hardliners like Che Guevara and Raoul Castro opposing it." Helms thought it was encouraging that Castro had asked Howard for an appraisal of Khrushchev. She had told Castro he was a shrewd politician who would dispose of him when he was no longer needed. Upon hearing this, Castro had nodded his head "as if in skeptical agreement."

The New York attorney James Donovan had also developed a relationship with Castro while negotiating to secure the release of Cuban exiles captured at the Bay of Pigs. In January 1963, he returned to Cuba to arrange the release of several imprisoned U.S. citizens. During what he called a "most cordial and intimate conversation" with Castro and his trusted aide and interpreter, the Boston-trained physician Dr. Rene Vallejo, Castro had invited him to return to Cuba with his wife for another visit, and had given Donovan the impression that he wanted to discuss "the future of Cuba and international relations in general." While accompanying Donovan to the airport, Vallejo raised the subject of re-establishing diplomatic relations.

When Kennedy heard about Donovan's experiences, he told Gordon Chase, the National Security Council aide responsible for Latin America, that they should "start thinking along more flexible lines," and not insist that Castro make a clean break with Moscow as a precondition for talks. He recommended that Donovan postpone what he called "his week-long walk along the beach with Castro" until they could debrief him. After that, he said, he might want to give Donovan "some flies to dangle in front of Castro." Chase concluded his memorandum of their conversation: "The above must be kept close to the vest. The President, himself, is very interested in this one."

Donovan returned in April and had two long conversations with Castro. Vallejo claimed that although Castro wanted to develop a relationship with the United States, other officials in his government were opposed and Castro feared they might rebel. But Castro still believed he and Donovan could negotiate a "reasonable relationship" between their nations. After being briefed about these conversations, Kennedy expressed more interest in pursuing a demarche with Cuba, discussing it with the CIA director, John McCone, five days later. McCone suggested two courses of action: engaging Castro in negotiations "with the objective of disenchanting him with his Soviet relations, causing him to break relations with Khrushchev," or continuing their current policy of supporting hit-and-run sabotage raids by Cuban exiles—of exerting "constant pressure of every possible nature on Khrushchev to force his withdrawal from Cuba, and then to bring about the downfall of Castro by means which could be developed after the removal of the Soviet troops." Kennedy decided to keep the Donovan channel open and pursue both strategies at once.

This remained his policy when Attwood met with Lechuga at Lisa Howard's cocktail party on September 23. After Attwood described his 1959 conversations with Castro, Lechuga suggested that Castro might be ready to talk again, particularly with someone he knew and trusted, and said there was a good chance that Castro would invite him to Havana. Attwood explained that since he was a diplomat instead of a journalist he would need official authorization, and promised to contact him when he had an answer. The next day, Bobby told Attwood he was concerned that he might be identified if he visited Cuba. He proposed holding the meeting in Mexico or at the United Nations instead and encouraged him to continue the conversation. Three days later, Attwood ran into Lechuga at the UN, relayed Bobby's comments, and said that if Castro or his personal emissary had something to tell the president, they could meet somewhere outside Cuba.

THE WESTERN TOUR

Despite his New Frontier rhetoric, Kennedy preferred oceans to mountains, golf courses to prairies, sailing to hunting, and swimming to fishing. He was the most widely traveled man to become president but had probably crossed the Atlantic more than the Continental Divide, and was more comfortable in Europe than in the American West. The West was also tricky for him because local dignitaries invariably presented him with cowboy hats or Indian war bonnets, and he disliked wearing anything on his head, particularly something making him appear ridiculous. When a delegation of Indian chiefs in Idaho gave him a feathered war bonnet during a campaign stop, he had finessed the situation by joking, "The next time I watch television, I'm going to root for our side," but he was certain to face more headdresses and cowboy hats on his Western conservation tour.

No one on his staff or in the press corps believed he was motivated by a love for the region or an interest in ecology; everyone understood that this "nonpolitical" trip was entirely political, his first campaign foray of the 1964 election. Before leaving, he had armed himself against a skeptical press corps that was mocking him as "Johnny Appleseed" and "Paul Bunyan" with a repertoire of self-deprecating jokes such as "Mr. Chairman, my fellow nonpartisans," and "It is obvious that this is a nonpartisan trip—I'm not going to a single state I carried." But he was serious about drawing large and enthusiastic crowds, and told Jerry Bruno, who was advancing the trip, "I want the crowds—I want those crowds to be there!"

The day before he left for the West, the Senate ratified the Limited Test Ban Treaty by a vote of eighty to nineteen, a larger margin than had been anticipated and one making it easier for him to pursue more agreements with Moscow. When he embarked on the tour, the NBC correspondent Sander Vanocur thought he seemed happier than he had in months, and the test ban victory was undoubtedly a factor.

He stopped in Milford, Pennsylvania, to speak at a ceremony honoring the descendants of Gifford Pinchot, Jr., the first head of the United States Forest Service. They had donated Grey Towers, their family's chateau-style mansion, to the Forest Service as a training center, and he had added the ceremony to his schedule because it fit with the conservation theme and Pinchot had been the uncle of his lover Mary Meyer and her sister, Tony, Ben Bradlee's wife, and he was curious to see where they had spent their childhood summers. Both women joined him on the flight to Milford. It was the first time he had seen Mary since Patrick's death, and Tony admitted to feeling a "little rivalry" with her sister.

He delivered a plodding speech to ten thousand spectators filling a hillside facing Grey Towers. While speaking of his administration's creation of three National Seashores, he said, "I don't know why it should be that six or seven percent only of the whole Atlantic Coast should be in the public sphere and the rest owned by private citizens and denied to many millions of our public citizens." The fact that much of the remaining 93 percent of coastline was in the hands of old-money families like the Pinchots, and new-money ones like the Kennedys, somewhat undermined the nobility of his statement. After finishing, he turned to Mary and Tony's mother, Ruth Pinchot, and asked to see her house, a summer bungalow near the estate. Forest Service officials had spent weeks preparing to bore him with a lengthy tour of Grey Towers and were crestfallen when he raced through the mansion to leave time for visiting Ruth's modest cottage. The New Deal had made Pinchot a fierce right-winger, but he turned on the charm and she showed him what he had come to see, photographs of her attractive daughters as little girls. She told friends that she had atoned for welcoming the devil into her house by doubling her contributions to conservative causes.

He flew on to Ashland, Wisconsin, where he made a lame joke about Calvin Coolidge, and then to the University of Minnesota Field House in Duluth, where he gave a speech that Vanocur called "dreadful" and "one of the worst reporters could remember." Even Bradlee's magazine was critical, with *Newsweek* reporting,

"The message that he brought to the people made heavy listening and the President's obvious unfamiliarity with the subject was uncomfortable." A large crowd turned out the next morning at the Grand Forks airport, pushing down an airport fence to get at him. But at the University of North Dakota Field House he droned on about conservation, a funereal atmosphere descended on the audience, and reporters ranked his speech the worst of his presidency. Jerry Bruno had turned out the crowds, but even he was disappointed by their lack of enthusiasm, calling them "unresponsive and restless." The president would try different themes, he said, "but the sense of emotional attachment just wasn't there."

There was something petulant about his performances, as if he were a sulky child being forced to visit some distant and tiresome relations. Not only did conservation and natural resources bore him, but he had left Washington during a busy and momentous week. The House was voting on his tax cut, liberals on a House Judiciary subcommittee were adding tough provisions to his civil rights bill, a dialogue with Castro suddenly seemed possible, two important fact-finding missions were heading to Birmingham and Saigon, and a delegation of American grain traders was meeting with its Soviet counterpart in Canada to discuss a sale of American wheat, a deal that would require his approval and was certain to be controversial. He had once said that he wanted to be president because the White House was "the center of action." This week, when the action in Washington was frenetic, he was thousands of miles away, lecturing restless audiences in states that would probably go Republican anyway. He was also missing Caroline's first day back at school, and while he was in Grand Forks, she and her classmates rode the Goodyear blimp, an excursion that had almost been canceled after a sniper fired .22-caliber bullets into the aircraft. When the excursion ended, Jackie told a Goodyear representative that her son was "just crazy about planes" and would probably become a pilot.

KENNEDY ARRIVED IN BILLINGS, MONTANA, on a Big Sky day of brilliant sunshine, low humidity, and razor-sharp shadows. Seven thousand people in a city of fifty-three thousand had packed the Yellowstone County Fairgrounds grandstands. More milled around the parking lot, kicking up dust and passing a girl head over head so she could shake his hand. He thanked Senator Mansfield for introducing him by praising "his high standards of public service" and his role in ratifying the test ban treaty. Until now, he had avoided talking about the treaty on the assumption it would be unpopular in these Goldwater strongholds. But when he said that the treaty would "bring an end, we hope, for all time to the dangers of radioactive fallout," and represented "a first step towards peace, and our hope for a more secure world," there were loud cheers and applause, and the reporter Peter Lisagor noticed a look of total surprise on his face.

He immediately discarded his prepared text and spoke extemporaneously about peace, the treaty, and nuclear war. Suddenly, he was campaigning again, pumping his fist up and down and stabbing the air with his forefinger as he said, "What we hope to do is lessen the chance of a military collision between these two great nuclear powers which together have the power to kill three hundred million people in the short space of a day." When he described his treaty as "a chance to avoid being burned," the cheers and applause grew even louder. Vanocur called the speech "an exercise in political discovery," saying that if he had won reelection reporters would have called it the moment when he discovered a winning strategy.

Throughout his career Kennedy had demonstrated a talent for recognizing and profiting from revelatory moments like this one. During his 1946 congressional campaign he had slogged through a banal speech about patriotism and the sacrifices of war to an audience of Gold Star Mothers. Sensing their disappointment, he abandoned his text and said, "Well, I think I know how you ladies feel. My mother, too, lost a son in the war." The women wept and rushed to the podium to grab his hand and hug him. Powers thought it was the moment he won the election. It was also, like his speech at Billings, a textbook example of Walt Rostow's observation "A politician is a communicating instrument both ways. He receives and sends communications, words, images, actions. Kennedy was awfully good at it."

While running for president, Kennedy would read placards, study expressions, and often replace a prepared speech with an extemporaneous one that he believed would resonate with a particular audience. The students listening to him speak on the steps of the University of Michigan Student Union during the 1960 campaign were so boisterous and enthusiastic that he abandoned his speech and shouted, "How many of you who are going to be doctors are willing to spend your days in Ghana? . . . How many of you are willing to work in the Foreign Service and spend your lives traveling around the world? . . . On your willingness to contribute part of your life to this country I think will depend the answer of whether a free society can compete." His aide Richard Goodwin, who saw the performance, believed that he had "inadvertently, intuitively . . . tapped into a still-emerging spirit of the times." After witnessing similar moments, Eleanor Roosevelt told Schlesinger that he reminded her of her husband because both seemed to gain strength in the course of their campaigns. Great leaders drew vitality and strength from their crowds, she said, and Kennedy was the first man she had seen since FDR to have that quality.

Roosevelt had understood that the Depression-battered American people longed for "freedom from want." At the Yellowstone County Fairgrounds, Kennedy learned that they wanted freedom from the fear of a nuclear war. Montanans living in the shadow of the Cuban missile crisis and surrounded by Minuteman launching pads, prime Soviet targets, were not interested in hearing him pontificate about dams, conservation, and the joys of the outdoors, subjects they understood better than he did. They wanted to hear about peace.

He concluded his Billings speech with a reference to the high court of history, saying, "I am confident that when the role of national effort in the 1960s is written, when a judgment is rendered whether this generation of Americans took those steps . . . to make it possible for those who came after us to live in greater security and prosperity, I am confident that history will write that in the 1960s, we did our part."

On the flight to Jackson Hole he told Secretary of the Interior Stewart Udall that he was looking forward to running against Goldwater, whose opposition to the test ban treaty was at odds with the concerns of voters like those in Billings. It would be "quite a campaign," he said.

The Jackson Lake Lodge had magnificent views of the Grand Tetons' spiky peaks, but his only concession to one of the West's great wonders was to train his binoculars on a distant moose while standing behind his cabin's picture window. While flying to Great Falls the next morning he decided to ditch his prepared speech, a dull recitation of his "nine-point program" for resource development, and talk about peace and education. He scribbled down some ideas and facts, writing, "12 million boys and girls under 18 live in families whose total income is $3,000 a year or less."

An Indian chief welcomed him at the airport. Each had dressed in a traditional costume: the chief in skins and feathers, Kennedy in his city-slicker regalia of white shirt with French cuffs, dark tailored two-button business suit (chosen in part because it masked the outline of his back brace better than a three-button model), white handkerchief in his breast pocket, polished handmade shoes, and a sober tie anchored by a *PT 109* clasp. Politicians crossing the Continental Divide usually abandoned or loosened their ties, but Kennedy never dressed down. He had explained his reasoning to Charlie Bartlett as they were leaving Washington to fly to Wisconsin and campaign in its 1960 primary. Pointing to several overcoats, he asked which one he should wear. Bartlett recommended the tweed one because it looked "more like Wisconsin." He disagreed. "I've got to take the black one because that's the coat I always wear," he said, "and the most important thing when you are in one of these things is always to be yourself."

Before embarking on the conservation tour he had told Jerry Bruno that while he was in Great Falls he wanted to visit Mike Mansfield's father, who was in failing health. Mansfield was almost moved to tears when Bruno informed him of this. "Did the President *really* say that?" he asked. "Would you thank him for me? Tell him I really appreciate that." On his way into town, Kennedy stopped at Patrick Mansfield's small wood-frame bungalow and met the nineteen Mansfield relatives who had gathered to greet him. They included Mike Mansfield's brother Joe, a captain in the Great Falls Fire Department. After leaving the house, Kennedy said, "I wonder how many majority leaders in the U.S. Senate have had a brother working in the hometown fire department. And that fellow wouldn't take a job in Washington for any amount of money."

Instead of reading his prepared speech at the Great Falls High School Memorial Stadium and saying, "I am delighted to be in Great Falls, the heart of the first fully operational wing in the country consisting of one hundred and fifty Minuteman missiles," he spoke about the dangers those missiles posed. He reminded the audience that their state had "concentrated within its borders some of the most powerful nuclear systems in the world," making it impossible to ignore "how close Montana lives to the firing line." In distance, they were "many thousands of miles from the Soviet Union," but "in a very real sense . . . [they were] only thirty minutes away." His job, he said, was "to make sure that those over one hundred Minuteman missiles which ring this city and this state remain where they are." He praised the test ban treaty as "a step toward peace and a step toward security . . . that gives us an additional chance that all of the weapons of Montana will never be fired," and concluded by speaking of human resources instead of natural ones, decrying the fact that children growing up in poor homes were less likely to complete high school or attend college. In his opinion, the nation should concern itself "with this phase of our resource development, our children."

At an afternoon groundbreaking for the nation's largest nuclear power plant, in Hanford, Washington, he said that he had strongly supported the test ban treaty, and "it may well be that man recognizes now that war is so destructive, so annihilating, so incendiary, that it may be possible . . . for us to find a more peaceful world. That's my intention."

Salt Lake City had voted overwhelmingly for Nixon in 1960. Its mayor had endorsed the right-wing John Birch Society, and its most prominent political leader, former secretary of agriculture Ezra Taft Benson, was an elder in the Mormon Church and a confirmed Birchite. Kennedy was presumed to be so unpopular that his decision to speak in the Mormon Tabernacle to a largely Mormon audience was being compared to his appearance at a 1960 convention of Protestant ministers in Houston, during which he had explained why his Catholic faith should not disqualify him from the presidency. Yet the largest and most enthusiastic crowd of his trip cheered him as he rode through downtown Salt Lake City at dusk in an open limousine, and eight thousand people had filled the Tabernacle to capacity and a similar number had packed a nearby hall and the Temple grounds, where loudspeakers would broadcast his speech.

He received a five-minute standing ovation when he took the podium. Instead of pandering to this conservative audience, he delivered a blistering attack on Goldwater's simplistic foreign policy, receiving sustained applause when he criticized his "black-and-white choice of good and evil." He urged these conservative Mormons to recognize "that we cannot remake the world simply by our own command," and asserted that "every nation had its own traditions, its own values, its own aspirations. . . . We cannot enact their laws, nor can we operate their governments or dictate our policies."

The applause was even louder when he proclaimed that the test ban treaty meant a "chance to end the radiation and the possibility of burning." He mentioned that he had just flown over the Little Big Horn, where Indians had killed General Custer and several hundred of his men. After calling it "an event which has lived in history," he reminded them that in the case of a nuclear war, "We are talking about two hundred million men and women in twenty-four hours," adding, "I think it is wise to take just a first step and lessen the possibility of that happening."

Among those applauding had to be people who had heard him deliver a hawkish cold war speech here in 1960, during which he had called Khrushchev "the enemy" and excoriated the Communists for seeking "world domination." Tonight, he quoted Brigham Young's commandment to his followers to "go as pioneers to a land of peace." When he finished, the Mormon Tabernacle Choir burst into the "Battle Hymn of the Republic," thunderous applause shook the hall, and the cheers were the loudest Bruno had ever heard him receive. While he was still on the stage, the United Press International correspondent Merriman Smith rushed up and said, "That was a great speech, Mr. President." Peter Lisagor overheard Smith and thought his praise was unseemly and unethical, but admitted feeling the same way.

Like Billings and Great Falls, Salt Lake City had demonstrated that the test ban treaty had support across the political spectrum, and that peace could be a powerful issue in 1964. Bruno thought that the best political advisers in the world could not have persuaded him any better to run on a peace-and-disarmament platform. Vanocur concluded, "If JFK had any doubts about his reelection—and I think he had none—they were dispelled by this trip."

He was ebullient throughout the rest of the tour. At an airport ceremony requiring him to push a button activating a generator at a dam 150 miles away, he joked, "I never know when I press these whether I'm going to blow up Massachusetts or start the project." While waiting for a disembodied voice to announce over the loudspeakers that the generator had engaged, he said, "If we don't hear from him it's back to the drawing boards." When the announcement finally came, he deadpanned, "This gives you an idea of how difficult it is to be president." He arrived at the lodge in Lassen National Park in such a good mood that he allowed himself to be photographed feeding a tame deer—the kind of staged scene he usually avoided—and gave the deer so much of the bread in his cabin that there was no toast the next morning. After a speaker introducing him in Tacoma praised Mount Rainier, he invited everyone to travel east and marvel at "the Blue Hills of Boston, stretching three hundred feet up, covered in snow." He told another audience, "I do not think that these trips do very much for people who come and listen . . . but I can tell you that they are the best educational three or four days for anyone who holds high office in the United States."

During a 1949 debate over federal funding of low-cost housing for veterans, he had shocked his fellow congressmen by denouncing the American Legion for opposing the measure because it wanted to curry favor with real estate and construction interests, declaring on the floor of the House, "The leadership of the American Legion has not had a constructive thought for the benefit of this country since 1918." His staff and friends had urged him to apologize and retract the statement. Instead, he attacked the powerful Legion again. After veterans and even Legion members rallied around him, he told Powers that the experience had taught him that "more often than not, the right thing to do is also the right thing politically." His Western tour had taught him that ending the cold war might also be the right thing politically.

He spent Sunday in Palm Springs relaxing at the singer Bing Crosby's ranch. He swam, watched football, and probably also watched an interview with Everett Dirksen on ABC's *Issues and Answers*. Asked what issue was most likely to "sink" the president in the election, Dirksen named the budget, specifically "a recurring deficit" and "public debt."

While rehashing the trip with his advisers around Crosby's pool, he asked Bruno how he had turned out such big crowds. "It's because they really like you, Mr. President," Bruno said. (After Bruno returned to Washington, he asked Lincoln if Salt Lake City had pleased him. She replied, "Jerry, he is very, very happy." When Mansfield returned he told his secretary, "Thank God, he got out of the state without being harmed.")

The darkest immediate cloud on Kennedy's horizon was Jackie's cruise. Angry letters were deluging the White House, attacking her for vacationing so soon after Patrick's death, feeling well enough to travel but not to resume her duties as First Lady, and not choosing to holiday in the United States. While at Crosby's ranch, Kennedy drafted a press release that portrayed the cruise as a wholesome family excursion, writing, "W.H. announced that Mrs. Kennedy would join Prince and Princess Radziwill, her sister, on a cruise in the Mediterranean. Mrs. Kennedy will be accompanied by her son John—and the Radziwills by their two children. They will travel on the _____ owned by Mr. Onassis which has been secured by Prince Radziwill." Very little in his draft was or would prove to be true. She was not bringing John, nor were the Radziwills planning to include their children. Saying that Prince Radziwill had "secured" the yacht implied that he had chartered it and that Onassis would remain behind.

Back in Washington the next morning he edited the release so that Salinger could deliver it at a noon briefing. When he finished, it read (with the passages he had crossed out in brackets, and his handwritten additions in italics) *"while Mrs. Kennedy is visiting Greece she* will accompany her sister and brother-in-law Prince and Princess Radziwill on a [ten day] cruise in the Eastern Mediterranean aboard the yacht Christina. [Mrs. Kennedy will be accompanied by her son, John Jr., and the Radziwills by their children.] The yacht has been secured by Prince Radziwill for this cruise from her owner, Aristotle Onassis. [The cruise will begin October 1st.] Mrs. Kennedy plans to depart tomorrow evening at 10."

It was more accurate than his first effort but still gave the impression that the cruise was a Radziwill production, with Onassis merely supplying his yacht. Pamela Turnure joined Salinger at the briefing and said it was "possible some people will join the cruise," but because the list had not been finalized she would not be announcing their names. Asked if Onassis would be on board, she replied, "Not to my knowledge."

That morning Kennedy scribbled the kind of to-do list that people compile after being away. Underneath a reminder to tell Lincoln to "get moccasins darkened," he wrote, "Study of Cuba—previous administration," evidence that he was monitoring the conversations between Attwood and Lechuga.

He ran into Arthur Schlesinger as he was heading upstairs with Jackie and the children for lunch. After Caroline curtsied, John copied her, leading Jackie to say, "I think there's something ominous about John curtsying," and John to protest indignantly, "Mummy, I wasn't curtsying, I was bowing." Kennedy generously praised Schlesinger's Salt Lake City speech even though he had discarded most of it. Later that day, Schlesinger handed him a memorandum describing a proposed agreement with Harvard University for his presidential library. Kennedy objected to its stipulation that Harvard would turn over the land whenever "the President" requested it. Despite his successful Western trip he was taking nothing for granted. "What if I'm no longer president?" he asked Schlesinger. "We've been assuming this would be a two-term proposition. What if it isn't?" Schlesinger assured him that Harvard would turn over the land even if he served only a single term, but he still insisted on changing the language so it read whenever "President Kennedy" requested it.

PART FOUR

October 1–31, 1963

DAYS 53–23

WASHINGTON, ARKANSAS, AND CAMP DAVID

J ackie had canceled her official engagements until January, but she decided to make an exception for Emperor Haile Selassie of Ethiopia and welcome him when he arrived at Union Station on Tuesday by chartered train from Philadelphia. The hairdresser Kenneth Battelle had flown from New York that morning and given her a sophisticated cut and style more suited to a jet-set cruise than to a First Lady who was in mourning and preparing to greet an emperor who traced his lineage back to King Solomon and the Queen of Sheba, and whose subjects approached him on their hands and knees. After seeing what Battelle had done, Kennedy summoned him back upstairs and asked, perhaps in jest, "What are you trying to do, ruin my career?" Battelle combed out her hair and gave her a pageboy. Kennedy also vetoed her hat as too flashy, and a photograph of them welcoming the emperor shows her wearing a black woolen suit and black pillbox hat.

He usually walked several paces ahead at ceremonial events, but at Union Station a reporter noted that "he gently guided her ahead of him . . . and if she dropped her yellow gloved hand from his arm, he placed his hand on her arm." A military band played, cannons boomed, and she presented the emperor and his granddaughter Ruth Desta with a bouquet of roses and informed them that she had broken mourning to greet them. The president hailed Selassie as "a man whose place in history is already assured," an honor never far from his mind.

They rode to the White House in an open limousine. The five-foot-tall emperor wore a field marshal's uniform plastered with ribbons and medals and stood erect in the backseat. Kennedy remained seated to avoid towering over him. Jackie and Ruth Desta followed in a bubbletop limousine. After discovering they were both keen horsewomen and painters, Jackie invited her and the emperor to tea in the family quarters. Haile Selassie used the occasion to present her with a full-length leopard-skin coat, perhaps chosen to trump the one she had received from his archenemy, President Aden Daar of Somalia. She slipped it on and, because they were speaking French, said, "*Je suis comblée* [I am overcome]." She hurried downstairs and found her husband in the Rose Garden. "See, Jack, he brought it to me!" she exclaimed. "He brought it to *me!*"

"I was wondering why you were wearing a fur coat in the garden," he said dryly.

Before leaving for Athens, she handed Chief Usher J. B. West a stack of prewritten postcards addressed to John and Caroline (she did not trust the foreign mails), and gave Evelyn Lincoln a letter in a sealed envelope with instructions to deliver it to her husband the following day.

DURING A WEDNESDAY MORNING meeting in the Cabinet Room, McNamara and Taylor reported on their mission to South Vietnam. General Krulak had overseen the drafting of their official report, consulting at every step with Bobby, who had in turn briefed the president. Bobby then relayed the president's comments back to Krulak, a process guaranteeing that the final report would be written to his specifications and include an optimistic assessment of the military situation, one justifying the withdrawal of some U.S. advisers. McNamara had made it clear to the aides accompanying him on the trip that this was the goal, leading McGeorge Bundy's older brother, Assistant Secretary of Defense William Bundy, to write, "All through the Saigon briefings and in the field, the question at the top of McNamara's mind . . . [was]: Could the U.S. look forward to a reduction in its military advisors by the end of 1965?"

McNamara and Taylor affirmed in their report that "the military campaign has made great progress and continues to progress." They acknowledged "serious political tensions in Saigon," but found "no solid evidence of the possibility of a successful coup . . . although assassination of Diem or Nhu is always a possibility." They were guardedly optimistic, writing, "The military program in Vietnam has made progress and is sound in principle." The political situation remained "deeply serious," but had "not yet significantly affected the military effort, but could do so at some time in the future." They recommended that "a program be established to train Vietnamese so that essential functions now performed by U.S. military personnel can be carried out by Vietnamese by the end of 1965."

An earlier draft of their report had recommended that the Defense Department "announce in the very near future presently prepared plans to withdraw 1000 U.S. military personnel by the end of 1963," adding that "this action should be explained in low key as an initial step in a long-term program to replace U.S. personnel with trained Vietnamese without impairment of the war effort." This passage had alarmed Averell Harriman's assistant William Sullivan, who told McNamara that pulling out all the U.S. advisers by the end of 1965 was "totally unrealistic," and threatened to write a dissenting report. To placate him, McNamara and Taylor eliminated the recommendation to withdraw a thousand advisers.

As soon as Kennedy noticed the omission, he suspended the meeting and took McNamara and Taylor into the Oval Office. When they returned, McNamara announced that the report now contained a troop-withdrawal schedule. Kennedy asked McNamara if reducing the number of advisers was dependent on military progress. "No. No, sir," McNamara said emphatically, adding that even if the military campaign went beyond 1965, "we believe we can train the Vietnamese to take over the essential functions and withdraw the bulk of our forces. And this thousand is in conjunction with that."

"What's the point in doing it?" McGeorge Bundy asked skeptically.

"We need a way to get out of Vietnam," McNamara said. "This is a way of doing it."

Taylor backed him up. He had asked the U.S. officers whom he interviewed, "When can you finish this job in the sense that you will reduce this insurgency to little more than sporadic incidents?" Most had said a year would be "ample time," assuming there were "no new major factors."

"Well, let's say it anyway," Kennedy interjected. "Then in '65 if it doesn't work out [unclear audio], we'll get a new date."

McNamara emphasized that the withdrawal was not contingent on winning the war, merely on completing the training of the South Vietnamese army, adding, "The only slightest difference between Max and me in this entire report is in this one estimate of whether or not we can win the war in '64 in the upper [unclear] territories and '65 in the [unclear]. I'm not entirely sure of that. But I am sure that if we don't meet those dates, in the sense of ending the major military campaigns, we nonetheless can withdraw the bulk of our U.S. forces, according to the schedule we have laid out . . . because we can train the Vietnamese to do the job."

Taylor now defined "victory" in terms making the withdrawal of the advisers justifiable under most circumstances, saying, "It ought to be very clear what we mean by victory or success. That doesn't mean every Viet Cong comes in with a white flag, but that we do suppress this insurgency to the point that the national security forces of Vietnam can contain [it]."

Chester Cooper, a CIA officer serving in the State Department as an assistant for policy support, was working in a basement office in the White House that morning. He protested when McGeorge and Bill Bundy brought him the final draft of a press statement announcing that the U.S. military mission in Vietnam would end in 1965. Bill Bundy, in a tone of voice that Cooper described as reflecting his "utter exasperation," said, "Look, I'm under instructions," meaning that the president had insisted on including this passage in the report. McGeorge Bundy asked McNamara to persuade Kennedy to remove the pledge to withdraw in 1965, but as Cooper wrote later, "McNamara seems to have been trapped," because "the sentence may have been worked out privately with Kennedy, and therefore imbedded in concrete."

After hearing more protests during a National Security Council meeting that afternoon, Kennedy demanded that everyone support his policy. "Reports of disagreements do not help the war effort in Vietnam," he said. "We must all sign on and with good heart set out to implement the actions decided upon."

McNamara suggested announcing the withdrawal timetable in order to "set it in concrete." Kennedy agreed, but wanted it presented to the press as something that McNamara and Taylor had proposed. As McNamara left the Cabinet Room to brief reporters, Kennedy shouted after him, "And tell them that means all of the helicopter pilots too."

McNamara's statement was front-page news. He informed reporters that "the military program in South Viet Nam has made progress and is sound in principle, though improvements are being energetically sought," that "Secretary McNamara and General Taylor reported their judgment that the major part of the U.S. military task can be completed by the end of 1965," and that "by the end of the year, the U.S. program for training Vietnamese should have progressed to the point where one thousand U.S. military personnel assigned to South Viet Nam can be withdrawn."

Some of those attending the October 2 meetings understood that the policy that Taylor and McNamara had proposed, and that Kennedy had approved, had been Kennedy's policy all along. Deputy Secretary of Defense Gilpatric said that McNamara told him afterward that the withdrawal "was part of a plan the President asked him to develop to unwind the whole thing."

After listening to a recording of the October 2 meeting thirty years later, McNamara found that it confirmed his impression that the decision to announce the withdrawal had divided the president's staff. "Many, many were opposed to approving a plan to remove all advisors and all military support within two years by the end of '65. Many, many were opposed to withdrawing a thousand within ninety days. And then after that decision was made, many, many were opposed to announcing it," he said. "And he [Kennedy] went through those controversies and the tape is very clear on this. First, the controversy over whether to establish the plan and have it as an official government policy. And second, the controversy over whether to put it in concrete by announcing it. He did both." McNamara believed he had done this because "he believed the primary responsibility of a president was to keep the nation out of war if at all possible."

JACKIE HAD BEEN CAREFUL not to spoil John and Caroline, but the moment she left for Greece, Kennedy asked his driver Muggsy O'Leary to buy some toy horses for Caroline, and sent out Lincoln to buy model planes so he could give one to John when he dashed into his bedroom every morning. John was too young for school, so he received the most attention. Kennedy played with him before his first meeting of the day, swam with him before lunch, played games of "through the tunnel and under the mountain," standing with his legs apart so John could crawl underneath, tickled him until he wet his pants, and let him ride along to Andrews and Camp David in the helicopter, putting on a helmet and touching the controls. He told a friend, "I'm having the best time of my life."

He brought John along on Wednesday for the first leg of a trip to Arkansas, taking him to Andrews by helicopter and letting him sit in the presidential compartment on Air Force One. He was going to dedicate a dam that lay within the congressional district of Wilbur Mills, the powerful chairman of the House Ways and Means Committee, and to gain a sense of how much his civil rights bill had damaged his chances of winning the state. Accompanying him was Senator William Fulbright of Arkansas, a Rhodes scholar, an internationalist, and a liberal in everything but civil rights. Two years earlier, Fulbright had seized the opportunity of sharing a flight with him to give him a memorandum opposing the Bay of Pigs operation and recommending a policy of isolating and containing the Castro regime. After reading it, Kennedy had invited him to attend the final Bay of Pigs review. Fulbright denounced the invasion as a violation of the nation's moral principles. Everyone in the room, including Kennedy, ignored him.

During their flight to Arkansas on October 3, Fulbright urged Kennedy to skip Dallas when he visited Texas. Fulbright's liberal positions on foreign affairs had made him persona non grata in the city, the wealthy Hunt family had funneled money to his opponents, and the *Dallas Morning News* had called him a "red louse." The attacks had so unnerved him that he steered clear of the city. He told Kennedy it was "a very dangerous place," adding, "*I* wouldn't go there. . . . Don't *you* go."

If Kennedy had harbored any doubts about visiting Dallas, an article that week in *Time* titled "Box Score for '64—Can Anybody Beat Kennedy?" would have dispelled them. It reported that although most political observers considered him a sure winner in 1964, a state-by-state survey by its correspondents indicated that Goldwater would give him "a breathlessly close contest." The article came with a box score showing him losing the South to Goldwater, winning most Northeastern states, some Midwestern ones, and California. The outcome might be decided by Texas, but because Vice President Johnson was "not the power he once was," *Time* said, Kennedy could "only be rated even there." If he won Texas, he would have 280 electoral votes, 10 over the 270 he needed, but if Goldwater won the state he would have 266 votes, "with an excellent chance for picking up the necessary additional four from among the Kennedy-hating unpledged electors of Alabama and Mississippi."

Kennedy found the article so unsettling that he had raised it with his political advisers on October 2. He did not usually tape meetings concerning politics, but he neglected to switch off the microphone, inadvertently recording this one. Because the participants kept moving around the room, only snatches of their sentences are sometimes audible. He began by asking, "Did you read that *Time* magazine yet?" Referring to Goldwater, he said, "I guess he's a Puritan, so anybody who's got any girls, just play it more quiet." Because Goldwater did not fool around with women, Kennedy assumed he would be less tolerant of people (such as himself) who did, and said, "I just figure that a guy who's getting laid is not going to go after a guy who's getting laid." Speaking of a staffer who liked flight attendants, he said, "He ought to look like he's all business. If he's parading stewardesses around he's going to make all the other guys sore." Returning to the *Time* survey, he called the writers and editors responsible for it "those cocksuckers," and complained, "I thought I was a sure thing." He insisted that even if he lost the West, he could still be reelected, "if I win California and Texas."

THE ARKANSAS CROWDS WERE large and friendly, but Fulbright was alarmed by how freely the president mingled with people at Heber Springs, where, he noted, "any one of a thousand or two thousand could easily have done him harm . . . because the poor Secret Service were lost in the crowd." There were no boos, only a few hostile placards, and he received loud applause when he mentioned the test ban treaty. An editorial in the friendly *Arkansas Gazette* predicted that he was "destined to join the silent company of great Presidents."

The next day he met in the White House with Governor John Connally of Texas, who was even less enthusiastic than Fulbright about his trip to Texas, although for different reasons. The Kennedy-Connally relationship had been one of dramatic fluctuations. At the 1956 convention, Connally had persuaded the Texas delegation to back Kennedy for the vice presidency, but four years later, while serving as Johnson's de facto campaign manager, he had initiated a whispering campaign about his health. He redeemed himself by working hard for the ticket, and Kennedy made him secretary of the Navy, a post he held for only a year before resigning to run for governor. Once Connally moved into the governor's mansion, Kennedy began badgering him to arrange a presidential trip to the state. Connally faced reelection in two years and was afraid that being seen as close to the president would be a liability. He stalled before finally proposing a low-key, nonpolitical trip that skipped Dallas, where he feared embarrassing signs and noisy pickets. Kennedy agreed to the plan but insisted on including Dallas.

Connally stopped in Dallas on his way to Washington to confer with its civic leaders and apologize for inflicting the president on them. He compared himself to a ship's captain faced with an admiral demanding to come aboard, and promised not to become "Kennedy's errand boy." Like him, they feared an incident similar to the infamous attack on Lyndon and Lady Bird Johnson during the 1960 campaign that had besmirched their city's reputation. Connally went to the Capitol before coming to the White House and told the Texas congressional delegation that he thought the president's visit was a mistake. He was coming to Texas to raise money, he said, yet his strength lay among people without any money, "Negroes and brass collar [working-class] Democrats."

"How about those fund-raising affairs in Texas, John?" Kennedy asked as soon as Connally sat down in the Oval Office.

Holding four would be a mistake, he said, and would not raise any more money than a single properly managed dinner. Because the president had not made a "real visit" to Texas since taking office, if he held multiple events during his first trip he might be seen as "trying to financially rape the state."

Kennedy was taken aback by the strong language and protested that he was coming more to win over the business community than to raise money. Connally argued that the place to do that was a nonpolitical event, not a fund-raiser that his enemies were sure to boycott. Texans were a courteous and hospitable people, he said, and more likely to honor him as their president instead of as a politician hunting for donations. He proposed nonpartisan speeches in Houston and San Antonio, then a luncheon in Dallas followed by a political fund-raiser in Austin. Kennedy capitulated, and Connally magnanimously said that *he* believed he would win Texas, although it might be close.

"We *shouldn't* have a hard race in Texas," Kennedy complained, irked by the notion of struggling to win his vice president's native state.

Connally implored him to bring the First Lady. "The women want to see her. They want to see what her hairdo looks like and what her clothes look like. It's important to them."

"I would hope that she would come," he said wistfully.

KENNEDY MET with his Vietnam advisers again on Saturday morning for a further discussion of the McNamara-Taylor report. The report had presented

The Truman Library commissioned Elaine de Kooning to paint a portrait of President Kennedy. She became so consumed by the challenge of capturing his "essence" in a single picture that she spent 1963 painting only him, papering the walls of her studio with his likenesses and falling, she admitted, "a teeny little bit in love with him." *(Alfred Eisenstaedt/Time & Life Pictures/Getty Images)*

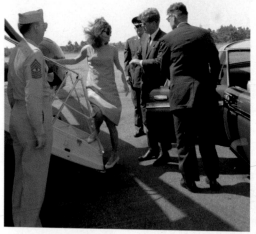

JFK bringing Jackie to their rented house on Squaw Island from the Otis Air Force Base Hospital on Cape Cod following the death of their infant son Patrick. Presidential adviser Arthur Schlesinger, Jr., noticed them becoming "extremely close and affectionate" following the tragedy. *(Photograph by Cecil Stoughton, White House/John F. Kennedy Presidential Library and Museum, Boston)*

The Kennedy family on the terrace of the Squaw Island house less than a week after Patrick's death. JFK had brought more of the family dogs up from Washington in hopes that they might distract Jackie and the children from their grief. *(Photograph by Cecil Stoughton, White House/John F. Kennedy Presidential Library and Museum, Boston)*

JFK confers in the Oval Office on August 15 with his newly appointed ambassador to South Vietnam, Henry Cabot Lodge. Kennedy taped the meeting without Lodge's knowledge, and one of the wires running from the table to the floor probably led to a tape recorder in the basement. *(Photograph by Robert Knudsen, White House/John F. Kennedy Presidential Library and Museum, Boston)*

A guest remembered the Squaw Island house as being "full of sadness" during the weekend of August 24 and 25. Caroline was particularly distressed by her brother's death, and her father was the only one who could cheer her up. *(Photograph by Cecil Stoughton, White House/John F. Kennedy Presidential Library and Museum, Boston)*

By the summer of 1963, John F. Kennedy, Jr., had become a rambunctious and personable little boy—"friendly, uninhibited, and unspoiled," according to journalist Laura Bergquist, who sensed a "joyous, funny . . . even sensuous" relationship between father and son. *(Photograph by Cecil Stoughton, White House/John F. Kennedy Presidential Library and Museum, Boston)*

JFK meets in the Oval Office with the leaders of the March on Washington on August 28. Earlier that afternoon he had stood at an open window, gripping the sill so hard that his knuckles turned white as he listened to the strains of "We Shall Overcome" wafting over from the Lincoln Memorial and telling a black White House usher, "Oh, Bruce, I wish I were out there with them!" *(Photograph by Cecil Stoughton, White House/John F. Kennedy Presidential Library and Museum, Boston)*

JFK cruises on the *Honey Fitz* during the Labor Day weekend. His health that summer was the best of his presidency. One physician recalled him as "bursting with vigor." *(Photograph by Cecil Stoughton, White House/John F. Kennedy Presidential Library and Museum, Boston)*

During a Labor Day interview with CBS newsman Walter Cronkite, Kennedy leveled his harshest criticism yet at South Vietnam's president Ngo Dinh Diem. Cronkite believed that his comments "effectively pulled the rug out from under Diem and changed the course of events in South Vietnam." *(Photograph by Cecil Stoughton, White House/John F. Kennedy Presidential Library and Museum, Boston)*

Kennedy meets at the White House on September 6 with Arizona Republican senator Barry Goldwater, his likely opponent in the 1964 presidential election. Although the two had become friends while serving in the Senate, JFK relished the thought of running against Goldwater, telling a friend that he could beat "good old Barry" without leaving the Oval Office. *(Photograph by Cecil Stoughton, White House/John F. Kennedy Presidential Library and Museum, Boston)*

The Kennedy children and their families gathered at Hyannis Port on September 7 to celebrate their father's birthday. There were funny hats, noisemakers, and a "Happy Birthday" tablecloth, as if they were still Joe Kennedy's little boys and girls. *(Photograph by Cecil Stoughton, White House/John F. Kennedy Presidential Library and Museum, Boston)*

Presidential friend and adviser Dave Powers welcomes the actress and singer Marlene Dietrich to the White House on September 10. The year before, Kennedy had received Dietrich in the upstairs family quarters and they had slept together. This time he scheduled only a brief afternoon meeting in the Oval Office, even though Jackie was away in Newport. It was perhaps an example of his attempts to curb his womanizing following the death of his son. *(Photograph by Robert Knudsen, White House/John F. Kennedy Presidential Library and Museum, Boston)*

JFK and Jackie invited Ben and Tony Bradlee to Newport for the Kennedys' tenth wedding anniversary. Jackie was not a keen golfer but gamely tagged along. *(Photograph by Robert Knudsen, White House/John F. Kennedy Presidential Library and Museum, Boston)*

On his way west for a tour stressing conservation, JFK stopped in Milford, Pennsylvania, on September 24 to speak at a ceremony honoring the descendants of Gifford Pinchot, Jr., the first head of the U.S. Forest Service. The family had donated its chateau-style mansion to the Forest Service for use as a training center. However, Kennedy probably added the ceremony to his itinerary because Pinchot had been the uncle of his lover Mary Meyer and her sister, Tony, Ben Bradlee's wife, and he was curious to see where the Meyer girls had spent their childhood summers. He is standing between Mary Meyer and her mother. *(Photograph by Cecil Stoughton, White House/John F. Kennedy Presidential Library and Museum, Boston)*

JFK speaks in Washington State during his Western conservation tour. He began the trip by delivering dull prepared speeches, but after discovering in Billings that the crowds wanted to hear about peace and the nuclear test ban treaty rather than conservation, he spoke extemporaneously about those subjects, receiving prolonged cheers and applause. *(Photograph by Cecil Stoughton, White House/John F. Kennedy Presidential Library and Museum, Boston)*

Emperor Haile Selassie of Ethiopia arrived in Washington, D.C., for a state visit on October 1, the same day that Jackie was leaving for Greece, where she would cruise with Aristotle Onassis and others aboard his sumptuous yacht. Before she departed, Selassie presented her with a magnificent leopard-skin coat and gave John a carved Ethiopian warrior. *(Photograph by Cecil Stoughton, White House/John F. Kennedy Presidential Library and Museum, Boston)*

JFK signs the ratification instruments for the limited test ban treaty in the White House Treaty Room. Presidential adviser Ken O'Donnell believed that this ceremony provided Kennedy with "the deepest satisfaction of his three years at the White House." *(Photograph by Robert Knudsen, White House/John F. Kennedy Presidential Library and Museum, Boston)*

Jackie was determined not to spoil John and Caroline, but the moment she left for Greece, Kennedy ordered a large supply of toys so that he could give the children something when they dashed into his bedroom every morning. He played with them often throughout the day and told a friend, "I'm having the best time of my life." *(Photograph by Cecil Stoughton, White House/John F. Kennedy Presidential Library and Museum, Boston)*

Jackie returned to Washington on October 18. When Kennedy reached the top of the metal staircase, she reached out with a white-gloved hand to caress his neck and draw him inside. *(Photograph by Abbie Rowe, White House/John F. Kennedy Presidential Library and Museum, Boston)*

After his father was incapacitated by a stroke, Kennedy initiated the custom of kissing him on the head. He visited him for the last time on October 20 in Hyannis Port. *(Photograph by Cecil Stoughton, White House/John F. Kennedy Presidential Library and Museum, Boston)*

During JFK's last November weekend at Wexford, the house that Jackie had insisted they build in the Virginia hunt country, one of the ponies tried to eat all of the sugar cubes that Kennedy had been trying to feed him. *(Photograph by Cecil Stoughton, White House/John F. Kennedy Presidential Library and Museum, Boston)*

The Kennedy family attended a performance of Scotland's famed Black Watch regiment on the White House lawn on November 13. The Black Watch returned two weeks later to play the bagpipes at JFK's funeral, at which his children would wear the same matching blue overcoats. *(Photograph by Robert Knudsen, White House/John F. Kennedy Presidential Library and Museum, Boston)*

Kennedy with astronauts Gus Grissom and Gordon Cooper outside the Saturn Control Center during his visit to Cape Canaveral on November 16. Five days later he met Cooper in San Antonio and invited him to accompany him to Dallas the next day. Cooper declined because he was due at Cape Canaveral. Had he gone, he would have ridden in the presidential limousine, probably sitting in the backseat between Jack and Jackie. *(Photograph by Cecil Stoughton, White House/John F. Kennedy Presidential Library and Museum, Boston)*

Kennedy made the Secret Service nervous by insisting on standing directly underneath the Saturn rocket. Looking up, he rocked back and forth on the balls of his feet and murmured, "When this goes up we'll be ahead of the Russians. . . . When this goes up we'll be ahead of the Russians. . . ." *(Photograph by Cecil Stoughton, White House/John F. Kennedy Presidential Library and Museum, Boston)*

Prior to embarking on the longest motorcade of his presidency, Kennedy shakes hands with the crowd welcoming him to Tampa on November 18. *(Photograph by Cecil Stoughton, White House/John F. Kennedy Presidential Library and Museum, Boston)*

After being presented with the official White House Thanksgiving turkey, Kennedy decided to spare the beast, saying in a mock-serious tone of voice, "It would be a shame, a terrible shame to interrupt a great line like Tom's. We'll just keep him." *(Photograph by Cecil Stoughton, White House/John F. Kennedy Presidential Library and Museum, Boston)*

Jackie sits between her husband and Vice President Lyndon Johnson at a Chamber of Commerce breakfast in Fort Worth on the morning of November 22. *(Photograph by Cecil Stoughton, White House/John F. Kennedy Presidential Library and Museum, Boston)*

Jack and Jackie arrive at Love Field in Dallas on November 22.

*(Photograph by Cecil Stoughton, White House/John F. Kennedy
Presidential Library and Museum, Boston)*

him with three options: apply selective pressures such as withholding U.S. subsidies for commodity imports and suspending aid to the South Vietnamese Special Forces, reconcile with Diem, or encourage a coup. McNamara and Taylor dismissed reconciliation as an ineffective strategy, saying it would indicate to Diem that the United States "would sit still for just about anything he did." They rated the prospects for a successful coup as low because Diem and Nhu had established a "praetorian guard" to protect themselves, while the generals appeared to have little stomach for a coup.

Kennedy approved "selective pressures." He understood that the generals would view the pressures as endorsing a coup, and Bundy sent Lodge a cable instructing him to pursue an "urgent covert effort . . . to identify and build contacts with alternative leadership."

The White House had announced on Wednesday that Taylor and McNamara had proposed a withdrawal schedule, and that the president had approved making their recommendation public. Kennedy formally approved their recommendations on Saturday, but according to a National Security Action memorandum, "directed that no formal announcement be made of the implementation of plans to withdraw 1000 U.S. military personnel by the end of 1963."

He concluded the Saturday meeting by saying, "Our decision to remove a thousand U.S. advisors by December of this year should not be raised formally with Diem. Instead the action should be carried out routinely as part of our general posture of withdrawing people when they are no longer needed." In other words, the withdrawal would occur whether or not Diem made any reforms.

Before flying to Camp David to spend the weekend with Caroline and John, he tried on a selection of hats from the desperate hatters of Danbury, Connecticut. His refusal to hide his thick chestnut hair under a hat had been a catastrophe for this important Connecticut industry. (Dave Powers had once joked that "if you put a hat on a Kennedy, you lose three quarters of the head, all of the charisma.") To placate Secretary of Health, Education, and Welfare Ribicoff, a former Connecticut governor, he had agreed to wear a hat from time to time. He lined up the candidates from Danbury and asked his aides to choose their favorites. After each picked out a different one, he told them, "You remind me of my Vietnam advisors."

Monday, October 7

WASHINGTON

Kennedy signed the instruments of ratification for the Limited Test Ban Treaty in the White House Treaty Room, a small and once neglected space in the second-floor family quarters that Jackie had redecorated in high Victorian style with deep green walls, floor-to-ceiling burgundy drapes, furniture from the Grant administration, and a painting of the signing of the Peace Protocols ending the Spanish-American War. He orchestrated the signing as if arranging its participants for another historic portrait, placing himself in the center of the room, sitting behind a handsome antique table he had ordered brought in for the occasion. Resting on it were four leather-bound copies of the instruments of ratification and a holder with pens standing upright like arrows in a quiver. Sixteen government officials and congressional leaders who had been instrumental in negotiating the treaty and shepherding it through the Senate stood in a semicircle behind him, hands clasped in front of sober suits, their expressions grave.

He used sixteen pens to sign four copies. He handed the first pen to Senator Fulbright, the next to Mansfield, the third to Dirksen. After passing out the rest to Harriman, Rusk, Johnson, and others, he realized that he had neglected to keep one for himself. He reopened one of the folders and added a flourish to his signature. As he slipped the pen into his breast pocket he smiled and said, "This one is mine." He gave it to Jackie.

Sorensen believed that "no single accomplishment in the White House" gave Kennedy "greater satisfaction" than the ratification of the test ban treaty. According to O'Donnell, the ceremony provided him with "the deepest satisfaction of his three years at the White House" because he believed that the treaty made it less likely that millions of innocent children would perish in a nuclear war. As he and Bobby spoke in his bedroom during the Berlin crisis, when the two powers appeared close to a nuclear exchange, his eyes had teared up and he had said, "It doesn't matter about you and me and the adults so much, Bobby. We've lived some good years. What is so horrible is to think of the children who have never had a chance who would be killed in such a war." On October 20, 1962, just before announcing a naval blockade of Cuba that might provoke the Soviets into mounting a surprise nuclear attack, he had summoned Jackie and the children back from the Virginia countryside so they could spend what might be their final days together, and be close to the White House shelter in case they had only a few minutes' warning. While swimming with Dave Powers that evening he said, "Dave, if we were only thinking of ourselves, it would be easy, but I keep thinking about the children whose lives would be wiped out." On Saturday, October 27, the most perilous day of the crisis, he told his mistress Mimi Beardsley, "I'd rather my children be red than dead." Making the fate of his children weigh on him even more heavily was his suspicion that the Soviets had sent the parts for a nuclear bomb in diplomatic pouches and assembled them on the top floor of their Washington embassy. When he sensed that the reporter Hugh Sidey was skeptical, he said in a stern voice, "That's what they tell me. Do you know something that I don't?"

The signing ceremony was also satisfying because he considered the test ban treaty a first step toward his goal of settling the cold war during his second term. Others shared his optimism. After conferring with him in early October, the British foreign secretary, Sir Alec Douglas-Home, had told reporters, "We have begun the process of reaching a détente with the Soviet Union," and suggested in an address to the General Assembly that the world was witnessing "the beginning of the end of the cold war." Since 1947, the editors of the *Bulletin of Atomic Scientists* had displayed a doomsday clock on their cover, showing how near the world was to the midnight of a nuclear war. They started their clock at seven minutes to midnight and reset it three times between 1947 and 1963. It fell to a low of two minutes to midnight in 1953 when the United States and the Soviet Union tested atomic weapons within a nine-month period. After Congress ratified the test ban treaty, the editors pushed the minute hand back to 11:48 p.m., the furthest it had yet been from midnight.

Kennedy had written to a friend in 1954, "I firmly believe that as much as I was shaped by anything, so was I shaped by the hand of fate moving in World War II. . . . The war made us. It was and is our greatest single moment. The memory of the war is a key to our characters." It was also the key to understanding why the test ban treaty meant so much to him.

Following his rescue after the sinking of *PT 109*, he had been given command of *PT 95*, a torpedo boat converted into an unwieldy gunboat. Despite its slow speed he drove it close to shore to attack Japanese positions and barges, coming under heavy fire while rescuing a detachment of marines who had made a diversionary raid on Choiseul Island. He witnessed the deaths of several wounded men, one of whom died in his bunk, and would later cite Choiseul as an example of how "men tend to like the idea of war until they have tasted it." Before the marines landed they had been raring to go, he said, but after they had been behind enemy lines, their appetite for combat had "somewhat diminished."

His letters from the Pacific reflected a growing cynicism with the top brass, armchair patriots, and war in general. His remark in one letter that "all war is stupid" appeared in different guises in others. He told a Navy friend, "War will exist until that distant day when the conscientious objector enjoys the same reputation and prestige that the warrior does today," and told his lover Ingrid Arvad, "This war here is a dirty business. It's very easy to talk about the war and beating the Japs if it takes years and millions of men, but anyone who talks like that should consider well his words." After complaining about those who made "thousands of casualties sound like drops in the bucket," he added, "But if those thousands want to live as much as the ten [surviving crewmen of *PT 109*] that I saw, the people deciding the whys and wherefores had better make mighty sure that all this effort is headed for some definite goal, and that when we reach that goal we may say it was worth it." In a letter to his family, he displayed a suspicion and distrust of senior officers that would later influence his interactions with the Joint Chiefs. Describing the inspection of his unit by Admiral Halsey, he wrote, "He said we were a 'fine looking crowd,' which was obviously a lie—and said it was 'a privilege for us to be where we are'—which made me edge away from him in case God hit him with lightning."

After coming home on medical leave, he and Chuck Spalding went to a restaurant in Palm Beach where the roof could be retracted on balmy nights so patrons could dine under the stars. For an entire hour he sat in silence, an anguished expression on his face. Spalding imagined him pondering "the terrific discrepancy between people at home dressed in white jackets and bow ties, looking like asses and . . . thinking of the nonsense of people being killed, somebody having his leg blown off."

He told a friend that his brother's death had "savaged" his family and "sucked all the oxygen out of our comfortable and smug assumptions." As a result, he said, "We sons and daughters no longer have that easy, witless, untested, and meaningless confidence on which we'd been weaned before the war," and finally understood "that there is nothing inevitable about us. And that's a healthy thing to know."

In the spring of 1945, he reported for the Hearst newspapers on the United Nations conference in San Francisco, writing in one dispatch, "The world organization that will come out of San Francisco will be the product of the same passion and selfishness that produced the Treaty of Versailles." The only possible "ray of shining light," he said, was "the realization, felt by all the delegates, that humanity cannot afford another war." He urged veterans and servicemen to take an interest in the conference, because "any man who has risked his life for his country and seen his friends killed around him must invariably wonder why this has happened to him and most important what good it will do. . . . It is not surprising that they should question the worth of the sacrifice and feel somewhat betrayed."

Fifteen years later, he told Sidey that if he became president, war with all its "modern horror" would be his biggest concern if he got to the White House. When his postwar diary was published in 1995, Sidey wrote in an introduction, "If I had to single out one element in Kennedy's life that more than anything influenced his later leadership it would be a horror of war, and the even worse prospects in the nuclear age. . . . It ran even deeper than his considerable public rhetoric on the issue."

Kennedy was not a pacifist. But his experiences in the Pacific, his fear of a nuclear war, and his sensitivity to the suffering that modern warfare inflicted on noncombatants, particularly children, all pushed him in that direction. His closest advisers suspected this, particularly those who clashed with him over using military force in Laos, Vietnam, Berlin, and Cuba. McGeorge Bundy was not entirely joking when he told his assistant Marcus Raskin, "You know, there are only two pacifists here in the White House, you and Kennedy."

FIVE HOURS AFTER a ceremony marking Kennedy's greatest foreign policy triumph since the Cuban missile crisis, an event occurred that threatened to end his presidency in impeachment and disgrace. After a four double-martini lunch at his Quorum Club, Bobby Baker stumbled into Senator Mansfield's office and resigned as secretary to the Senate majority leader, hoping to halt a threatened Senate investigation into his murky business affairs. In fact, Baker had traded so many favors and involved himself in the public and personal lives of so many legislators it was only surprising that he had not been forced to explain himself sooner. His current problems stemmed from a lawsuit filed in federal court in early September by the Central Vending Corporation that accused him of accepting a $5,600 fee to place its machines into the plants of a major defense contractor, then double-crossing the company by pushing the machines of a rival company in which he had a financial interest. The lawsuit made a Senate investigation inevitable and prompted Mansfield to summon him to a meeting in Everett Dirksen's office at 3:00 p.m. on Monday. Also attending would be Senator John Williams, the Delaware Republican instrumental in bringing down President Eisenhower's chief of staff Sherman Adams for an influence-peddling scheme similar to Capital Vending.

Baker had raged against his fate during his boozy lunch, telling his companions, "My boss has abandoned me. The goddamn press is having a field day at my expense. There are so many people involved that if this thing keeps going it'll drag them down. . . . I'm gonna resign. Fuck Senator Williams."

He told Mansfield that quitting was preferable to meeting with Williams and dismissed his suggestion that he take a leave of absence because, as he explained later, "Somehow I got it into my head that should I resign, the entire Bobby Baker episode would magically disappear from the front pages and come to a grinding halt."

Three days later, Williams declared that the integrity of the U.S. Senate was at stake and introduced a resolution calling for an investigation. He said he would not repeat the "multitude of rumors" circulating about Baker's activities, but promised that they would be "fully checked," a statement guaranteed to unsettle Kennedy as well as Johnson, whose relationship with Baker had been so close that Baker was known as "Little Lyndon." The president and vice president were among the "many people involved" whom the scandal might drag down, and among the rumors that Williams intended to check were those surrounding the involvement of congressmen and White House officials with Quorum Club party girls such as Ellen Rometsch, and the allegation that Johnson had bought a large life insurance policy from a Maryland agent named Don Reynolds, who had then been required to purchase advertising on a Texas television station controlled by the Johnsons as a kickback.

After Williams announced his investigation, Baker received solicitous calls from Lady Bird Johnson and Bobby Kennedy, both obviously speaking as surrogates. Lady Bird said, "Bobby, Lyndon and I just want you to know we love you. You are like a member of the family and we are so grateful for all you've done for us. Our prayers are with you." Baker pictured Johnson at her side, "petrified that he'd be dragged down." Bobby Kennedy told Baker, "Bobby, my brother is fond of you and remembers your many kindnesses. I want you to know that we [the Justice Department] have nothing of any consequence about you in our files. . . . My brother and I extend our sympathies to you. I know you'll come through this."

Tuesday, October 8–Sunday, October 13

WASHINGTON AND CAMP DAVID

Kennedy brought John along to his pre-press-conference breakfast briefing on Wednesday morning. The boy went around the table shaking hands before climbing onto a chair being left vacant for George Ball and refused to leave. When his father opened with his customary "What have we got today?" question, he piped up, "I've got a glass of ice water."

The previous year, the *Look* photographer Stanley Tretick had proposed a photographic essay titled "The President and His Son." Kennedy responded through intermediaries that he liked the idea, but he kept postponing it. Laura Bergquist, who would write the text, thought he was reluctant because John had not yet begun talking, and Jackie considered her and Tretick "journalistic thieves," intent on sneaking photographs of her children. When Tretick heard about the Onassis cruise he called Lincoln to ask if he could shoot the story while Jackie was away. After Lincoln suggested calling back later, he asked if she meant after October 1. "Well, I didn't say that," she replied. "But it might be a good idea."

Salinger called Tretick on Tuesday to say he could begin photographing John and the president the next day. When he walked into the Oval Office on Wednesday morning, Kennedy told him, "We'd better get this out of the way pretty quick. Things get kind of sticky when Jackie's around." Bergquist was in New York meeting a deadline, but Kennedy insisted she had to witness the shoot to get "the mood of the boy," forcing Tretick to spend the day sitting outside the Oval Office, waiting for her to arrive.

Kennedy was in high spirits when he met with Heller to prepare for his press conference. He had already thought up some amusing ripostes and promised "the six o'clock comedy hour." He had called the conference to announce his decision to approve the sale of surplus U.S. wheat to the Soviet Union. Republicans had denounced the deal, with Nixon calling it "a major foreign policy mistake . . . even more serious than fouling up the Bay of Pigs." The deal made economic sense, but some of his advisers considered it a grievous political error that would antagonize Poles and other blue-collar ethnics. Johnson told O'Donnell that it was "the worst political mistake" the president had ever made.

Kennedy opened the press conference by rebutting the most common objections to the wheat deal, pointing out that the grain would be transported in American ships, the nation had a huge wheat surplus, the Soviets would pay cash, the deal would help the U.S. balance of payments, and the nation's allies were already selling U.S. grain to the Russians anyway. A more revealing argument lay buried in a letter that he sent to Congress in which he called the deal "one more hopeful sign that a peaceful world is both possible and beneficial to us all," and said that prohibiting it would cause Soviet leaders to conclude that the United States was "either too hostile or too timid to take any further steps toward peace . . . and that the logical course for them to follow is a *renewal* [emphasis added] of the Cold War."

A reporter asked him about Eisenhower's recent statement that he was unclear about Goldwater's stand on various issues. "I don't think Senator Goldwater has been particularly deceptive," he said. "I think he has made very clear what he's opposed to. . . . I have gotten the idea. I think President Eisenhower will as time goes by."

He danced around the question of whether Goldwater had sewn up the Republican nomination, but made his preference for running against him so obvious that a *New York Times* headline the next day would read, "President Nudges Goldwater's Hat—Says He Thinks Senator Can Be G.O.P. Nominee." His hope that Goldwater would win the nomination was an open secret. "Give me good old Barry," he had told Fay, adding that then he could campaign without leaving the Oval Office. (He feared Governor Romney of Michigan the most. "No vice whatsoever, no smoking, no drinking," he said to Fay. "Imagine someone we know going off for twenty-four to forty-eight hours to fast and meditate, awaiting a message from the Lord on whether to run or not to run. Does that sound like one of the old gang?") He also preferred Goldwater because they had become friends while serving together in the Senate (Goldwater had praised his inaugural address, albeit condescendingly, saying, "God, I'd like to be able to do what that boy did there"), and he anticipated a clean campaign focused on their ideological differences. In fact, he felt so comfortable around Goldwater that when he arrived at the Oval Office for a meeting and found him sitting in his favorite rocking chair, he told him, "Keep your seat, Barry. And you can have this fucking job, too. If you want it."

WINSTON CHURCHILL'S SON, RANDOLPH, was staying in Washington with Kay Halle. He called Kennedy on Tuesday to report that Prime Minister Macmillan had been rushed to a London hospital for an emergency prostate operation and would be resigning within twenty-four hours. Kennedy invited him to come to the White House with Halle after the press conference, and they arrived just as John was poking his head out of a secret door in the kneehole of the desk as his father said, "I'm a great big wolf and I'm going to eat you up in one bite!" Caroline walked into the room, her shoulders hunched like a miniature version of her father's, and he told Halle, "You know, I've been taking care of the children because Jackie is away, and I'm having the most marvelous time."

He invited Tretick and Bergquist to join them. They came in as John was careening merrily around the room in his pajamas. Bergquist called it "a sight to gladden the eye and camera."

"What do you think of him?" Kennedy demanded. Before anyone answered, he asked, "Isn't he a charge?"

He struck Tretick as more interested in what they thought of John than in the photographs. Bergquist did not usually warm to small children, but she thought the boy was "an instant beguiler" and "not gorgeous" but "friendly, uninhibited, and unspoiled." Kennedy grabbed him, pulled up his pajama shirt, and began caressing the bare skin above his fanny, and she sensed a "joyous, funny, mutually fascinated, male-to-male, even sensuous" relationship.

John wiggled free and disappeared beneath the desk. He threw open the little door, poked his head out, and Tretick, almost faint with joy, took what he predicted would be "a hell of a picture."

Churchill was already four sheets to the wind. He asked a steward for a bottle of scotch that Kennedy eyed nervously, fearful it might appear in one of the photographs. To distract Churchill from the bottle, he asked John to tell Churchill a secret. The boy whispered some unintelligible words into Churchill's ear. Churchill slapped his head and exclaimed, "Oh no! No! No! No! Not *that*!" Bergquist and Tretick hung around on Thursday and Friday. They were there when John stood outside the Oval Office gaily chanting "G'myko! G'myko!" as the Soviet foreign minister conferred with his father, when he tried on Maxwell Taylor's gold-braided hat and imitated a chimpanzee, and when he went racing through the West Wing after someone had said he was cute, shouting, "I'm cute! I'm cute!"

Bergquist claimed she was not a "gung-ho idolater" but still considered Kennedy "a fascinating human animal," and "one of the smartest, quickest, funniest human beings" she knew. Because he was easily bored, she always saved her best jokes for him and came expecting lots of lighthearted banter. The Tretick photo shoot was different. She had not seen him in a year and sensed an unusual sadness and "a somber, sobering quality," telling a friend that there had been something "remote and tragic" about him. (Nine months later she shared her impressions with Jackie, who said, "Oh, you caught that, because that was very true about him.") The day after Tretick finished the shoot, Ted Sorensen told an interviewer that the president was "subject to moods" and sometimes discouraged by his inability to get things done as he would like. "He's exuberant at times. He's discouraged at times," he explained. "There are events which interest him and those that bore him. There are those which make him sad. And nothing is done by anyone else to dispel them, I suppose."

He had been riding an emotional roller coaster since the beginning of the summer. He had delivered his landmark American University and civil rights speeches, traveled to Germany and Ireland, and enjoyed the best weekends of his life on the Cape. Then had come the test ban treaty, the death of his son, the infighting among his advisers over Vietnam, his triumphant Western tour, and Jackie's perilous cruise. By the time Bergquist saw him, it appeared unlikely that Congress would pass his tax-cut and civil rights bills before the end of the year, Khrushchev had yet to respond to his proposal for a joint lunar mission, Prime Minister Harold Macmillan, the only foreign leader he counted as a genuine friend, was ill, and hearings into the Bobby Baker affair threatened to embroil him in the kind of scandal that had doomed Macmillan.

Bergquist was also shocked to find herself facing "a very serious preoccupied man who was obviously beginning to look middle-aged." Kennedy monitored his appearance so carefully that he must have been aware of this, and it may have contributed to his moodiness. He weighed himself after every swim, and Powers sensed a correlation between his mood and his weight. He had recently complained to Fay that his face was showing his weight and he was getting what he called "full jowls." (He should have been more concerned about his cholesterol, since an October 12 laboratory report showed it at 353, a dangerously high level.) Jackie's secretary Mary Gallagher had detected some reddish highlights in his hair at his birthday party in May. Photographs taken later that summer show his hair flecked with gray, but by October she was noticing more highlights. Like all the Kennedys, he was a fanatical sun-worshipper. The phrase "a healthy tan" was common in the sixties, and a deep one helped refute the rumors that he was sickly. His tan had to be dark in order to be visible on black-and-white television, and during the campaign he had ordered Lincoln to schedule a day off every week, preferably at a beach. When he was a young man a friend had chided him for spending so much time in the sun at Palm Beach so he could "look so handsome at these parties you go to." He had replied, "It's not only that I want to look that way, but it makes me feel that way. It gives me confidence, it makes me feel healthy."

He could keep up his tan during the winter at Palm Beach and during the summer on Cape Cod, but if being tanned really *did* make him happy, it made sense that he might feel lower in the autumn, when it was hurricane season in Florida and the sun in Hyannis Port was too weak to darken his skin.

AS SOON AS Foreign Minister Andrei Gromyko arrived for a meeting on October 10, Kennedy said, "Why don't we go out on to the terrace and talk one-to-one without interpreters?"

Gromyko spoke excellent English, so if Kennedy had merely wanted to hold a confidential conversation without interpreters, he could have sent them out of the room for a few minutes. He took Gromyko outside because what he wanted to say was so sensitive that he did not want to be overheard by Ambassador Dobrynin, Dean Rusk, or Llewellyn Thompson, who were also attending the meeting, or by any listening devices, including the microphone he had just activated. Rusk had displayed a similar caution when meeting with Gromyko at the United Nations the previous month. After reporting that the president wanted to build on the success of the test ban treaty, he had asked him, "Could we go for a ride out of town and carry on our conversation?" While walking along a suburban road without interpreters, Rusk told Gromyko that the president wanted to reduce the size of U.S. forces in Europe, news that would have dismayed America's NATO allies. Gromyko later wrote that the issue of U.S. troop levels in Europe had been present "visibly or invisibly at almost every U.S.-Soviet meeting since the war," and the fact that Kennedy was suddenly ready to discuss reducing U.S. forces had "seized our attention."

Kennedy and Gromyko had met several times during his presidency, most recently during the Cuban missile crisis, when he had impressed Gromyko with his candor by admitting that the Bay of Pigs had been a mistake, telling him, "I don't deny that the Cuban problem is a serious one, but I am restraining those who are in favor of actions which could lead to war."

Standing with Gromyko on the terrace outside the Oval Office, he again spoke candidly. "The fact is, there are two groups of the American population which are not always pleased when relations between our two countries are eased," he said. "One group consists of people who are always opposed to improvement for ideological reasons. . . . The other group are people of 'a particular nationality' [Gromyko assumed he was speaking of the 'Jewish lobby'] who think that, always and under all circumstances, the Kremlin will support the Arabs and be the enemy of Israel. . . . That is the reality. But I think it is still possible to improve relations, and I want Moscow to know that."

Gromyko said the Kremlin understood his situation, and that the positive reaction of the American public to the resolution of the Cuban crisis had shown that these two groups were a minority.

"I just wanted you to know some of the difficulties the President of the United States has to face when dealing with the questions of Soviet-U.S. relations." He also wanted Khrushchev to understand why, having signed the test ban treaty, installed the hotline, approved the wheat deal, proposed a joint moon mission, and entered into talks to ban nuclear weapons from space, he felt it necessary to slow down the pace for a while. His caution was a good example of what Walt Rostow considered one of his greatest strengths: a sense of history consisting "of a sense of the scale and timing of the problems he confronted, versus the capacities . . . of the United States."

He and Gromyko rejoined the others and held an unproductive discussion about arms control and a nonaggression pact, but agreed on a direct New York–Moscow air route and the establishment of consulates in Leningrad and Chicago—secondary issues but ones keeping the atmosphere of détente alive. "I don't want you to get discouraged," Kennedy said after they finished. "You may not be conscious of much progress where you sit, but we've been pulling and hauling around the United States for the last three months. . . . And we think, for us, we've made some progress in our relations with the Soviet Union. We may not get the German question disposed of and may not have solved all the matters, but considering some of the difficulties that both of our countries face—and internally and externally—it seems to me we've done pretty well. So I'm rather encouraged, not discouraged. I don't want you to be discouraged."

"Well, there is improvement in some things," Gromyko conceded.

Referring to Khrushchev's desire for more agreements, Kennedy said, "There is only a certain tempo which you can move in these matters." After mentioning the test ban and the wheat deal, he added, "Do you realize that in the summer of 1961, the Congress unanimously passed resolutions against trade with the Soviets and now we're going ahead, we hope, with this very large trade agreement that represents what's changed in American policy. . . . That's progress. We're talking about next week with going ahead with this matter on space, we're talking about getting the civil air agreement settled, we've got good communications. . . . I agree we haven't settled Berlin but considering that we've got a lot of problems, we've—you've taken some of your troops out of Cuba so it's less of a problem for us here—that's some progress."

"You are right, Mr. President. There is a change in the atmosphere."

As they were talking, one of Kennedy's children shouted "Daddy!" He told Gromyko to open the door so they could come in.

"Want to say hello to the minister?" he asked.

"They are very popular in our country," Gromyko said.

"His chief is the one who sent you Pushinka," he reminded them. "You know that? You have the puppies."

A reporter meeting the usually dour Gromyko afterward described him being in a relatively jovial and loquacious mood. He even cracked a joke about flying to the moon instead of returning to Moscow. The *Washington Post* took his high spirits as a sign that the Soviet Union was "eager to maintain a show of forward momentum in improving relations."

The same day that Kennedy met Gromyko, he received a letter from Khrushchev that was published in *Pravda* and U.S. newspapers. Khrushchev wrote that it was important "to develop further the success we have achieved, to seek solutions of other ripe international questions," and expressed hope that the test ban treaty "should become the beginning of a sharp turn toward broad relaxation of international tension." Ten days later, the State Department drafted a reply from Kennedy that read, "I am convinced then that the possibilities for an improvement in the international situation are real." The opportunities might be "fragile ones," he said, but the two powers should "move forward, lest our hopes of progress be jeopardized." Kennedy signed off on the letter, and McGeorge Bundy scrawled on its bottom, "Approved. Let's get it out." The State Department never sent it, an inexplicable error not coming to light until December. A "clerical misunderstanding" was blamed, an explanation that strains credulity.

Earl Blaik and Kenneth Royall followed Gromyko into the Oval Office to report on their mission to Birmingham. Mayor Boutwell had brought an all-white delegation to the airport to meet them, and after some perfunctory handshakes had declared that blame for his city's racial strife lay with "professional outsiders who thrive on the fruits of tension and unrest." Boutwell had also called their mission "advisory"—meaning he would not be bound by their recommendations—and accompanied them to an exclusive whites-only club for lunch.

During the next several days they had met five hundred prominent whites and blacks, but never in an integrated group. (They may have also informed Kennedy that while they were in the city two bombs exploded in a middle-class black neighborhood, a Klan wizard posted bail for two white men charged with possessing dynamite, and Alabama state troopers flew Confederate battle flags while patrolling black neighborhoods.) In an effort to lighten their dispiriting report, Blaik asked Kennedy, "How is your sense of humor?" and went on to describe a sign he had seen proclaiming "Kennedy for King—Goldwater for President." There was a long pause until Kennedy got the "joke"—the sign had meant he was "for" the Reverend Martin Luther King, Jr.

IN DECEMBER 1955, six years before Kennedy established the President's Commission on the Status of Women and gave it the task of making recommendations "for overcoming discrimination in government and private employment on the basis of sex," he had sat by the pool in Palm Beach reading the second volume of a biography of his hero Lord Melbourne, the nineteenth-century British statesman known for his hedonism, intellect, and aristocratic style, and writing in a notebook that one reason he found European history more interesting than American was that American women were by comparison "not glamorous." Instead, they were "either prostitutes or housewives," who did not "play much of a role in [the] cultural or intellectual life of [the] country." It was not that surprising an observation for a man who had grown up at a time when most women *were* housewives, and who had attended an all-male prep school and college, served in a military that segregated the sexes, and spent fourteen years in Congress with few female members.

The man who received the eighty-six-page report from the Status of Women Commission at an East Room ceremony on Friday, October 11, was not that different from the misogynist of 1955. The previous month he had welcomed a delegation of female delegates to the United Nations General Assembly to the White House. Their spokesman, the elderly Daw Mya Sein of Burma, answered his greeting by saying, "Thank you very much, Mr. President, for receiving us here today. And I hope in a few years' time that a woman president will be standing just where you are now, welcoming the *men* delegates to the United Nations." Without missing a beat, he replied, "Madam, you are raising the standard of rebellion in the royal pavilion."

His quick comeback impressed the U.S. delegate Marietta Tree, but she was disappointed when he followed it by saying, "I never know whether women want to be referred to as women or as politicians." Deputy Assistant Secretary of State Katie Louchheim muttered, "If they are politicians, they don't care." He had once made a similar observation to Tree, saying, "I don't know how to treat women politicians—as women or as politicians," so he obviously considered it a clever riposte. Tree had the same reaction as Louchheim, that women "just thought of themselves as people involved in politics." It confirmed her impression that Kennedy was "quite uneasy with women who were involved with politics," and that "for the most part, women were a necessary adjunct to his life, he simply enjoyed their beauty and charms without particularly [enjoying] . . . their intellectual side or their counsel." Nancy Dickerson had a similar take and thought that although he had "great sex appeal" he was also "the complete male chauvinist." He loved being around women and sometimes asked for their opinions, she said, but "thought it ridiculous to pay them the same [attention] as men." Earlier in his term she had shared a flight with him on Air Force One to New York, where he was speaking at a convention of women in radio and television. He showed her his speech and asked for suggestions. She urged him to say, "Let's get women off the weather beat and let them be newscasters." He looked shocked, she recalled, "as if I was certifiable."

Jackie encouraged his prejudices, once asking him why women like Madame Nhu and Clare Boothe Luce (the former congresswoman, U.S. ambassador to Italy, and wife of the publisher Henry Luce), who were both obviously "attractive to men," also had "this queer thing for power"—an attribute that she called "unattractive in a woman." He told her, "It's strange, but it's really because they resent getting their power through men." As a result, he thought, they ended up hating men.

While he was in New York that autumn Kennedy had asked the noted journalist Clayton Fritchey, who was serving on Adlai Stevenson's staff, to explain why Stevenson appealed to so many women, Jackie included. "Look, I may not be the best-looking guy in the world," Kennedy said, "but, for God's sake, Adlai's half-bald, he's got a paunch, he wears his clothes in a dumpy kind of way. What's he got that I haven't got?" The difference, Fritchey explained, was that although they both loved women, Adlai also liked them, and gave them the impression that they were "intelligent and worth listening to."

"I don't say you're wrong, but I'm not sure I can go to those lengths," he admitted.

Assistant Secretary of Labor Esther Peterson, the highest-ranking woman in the administration and vice chair of his Commission on Women, thought his attitudes toward women compared poorly with those of Bobby, who never gave her the feeling that he was treating her differently because she was a woman. But when he walked into the East Room to accept Peterson's report, he immediately noticed that men had taken all the front-row seats while the women sat or stood in the rear. He said, "Gentlemen, we are here to talk about the status of women," and led two female legislators to seats that men had hastily evacuated. That accomplished, he offered the women a few extemporaneous banalities, praising their report as "very useful" and declaring, "I think we ought to look as a society at what our women are doing and the opportunities before them." Flummoxed about what else to say, he recited his favorite all-purpose line, recounting how the

Greeks had defined happiness as "the full use of your powers along lines of excel-lence," and wondered if American society afforded women this opportunity, although the report that he was praising proved that it did not.

TRETICK WAS ECSTATIC about the photographs but still lacked a good color shot for the cover. On Friday, he persuaded Kennedy to sit on a bench in the Rose Garden with his son, but the light was harsh, the boy restless, and the session ended abruptly when Taylor and McNamara arrived for a briefing. After Kennedy brushed off Tretick's request for another sitting, Bergquist asked if he had seen the recent photograph of the Nixons in Berlin. She said it showed the Nixons and their girls standing "like waxwork dummies" and gazing at the Wall with "glazed, uneasy smiles." If he would give Tretick one more session, she'd bet his photographs could easily beat that sorry Nixon picture.

"Was it really that bad?" he asked, grinning broadly before inviting them to fly to Camp David in the morning so Tretick could try again.

Schlesinger ran into him on Friday evening, and asked after Jackie. He said she was enjoying herself and admitted having pressured Roosevelt into accom-panying her. As Schlesinger was leaving, he called out wistfully, "What are you doing tonight?" Schlesinger noted in his diary, "I hate to repeat the cliché about the loneliness of the job, but it *is* a lonely job."

John and Caroline had flown to Camp David the night before and met him at the landing pad. He had brought a life-sized toy parrot with a tape recorder embedded inside that he hoped would distract John long enough for Tretick to get his cover shot. He placed it on the tarmac in front of the helicopter, pushed a button, and the parrot said, in Kennedy's flat Boston accent, "My name is Polly Parrot. Would you like to fly with me in my helicopter?" John answered, "Hi, Poll Parrot, would you like a stick of gum?" and dashed off before Tretick could raise his camera.

Father and son finally posed together on a wrought-iron bench. John stood with his hand on his father's shoulder, and both flashed their toothy Kennedy smiles. It would appear on the cover of the December 3, 1963, issue, available on newsstands November 18. Kennedy obtained copies of the photographs several weeks earlier and showed them off around the White House, becoming "quite a bore on the subject," according to Tretick. Kennedy had expected Jackie to be furious. Instead, she said wearily, "No, Jack. I guess it's your year. You can use the children any way you want, and if you want me to pose in the bathtub for photographs, I suppose I should do that, to help out."

Her cruise was proving as embarrassing as he had feared. She was photographed sightseeing in Istanbul, exploring ruins in Crete, and zipping around on speedboats. A *Newsweek* article titled "Caesar's Wife" suggested that the trip had exhausted her immunity from criticism. Other articles reported that the "Millionaire Greek ship owner" had ordered forty-four pounds of lobster for a gala shipboard dinner and given her command of his "floating pleasure dome." The chairman of the Republican National Committee denounced "all-night parties in foreign lands," and a GOP congressman criticized her for accepting "the lavish hospitality of a man who had so defrauded the American public."

Communication proved difficult. The Greek switchboards dropped connections and one late-night call was routed to a Mrs. Kennedy married to a Foreign Service officer in Athens. After a paparazzo with a telephoto lens snapped her in a bikini, Kennedy called, read her some of the articles, and suggested she come home early. When she protested that it would be difficult to get ashore, he said, "You're a good swimmer, Jackie."

Her friend Princess Irene Galitzine was also aboard, giving the cruise an additional jet-set patina. Galitzine was descended from Russian nobility and had become one of Italy's most famous designers on the strength of launching a line of "palazzo pajamas," colorful silk evening trousers that had become the rage after Claudia Cardinale wore a pair in the first Pink Panther movie. The Italian industrialist Gianni Agnelli had introduced the two women during Jackie's holiday in Amalfi, and Galitzine had been mesmerized by how her irregular teeth, large mouth, and big feet added up to something "inexplicably fascinating and beautiful." During the cruise she noticed that Jackie would sometimes lock herself in her cabin after dinner with a glass of champagne. Jackie explained that she was writing to her husband and when she did this she felt as if she were talking to him. She expressed sentiments in her letters that she found too hard to tell him in person, writing, "I loved you from the first moment I saw you," and "If I hadn't married you my life would have been tragic because the definition of tragedy is a waste. But ten years later I love you so much more." In similar letters from Italy she had written, "I think that I am lucky to miss you—I know that I always exaggerate but I pity everybody else who is married," and concluding, "I'll show you how much I love you when I get back."

The cruise ended on October 13, but she decided to extend her holiday by accepting an invitation from King Hassan of Morocco to visit Marrakech. The king sent his private jet to collect her and installed her in a guest palace. Kennedy asked a military aide to ascertain its size and appearance, no doubt praying that it would be small and modest. She shopped in the bazaars, admiring brass pots, rugs, and leather goods that the *New York Times* speculated would be sent to her as gifts. It was also reported that the king had flown in hairdressers from Paris who had given her "a Parisian style to suit her personality."

CAMP DAVID AND WASHINGTON

On Monday, Salinger announced that the president had decided to stay at Camp David with his children because it was a lovely day and he had no pressing engagements in Washington. Articles that morning in the *New York Times* and the *Washington Post,* ones he surely read, summarized the findings of a Louis Harris poll surveying the racial attitudes of white Americans. The poll confirmed what he had told Birmingham's white leaders: that providing equal access to public accommodations and university classrooms was easy compared with integrating neighborhoods and public schools. It reported that although 71 percent of whites, including a solid majority in the South, believed that "Negroes are discriminated against," many thought that they were partly to blame. Sixty-six percent thought they "had less ambition" than whites, and 55 percent cited their "looser morals." The poll concluded that "substantial numbers of white people in both the North and the South still believe the composite stereotype of the Negro as lazy, unintelligent and inherently inferior to whites."

A Gallup poll released that weekend showed Kennedy's approval rating falling to 57 percent nationally, the lowest level of his presidency, and dropping in the South from 50 to 35 percent after he submitted his civil rights bill. There was better news in a second Harris poll appearing in the *Washington Post* on Monday. It reported that although he had lost the support of 6.5 million Americans who had voted for him in 1960, he had gained the backing of 11 million who had voted for Nixon, meaning that if the election were held that day, he would defeat a

Republican opponent by 4.5 million votes. His prospects in the Electoral College were less encouraging, with Harris predicting the loss of half of the Southern states he had won in 1960, a dismal showing that *Newsweek* blamed on his being "the most widely disliked Democratic President of this century among white Southerners."

His civil rights bill remained stalled in the House Judiciary Committee, where a subcommittee dominated by liberals had added provisions making it too extreme to appeal to Republican moderates, many of whom represented districts containing the very white-middle-class voters that the Harris poll had identified as opposing discrimination in theory yet resisting the integration of their own neighborhoods and schools. The liberals had added a Fair Employment Practices Commission (FEPC) to the bill, a more expansive definition of "public accommodations," and a clause permitting the Department of Justice to bring suit in federal court on behalf of individual Americans whose rights were being infringed. Writing about the impasse in the *New York Times*, Anthony Lewis cautioned that "by pressing for all they [the liberals] want, they risk alienating the votes needed to pass anything at all." Southern Democrats on the Judiciary Committee confirmed the folly of the liberals' position by announcing their intention to vote for the bill because they were certain that it would be easily defeated on the House floor.

Bobby Kennedy testified before the House Judiciary Committee on Tuesday. He criticized the liberals' additions to the public accommodations section, arguing that they would lead to the regulation of law firms, medical practices, and other private entities, but then surprised the committee by endorsing an FEPC. It was a shrewd compromise. By capitulating on the issue that meant the most to the civil rights movement, he and the president were making it harder for liberals to demand a bill incorporating everything they wanted. The *Detroit Free Press* called it "politics in its purest definition—the art of the possible," and the *Atlanta Constitution* declared, "There always comes a time in the legislative process for compromise." Two days after Bobby's testimony, Representative William McCulloch of Ohio, the ranking Republican on the House Judiciary Committee, reported an "improved climate" for a bipartisan bill. A spokesman for the Washington NAACP attacked the compromise as a "sell out," but given the polls showing that a majority of Americans believed the president was moving too fast on civil rights, it was a courageous one.

KENNEDY'S BACK HAD continued bothering him during the weekend, and he asked Dr. Kraus to meet him at the White House when he returned from Camp David. Kraus noted that he was experiencing discomfort on his left side, and told him that if he resumed his full exercise program, his pain would disappear. He again urged him to discard his back brace. Kennedy promised to get rid of it on January 1, 1964, making it a New Year's resolution.

IN THE SPRING OF 1964, Jackie would tell Father Richard McSorley, a Jesuit priest at Georgetown University who had become her confidant, "I was melancholy after the death of our baby and stayed away last fall longer than I needed to. I could have made his life so much happier, especially for the last few weeks. I could have tried harder to get out of my melancholy." Her comment about staying away too long probably referred to the weeks she had spent in Newport in September, her cruise, and her decision to add an excursion to Morocco, a change of plans enabling her to skip the October 15 state dinner for Prime Minister Seán Lemass of Ireland, an event that may have meant more to her husband than any of his presidency.

There were no real foreign policy reasons for giving Lemass a state visit, and Kennedy was doing it to thank him for his hospitality in Ireland the previous summer. The Irish ambassador to Washington, Thomas Kiernan, believed that this trip had changed Kennedy's feelings about his ancestral homeland. Before, Kiernan said, his "Harvard attitude" and desire "to be accepted as part of the establishment" had led him to side with Great Britain in disputes between the two nations. These prejudices began falling away in Ireland. As he and Kiernan flew from Dublin to Galway by helicopter, he had pointed out the largest houses and asked how much they would cost. Back at the White House, he had shoved a picture postcard of his family's ancestral home into the frame of his bedroom mirror, adding it to a postcard that Caroline had sent him from Amalfi, a snapshot of her standing in her mother's shoes, and a Polaroid photograph of Jackie— all thrust into the mirror at odd angles and resembling the kind of collage found on any family refrigerator.

Jackie was willing to indulge his affection for Ireland, up to a point. When

Kiernan presented him with the Kennedy coat of arms, she had it mounted on a seal ring that he mischievously used on a letter to Queen Elizabeth. She decided things were going too far when he asked Kiernan to track down *her* coat of arms. She complained that he wanted to put her Irish crest on his cufflinks, on everything, and Kiernan sensed that the Irish were "getting her down." Kennedy's insistence that the three days he had spent in Ireland had been the happiest of his life could not have helped, since these were also three days that he had spent without her. So instead of attending the Lemass dinner she stayed in Morocco, where it was reported that "like a desert queen she sat before a low table covered with a lace tablecloth and was offered sweet mint tea in golden glasses."

Lemass received the full treatment: a multigun salute, honor guard, and motorcade in an open car. After the state dinner, Kennedy invited a dozen guests upstairs to the family quarters to continue the party. The Air Force string band played Irish melodies, Gene Kelly danced, and Dorothy Turbidy, a Kennedy family friend who had accompanied Lemass from Ireland, sang "The Boys of Wexford," the same song that children from that town had sung to welcome Kennedy to Dublin. Its subject was bleak but stirring—a battle during the 1798 Irish Rebellion when Irishmen armed only with pikes and pitchforks had defeated the British at Wexford, only to be wiped out days later. After noticing how much the song had moved him, Eunice had bought a recording to give him for Christmas. Turbidy sang "Wexford" well, according to Kennedy's former Navy buddy, Assistant Secretary of the Treasury James Reed, but it was a sad song, and despite having known Kennedy for years, Reed thought he had never seen such sadness so plainly visible on his face.

The next day Kennedy became the first American president to host a Communist head of state at the White House. Inviting Josip Broz Tito of Yugoslavia to Washington had been a brave move, particularly a year before Kennedy would be seeking reelection, but the way Kennedy treated Tito was not. The result was a half-profile in courage. After leading the most effective anti-Nazi partisan movement of World War II, Tito had broken with the Soviet Union in 1948 and accepted U.S. aid under the Marshall Plan. Truman and Eisenhower had provided Yugoslavia with economic assistance and, after declaring that he did not consider Tito a Soviet puppet, Eisenhower had invited him to the White House, only to rescind the invitation following protests from Congress. Kennedy faced similar pressures. Republicans denounced him for hosting a Communist, with Goldwater declaring, "To the disgrace of every living American, we are welcoming this tyrant to the American capital."

Kennedy attempted to make Tito's visit as brief and invisible as possible. There were no pictures of him welcoming the Yugoslav leader, and the official photograph showed them on opposite sides of a vast conference table, with only the back of Kennedy's head visible. Hundreds of Yugoslav Americans picketed the White House, leading Kennedy to complain that every hour Tito remained in town was costing him ten thousand votes. The State Department described their talks as "cordial and frank," but there were rocky moments. Tito realized that he was not getting a first-class welcome, and when Kennedy tried to pump him for information about the Latin American nations he had just visited, he made a pompous disclaimer about never taking an interest in the internal politics of a host nation. Kennedy quickly changed course, becoming chummy and making him feel they were two sophisticated men who could speak frankly. "Look, I asked for your opinion, I didn't ask you for a report," he said. "Now come on and tell me, who's winning in the Communist party apparatus in Latin America, the Chinese or the Russians?" Tito replied, "Well, if you're really going to put it that way, I will tell you."

Jackie called before leaving Morocco to say she was furious that de Gaulle—that "spiteful man"—had refused to sign the test ban treaty. She claimed that she never wanted to go near the French again, adding that she had decided against making a brief stop in Paris on the way home.

"No, no, you mustn't be like that," he said. "Don't you see that you're the one avenue that's open [to de Gaulle and the French], and they think I'm a so-and-so but they think you're nice because you like France." Repeating the maxim that had guided him through the Cuban missile crisis, he urged her to remember that "you must always leave an avenue open." She changed her mind and flew through Orly. During a short layover she chose a dozen silk ties for him from a collection that she had asked Dior to messenger to the airport, and accepted a large bouquet of roses and orchids sent by de Gaulle.

The moment her private plane landed in Washington, Caroline and John dashed up the metal staircase and disappeared inside. Caroline carried a clay bird's nest she had made in pottery class, taking to heart her mother's advice not to buy things for people, but to learn something from memory or make something. When Kennedy got to the door she reached out with a white-gloved hand to caress his neck and draw him inside. Caroline recited a French sentence she had memorized for the occasion, saying, "*Je suis content de te revoir.*" Kennedy's French was so rudimentary that he thought "*content*" only meant "contented" and told Caroline it was too weak for the occasion. The family emerged together. King Hassan's Parisian hairdresser had given Jackie a simple, straight cut. Perhaps she was making amends for the Battelle hairdo.

Later that evening she told him, "I'll never be away again at such important moments of accomplishment." Referring to the test ban treaty ceremony, she added, "Everyone needs to have support and pride from those they love when they have accomplished something great." Still, she took the children to Camp David the next day, leaving him alone on the eve of his departure for a two-day trip to New England.

On Friday morning, an editorial in the right-wing *Delaware State News* declared, "Yes, Virginia, there is a Santa Claus. His name right now happens to be Kennedy—let's shoot him, literally, before Christmas." That afternoon, Kennedy addressed members of the National Trust for Historic Preservation. Standing on a platform on the South Lawn, he recited a passage from a poem by Edna St. Vincent Millay: "Safe upon the solid rock / the ugly houses stand. / Come see my shining palace. / It is built upon the sand."

ORONO, BOSTON, AND CAPE COD

Kennedy's Western tour had demonstrated that Americans could become as weary of a cold war as a hot one. The test ban treaty ratification battle had demonstrated the importance of convincing Congress that an agreement with the Soviet Union need not compromise national security. He combined these lessons in a speech that he delivered at the University of Maine's Alumni Stadium in Orono on Saturday morning. After speaking of "new rays of hope on the horizon," he cautioned that "we still live in the shadows of war," and promised to maintain "our readiness for war" but pursue "every avenue for peace." After recounting how one German statesman had asked another shortly after the start of the First World War, "How did it all happen?" only to have the other reply, "Ah, if only one knew," he said, "If this planet is ever ravaged by nuclear war, if three hundred million Americans, Russians, and Europeans are wiped out by a sixty-minute nuclear exchange, if the pitiable survivors of that devastation can then endure the ensuing fire, poison, chaos, and catastrophe, I do not want one of those survivors to ask another, 'How did it all happen?' and to receive the incredible reply, 'Ah, if only one knew.'" He received a standing ovation for what would be called a major foreign policy speech and the opening salvo of his campaign—a warning to those opposing détente that they were making more likely a nuclear conflagration that could kill millions of Americans.

Two hours later he walked into Harvard's Soldiers Field stadium during the early minutes of the Columbia game. Spectators jumped up, pointing and cheering, and the Harvard band played "Hail to the Chief." His own Harvard football career had been a fiasco. He had reported weighing 150 pounds and was demoted during the season first to the "B" and then to the "C" freshman team. But his enthusiasm for the game had remained undiminished, and he smoked a cigar, waved to a friend's son as he came off the field, and applauded enthusiastically when a Harvard field goal tied the score. He had decided to attend at the last minute, leaving the Secret Service no time to screen his neighbors in the stadium. He sat between Larry O'Brien and Dave Powers, high on the fifty-yard line and surrounded by Harvard students.

Near the end of the first half he turned to O'Donnell and said, "I want to go to Patrick's grave, and I want to go there alone, with nobody from the newspapers following me." He stayed for the halftime show, laughing when the Columbia band performed a spoof about a presidential candidate named "J. Barry Silverwater." Police blocked the exits from the parking lot to prevent anyone following him to the cemetery. The trip was less spontaneous than it appeared. He had designed Patrick's headstone, giving Lincoln a sketch and instructing her to have it installed before October 19. He had also brought along a bouquet of yellow chrysanthemums. After standing silently for several minutes at the grave, he said, "Patrick seems so alone here," and wondered if he would be buried alongside him.

He had several hours before he was due at the All New England Salute Dinner, a fund-raising event at the Commonwealth Armory. While heading back to his hotel he asked his driver to stop at one of his favorite haunts, the Boylston Street Schrafft's. A waitress cried, "Oh, my God, it's the President!" and dropped a glass. A teenage soda jerk kept saying, "Look who's here. . . . Look who's here."

He signed menus and napkins, ate a butterscotch sundae, ordered a chocolate frappe to go, and chatted about old times with Thomas Pellegriti, who had driven him during his congressional campaigns and now managed the restaurant. As he began walking down Boylston Street there were shouts of "That's the President!" accompanied by the *bang* of fender-benders as drivers took their eyes off the road.

His impromptu walk was another security headache for the Secret Service and Boston police during a day that had already demonstrated how difficult it was to protect a president who was determined to move about freely and spontaneously. At Logan Airport he had walked straight through the honor guard and around the Secret Service to shake hands with mechanics. While being driven to his hotel he had insisted on stopping to greet a group of nuns standing outside their convent. He had slipped out a side entrance of the hotel with a small contingent of Secret Service agents, leaving police and reporters to make a mad dash to the Harvard Stadium, and while riding to the armory that evening he stood in the back of an open car in a dinner jacket, waving at crowds three deep and insisting on traveling so slowly that he arrived twenty minutes late.

He flew to Hyannis Port by helicopter on Sunday morning, landing on the lawn of his parents' home. He took his father for a gentle excursion on their power boat, and they later watched a football game on television. He asked the family chauffeur if he was getting "the best care," adding simply, "I miss him." During the afternoon he crossed the street to visit Larry Newman and his daughter Leighlan ("Lee-Lee"), who had nicknamed him "Mr. Kissable." She rushed up and grabbed his legs, then climbed into his lap as he and her father discussed Vietnam. He told Newman that MacArthur and de Gaulle had used identical words to warn him against committing U.S. forces to a land war in Asia. "The first thing I do when I'm reelected, I'm going to get the Americans out of Vietnam," he said. "Exactly how I'm going to do it, right now, I don't know, but that is my number one priority—get out of Southeast Asia. . . . We are not going to have men ground up in this fashion, this far away from home. I'm going to get those guys out because we're not going to find ourselves in a war it's impossible to win." As he left he smiled and said, "I'd like to be around when Lee-Lee's ten or fifteen years older."

The weather was too cool for his father to sit on his porch Monday morning, so he climbed to his second-floor room to kiss him good-bye. After he left the room, Nurse Dallas wheeled Joe Kennedy's bed to the doors opening onto the balcony so he could watch his son's helicopter lift off. Moments later she heard the elevator door open and looked over her shoulder to see the president pressing a finger to his lips. He touched his father lightly on the shoulder and said, "Look who's here, Dad." He kissed him again and whispered, "Mrs. Dallas, take good care of Dad before I come back."

Tears filled his eyes as his helicopter rose above the house. "He's the one who made all this possible," he told Powers, "and look at him now."

Monday, October 21

WASHINGTON

A front-page article in the Sunday, October 20, *New York Times* by the noted journalist Homer Bigart that described the desperate poverty in eastern Kentucky had left Kennedy so dismayed that it was almost all he wanted to talk about with Walter Heller on Monday. Bigart reported that unemployed coal miners and subsistence farmers faced "another winter of idleness and grinding poverty," and wrote of "the pinched faces of hungry children," "listless defeated men," a tar-paper-shack school "unfit for cattle" where "daylight shone through gaping holes between rotting planks," and "pot-bellied and anemic" children hauling water from a creek "fouled with garbage and discarded mattresses," so hungry they ate the dirt from chimneys.

Kennedy had witnessed poverty like this while campaigning in the 1960 West Virginia primary. Although he had seen wretched people in postwar Berlin, Asia, and Latin America, West Virginia was the first time he had faced abject poverty in his own country, and he often referred to the "blight" of poverty in the state during the general election, speaking about children sharing their school lunches with their parents, and families receiving "surplus food packages and no hope for the future." He delivered an inaugural address with more references to poverty, hunger, and suffering than those given by FDR, Eisenhower, Truman, or any president to follow. After declaring that "man holds in his mortal hands the power to abolish all forms of human poverty and all forms of human life," he had pledged to "assist free men and free governments in casting off the chains of poverty." His first official act as president had been to sign an executive order doubling the food rations supplied to four million poor Americans. Hunger and poverty continued to concern him, and in his 1963 State of the Union address he had said, "Tax reduction alone is not enough . . . to improve the lives of thirty-two million Americans who live on the outskirts of poverty," "The quality of American life must keep pace with the quality of American goods," and "This country cannot afford to be materially rich and spiritually poor."

In the spring of 1963, Heller had sent him a memorandum titled "Progress and Poverty," warning that America was experiencing a "drastic slowdown in the rate at which the economy is taking people out of poverty." Throughout the spring and summer he and Heller discussed how to remedy this. Heller admitted that although the tax cut might create several million jobs it would not help the poorest of the poor—"those caught in a web of illiteracy, lack of skills, poor health, and squalor." He gave Kennedy an economic and statistical analysis of this group and suggested an "attack on poverty." At a cabinet meeting that fall, Kennedy announced that "disadvantaged groups other than Negroes now deserve our attention," and after reading the testimony Heller was proposing to give to the Senate Finance Committee in support of the tax cut, he said, "Walter, first we're going to get your tax cut, and then we're going to get my expenditure program [his attack on poverty]."

He told Heller during their meeting on October 21 that in light of the Bigart article he had decided that attacking poverty would be a major theme of his reelection campaign, and he planned on traveling to poverty-stricken areas to "arouse the American conscience." Heller wrote in a memorandum, "It's perfectly clear that he is aroused by this, and if we could really produce a program to fill the bill, he would be inclined to run with it."

GOOD HOUSEKEEPING MAGAZINE had commissioned the best-selling author and columnist Jim Bishop to write "A Day in the Life of President Kennedy." Bishop arrived at the White House on Monday with his wife, Kelly, puzzled that the president had agreed to let them snoop around and interview his staff and family for an article appearing in a magazine that even he dismissed as "a publication for women, replete with recipes, patterns, deodorants, and articles about what to do with your cheating husband." Bishop probably didn't want to admit that Kennedy was cooperating because he anticipated an article as uncritical and flattering as his "A Day in the Life of President Eisenhower."

Bishop arrived at the White House a skeptic who believed the problem with Kennedy was that "one never knew how much of the warmth was real." He had expected a perfunctory meeting lasting a few minutes. Instead, Kennedy stuck out his hand and said "Jim," as if they were old friends, and "Kelly" before he could introduce his wife. He suggested that since Bishop's ancestors had also come from County Wexford he might like to see his photographs of his recent trip there. As they leafed through his scrapbook he smiled at Kelly and said, "He ought to get a book out of this, don't you think?"

Bishop protested that he was writing only an article.

"Stretch it a little and you'll have a book." Turning to Kelly, he said, "You speak to him."

Jackie would have resented Bishop's intrusion at the best of times. His presence this week was particularly unwelcome. She had returned from her trip feeling guilty and eager to build on the new intimacy she sensed between herself and her husband. A number of observers had noticed their relationship changing for the better. The reporter Helen Thomas thought they had "grown closer" after Patrick's death and "appeared genuinely affectionate toward each other." Roswell Gilpatric would later say, "You could see now that he liked being with her. . . . I think their marriage was really beginning to work out." Jackie agreed, telling Father McSorley, "It took us a very long time for us to work everything out, but we did, and we were about to have a real life together." Because these statements were made after Dallas, they cannot escape the suspicion that they were motivated by a desire to paint the couple's final days together as happy ones. There may have been some wishful thinking and exaggeration, but there is enough contemporaneous evidence to confirm their essential truth.

On Monday, with her privacy already under assault from Jim and Kelly Bishop, Jackie called J. B. West into her bedroom and said in her trademark whisper, "Oh, Mr. West, I've gotten myself into something. Can you help me get out of it?" She explained that although she had invited Princess Galitzine to stay at the White House, "now *we've* changed our minds," and she wanted to rescind the invitation so she and the president could spend the next several nights alone. "Could you help us cook up something so we can get out of having her as a houseguest?" she asked. Before he could answer, she continued, "Would you fix up the Queen's Room and the Lincoln Room so that it looks like we're still decorating them, and I'll show her our guest rooms are not available?"

West had the furniture covered with drop cloths, the rugs rolled up, and buckets of white paint and dirty brushes set out. As a finishing touch, he scattered around ashtrays filled with butts left by the imaginary workmen. When Princess Galitzine came to dinner, Kennedy walked her down the East Hall, stopping to point out the renovations in the Queen's Room and say, "And you see, this is where you would have spent the night if Jackie hadn't been redecorating again."

Tuesday, October 22–Friday, October 25

WASHINGTON

Kennedy told Evelyn Lincoln that Tuesday had been so awful that he felt like "packing his bags and leaving." During dinner with Jackie and the Bradlees he complained about it being "miserable" from start to finish. The Birmingham Police Department continued refusing to hire a Negro officer, and liberals on the Judiciary Committee continued pushing a civil rights bill that could not pass the House. His invitation to the Bradlees had been the usual last-minute summons, tendered at the end of the day when he wanted to relax, celebrate, bitch, or do all three. His agenda that evening included Jackie's cruise and the Bobby Baker scandal. Before the Senate Rules Committee began taking testimony, he hoped to persuade Bradlee (and *Newsweek*) that rumors of sexual misbehavior by anyone in the White House were unfounded. He told Bradlee that he had always viewed Baker "primarily as a rogue, not a crook," adding, "He was always telling me where he could get the cutest little girls, but he never did." Bradlee noted that Kennedy had appeared "reluctant to take reports of Baker's sexual adventures too seriously, or the trouble he [Baker] might get into as a result of them," and had been "briefed to the teeth."

Kennedy said he was certain Johnson had not been "on the take" while he was vice president, but before that, he was "not so sure." This comment prompted a discussion of what Bradlee called Washington's "new, sophisticated immorality," the practice of currying favor with congressmen by paying their law firms exorbitant fees for make-work projects, and steering contracts to firms in which an elected official had a financial interest.

Kennedy said he had just learned that J. Paul Getty, one of the richest men in the world, had paid only $22,000 in taxes the previous year. Bradlee replied that if he wanted to get a tax-reform bill through Congress, he should give this kind of information to *Newsweek*. "Maybe after 1964," he said, a phrase Bradlee had noticed him using more often these days. Most presidents enjoy their greatest successes during their first term, but because Kennedy's victory had been so narrow, Schlesinger believed that he was "looking forward increasingly to his second term as his big season of accomplishment." When Kermit Gordon described what he called an "especially noxious subsidy situation"—a case in which the beneficiaries of the subsidy were those who were already the richest in the business—Kennedy said, "I am looking forward to the second term, when I can really take this government to pieces and stop this sort of thing."

During dinner Jackie called Onassis "an alive and vital person," and praised her husband for being "really nice and understanding." Sensing that she was remorseful about the bad publicity surrounding her cruise, Kennedy joked that this might be a good time to capitalize on her guilt. "Maybe now you'll come with us to Texas next month," he said.

"Sure I will, Jack," she said, flipping open a red leather appointment book and writing "TEXAS" across three days in November.

DURING THE WEEK KENNEDY grilled his staff about their encounters with the Bishops. Evelyn Lincoln passed along a tidbit that she knew would delight him. Bishop had recounted that while he was researching "A Day in the Life of President Eisenhower," the president's secretary Ann Whitman had told him that Ike often sat at his desk for hours on end with nothing to do, becoming so bored that he would plaintively ask for something to keep him busy. "I told Mr. Bishop," she said firmly, "that was *not* the case with President Kennedy."

He was unhappy that George Thomas had told Bishop that he owned twenty-five pairs of shoes. "Don't you see how most of the people who own only one pair of shoes might resent my having twenty-five?" he asked him. "Even if it were true?" Thomas had also revealed that he sometimes went through five shirts a day, changed his entire wardrobe between meetings, and to facilitate this, Thomas would hang a new set of clothes in the small bathroom off the Oval Office so he could dart in and replace a blue suit with a brown one, complete with matching tie, shoes, and shirt. Bishop, incurious to a fault, had failed to ascertain whether vanity, a fetish for clean clothes, or a desire to match his wardrobe to a visitor's position or personality lay behind all this frantic wardrobe-changing.

Bishop interviewed Jackie during a chaotic Wednesday morning. As they spoke, John dashed from the bathroom naked and one family dog bit another. He found it odd that she answered his questions while staring at Kelly as if he were invisible. He asked her for a "word portrait" of an average evening at home with the president. With a fixed smile, she described him bringing his "home-work" upstairs to the family quarters and reading it—a response in keeping with her rule of "minimum information with maximum politeness."

She informed Bishop that she planned to accompany her husband to Texas the next month. He wondered if that meant parades and all. "Parades and chicken banquets," she insisted.

ON WEDNESDAY IT SEEMED POSSIBLE that the Baker scandal and a coup in South Vietnam might reach a climax simultaneously.

Following a two-hour executive session, the chairman of the House Rules Com-mittee told reporters, "We'll start with Baker. Where it spreads from there we don't know," and the *Washington Post* pointed out that the Senate resolution mandated "an investigation of any possible conflicts of interest or other improprieties."

According to a cable from the CIA station chief in Saigon, "Highly reliable source reports coup imminent led by Lt. Col. Pham Ngoc Thao." The source, however, feared the "coup may fall apart en route." Kennedy received a cable from Lodge the same day warning that, "in the contest with Viet Cong, we are at present not doing much more than holding our own," and reporting that because of recent restrictions on U.S. aid to the regime, "experienced observers believe that our actions are creating favorable conditions for a coup. . . . Although I as yet see no one who looks as though he means business in this regard."

Kennedy decided to send his Harvard roommate Torbert ("Torby") Macdon-ald to Saigon to warn Diem that a coup was imminent and his life might be in danger. Following Kennedy's script, Macdonald told Diem, "They're going to kill you. You've got to get out of there temporarily to seek refuge in the American embassy and you must get rid of your sister-in-law [Madame Nhu] and your brother [Nhu]." After he returned, Macdonald told Kennedy, "He just won't do it. He's too stubborn."

DURING A TWO-HOUR CONFERENCE with House leaders and ranking members of the Judiciary Committee on Wednesday, Kennedy tried to hammer out a compromise civil rights bill satisfactory to moderate Republicans and liberals. The House minority leader, Charles Halleck of Indiana, was the key to any deal, and Kennedy had convened the meeting to discover what he would accept. Halleck complained to Kennedy that liberals on the Judiciary Committee, Republicans and Democrats alike, had loaded the bill with provisions "way beyond anything you asked, and way beyond anything we ought to do," with the result that moderate Republicans such as himself risked being targeted as "goats" for emasculating the bill.

"*We're* the goats," Kennedy said, reminding him that liberals and civil rights leaders had criticized his original bill for being too cautious.

Halleck said he had been courageous to introduce the bill. He flattered Halleck in return, and within two hours they had sketched out a compromise. After the others left, Halleck told Kennedy, "The colored vote in my district doesn't amount to a bottle of cold piss." He wanted to pass a civil rights bill anyway because whenever he went to Warm Springs, the Georgia resort made famous by FDR, none of the restaurants would serve his Negro driver. "Once in a while, a guy does something because it's right," he explained.

On Wednesday evening Kennedy invited the Bradlees to their second dinner in a row. By the time he joined them, Jackie had put on a dress from King Hassan and was imitating the bumps and grinds of a Moroccan dancer. She complained that Bishop was "prying awfully deep," even trying to get her maid to reveal what she wore to bed and who slept where. "Never mind," he said. Bishop was writing a lead story, "and the way things are going for us right now, we can use anything we can get. Anyway, we have the right of clearance. . . . That's a great thing—that right of clearance."

He mentioned that the *Washington Post* had run a photograph of Bobby Baker's house, and Bradlee said he understood that when the photographer rang the bell, two women in evening dresses had opened the door.

"Did they get their pictures?" he asked.

While walking to the White House theater to watch the new James Bond movie, *From Russia with Love,* they discussed who he wanted to succeed him in 1968. After everyone had vetoed Johnson, Jackie asked, "Well, who then?"

"It was going to be Franklin [Roosevelt]," he said mischievously, "until you and Onassis fixed that."

He seldom sat through an entire film, but he watched this one to the end. Bradlee thought he liked the cool sex and brutality. As they were leaving, he announced that he and Jackie were going to take a holiday out West the following summer. He was thinking of Montana, where he had received such a good reception, but not Wyoming, too many "cold bastards" there.

At a meeting on Thursday with Rusk, Taylor, and Gilpatric, he approved a schedule for redeploying U.S. forces from Europe that was in line with Rusk's assurances to Gromyko during their secret walk. He agreed to a reduction of 30,000 troops from U.S. logistical forces in Europe, 10 percent from headquarters staff, and the return, with the minimum explanation possible, of units sent to bolster U.S. forces during the 1961 Berlin crisis. A National Security Action Memorandum summarizing his decisions stated that the "possible redeployment of U.S. forces under consideration within the government should not be discussed publically nor with our allies until a decision has been made and politico-military plan for action approved. Even then, whenever possible[,] action of low visibility should be taken without public announcement."

He took another step toward reducing cold war tensions during a Thursday meeting with Jean Daniel, the noted French journalist who edited the Socialist newsweekly *L'Observateur.* After Attwood learned that Daniel would be traveling to Cuba in early November and hoped to interview Fidel Castro, he had asked Bradlee to persuade Kennedy to see him before he left. They met alone in the Oval Office for thirty minutes. Kennedy did not activate the hidden microphone, but Daniel took what he called "very specific" notes.

Kennedy began by saying that he had decided that worrying about the state of Franco-American relations was a waste of time, and that General de Gaulle's "rather incomprehensible" strategy required a certain amount of tension with the United States—tension that de Gaulle needed, he added facetiously, "to restore to Europe the desire to think for itself and renounce its torpid dependence on American dollar aid and political guidance!"

Daniel asked what he expected from de Gaulle's visit this winter. "Absolutely nothing!" he said, smiling. But he was looking forward to it anyway because de Gaulle was a "historic figure," and perhaps "the strangest great man of our time."

During a break from negotiations over the Panama Canal with President Roberto Remon, Kennedy had told Deputy Special Assistant for National Security Affairs Carl Kaysen that he felt the talks were going badly: "He says we've been screwing them all these years, and I agree." He apparently felt the same way about pre-Castro Cuba. Knowing that Daniel was certain to repeat his remarks to Castro, he now delivered an extraordinary denunciation of America's earlier Cuban policies:

> I believe there is no country in the world, including all the African regions, including any and all the countries under colonial domination, where economic colonization, humiliation and exploitation were worse than in Cuba, in part owing to my country's policies during the Batista regime. I believe that we created, built and manufactured the Castro movement out of whole cloth and without realizing it. I believe that the accumulation of these mistakes has jeopardized all of Latin America. . . . I can assure you that I have understood the Cubans. I approved the proclamation which Fidel Castro made in the Sierra Maestra, when he justifiably called for justice and especially yearned to rid Cuba of corruption. I will go even further: to some extent it is as though Batista was the incarnation of a number of sins on the part of the United States. Now we shall have to pay for those sins. In the matter of the Batista regime, I am in agreement with the first Cuban revolutionaries. That is perfectly clear.

He paused, and after noting Daniel's amazement continued:

> But it is also clear that the problem has ceased to be a human one, and has become international—that is, it has become a Soviet problem. I am the President of the United States and not a socialist; I am the President of a free nation which has certain responsibilities in the Free World. I know that Castro betrayed the promises made in the Sierra Maestra, and that he has agreed to be a Soviet agent in Latin America. I know that through his fault—either his "will to independence," his madness or communism—the world was on the verge of nuclear war in October 1962.

Referring to Castro's recklessness during that crisis, he said, "I must say, I don't even know if he realizes this or even cares about it," adding, "You can tell me whether he does when you come back." Speaking as much to Castro as Daniel, he warned that Latin American nations "are not going to attain justice and progress . . . by going from economic oppression to a Marxist dictatorship which Castro himself denounced a few years ago." Then he held out the carrot, saying, "The United States now has the possibility of doing as much good in Latin America as it has done wrong in the past; I would even say that we alone [i.e., not the Soviet Union] have this power—on the essential condition that communism does not take over there."

He rose, signaling that the conversation was over. Before leaving, Daniel posed two questions, both obvious negotiating points that Castro would want answered.

Could the United States tolerate "economic collectivism"? he asked. In other words, did Castro have to renounce communism as well as subversion?

"What about Sekou Toure [the Marxist leader of Guinea]? And Tito? I received Marshal Tito three days ago and our discussions were most positive."

Daniel inquired about the American economic blockade. Kennedy said it would continue as long as Castro was attempting to subvert other Latin American nations. The deal he was proposing was clear: if Castro stopped trying to export communism to other nations and became the Tito of the Caribbean, then like Tito he could receive U.S. recognition and aid. As they parted, Kennedy said he wanted a report when Daniel returned from Havana, adding, "Castro's reactions interest me."

ON THURSDAY, BISHOP ANNOUNCED that he had collected enough anecdotes and observations for a small book. He and Kelly would fly to Aruba and while closeted in a hotel finish the article and book in a couple of weeks. He would send Kennedy a carbon copy so he could correct factual errors and identify any observations that he found "hurtful and unfair." If Bishop agreed, he would remove or change them.

"If it gets here before Jackie and I leave for Texas, I'll take it with me," Kennedy said. Bishop was perplexed by his urgency, writing later, "For a reason beyond my divination, he was eager for the little book." But Kennedy's motives were not hard to divine. Bishop had written a laudatory article about Eisenhower and he wanted no less for himself. Anticipating correctly that the book would be flattering, he wanted it published as soon as possible as an antidote to Lasky's venomous tome. Before Bishop left, he questioned him closely about his best-selling book, *The Day Lincoln Was Shot*. "My feelings about assassination are identical with Mr. Lincoln's," he said. "Anyone who wants to exchange his life for mine can take it. They just can't protect [me] that much." Bishop thought he "seemed fascinated, in a melancholy way, with the succession of events of that day which had led to the assassination."

Kennedy woke Friday to front-page articles reporting that Dallas had been flooded with handbills carrying his photograph and captioned "Wanted for Treason," and that protestors had heckled and attacked Adlai Stevenson when he delivered a speech at an event in the Dallas Municipal Auditorium celebrating United Nations Day—not that surprising a reaction in a state whose legislature had passed a law that made flying the United Nations flag a criminal offense.

Stevenson had celebrated the new spirit of détente in his speech, saying, "We may be moving into a new era," and calling the atmosphere in the United Nations the best since its founding. There were loud catcalls and boos, and fistfights between hecklers and supporters. "They fear to hope," he said of his opponents. "And if anything, this eighteenth anniversary of the United Nations is an occasion that offers hope." An angry crowd surrounded him as he was leaving. Two men spat in his face and the wife of an insurance executive smacked him over the head with a sign proclaiming "If You Seek Peace, Ask Jesus." "We are patriots," she explained. "I just can't understand all these liberals and their ideas." She later blamed "a group of Negroes" for pushing her toward Stevenson.

Kennedy asked Schlesinger to call Stevenson and congratulate him for keeping his cool. Schlesinger was close to Stevenson, but the fact that Kennedy did not make the call himself was more evidence of their complicated relationship. Stevenson tried making light of the confrontation but finally said, "You know, there was something very ugly and frightening about the atmosphere. Later, I talked with some of the leading people out there. They wondered whether the President should go to Dallas, and so do I." Knowing Kennedy would dismiss any warning about physical danger, particularly one emanating from Stevenson, Schlesinger decided against relaying it.

As Kennedy was reading about these events in Dallas, a bomb threat delayed Tito's departure for Europe on the *Rotterdam*. Tito had previously complained to the chief of protocol, Angier Biddle Duke, about the placards carried by pickets outside the Waldorf-Astoria calling him a "Murderer" and "Red Pig." As he and Duke were driving to the pier, Duke spread out the *Herald Tribune*, pointed to a photograph of Stevenson being assaulted in Dallas, and said it proved there had been nothing special in Tito's treatment, adding, "This is how we treat our own distinguished national leaders."

Later on Friday, Kennedy received a cable from Lodge responding to his concerns that the coup might fail. Lodge reported that the generals were "seriously attempting to effect a change in the government," and argued against thwarting them because it was "at least an even bet that the next government would not bungle and stumble as the present one has."

Sending a Republican to Saigon, particularly one this headstrong and self-assured, must have again seemed less clever than it had last summer. In a cable signed by Bundy, Kennedy told Lodge, "We are particularly concerned about hazard that an unsuccessful coup . . . will be laid at our door by public opinion almost everywhere. Therefore . . . we would like to have option of judging and warning on any plan with poor prospects of success. We recognize that this is a tall order, but President wants you to know of our concern."

During a morning meeting with his foreign policy advisers, Kennedy doodled "Lodge," "Coup," and "Degree of Correctness" three times down the page. After attending a White House luncheon for Radio Free Europe, he spent the afternoon upstairs, writing and circling "coup," "press problems," and "coup plans."

Jackie's dressmaker Oleg Cassini had told Prime Minister Harold Macmillan that he believed the Kennedys had acquired something the British had lost, "a casual sort of grandeur about the evenings, always at the end of the day's business, the promise of parties, the pretty women and music and beautiful clothes and champagne." Being invited to one of their casual White House dinners was a coveted honor, and the fact that Britain's ambassador, David Ormsby-Gore, was such a frequent guest grated on the French ambassador, Hervé Alphand. Jackie finally invited him and his wife to dinner on Friday evening because she thought he was about to explode.

Her fondness for French history, culture, and cuisine did not, surprisingly, encompass the French people. She considered them "really not very nice" and could not think of a single French person she liked, except for a few "very simple" ones. Aside from the nonsimple Alphands, she also invited the Roosevelts and Princess Galitzine. Kennedy arrived for the evening in high spirits because William McCulloch, the ranking Republican on the House Judiciary Committee, had just announced that he would send the compromise civil rights bill to the House floor. He liked to tease when he was in a good mood. He told Alphand he was wearing the same shirt he had just seen on Ambassador Ormsby-Gore, and kidded Roosevelt about their recent weight-loss competition. After dinner, he offered Alphand the same analysis of Franco-American relations he had given Daniel, telling him that de Gaulle needed to provoke "an atmosphere of tension" to pursue his policy of independence. "Certainly not, Mr. President!" Alphand exclaimed indignantly. Surely a "free and responsible ally" was preferable to "an obedient servant."

Jackie told Alphand that the French author André Malraux had sent her a fine piece of jewelry to honor the birth of her third child, and although she had been happy to receive it, she hoped he would agree to take it back. Alphand noticed that mentioning Patrick had almost brought her to tears. He wrote in his diary that she remained gripped by "*une profonde et grande emotion.*" He also noted that he had heard rumors of Kennedy's womanizing. "The President's desires were difficult to satisfy," he wrote, and raised fears of scandal, which might happen "because he does not take sufficient precautions in this Puritan country."

The Roosevelts mentioned the attack on Stevenson in Dallas and urged Jackie to be careful. She said she wished she could take a "pass" on the trip but Jack wanted her there. The next day, she told the Secret Service agent Clint Hill that the Roosevelts had tried to talk her out of going to Dallas, and asked his opinion. He thought she was fishing for an excuse to back out of the trip and joked that she wanted to avoid going to the Johnsons' ranch. "Well, that is rather frightening in and of itself," she admitted before turning serious and asking, "Do you think the climate in Dallas is so hostile . . . so hostile to the President that the people could mistreat us like they did Adlai?" Hill said there had been no more threats against her husband in Dallas than anywhere else in the South, a remark that was less reassuring then he meant it to be.

AMHERST AND ATOKA

Kennedy criticized the speech that Sorensen had written for him to deliver at the groundbreaking ceremonies for the Robert Frost Library at Amherst as "thin and stale," and asked Schlesinger to revise it with an eye to including the "poetry and power" theme of Frost's Inauguration Day poem. He liked Schlesinger's version better—despite complaining that some of it "sounded too much like Adlai"—and invited him to fly to Amherst so they could revise it on the plane

He probably cared more about the Amherst speech than any other he delivered that fall. Its theme was the importance of the arts in the life of a great nation, a concept he had championed not only because of Jackie's interest in the arts but because he believed that like sports, military power, economic strength, and scientific achievement, the arts were a barometer of national excellence, and flourished under a great leader. To promote them he had made a big production of choosing new volumes for the White House library; woven poetry and excerpts from literature into his speeches; invited artists, writers, and classical musicians to the White House; proposed a national cultural center in Washington (the future John F. Kennedy Center for the Performing Arts); and established the Presidential Medal of Freedom for "especially meritorious contribution to . . . cultural or other significant public or private endeavors," designing the award himself and nominating its first twenty-two recipients. There was a resulting boom in museum attendance and interest in the arts, leading the historian and critic Lewis Mumford to praise him as "the first American president to give art, literature, and music a place of dignity and honor in American life."

In "The Arts in America," an article Kennedy wrote for *Look* in 1962, he called the arts "very close to the center of a nation's purpose," "a test of the quality of a nation's civilization," and the incarnation of "the creativity of a free society." He recounted how the distinguished artist George Biddle had attended a meeting at the White House during which FDR told the British ambassador that he was looking forward to the day when contemporary paintings hung on the walls of every American classroom, and quoted Biddle as saying that "Roosevelt had little discrimination in his taste in painting and sculpture.... [But] he had a more clear understanding of what art could mean in the life of a community—for the soul of a nation—than any man I have known." It was a comment that also applied to Kennedy, who had promoted the arts despite his own middlebrow tastes and a restlessness that sometimes became apparent when he attended the very cultural events he was sponsoring. (August Hecksher, who advised him on artistic matters, said later, "I don't think he liked music. Sitting on those little White House chairs in the East Room was really physically painful.") Kennedy would also echo Roosevelt's comment about hanging great works of art in every classroom when he told the French author Romain Gary, "Your children live on streets like the Rue Anatole, Boulevard Victor Hugo, Avenue Valery.... Our streets all have numbers. We have enough great names to replace them: Hemingway Square, Melville Boulevard ... I would like to see a twelve-year-old boy come home and tell his mother, when she scolded him for being late, 'I was playing baseball on William Faulkner Avenue.'"

His second reason for wanting to deliver a brilliant speech at Amherst was that he had treated Robert Frost shabbily in the final weeks of the poet's life, and attending the groundbreaking for his library was a kind of posthumous apology. Frost had visited the Soviet Union during the summer of 1962, met with Khrushchev, and upon his return recklessly told reporters at an airport press conference that Khrushchev thought Americans "were too liberal to fight," and would "sit on one hand and then the other." A resulting *Washington Post* headline declared, "Frost Says Khrushchev Sees US as 'Too Liberal to Defend Itself.'" Kennedy was so furious that he refused to speak to Frost again, even when he was on his deathbed, even after numerous entreaties from his family and friends, including Secretary of the Interior Stewart Udall, who had introduced them.

Udall considered his pettiness "cold and unfeeling" and was still upset about it when he flew with him to Amherst. During the flight he reminded him of his cruelty to Frost, albeit in a lighthearted way by remarking that the poet's elderly daughter did not hold either of them "in high regard," adding, "Well, Mr. President, if you see me wrestling on the ground with someone, you'll know that I'm wrestling with Leslie Frost."

"Well, Stewart," he said, "we'll give you the benefit of the doubt."

Fog forced Air Force One to circle for an hour, giving him time to tinker with his speech and complain to Schlesinger that Eisenhower's memoirs had been excessively self-righteous. "Apparently he never did anything wrong," he said. "When we come to writing the memoirs of this administration, we'll do it differently." When Schlesinger noted this in his diary, he did not explain who Kennedy had meant by "we." Both of them collaborating on a memoir, or writing competing accounts of the administration? Or was it the royal "we"?

After Schlesinger left his compartment, he told Assistant Treasury Secretary Jim Reed, who had joined the party because he was an Amherst alumnus, "I really don't think too much of this speech." He added a preamble about education and poverty, and revised it some more. He eliminated Schlesinger's "Too often we do not honor our artists until they are dead and can disturb us no longer," perhaps because it was uncomfortably close to how *he* had treated Frost in his final months. He cut laborious passages such as "He carved his poetry in materials as subtle as the colors of this New England Indian Summer, and as enduring as the granite of his New Hampshire hills." He replaced Schlesinger's "unchallengeable figures of our time," with "granite figures of our time," his "the loveliness of our national environment" with "the beauty of our natural environment." In places, he turned Schlesinger's ham-fisted prose into poetry, replacing "when power intoxicates, poetry restores sobriety" with "when power corrupts, poetry cleanses."

By the time his helicopter set down on Amherst's Memorial Field, the fog had lifted and it had become a gorgeous Indian summer day. He spoke first in the Amherst College cage, a sprawling athletic structure with dirt floors and hanging nets. Delivering a prepared speech always made him more nervous than speaking extemporaneously, and his hands never stopped moving. He fiddled with his pages or stabbed the air with a forefinger, as much to release tension as punctuate his words.

He based his opening remarks on the notes that Reed had just seen him write and memorize. They expressed his newfound interest in the connection between poverty and education, and the barriers that kept poor children from attending institutions like Amherst. After telling the students and alumni that Woodrow Wilson had once said, "What good is a political party unless it is serving a great national purpose?" he asked, "And what good is a private college or university unless it is serving a great national purpose?" He declared that "privilege is here, and with privilege goes responsibility." After reminding them that "private colleges taken as a whole draw fifty percent of their students from the wealthiest ten percent of the nation," he cited the statistics he had used during his conservation tour to draw connections between poverty, lack of education, and unemployment. He decried America's shocking disparity in income, pointing out, "In 1958, the lowest fifth of the families in the United States had four and a half percent of the total personal income, the highest fifth, forty-four and a half percent," and adding, "There is inherited wealth in this country and also inherited poverty. And unless the graduates of this college and other colleges like it who are given a running start in life—unless they are willing to put back into our society these talents . . . to put those qualities back into the service of the Great Republic, then obviously the presuppositions upon which our democracy is based are bound to be fallible."

Speaking of Frost, he said, "The men who create power make an indispensable contribution to the nation's greatness, but the men who question power make a contribution just as indispensable . . . for they determine whether we use power or power uses us. It is hardly an accident that Robert Frost coupled poetry and power, for he saw poetry as the means of saving power from itself. When power leads men towards arrogance, poetry reminds him of his limitations. When power narrows the areas of man's concern, poetry reminds him of the richness and diversity of his existence. When power corrupts, poetry cleanses. For art establishes the basic human truth which must serve as the touchstone of our judgment."

His homage to Frost completed, he offered a vision of what poetry tempered by power might accomplish that amounted to a litany of what he intended to accomplish during his second term. He said:

> I look forward to a great future for America, a future in which our country will match its military strength with our moral restraint, its wealth with our wisdom, its power with our purpose. I look forward to an America which will not be afraid of grace and beauty, which will protect the beauty of our natural environment, which will preserve the great old American houses and squares and parks of our national past, and which will build handsome and balanced cities for our future.
>
> I look forward to an America which will reward achievement in the arts as we reward achievement in business or statecraft. . . . And I look forward to an America which commands respect throughout the world not only for its strength but for its civilization as well. And I look forward to a world which will be safe not only for democracy and diversity but also for personal distinction.

The *New York Post,* then a left-wing publication, praised his words in an editorial as "a thousand light years away from the usual banalities uttered by politicians on such occasions," adding, "rarely has a man wielding enormous power saluted the poet in phrases so cadenced or celebrated his role in terms so perceptive and profound."

He went from the field house to the site of the future Robert Frost Library, where ten thousand people, three times the number predicted, sat above him on the sunny slopes of College Hill. He recounted Frost's post-inauguration admonition to him, saying, "He once said to me not to let the Harvard in me get to be too important. So we have followed that advice." Before leaving, he told Kay Morrison, Frost's long-serving secretary, "We just didn't know he was so ill." It was not true. Frost had lingered in the hospital for weeks, and Kennedy had been informed of his condition.*

Jim Reed had been with him until he returned to Washington that afternoon,

---

* A December 14, 1962, letter to Kennedy from the president of Frost's publisher, Holt, Rinehart and Winston, informed him that "Robert had a serious operation on Monday, at Peter Brigham Hospital, where he will be recuperating for several weeks."

and transferred to a helicopter flying him to his new weekend house in Atoka. During all that time Reed remembered him being "in high good humor and high fettle," a surprising observation since minutes before leaving the White House for Amherst, he had learned that his worst fears about the Bobby Baker investigation were being realized. In an exclusive story appearing on the front page of the *Des Moines Register,* headlined "U.S. Expels Girl Linked to Officials—Is Sent to Germany After FBI Probe," the investigative reporter Clark Mollenhoff wrote, "A Senate Committee will hear next week about the friendship of several congressional figures with an exotic 27-year-old German girl who was expelled from the country last August." An "outline" of her activities would be provided to the Senate Rules Committee, Mollenhoff said. "However, the evidence also is likely to include identification of several high executive branch officials as friends and associates of the part-time model and party girl." He added that she was the wife of a West German army sergeant and had been deported on August 21 at the request of the State Department. An investigation had established "that the beautiful brunette . . . was associating with congressional leaders and some prominent New Frontiersmen from the executive branch of government." An "incomplete list of her government friends" had been supplied to Senator Williams (who was obviously Mollenhoff's source), and he planned to share it with the Senate Rules Committee on Tuesday.

During the flight back from Amherst, Kennedy could contain himself no longer. He mentioned the Baker scandal to Schlesinger, and after pretending to be ignorant about the identities and activities of Baker's party girls, casually remarked that the scandal "might be the Profumo affair of this administration." Schlesinger had not read Mollenhoff's story and said he understood that the scandal involved money, not sex. Kennedy replied that when a newsman rang the door at Baker's town house, one allegedly occupied by his secretary, a girl in a negligee had answered the door.

After he landed on the meadow below his new home, his official schedule noted "no further activity recorded this date." In fact, he was on the telephone almost constantly throughout the afternoon and evening. Evelyn Lincoln's phone logs show that between 4:16 and 8:45 p.m. he spoke with O'Donnell six times, Bobby six times, once with J. Edgar Hoover, and twice with Edwin Guthman, who handled press relations for the Justice Department.

According to the FBI file on Ellen Rometsch, O'Donnell called the Bureau at

5:00 p.m., "and asked to be briefed on the information developed by the FBI in our investigation last summer concerning Ellen Rometsch, and whether there was any information to the effect that she had been involved with anyone at the White House." Fifteen minutes later Bobby called the FBI agent Alex Rosen, and, referring to the *Des Moines Register* article, said he was contacting Clark Mollenhoff to tell him there was "no substance" to allegations about the involvement of any White House personnel with Rometsch, and that he had requested that the FBI conduct a further investigation to substantiate this. The president himself called Hoover, prompting Rosen to note, "Pursuant to the Attorney General's request and the Director's subsequent conversation with the President, we instituted investigation to locate and re-interview subject Ellen Rometsch." At 9:00 p.m., O'Donnell supplied Rosen with Rometsch's address in West Germany.

Assistant Director Cartha DeLoach reported that his agents had received "a considerable number of telephone calls over the weekend" regarding the Mollenhoff story and Ellen Rometsch, including five from the press secretary Ed Guthman. During his first call, Guthman had asked DeLoach to persuade the New York *Daily News* not to carry the Mollenhoff story. DeLoach refused, and in subsequent calls Guthman asked him to prevent the AP from picking up the article. DeLoach explained that he did not have the personal contacts at the AP to accomplish this, adding that "it was not within the province of the FBI to kill the story." During their final conversation Guthman told him, "The President was personally interested in having this story killed." DeLoach replied that the FBI had interviewed Rometsch in July and furnished the results to the attorney general. He advised Guthman to make his own statements to the press "without dragging the FBI into this matter."

JACKIE HAD PROPOSED BUILDING a home in Atoka after they had been unable to extend the lease on their rented house in the Virginia hunt country. He resisted at first, but capitulated after she went into a sulk. (She knew he could not tolerate a sulker, a weakness Billings called his Achilles heel.) He insisted on a modest house. She agreed to keep it under $40,000, but the cost rose to $60,000, then to almost $100,000 by the time it was completed. When he brought Bartlett to see the foundations he was already in despair. The hills were claustrophobic, the grass brown, the trees bare. "Can you imagine me ending up in a place like this?" he asked.

He had agreed to build the house before he or Jackie had visited Camp David, the presidential retreat in the wooded hills of northwestern Maryland. They had assumed that because the Eisenhowers had loved Camp David so much, they would naturally hate it. They were pleasantly surprised when they finally went and returned often, leading him to ask Jackie, "Why are we building Atoka when we have this wonderful place for free?" She had a similar reaction, telling Chief White House Usher West, "If only I'd realized how nice Camp David really is, I'd never have rented Glen Ora or built Wexford," the name she had given their new house, hoping it would persuade her husband to like it.

Wexford had been completed that summer, but instead of immediately moving in, they had rented it to strangers, an arrangement a reporter likened to a woman allowing someone else to wear her new mink coat first. While driving with West to the warehouse where they stored their furniture in order to choose some items for Wexford, she asked him if a president had ever sold a house while he was in office. West was not sure. "Well, do you have any idea what the repercussions would be if I were to sell Wexford?" she asked. He guessed that she would realize twice what they had paid for it.

She could have gone to Wexford while he was in Boston. Instead, she had taken the children to Camp David because she wanted them to experience their new house for the first time as a family. She was so concerned that he might find an excuse to avoid coming that weekend that she persuaded Princess Galitzine to join them, telling her, "John detests the country and loves the ocean and doesn't want to come. But if *you* come it may persuade *him* to come." She may have also wanted Galitzine as a counterweight to Lem Billings, who had accompanied Kennedy to Amherst and would be coming with him to Wexford. For thirty years he had been a constant Kennedy family houseguest at Palm Beach, Hyannis Port, or wherever Jack and Jackie happened to be living. He had arrived at the White House a week after the inauguration, moved some clothes into a third-floor room, and came and went at will, often tagging along to Virginia and the Cape, prompting her to whisper to West in mock despair, "Oh, Mr. West, he's been a houseguest every weekend since I've been married." She tolerated his constant presence—she had no choice—but if there was ever a weekend when she might have wished he might stay away, it could have been this one.

It would have been surprising had she *not* been jealous of her husband's relationship with Billings. They had roomed at Choate, traveled across Europe as students, lost their virginity to the same prostitute, and exchanged hundreds of candid letters (during their courtship, Jack had sent her one postcard). Their love affair was platonic for Kennedy, but more complicated for Billings, who was a closeted homosexual. He had made a pass when they were teenagers that Kennedy had rebuffed, but it had not damaged their relationship, and for Kennedy to continue their close friendship throughout his political career, at a time of great homophobia, was both reckless and courageous. His fondness for Billings puzzled outsiders. Eunice called it "more than a friendship," adding, "it was a complete liberation of the spirit. . . . [Jack] was a completely liberated man when he was with Lem." Kennedy knew that Billings had not only loved him longer than anyone outside of his own family, he loved him for himself. Billings claimed to know more about Kennedy's personal life than anyone else, including members of Kennedy's family, once saying, "He never had any secrets from me." There is no evidence that Billings knew about Ellen Rometsch. But if Kennedy did confide in anyone that weekend, it would have been him.

The weekend could not have been more ill-timed. Aside from worrying about a potential scandal that might lead to his impeachment, Kennedy was monitoring an imminent coup in Vietnam that might become his next Bay of Pigs. He had too much on his mind to pretend he liked a home that he had never wanted to build and that had not turned out very well. But despite his reservations, Billings sensed that he was still excited by the prospect of seeing it for the first time, "because it was brand new and his own possession." If so, his excitement was short-lived. There was nothing grand or distinctive about the fifteen-room yellow stucco ranch house stretching like a barracks across a small rise grandiloquently known as "Rattlesnake Mountain." His own parsimoniousness, not Jackie's design, was largely to blame. The house had a fine view of the Blue Mountains, a stable for Jackie's horses and the children's ponies, and a handsome flagstone terrace, but its interior was disappointing. There were not enough closets or spare bedrooms for his liking, and he considered the collection of suggestive Mogul miniatures that Jackie had hung in the dining room in questionable taste. Nor did Wexford impress Princess Galitzine, who was surprised to find a "modest house without a butler, gardener, or even a garden."

Jackie was riding when Galitzine arrived, so he fixed her a Bloody Mary and joked about picking up the telephone and calling Khrushchev. In an attempt to make conversation, she raised an uncomfortable subject: what he planned to do after 1968. "You'll be so young," she said. "Aren't you afraid of being bored?" He feared boredom almost as much as death and was probably not in a mood to joke about his post–White House years, which thanks to Ellen Rometsch might arrive sooner than the princess imagined, but he gamely played along, saying, "I'll probably nominate myself ambassador to Italy." Then he took her for a drive, stopped for ice cream, and had to borrow money from his Secret Service agents to pay for their cones.

He maintained the easy banter throughout dinner and a screening of home movies of Jackie's cruise. "Next year, when I'm reelected, Jackie will stay at the house with the kids and I'll come on the boat," he joked, adding that he hoped Galitzine would join him and introduce him to her friends.

After the Onassis film, he screened one of his televised debates with Nixon. It is hard to imagine what possessed him to show it. Jackie and Billings had seen the debates live, and had probably watched the film several times. Perhaps he wanted to impress Galitzine or revisit happier times. He was suddenly no longer "the jokey, affectionate playboy" Galitzine had seen earlier that evening. Instead, he stared at the screen transfixed, reminding her of a boxer preparing to enter the ring. During his 1946 campaign, Jim Reed had noticed that he sometimes became so engrossed in a conversation that he was oblivious to his food, pulling a caramel from his pocket and chewing on it while spooning soup, or popping a marshmallow into his mouth while eating roast beef. As the film flickered across the screen, he grabbed Galitzine's glass of champagne and drained it.

WASHINGTON

E velyn Lincoln wrote in her diary, "The President came in all excited about the news reports concerning the German woman and other prostitutes getting mixed up with government officials, congressmen etc. He called Mike Mansfield to come to the office to discuss the playing down of this news report."

Kennedy's appointment book is blank from the time he returned from Wexford on Monday until one o'clock, when he went to the pool. A note says, "Staff members conferred with the President." The reporter Dan Oberdorfer writes in his biography of Mansfield that "alerted by the administration," Mansfield invited J. Edgar Hoover to his home on Monday afternoon, "where a meeting between Hoover, Mansfield and Dirksen would not attract attention from reporters who were swarming around the story." Lincoln's diary suggests that sometime that morning it was the president who alerted Mansfield.

Bobby was given the task of persuading Hoover to see Mansfield and Dirksen. He called Hoover into his office at the Justice Department, and according to a memorandum written by Hoover, informed him that he and the president "had discussed the Ellen Rometsch case and the aspects of it which tied into the Bobby Baker case" and wanted him to meet with Mansfield and Dirksen about the matter before the Senate began its hearings tomorrow. Hoover also noted that the president had asked him to see Mansfield when they spoke by telephone on Sunday.

Hoover suggested that since the FBI had already submitted a complete report on Rometsch in July, Bobby should simply read it out loud to Mansfield and

Dirksen. Bobby argued that it would be better if the senators saw Hoover person-ally, since they were primarily interested in any breach of security in the Rom-etsch case (which was not entirely true) and would give more credence to whatever he told them in person (which was true). Once Bobby had squirmed and groveled enough, Hoover called Mansfield and arranged to meet him and Dirksen at Mansfield's home. Mansfield and Dirksen left no record of what transpired. Dirksen died in 1970, and when Oberdorfer asked Mansfield about the meeting during a 1999 interview, he would only admit to having "a very faint memory" of it. Because Mansfield had an excellent memory, and this had been the only time he and Hoover had met, Oberdorfer was skeptical, and suggested he wanted to forget what had occurred because of its "seamy nature."

According to Hoover's memorandum, the only firsthand account of the encounter, he read Mansfield and Dirksen the July FBI report on Rometsch. They asked him "a number of questions" that he answered "to their satisfaction." He stated that the Bureau had reopened the case "in view of the current public-ity," but could "assure them there had been no breach of security." Although the Bureau had found "no connection" between Rometsch and anyone in the White House, he said that a number of congressmen had been clients of these "call girls," a statement he must have known would make them reluctant to pursue the sexual aspects of the scandal. When Mansfield expressed shock that immo-rality was so common among congressmen, Hoover suggested that he and Dirk-sen persuade members of their respective parties "to cut out the hi-jinks."

Hoover told Bobby afterward, "Senator Mansfield and Senator Dirksen were perfectly satisfied and willing to keep quiet." While Hoover was still in his office, Bobby telephoned O'Donnell and said, "Everything is well in hand." At the end of the call, Hoover noted, "Mr. O'Donnell extended an invitation from the Presi-dent for me to have luncheon with the President on Thursday, October 31, 1963, at 1:00 P.M., which I accepted."

Bobby Baker would later claim that by accepting Hoover's assurances about Rometsch, Mansfield and Dirksen had saved Kennedy's presidency. "Had they not had that meeting, and had the people who had relations with Ellen Rometsch been called to testify," he told Oberdorfer, ". . . you guys in the press would have had the greatest field day in your history." Kennedy had visited Mansfield's ail-ing father in Great Falls because he was a thoughtful and humane man. He had offered Dirksen's Democratic opponent tepid support because he liked Dirksen, and needed his help to move his legislative agenda through Congress. Had he been a different kind of man and politician, Dirksen and Mansfield might have been less inclined to accept Hoover's assurances, and allowed the Rules Committee to investigate Baker's sexual shenanigans.

Every newspaper that Kennedy read on Tuesday provided an opportunity for him to ponder his narrow escape. Unaware that the Rules Committee would not be exploring the party-girl aspect of the Baker scandal, reporters and congressmen considered Rometsch big news. The *Evening Star* published an eye-catching photograph of "the mysterious German beauty" who had been deported for "personal misbehavior." The *New York Times* ran a photograph of her underneath the headline "Baker Inquiry Is Asked If German Woman's Ouster by U.S. Involved Security," and reported that Representative H. R. Gross of Iowa had given a speech on the House floor Monday demanding to know "if there was any element of security violation" involved in her "speedy" deportation.

On the same day that Kennedy's humanity and sensitivity may have saved his presidency, he displayed these same qualities in a note to George Kennan, the eminent diplomat and historian whose last posting had been as ambassador to Yugoslavia. Kennan had sent him a handwritten letter praising his deft handling of Tito during the state visit. After noting that his sincerity could be "credited" since he was fully retired, he wrote, "I am full of admiration, both as a historian and as a person with diplomatic experience, for the manner in which you have addressed yourself to the problems of foreign policy with which I am familiar. I don't think we have seen a better standard of statesmanship in the White House in the present century. . . . Please know that I and many others are deeply grateful for the courage and patience and perception with which you carry on." Coming from the man who had invented the cold war strategy of containment and won a Pulitzer Prize for history (and would be called, at his death, "the American diplomat who did more than any other envoy in his generation to shape United States policy during the cold war"), it was an impressive testimonial, and for a president who cared so deeply about the verdict of history, a gratifying early review. He responded on October 28, addressing Kennan as "George" for the first time and writing, "It was uncommonly thoughtful for you to write me in this personal way," and promising to keep his letter "nearby for reference and reinforcement on hard days."

At an afternoon meeting on Monday, Kennedy and a majority of Democrats on the House Judiciary Committee formally agreed on a civil rights bill that would attract enough Republicans to win a floor vote. It was stronger than the administration's initial bill and contained an FEPC provision, but weaker than what the liberals had wanted. Kennedy had to play some political hardball to achieve the compromise. When the Illinois congressman Roland Libonati persisted in raising objections, he suspended the meeting and left the room to call Mayor Richard Daley of Chicago. "The Judiciary Committee is trying to get a civil rights bill together and Roland Libonati is sticking it right up us . . . ," he said, "standing with the extreme liberals who are gonna end up with no bill at all."

"He'll vote for it," Daley promised. "He'll vote for any goddamned thing you want." He asked Kennedy to pass the phone to Libonati so he could deliver the news in person. Kennedy balked at such naked steamrolling and suggested that Daley call him later. "That's better," Daley agreed. "But he'll do it. The last time I told him, 'Now look it, I don't give a goddamned what it is, you'll vote for anything the President wants and . . . that's the way it's gonna be.'"

"That'd be good," Kennedy said.

After the Judiciary Committee left, Caroline and John came into his office to model their Halloween costumes. "Do you think he will know who we are?" Caroline asked Lincoln. She assured them he would be fooled. "Why, it's Sam and Mary!" he exclaimed. He called his father in Hyannis Port and handed them the receiver so they could shout "Trick or Treat!"

Cecil Stoughton took a photograph. It showed the president seated at his desk laughing. Caroline was a witch and held a live black cat in one hand. John was a panda, "Peter Panda." Their costumes were cheap plastic ones, the kind sold at Woolworth's that any middle-class kid might wear.

LINCOLN WROTE IN HER DIARY that Tuesday had "started off with a bang." There was a Legislative Leaders Breakfast, a final bipartisan meeting of House leaders prior to the Judiciary Committee's vote on the civil rights bill, and a cabinet meeting during which Kennedy scrawled "POVERTY" in a bold hand on a yellow legal pad, repeatedly circling and underlining it.

The Democratic and Republican House leaders agreed to support his compromise civil rights bill, and the Judiciary Committee approved it by a vote of 23 to 11. Fourteen Democrats and 9 Republicans voted in favor; all but one came from the North. (Despite Daley's arm-twisting, Libonati voted against it.) The bill faced more hurdles in the House and had to clear the Senate, where Southern Democrats were threatening a filibuster, but Kennedy had won an important battle. Faced with choosing between a bill that stood little chance of passage but would have made him a hero to the civil rights movement and liberals, and one that was imperfect but might be enacted, he had chosen the pragmatic course. Anthony Lewis praised it in the *New York Times* as "a notable political achievement," and the *Boston Globe* called it a victory in a "showdown battle . . . for a compromise civil rights bill." It was also a victory for bipartisan cooperation and a president who had deftly engineered the compromise, but Halleck was the biggest hero. Some Republicans excoriated him for rescuing Kennedy's bill on the eve of a presidential election year and dealing a setback to the GOP's emerging Southern Strategy of opposing civil rights legislation in order to win formerly solid Democratic seats in the South and pick up white backlash seats in the North. An anonymous House Republican told a *Washington Post* columnist, "Kennedy's going to get whatever credit there is for passing a bill, so why should we get him off the hook? This will cost us ten to fifteen new members from the South . . . and prevent us from getting any benefit from Northern white reaction against civil rights."

Kennedy called Halleck that afternoon to thank him. "I got a lot of mad people up here," Halleck said. Kennedy commiserated, saying, "I got a lot of mad Negroes that are ready to come and throw rocks at me, but that's all right." Halleck said that he might not win reelection as minority leader, "but I don't give a damn."

That afternoon Kennedy convened an all-hands-on-deck meeting of his Vietnam advisers in the Cabinet Room that would prove to be his last opportunity to derail a coup.

Since he had told Lodge on August 15 that he would leave everything in his hands, he had made so many conflicting statements and vacillated so much that his advisers must have been uncertain whether he welcomed or dreaded a coup. He had approved the controversial cable of August 24 green-lighting a coup, but attempted to rescind it two days later. He had told Walter Cronkite that if Diem did not enact reforms and dismiss his brother, the United States might cease supporting his government, and then told Huntley and Brinkley that his administration would continue providing military and financial aid to Diem regardless of what he did. He had sent Krulak and Mendenhall to Vietnam to determine if Diem could win the war despite the political turmoil, and when they failed to agree he had sent McNamara and Taylor. The generals plotting against Diem had signaled that a coup was imminent, and then developed cold feet when he pulled back from the August 24 cable. They were encouraged by his public criticism of Diem to Cronkite, then discouraged by how quickly he retreated from it. But after he announced the withdrawal of U.S. advisers and took steps to curtail several assistance programs, they took heart and resumed their plotting.

Throughout all this he never questioned the morality of encouraging a coup against a long-standing U.S. ally. Instead, he pressed for continual, up-to-the-minute assessments of the odds that it would succeed, and if those odds were poor, how he could stop it. He had told Lodge in his August 28 "Eyes Only for Ambassador" cable, "We note that you continue to favor the operation; we also assume your concurrence . . . that if this operation [the coup] starts, it must succeed. But it remains unclear to us that balance of forces in Saigon yet gives high confidence of success, and we need daily assessment from you on this critical point. . . . More broadly, we are assuming that whatever cover you and we maintain, prestige of U.S. will necessarily be engaged in success or failure of this effort. Thus we ask you present estimate of latest point at which operation could be suspended and what would be consequences of such suspension." This cable was scarcely different from the one that Bundy, speaking for Kennedy, would send Lodge on Tuesday, October 29, following hours of discussions that afternoon.

Kennedy recorded the October 29 meeting, activating the hidden microphones in the Cabinet Room as William Colby, chief of the Far Eastern Division of the CIA, was reporting that the pro- and anti-Diem forces in and around Saigon appeared evenly balanced, with approximately 9,800 troops on each side. Bobby added to his brother's anxiety by saying, "We're putting the whole future of the country and, really, Southeast Asia, in the hands of somebody [General Don, the intermediary with Lodge for the plotters] that we don't know very well." Rusk said that if there was a substantial number of senior Vietnamese officers who believed they could not win the war under a Diem government, then the United States assumed a "heavy responsibility" by thwarting them. Taylor disagreed, saying he had found "absolutely no suggestion the military didn't have their heart thoroughly in the war." The CIA director, McCone, thought that even a successful coup "would seriously affect the war" and "might be disastrous."

Kennedy steered the conversation back to what really concerned him: the odds that a coup would succeed. If the forces in the Saigon area were "almost even," he said, then a coup was too risky and Lodge should discourage it.

McNamara pointed out that Lodge would resist this change in policy, "since we have . . . rightly or wrongly, I think, led him to believe that we would support a coup, or at least that we would keep hands off."

When the meeting reconvened later that afternoon, Kennedy said that since forces were almost equal, "there is a substantial probability that there'll be a lot of fighting—"

"Or even defeat," someone interjected.

"Or even defeat," he acknowledged. "We think it would be disastrous to proceed unless they can give us evidence that indicates that the majority strength is still in there."

The rest of the meeting was devoted to drafting a cable to Lodge that expressed his reservations, and his insistence that the chances of a coup succeeding must be high for Lodge to allow it to proceed.

McNamara pointed out that they could not ask Lodge to guarantee "a sure thing."

"That's right," Kennedy said, "and I understand that. But, I mean, we ought to have it that he is more convinced than not that it's going to [succeed]." Referring to Lodge, he said that if there was a bad outcome, it "looks to be his ass [because] he's for a coup." Based on Lodge's past performance, he acknowledged that he would probably resist or ignore any instructions from them to discourage a coup. "He's for it for what he thinks are very good reasons," he said. "I say he's much stronger for it than we are here, but well, I admire him his, his nerve if not his, his prudence."

He and Bundy had received a cable from Lodge on Tuesday stating, "It would appear that a coup attempt by the Generals' group is imminent; that whether this coup fails or succeeds, the USG must be prepared to accept the fact that we will be blamed, however unjustly; and finally, that no positive action by the US can prevent a coup attempt short of informing Diem and Nhu with all the opprobrium that such an action would entail. Note too Don's statement we will have only four hours notice. This rules out my checking with you between time I learn of coup and time that it starts. It means U.S. will not be able significantly to influence course of events."

In a reply from Bundy that Kennedy helped draft and was sent after the October 29 meetings, they told Lodge, "Believe our attitude to coup group can still have decisive effect on its decisions. We believe that what we say to coup group can produce delay of coup and that betrayal of coup plans to Diem is not our only way of stopping coup." They closed by saying, "We reiterate burden of proof must be on coup group to show a substantial possibility of quick success; otherwise we should discourage them from proceeding."

In his reply, Lodge called out Kennedy for his timidity and ethics. After conceding that it was important to "get best possible estimate of chance of coup's success," he contended that this was irrelevant since he did not think that "we have power to delay or discourage a coup." It would be, he cabled, "theoretically possible for us to turn over the information which has been given to us in confidence to Diem and this would undoubtedly stop the coup," but that "would make traitors of us." The bottom line, he argued, was that "we have very little influence on what is essentially a Vietnamese affair." Referring to Kennedy's demand that the plotters provide proof they could succeed, he said, "I do not know what more proof can be offered than the fact these men are obviously prepared to risk their lives and that they want nothing for themselves. If I am any judge of human nature, Don's face expressed sincerity and determination on the morning that I spoke to him." He concluded, "If we were convinced coup was going to fail, we would, of course, do everything we could to stop it."

This was not good enough for Bundy and Kennedy. In a sharply worded reply, they said they could not accept "that we have no power to delay or discourage a coup." Reminding him of his statement that he would do everything to stop a coup that they believed doomed to fail, they said, "We believe that on this same basis you should take action to persuade coup leaders to stop or delay any operation which, in your best judgment, does not clearly give high prospect of success." Feeling it necessary to defend their honor, they added, "We have never considered any betrayal of Generals to Diem."

ON OCTOBER 30, 1960, Kennedy had driven from Philadelphia to suburban Levittown for a campaign rally. The day was overcast and chilly and he was two hours late, but forty thousand people showed up and hundreds of thousands more lined his motorcade route. When he stopped to receive bouquets, women hurled themselves at his car and one even ended up in his lap. The next day, crowds in South Philadelphia's Italian and black neighborhoods hung out tenement windows, jammed sidewalks, and showered him with confetti and flowers.

Three years later to the day that he had received that exhilarating reception, he drove through the same South Philadelphia neighborhoods while traveling from the airport to a downtown hotel where he would speak at a fund-raising dinner for Mayor James Tate. His motorcade had been well advertised, the weather was fine, and he was traveling at rush hour through wards that had given him large pluralities in 1960. This time the crowds in the Italian neighborhoods were so small and unresponsive that one reporter called the reception among the poorest of his presidency. It was one thing for Kennedy to read about white backlash, but another to see it with his own eyes, and while he was sitting next to Congressman William Green, who had also been in the car with him in 1960 when that woman had vaulted into his lap. The turnout in black neighborhoods was even more disappointing, probably the result of local black leaders criticizing his civil rights bill as too timid.

His motorcade skirted Delmar Village, a middle-class housing development not unlike Levittown, where he had been hailed in 1960. In August, a mob of jeering and rock-throwing whites had attempted to prevent Horace and Sara Baker, the first blacks to purchase a home in Delmar, from moving in. The Bakers' new house was vandalized, and a hundred state policemen were mobilized to protect them. One thousand heads of families in Delmar issued a statement that deplored the violence but added, "We do not welcome the Baker family into our community." The family heads complained of "being forced to socially accept this family by law," and called for "boycotts of any business which serves or deals with them." The Baker incident had made the front pages of East Coast newspapers, where it had undoubtedly come to Kennedy's attention, perhaps contributing to his statement to the Birmingham whites that integrating public accommodations was "easy" compared with education and housing.

After such a disappointing welcome many politicians would have soft-pedaled their commitment to civil rights. When Kennedy spoke in Convention Hall that evening he called his bill "strong, just, effective, and reasonable," and a way "to secure for all Americans the rights and opportunities that they deserve." Referring to the speech that he had delivered in the same hall on October 31, 1960, he said that he still believed in an America where rights "are enjoyed by all regardless of their race." Progress had been made, he said, but the issue would "continue to be us with until all Americans of every race can regard one another with the quality for which this city is noted—brotherly love."

He flew back to Washington that evening with Governor David Lawrence of Pennsylvania. While eating snacks and drinking beer, he told a joke that Lawrence would call "one of the best stories" he had heard on the subject of integration.

After ascertaining that Lawrence remembered how to play knock-knock, he said, "Knock-knock."

"Who's there?" Lawrence dutifully replied.

"Iza."

"Iza who?"

"I's ya next door neighbah!"

Lawrence laughed while recounting the moment. "I's ya next door neighbor. I can hear him say it."

According to Larry Newman, Kennedy "wouldn't listen to a dirty joke, especially if it was an ethnic joke. And especially if there was a mimicked accent involved. He would simply say, 'I don't want to hear it,' and walk away." Given this, his "Iza" joke becomes even more inexplicable. Was he smarting from the poor turnout for his motorcade? Upset that he appeared to be losing the support of blacks *and* backlash whites? Did it prove that his civil rights education remained incomplete, or could never be completed? That *he* would have been among the whites telling pollsters that they wanted blacks to have equal rights, but did not want them next door? Perhaps he considered jokes like this one simply, as he had told George Taylor about the practice of segregating his campaign workers at lunch in 1946, "one of the things of the time."

The next day brought the most humiliating meal of his presidency, a private luncheon with J. Edgar Hoover that was partial payment for his role in persuading Mansfield and Dirksen to put Rometsch and the other party girls off limits during the forthcoming Senate hearings. The final bill for Hoover's services would presumably include keeping him in office past the mandatory government retirement age of seventy.

The conventional wisdom is that Kennedy had reappointed Hoover in 1960 because he feared that Hoover might leak damaging information about his personal life, including his dalliance during World War II with a Danish woman who had once allegedly traveled in Nazi circles. But he had also retained Hoover because he was a close friend of his father's and it would have been difficult for any president, particularly one who had won such a narrow victory, to cashier an icon like Hoover. The Washington attorney Clark Clifford, his principal adviser during the transition, had served in the Truman administration and by his own admission "despised and distrusted" Hoover. Yet even he had recommended reappointing him to avoid a partisan backlash during Kennedy's first months in office. Still, Kennedy fantasized about ridding himself of the man, once telling Fay, "I really am not in a position to do the things I'd like to do. I did not get a plebiscite from the people, and I have to really kind of balance things. . . . But come '64, I'm going to win big and do all the things that I've been unable to do— like getting rid of J. Edgar Hoover." He told Hilsman, "What we're going to do is this, we'll have the Army band walk down the side of the Mall playing 'The Star Spangled Banner,' and the Navy band on the other side. The Air Force band will parachute in, playing the national anthem as they descend. From a platform in the middle of the Mall, I will present Hoover with the Medal of Freedom and every other medal we can possibly think of. Then I will whisper in his ear, 'You're fired.'" In fact, he would not have needed to fire Hoover, just waited until his seventieth birthday on January 1, 1965, and staged an elaborate retirement ceremony.

Kennedy had ordered a microphone installed in the upstairs living quarters, but there is no evidence of his ever employing it, and his luncheon with Hoover was hardly an event he would have wanted to preserve for posterity. His predecessors had made these lunches with Hoover frequent affairs, and Hoover had reciprocated with gossip about other politicians and public figures that left them wondering what he had on them. Although he had probably collected more salacious information on Kennedy than any of his predecessors, Kennedy had lunched with him only five times since taking office, and just once in 1963.

The following week, Kennedy gave Bradlee an account of their luncheon designed to convince him that he had known nothing about Baker's girls until hearing about them from Hoover. He claimed that he had invited Hoover (this "awful bore") to lunch because he had learned that FDR had regularly entertained him and felt he should do the same, what with "rumors flying and every indication of a dirty campaign coming up." He recounted how Hoover had given him a full briefing on the hijinks between various U.S. senators and Baker's girls. Shaking his head in apparent amazement, he said, "Boy, the dirt he has on those senators. You wouldn't believe it." He also related how Hoover had brought a photograph of Rometsch that showed her to be "a really beautiful woman," and he had presumably feigned a similar innocence as Hoover passed a photograph of his former lover across the table at lunch.

PART FIVE

November 1–22, 1963

DAYS 22–1

Friday, November 1–Sunday, November 10

WASHINGTON, NEW YORK, AND ATOKA

Bundy woke Kennedy just after 3:00 a.m. to report that the South Vietnamese generals had launched their coup. Three hours later, a CIA cable described "heavy fighting including armor, small arms, and possible some light artillery vicinity Palace as of 1530 hours [Saigon time]." At an early morning White House staff meeting, Forrestal called the putsch "much better than anyone would have thought possible." Bundy said the action was an "acceptable type of military coup."

Kennedy convened his advisers in the Cabinet Room, and after hearing more optimistic reports he said, "I think we have to make it clear this is not an American coup." Among the cables to Lodge that he approved that morning was one urging him to persuade the generals to bear seven points in mind. These included: "Practical evidence of determination to prosecute war with renewed vigor; Reprisals at minimum; Safe passage for family [of Diem and Nhu] to exile; Humane treatment for arrestees."

He was presiding at a meeting on Saturday morning when Forrestal handed him a telegram reporting that Diem and Nhu had committed suicide after surrendering. He jumped to his feet and rushed from the room with what Taylor called "a look of shock and dismay on his face which I have never seen before." He was in turmoil all day. Schlesinger thought he looked "somber and shaken." Forrestal believed that the deaths "shook him personally," bothering him "as a moral and religious matter." Jackie noticed that he had "that awful look that he had at the time of the Bay of Pigs," adding, "I mean he was just—just wounded."

As shocked as he was by Diem's death, he could not have been entirely surprised. He had, after all, sent Macdonald on a secret mission to warn Diem that his life was in danger, and would later tell Cardinal Spellman of New York that he had known that Diem might be killed but could not control the situation.

He believed that devout Catholics like Diem and Nhu would not have committed suicide, and told McNamara, "We must bear a good deal of responsibility for it." He ranted to Fay about Madame Nhu. "She's responsible for the death of that kind man," he said. "You know it's so totally unnecessary to have that kind man die because that bitch stuck her nose in and boiled up the whole situation down there." While Jackie was at Wexford, he invited Mary Meyer to the White House for the first time since the previous spring. She signed in around one o'clock and stayed several hours. They may have resumed their affair, but it is also possible that he simply wanted her there to comfort him. He had not taken up again with Marlene Dietrich when she visited in September nor continued his affair with Mimi Beardsley after Patrick's death, so his encounter with Meyer may have also been innocent.

By the time he reconvened his advisers that afternoon, it appeared that Diem and Nhu had been executed while riding in the back of an army personnel carrier. "There is some question in some of our minds as to how much we want to know about this," Hilsman said. "It's becoming more and more clear that this is an assassination." McCone agreed, saying, "I would suggest that we not get into—into this story." After learning that General Duong Van ("Big Minh") Minh, who had led the coup, may have ordered the executions, Kennedy said in a soft voice, "Pretty stupid." A moment later he asked, "We haven't got any report on what public reaction [in Vietnam] was to the assassination, have we?"

"Jubilance in the streets," Hilsman said, adding that Lodge had been cheered publicly and might finally get a chance to be elected president . . . of South Vietnam.

"I'm not sure about that," Kennedy said.

After more speculation about the popularity of the coup, he asked, "What are we gonna say about the, uh, death of Diem and Nhu? We're not gonna say anything, right?"

Someone remarked that reporters were being told that the government was receiving conflicting reports about their deaths.

"We've already got an unfortunate event," he said. "Nonetheless, it'd be regrettable if it were ascribed, unless the evidence is clear ... to Big Minh and the responsible council of generals. I don't want it wrapped around him if we can help it."

Hilsman speculated that more information about those responsible for the murders of Diem and Nhu would surface within the next forty-eight hours.

"I'm sure Lodge must be aware that this is an unfortunate matter," Kennedy said, "and I suppose next they're going to make every effort to disassociate Big Minh and Conein [the CIA officer who had been the principal intermediary with the generals plotting the coup]." Speaking of Minh, he added, "If there was not responsibility on his part, that should be made clear."

"In other words, get a story and stick to it," Hilsman said.

Stepping back from what might be construed as an attempt to cover up Minh's role in the assassinations, he said, "It ought to be a true story ... if possible."

HE HAD DICTATED the college honors thesis that became his first book, *Why England Slept,* and dictated his contributions to his second, *Profiles in Courage.* When he began dictating his first speech to the House of Representatives, his secretary had expected "this green young legislator" to stumble over his words. Instead, she said, he sat back in his chair and a "stream of beautiful language" just "flowed out." Audiotapes of him dictating his Senate speeches show him seldom pausing or repeating himself, and delivering sentences shorn at birth of adjectives and qualifiers. When he could not dictate, he scribbled notes and delivered extemporaneous speeches that resembled his dictation, with "the words rolling out of his mouth as if he had written them weeks before," Lincoln said. He dictated his announcement that he was running for president two hours before delivering it and while a barber was cutting his hair, and dictated passages for his inaugural address while flying to Palm Beach. On November 4, he dictated some material for his memoirs. He said, "One, two, three, four," to check that the Dictaphone was working, then added the date because he assumed this would be one of many such recordings on this subject.

Diem's assassination had prompted him to consider his memoirs, perhaps because he knew that history would judge him harshly and he wanted to get his version of events down while it was fresh in his mind. He began, "Over the weekend, the coup in Saigon took place. It culminated three months of conversation about a coup (comma), conversation which divided the government here and in Saigon." He listed those opposing the coup—Taylor, Bobby, McNamara, and McCone—and those favoring it—Harriman, Ball, Hilsman, and Forrestal—and repeated his comment to McNamara that "we must bear a good deal of responsibility for it." He blamed it on the August 26 cable, and said, "In my judgment that wire was badly drafted (comma), it should never have been sent on a Saturday. I should not have given my consent to it without a roundtable conference in which McNamara and Taylor could have presented their views." If this was an accurate preview of his memoirs, they would have been memorably honest and unsparing.

Two minutes into his dictation, John came into the room and began shouting. Relieved to be distracted from accepting responsibility for his most ineptly managed crisis since the Bay of Pigs, Kennedy said, "Wanna say something? Wanna say something? Hello . . ."

"Hello," John obliged.

He quizzed his son about the seasons, asking him, "Why do the leaves fall?" "Why do the leaves turn green?"

After John left, he said, "I was shocked by the death of Diem and Nhu," praised Diem as "an extraordinary character" who had "held his country together," and called his death "particularly abhorrent." Because he could not bear to do anything for very long, his dictation lasted for only five minutes and twenty-one seconds.

He may have been atoning for his complicity in Nhu's and Diem's murders when he sent Secretary of the Interior Luther Hodges an uncharacteristically tough memorandum on Monday complaining about what he called an "inexcusable" outbreak of polio in America's Trust Territories in Micronesia. He demanded to know why, when the polio vaccine was widely available in the United States, "no action was undertaken between 1958 and 1963 when the spread of the disease became acute," and if "there is a difference in treatment for United States citizens in this country and the people for whom the United States is responsible in the Trust Territory." It was a scandal, but the fact he chose to address it today, and in such strong terms, and to demand that Hodges "expedite a complete investigation into the reason why the United States Government did not meet its responsibility in this area," suggests good works atoning for sin.

Also on Monday, Byron Skelton, the Democratic National Committeeman for Texas, sent Bobby a newspaper clipping headlined "5 Flags Upside-Down." The flags were outside the Dallas home of General Edwin Walker, who had been forced out of the Army in 1961 for disseminating right-wing propaganda to troops under his command in Germany. He was flying them to protest U.S. membership in the United Nations and the decision by Dallas officials to apologize to Stevenson. In a covering letter, Skelton wrote, "Frankly I am worried about President Kennedy's proposed visit to Dallas. You will note that General Walker says that 'Kennedy is a liability to the free world.' A man who would make this kind of statement is capable of doing harm to the President. I would feel better if the President's itinerary did not include Dallas. Please give this your earnest consideration."

While reviewing foreign policy issues with Bundy on Monday, Kennedy said he favored "pushing toward an opening toward Cuba" that would take Castro "out of the Soviet fold." That same day, Attwood called Bundy's deputy, Gordon Chase, to report that he had held further conversations with the Cubans about what he called "the accommodation approach to Castro" but did not want to discuss them on the phone. He did say, "The general tone seemed to be that Castro is interested, that other people in the [Cuban] hierarchy are opposed, and that the problem is sticky one."

On Tuesday, Attwood briefed Bundy and Chase in person about developments since his September meeting with Lechuga. He reported that following further conversations and telephone calls between himself, Lechuga, Lisa Howard of ABC, and Castro's confidant Dr. Rene Vallejo, the Cubans had decided against sending a senior official from Havana to participate in secret talks at the United Nations. Vallejo had called Howard to reaffirm that Castro was interested in the talks but could not leave Cuba to participate in them personally. On October 31, Vallejo had told Howard that Castro wanted to send a plane to Mexico City to collect a U.S. official (presumably Attwood) and fly him to a private airport in Cuba. Bundy and Chase asked Attwood to write a memorandum for the president summarizing all this. Bundy added that the president was more interested than the State Department in exploring the Cuban overture, but wanted a preliminary meeting at the UN between him and a Cuban official to agree on an agenda. At a Tuesday White House meeting on Cuba that the president did not attend, the CIA's deputy director for plans, Richard Helms, proposed that they slow down the pace of the Attwood initiative, "war game" the peace scenario, and "look at it from all possible angles" before making contact with Castro.

KENNEDY WAS IN AN EXPANSIVE MOOD when Ben and Tony Bradlee arrived on Tuesday evening for another last-minute dinner party. Although he had kept the Baker investigation from metastasizing into another Profumo scandal, it remained on his mind, and he invited everyone to guess who the "hidden Profumo" in his administration might be, knowing full well it was himself. Salinger and Gilpatric were among the names tossed out.

He recounted his luncheon with Hoover and spoke about seeing the photograph of Rometsch as if it had been the first time he had laid eyes on her. "Boy, the dirt he [Hoover] has on those senators," he said, shaking his head. "You wouldn't believe it."

Calls bringing good news kept interrupting the dinner. Another brief Berlin autobahn standoff had ended with the Soviets backing down, and early results in the off-year elections showed Democrats winning important contests in Kentucky and Philadelphia, although with narrower margins than Kennedy would have liked. "The way things have been going," he said, "to win in Philadelphia, Kentucky, and the autobahn adds up to a pretty good day."

He needled the Bradlees about their failure to enroll their daughter in a snobby dancing school, claiming that his father would have told him to leave town rather than accept such a snub. While puffing on one of the three cigars he chain-smoked that evening, he raised the surgeon general's long-awaited report on the link between cancer and smoking, saying he was concerned that it would reduce federal tax receipts and harm the economies of tobacco-growing states. He complained about a news photograph showing U.S. servicemen dancing with bar girls in Saigon. "If I was running things in Saigon," he said, "I'd have those G.I.s in the front lines tomorrow." A leftist government had recently assumed power in the Dominican Republic, and he was torn about whether to order the CIA to orchestrate an antigovernment student demonstration there. Bradlee asked how he would feel if the Soviets did the same thing here. He had no answer to this.

He invited Ambassador David Ormsby-Gore to dinner the following evening. After the test ban treaty had been initialed in Moscow, Ormsby-Gore had spent a weekend in Hyannis Port with him and Bobby, discussing further steps to improve U.S.-Soviet relations. Bobby had said that his brother should visit the Soviet Union, and over dinner on Tuesday, Kennedy reminded Ormsby-Gore of that conversation. "You know, I have made up my mind that one of the things I really must do is go to the Soviet Union," he said. "I believe that this would be in everybody's interest—whether I can do it before the presidential elections next year may be a bit doubtful . . . but sometime I am determined to go."

An article by Attwood appearing in the November 5 issue of *Look* titled "We Face a New Kind of World" claimed, "On balance, the state of the world, as seen from Washington, looks considerably more hopeful than it did three years ago." Attwood argued that the end of the European colonial empires had brought about "one of the most revolutionary periods in human history." During this period, he wrote, "the supremacy of the world's white, Christian minority" was vanishing and Americans should accept that "being the strongest power on earth doesn't mean that we can impose our system or our way of life on other countries." Kennedy liked the article so much that he asked the Democratic National Committee chairman, John Bailey, to send a copy to every member of the Senate and House, although one wonders how he squared Attwood's warning about imposing our system on other nations with promoting bogus student demonstrations in the Dominican Republic, and supporting the sabotage campaign of Cuban exile groups. Like many great men in the making, he wanted to be inspirational *and* successful—high-minded in public and pragmatic in private.

Hours after asking Bailey to distribute Attwood's lofty article, he flew to New York to accept the Protestant Council's first annual "Family of Man" citation, bestowed for his support of human rights. He had been battling Congress over cuts to his foreign aid budget and used his speech to the council to defend foreign assistance on practical and humanitarian grounds, painting it as an effective cold war weapon *and* a moral imperative. He criticized congressmen who found it "politically convenient to denounce both foreign aid and the Communist menace," and enumerated its economic benefits—a half million jobs created at home and the promotion of U.S. exports. But moments later he was insisting that "the rich must help the poor. The industrialized nations must help the developing nations." Referring to the Marshall Plan and the robust foreign aid program of the Eisenhower years, he said, "Surely the Americans of the 1960s can do half as well as the Americans of the 1950s. . . . I do not want it said of us what T. S. Eliot

said of others some years ago: 'These were a decent people. Their only monument: the asphalt road and a thousand lost golf balls.'

At a black-tie party afterward, William Styron was surprised to see him "quite
alone and looking abandoned." He greeted Styron and his wife, Rose, with "a
grand smile," Styron remembered, as if they were "long-lost loved ones," and
asked, "How did they get *you* to come here? They had a hard enough time getting
me." He was in an amiable mood, but Styron detected "an undercurrent of seri-
ousness, almost an agitation" when he spoke about civil rights. He asked Styron
if he was acquainted with any Negro historians and if he knew the black authors
James Baldwin and Ralph Ellison, and if he thought they might accept an invitation to the White House. Recalling their Labor Day conversation about the Nat
Turner rebellion, he said, "What a great idea for a novel. I hope it's done soon."
Styron felt himself being swept away by his charm, "overtaken by a grand effer-
vescence" that he compared to "being bathed in sparkling water." Kennedy was
distracted, turned away, and Styron never saw him again.

BY THE TIME KENNEDY spent his third straight weekend at Wexford, he
had either changed his mind about the house or decided to embrace it for Jackie's
sake. Salinger informed reporters that the family liked it so much that they had
decided to enlarge the stables and add a wing with more guest rooms and servants' quarters.

He arrived at Wexford early on Saturday afternoon with the Bradlees and the
photographer Cecil Stoughton. Jackie had organized an informal horse show to
entertain them, but the hill leading to the house was so steep and the road so rut-
ted from days of rain that none of her friends' horse vans could make it, leaving
her and Caroline as the only performers. It was a gorgeous day, sunny and cool.
He and the Bradlees sat on the stone wall of the patio, drinking Bloody Marys
and watching Jackie jump hurdles in the meadow below. Later they sat against
the wall of the house, sheltered from the wind, their faces tipped toward the weak
November sun. Jackie led John's pony, Leprechaun, up from the meadow and
handed her husband some sugar cubes to feed him. When the pony nudged him
onto his side, looking for more sugar, he threw an arm over his head. As Jackie
and the Bradlees collapsed in hysterics, he shouted at Stoughton, "Are you getting this, Captain? You're about to see a president trampled by a horse."

Stoughton also filmed him teaching Caroline how to swing a golf club, and John marching across the lawn, wearing an oversized helmet and carrying a toy rifle on his shoulder. He stopped to salute his mother with his left hand. She knelt down in her riding boots and jodhpurs to show him how to do it correctly, using his right. Tomorrow Daddy would be taking him to a ceremony (Veterans Day) where he would see real soldiers, she explained. They would be saluting Daddy, so perhaps he would want to salute him, too. Kennedy was concerned about John's fascination with guns and the military but reluctantly indulged it, buying him toy guns, letting him attend military ceremonies, and telling General Clifton, "I guess we all go through that. He just sees more of the real thing."

The family attended Sunday Mass at St. Stephen the Martyr Church in Middleburg and heard Father Albert Pereira preach a homily about Christian death and the high cost of elaborate funerals. In a nod to the president, he said, "The Saints today are the peacemakers." The church had opened in April and was purpose-built for the First Family, with a soundproof and bulletproof usher's room where the president could take calls. Pereira was one of the few clergymen with whom Kennedy felt comfortable discussing Catholic dogma and his faith (another was Cardinal Cushing), perhaps because he was an outspoken civil rights advocate who had proved his courage by playing a key role in integrating Middleburg's lunch counters. Before St. Stephen's opened, Kennedy had attended Pereira's services at the Middleburg Community Center, often arriving early for a private theological conversation. On November 10, Pereira gave him a Bible that he would carry to Texas, and that Johnson would use to take the oath of office.

Marie Ridder often went riding with Jackie and had known her and Jack for years. When she stopped at Wexford during one of these fall weekends (most likely the last one), Kennedy complimented the house within Jackie's hearing, and she thought they seemed "very cozy" together. Bill Walton confirmed her impression that Jack and Jackie's relationship had improved when they dined together a few days later, telling her that Jackie had taken him aside to say, "I think we're going to make it. I think we're going to be a couple. I've won."

ATOKA, ARLINGTON, AND WASHINGTON

M onday was "Daddies Day" at the White House school, when fathers attended classes with their children. Kennedy missed Caroline's first class, but before going to Arlington for Veterans Day ceremonies he joined the students at recess and praised their French teacher, Jacqueline Hirsh, for the "many miracles" she had worked with the children.

It was an ideal day for a military pageant, with bright sunshine and a brisk wind snapping the flags. He left John outside the amphitheater but soon changed his mind, telling a Secret Service agent, "I think he'll be lonely out there," and asking him to bring the boy inside. An agent who had seen the First Lady teaching John how to salute at Wexford leaned down as the color guard saluted the president and whispered, "Okay. Time to salute Daddy." This time, John used his right hand.

Kennedy found the ceremony so moving that he remained throughout the speeches instead of returning to the White House. While strolling down the rows of white gravestones with Representative Hale Boggs afterward, he said, "This is one of the really beautiful places on earth. I could stay here forever." Arlington remained on his mind all day, and he told Charlie Bartlett, "I suppose I'll have to go back to Boston because that's where my library is going to be." Then his face darkened and he added, "But of course I'm not going to have a library if I only have one term. Nobody will give a damn."

He returned to the White House as Hirsh was leaving. Knowing that Caroline was disappointed that he had missed her French class, he persuaded Hirsh to repeat it. As she held up pictures of objects, the children shouted their names in French. He felt sheepish that his command of the language was so poor that he had not known that a watermelon was *la pasteque.*

Hirsh took Caroline on an excursion every Monday afternoon and taught her a new French sentence. Jackie had promoted it as a way for her daughter to do something any ordinary child might do, such as shop at a store and travel by bus. Today Hirsh took Caroline and her ten-year-old son, Mike, to the National Zoo and taught her to say "We went to the zoo." Caroline and Mike returned to the Oval Office with balloons for her father and brother. Mike had broken his tooth playing football and the dentist had given him a temporary silver cap. When Kennedy noticed it he exclaimed, "My God, Mikey, you look like a Russian with that tooth!" Realizing that he had hurt the boy's feelings, he bent down, opened his mouth wide, and said, "Mike, you look into my mouth and you let me know which one of my teeth are capped. I had an accident too."

Caroline repeated her new French phrase, and he asked if it was the name of a bird. She informed him that it meant "We went to the zoo."

"Well, I think it's time I learned French." Turning to Hirsh, he asked, "If you gave me a French lesson how would you do it?"

She suggested he could start by reading the French edition of *Profiles in Courage.* He was already familiar with its contents, so they could concentrate on conversation and grammar. During each lesson he could summarize what he had read in French. He told her he wanted to be fluent by June, when he would be going to Normandy for the twentieth anniversary of D-Day. (He also wanted to surprise Jackie, whose facility with languages had left him somewhat jealous.)

He was serious enough to squeeze four lessons into the next ten days. He was a difficult student, self-conscious and restless, getting up and down, impatient to learn. "I can't wait to surprise the world," he told Hirsh. "It's always good to improve [at] anything." He ruminated a long time before producing a sentence that was grammatically correct but atrociously pronounced, and he interrupted so often that she warned that if he wanted to be fluent by June he would have to concentrate more. She praised his grammar and was honest about his accent. His goal, he said, was to sound like a French person and "to be able to do it [speak French] just perfectly." She estimated that might take at least a year. "I bet I do it in six months," he boasted.

THE DECEMBER 1962 CEREMONY at Miami's Orange Bowl honoring the Cuban exiles who had been captured during the Bay of Pigs operation and freed in exchange for a ransom of medicine and baby food had been emotional for Kennedy because he felt responsible for their captivity. After the brigade presented him with its flag he impulsively declared, "I can assure you that this flag will be returned to this brigade in a free Havana," but it soon became apparent that he and the exiles differed on what constituted a free Havana. For them, it was a city without Castro or communism, one liberated by a coup, counterrevolution, or invasion. As much as this scenario would have pleased him, he could imagine a resolution of the Cuban problem leaving Castro in power. Because he considered both outcomes acceptable, and prized success over ideology, since the spring of 1963 he had been following a two-track strategy of continuing clandestine attempts to destabilize and overthrow Castro while encouraging efforts to establish a dialogue.

These strategies converged on November 12, when he chaired a meeting of senior administration officials overseeing the CIA's anti-Castro campaign. Director McCone presented a dispiriting summary of the current state of play, admitting that Cuba's military remained loyal to Castro and its internal security forces well organized. Desmond Fitzgerald, who headed the CIA's Cuban task force, gave a discouraging update on the Agency's efforts to topple Castro. Casualties among CIA operatives in Cuba had increased, with twenty-five captured or killed, while the willingness of Canada, Spain, and the UK to continue trading with Cuba had diluted the impact of U.S. economic sanctions. He reported that the Agency continued to support autonomous anti-Castro groups mounting sabotage operations from bases outside U.S. territory, and listed four recent sabotage operations, but offered vague statements about their effect, justifying them as ways of "keeping up the pressure," raising "the morale of the people," and adding to Cuba's "growing economic problems."

Kennedy asked point-blank if the CIA's sabotage program was worthwhile. Rusk criticized it as counterproductive, and argued that it might weaken support for the exile groups within Cuba and result in the Soviets increasing troop levels on the island and staging more incidents on the Berlin autobahn. Despite these objections, the consensus at the meeting was that the CIA program should continue because it was low-cost, denied Castro essential commodities, and improved the morale of the anti-Castro Cubans.

Kennedy signed off on several sabotage operations scheduled for the weekend, but hours later he was pursuing the second track of his Cuban policy. Bundy called Attwood to deliver a message from the president that was so sensitive he said he could only communicate it orally. He told him that Kennedy wanted him to contact Castro's confidant, Dr. Rene Vallejo, and say that while it did not seem practical at this stage to send an American official to Cuba, the administration would like to begin the conversation by having Vallejo visit the United States and deliver any messages from Castro directly to Attwood. Bundy added, "In particular, we would be interested in knowing whether there was any prospect of important modification in those parts of Castro's policy which are flatly unacceptable to us: namely . . . (1) submission to external Communist influence, and (2) a determined campaign of subversion directed at the rest of the hemisphere. Reversals of these policies may or may not be sufficient to produce a change in the policy of the United States, but they are certainly necessary, and without [them] . . . it is hard for us to see what could be accomplished by a visit to Cuba." Kennedy was reiterating the conditions that he had asked Jean Daniel to communicate to Castro: cease the subversion and move out of Moscow's orbit. Attwood told Bundy he would ask Lisa Howard to call Vallejo before getting on the line himself and directing the conversation according to these guidelines. If Vallejo agreed to travel to New York, Attwood would come to Washington to receive instructions on how to handle the negotiations.

KENNEDY CONVENED THE FIRST formal meeting of his reelection team in the Cabinet Room on Tuesday afternoon. Attending it were his brother Bobby; his brother-in-law Stephen Smith, who would be managing the campaign; his political advisers Lawrence O'Brien and Ken O'Donnell; Ted Sorensen; John Bailey, who chaired the Democratic National Committee (DNC); DNC treasurer Richard Maguire; and Richard Scammon, the director of the Census Bureau. Vice President Johnson had not been invited.

Lincoln had noticed Johnson's name appearing less often on the lists of invitees to crucial policy and planning meetings in 1963. Her record of the private conferences between him and the president showed them meeting alone for more than ten hours in 1961, but for only seventy-five minutes in 1963. It is unlikely Kennedy simply forgot to invite him to the November 12 meeting, because he frequently complained about Johnson's sensitivity and must have known he would be hurt to be excluded from the first major planning session for the 1964 campaign. Johnson had left for his Texas ranch two days earlier but would surely have stayed in Washington to attend an important meeting like this one. Sorensen believed he had been excluded because he was "not part of the inner circle and did not have the warmest relations with—or full confidence of— everyone in that room," a polite way of saying that, as Sorensen well knew, Kennedy had little confidence in his ability to perform the only vice presidential duty that really mattered, assuming the presidency.

Their relationship had reached a nadir that fall after Johnson aligned himself with the hard-line Diem supporters in the administration and criticized the wheat deal. He sat silently at White House meetings, offering a few mumbled remarks or becoming infuriatingly loquacious. Kennedy may not have wanted him around because he was afraid that a man who considered himself more politically astute than anyone else in the White House would try to dominate the meeting, and perhaps because he was undecided about keeping him on the ticket. Even so, it was a curious omission, since the meeting concerned a reelection campaign in which Johnson's home state would play a key role. Kennedy even raised the subject of his forthcoming visit to Texas at the meeting, saying in an irritated voice that he would be seeking campaign funds as well as votes, and adding, "Massachusetts has given us about two and a half million, and New York has been good to us, too, but when are we actually going to get some money out of those rich people in Texas?"

Few believed that Kennedy would lose the election. McGeorge Bundy was even thinking ahead to a possible third term, telling Jackie that there might be such a demand for him to return to the White House that they should investigate the legality of him serving another term if it were not consecutive with the first two. The respected political commentator Stewart Alsop wrote in his November 2 *Saturday Evening Post* column that although Washington journalists who wanted to hype the forthcoming contest were offering scenarios for a Goldwater victory, hardly anybody believed it. "Goldwater doesn't have a prayer of beating John F. Kennedy in 1964," he said. "Neither does anyone else." He argued that Kennedy's Catholicism, which had cost him so many votes in 1960, was no longer a factor, nor were his youth and inexperience now that he had become "a middle-aged fellow with thickening jowls, a tendency to lose his reading glasses, [and] the remembered fear of nuclear war written clearly on his face."

A recent Gallup poll had Kennedy winning 58 percent of the national vote compared with Goldwater's 39 percent, with 6 percent undecided or voting for third-party candidates. The greatest threat to his reelection was that Goldwater would implode before taking the nomination, leaving him to face a more moderate Republican opponent such as Governor George Romney of Michigan or Governor Nelson Rockefeller of New York. Goldwater had already made some gaffes, promising to sell the popular Tennessee Valley Authority, and telling an interviewer, "You know I haven't got a really first-class brain."

Kennedy made it clear at the November 13 meeting that he intended to micromanage the Democratic convention, just as he had state visits and the design of Air Force One. He wanted a livelier convention, and said, "For once in my life I'd like to hear a good keynote speech." He also wanted a color film about the last four Democratic presidents. Only NBC broadcast in color, most Americans did not own color sets, and a color film would be more expensive, but he thought it would impress the delegates. "We'll run on peace and prosperity," he declared. "If we don't have peace we'd better damn well win the [cold] war." He went on to assess his chances in each state, showing a detailed knowledge of the key players and demonstrating that he really *could* have driven down that street in Boston and recalled which stores had displayed his posters in 1946.

He sounded less sure-footed when he shifted to the big picture. As if thinking out loud, he said, "But what is it that we can make them decide they want to vote for us, Democrats and Kennedy—the Democrats not strong in appeal obviously as it was twenty years ago. The younger people . . . what is it we have to sell 'em? We hope we have to sell 'em prosperity, but for the average guy that prosperity is nil. He's not unprosperous but he's not very prosperous. . . . And the people who are really well off hate our guts. . . . There's a lot of Negroes, [but] we're the ones that are shoving the Negroes down his throat. . . . We've got peace, you know what I mean, we say the country's prosperous and I'm trying to think of what else."

He passed out copies of Homer Bigart's article about poverty in Kentucky and said that as part of his prosperity theme he wanted to mount an attack on poverty. He would remind Americans that most poor people were white and would schedule photo opportunities with white coal miners in Appalachia and poor Negroes in Northern cities.

"I wouldn't do that, Mr. President," Scammon interjected. "You can't get a single vote more by doing anything for poor people. Those who vote are already for you. I was thinking of photographs with policemen in the cities. Then you should go to the new shopping centers on the highways. The votes you need, your people, men with lunch pails, are moving out to the suburbs."

Scammon's analysis fascinated him, and he asked how these new demographics might play out in 1964. Scammon spoke of Catholics buying suburban houses and suddenly becoming concerned about their property taxes.

He immediately got it: preventing these new suburban Democrats from turning into Republicans would be key to winning a landslide in 1964. He asked Scammon how many Democrats retained their party affiliation after moving to the suburbs, and at what rung on the social and economic ladder a Democratic family became Republican.

"It might be less than ten thousand dollars a year. I'll try to find out," Scammon promised.

"It's going to be a new kind of politics," he said.

"It's a new kind of country."

Wednesday, November 13

WASHINGTON

Kennedy stopped at Lincoln's desk to chat as she was reading the memorandums from the previous day's campaign meeting. She told him that staging a convention as electrifying as the one in 1960 would be difficult and that the next would not be as exciting because everyone knew what would happen.

"Oh, I don't know," he said. "There might be a change in the ticket."

The White House electrician and dog handler Traphes Bryant had noticed an increase in the barbed comments about Johnson that fall. He overheard a staffer saying that because FDR had dumped Wallace for Truman and still won reelection, voters would not hold it against Kennedy if he did the same to Johnson. Another asked, "How would you like to work for *him*?" Another said, "We've got to get that Texas cornpone out of here before he uses the vice presidency as a springboard into the White House in '68," and another claimed that even Jackie wanted the president to drop him, adding, "Jack won't pay any attention to her, of course, but for once she's right."

Kennedy had dismissed the rumors about Johnson being replaced at his October 31 press conference, and when Bartlett raised the possibility with him he angrily denied it. But if he *was* considering replacing Johnson, he would certainly not have announced it at a press conference a year before the election, or tipped his hand to Bartlett, Bradlee, Joe Alsop, or any of his other journalist friends. But Lincoln was in a different category, and he had such faith in her discretion and loyalty that she not only knew about his lovers but had acted as an intermediary, receiving their billets-doux at her home address.

After examining Kennedy on Wednesday, Dr. Burkley noted that he weighed 170½ pounds, had complained about "a slight ache in his right groin after resistive exercises," but insisted that he felt fine after taking a swim and using an anesthetic spray. He concluded that "his energy is excellent . . . and [he] now reports that he has resumed his full number 1 exercise program with 12½ pounds of weights."

Kennedy chaired an afternoon meeting to finalize his new program to alleviate poverty in eastern Kentucky that was attended by the state's governor and U.S. senators, the secretaries of agriculture and labor, and Undersecretary of Commerce Roosevelt. They agreed on an enhanced school lunch program, more public health services and surplus food, and initiatives to provide jobs and housing grants. The only proposal requiring congressional approval was an accelerated public works program. A week later, Roosevelt sent Kennedy a memorandum from his new office in Kentucky, reporting that the first emergency medical teams would be in the state by the end of the week, a survey of school lunches and a county-by-county survey of surplus food supplies would be on Kennedy's desk by December 5, food was being rushed to needy areas and distributed by surplus vehicles supplied by the federal General Services Administration, and the Kentucky Highway Commission and U.S. Forest Service would be hiring eight hundred men by the end of the month. It was testimony to how quickly a president can use his executive powers to ease suffering.

Later that afternoon, he and Jackie appeared together at a White House function for the first time since Patrick's death, watching a performance on the South Lawn by the Royal Highland Black Watch for an audience of underprivileged children. The commander of the Black Watch presented him with a ceremonial dagger and said that their motto was "Nobody wounds us with impunity." He replied, "I think that is a very good motto for some of the rest of us."

The family watched the piping and marching from the second-floor Truman Balcony. Caroline and John wore matching powder-blue overcoats with black velvet collars, the same ones they would wear when the Black Watch pipers returned to Washington twelve days later. Caroline threw her arm around her father's neck, and John crawled in and out of his lap. Afterward, Nanny Shaw brought them into the Oval Office in their pajamas to say good night. Kennedy lay on the rug so they could swarm all over him. Lincoln walked in and asked, "What would the people think if they saw the President down on the floor?" Looking up from the floor, he said, "After all, Mrs. Lincoln, I am also a father."

Lincoln and Shaw took the children into the Rose Garden. While John chased one of the family dogs, Caroline stared into the night sky and recited, "Star light, star bright . . ." but could not remember the rest of the ditty. He appeared silently behind her as she went on: "Star bright, star light . . ."

"First star I've seen tonight," Lincoln prompted.

"Up above the world so high," Kennedy said. "Why don't you go over and say that to Mommy?"

PRINCESS GALITZINE HAD MET the reclusive screen star Greta Garbo on a previous Onassis cruise and had renewed their friendship when Garbo attended a showing of her fashions in New York. Garbo had declined several invitations to dine at the White House, but after learning that Galitzine was coming on Wednesday she accepted on condition that the event would be small and discreet. Jackie invited her sister, Lee, and the Washington socialite Florence Mahoney. Kennedy asked Lem Billings, who had met Garbo in 1962 and claimed to have become her great chum while accompanying her on a driving tour of the Riviera the summer before. Ever since then, he had been regaling and perhaps irritating Kennedy with paeans to her beauty and humor.

One of Kennedy's least-appealing attributes was a fondness for practical jokes and a tendency to let them continue too long. A prime example was his treatment of Stevenson in Newport the previous year. The sky had been threatening, the seas rough, and the winds strong, but he summoned Adlai from Washington anyway. Oleg Cassini, who was his guest that weekend, had protested that it was a terrible day for flying. "Good. He'll be airsick," Kennedy said. Stevenson was green and mopping his brow as he disembarked from a helicopter. Kennedy proposed they talk while taking a cruise, a suggestion that Stevenson received with what Cassini called "horror in his eyes." The seas pitched and rolled, lightning flashed, and Kennedy sat with him in the stern, braving the weather without a jacket and forcing him to follow suit. When they docked, he said, "Well, Adlai, there's your helicopter waiting." As it strained to gain altitude, Cassini said, "Mr. President, that is truly cruel and unusual punishment."

"He could use it," Kennedy replied. "It's good for his health."

The previous weekend at Wexford he had persuaded Bradlee to participate in a prank on Torby Macdonald. At his urging, Bradlee had called Macdonald and, as Kennedy listened on an extension, warned him that *Newsweek* was preparing to run a Bobby Baker story that would link Macdonald to a minor lobbyist named Micky Weiner. As Macdonald became increasingly frantic, protesting that he barely knew Weiner, Kennedy put his hand over the mouthpiece and said, "Torb's hurting. Tuck it to him some more." Bradlee continued tormenting Macdonald, and Kennedy collapsed on the sofa, helpless with laughter.

Kennedy had invited Garbo to come early so he could brief her on the prank that he planned to spring on his best friend. When Billings arrived, he bounded over to Garbo and exclaimed, "Greta!" She turned to Kennedy with a puzzled look on her face and said, "I have never seen this man before." Billings was too mortified to eat. He listed everywhere they had been together, but she insisted she had never met this "Mr. Billings." As he became increasingly upset and disoriented, Kennedy was solicitous, suggesting that he might have met someone resembling Garbo. When he finally put his friend out of his misery, everyone laughed uproariously. Billings grinned, trying to be a good sport, but later called the prank "one of the worst things I ever went through in my life."

Garbo became inebriated and shouted, "I must go!" But she stayed and stayed. Jackie gave her a tour of the White House, and she took off her shoes and sat on Lincoln's bed. She refused an invitation to stay overnight because she feared it might have entailed what she called "a visit from the President." Kennedy usually retreated to his study after dinner. Tonight he remained at the party, pointedly telling Garbo that he never stayed with guests this long. Before she left he gave her one of his prized pieces of scrimshaw, prompting Jackie to remark, "He never gave *me* a whale's tooth."

WASHINGTON, THE MASON-DIXON LINE, MANHATTAN, AND PALM BEACH

Kennedy's sixty-fourth press conference was a grim affair. He was mad at Congress for cutting his foreign aid budget, and at the Soviets for arresting the Yale professor Frederick Barghoorn in Moscow on trumped-up espionage charges. These subjects and Vietnam dominated the conference. He sounded cool and reasonable in the transcript, but on television appeared nervous and tense. He cracked fewer jokes, he smiled less, and his voice trailed off. Asked about the purpose of the conference on Vietnam that his advisers were attending in Honolulu the next week, he offered a laundry list of goals, including "assess the situation," decide "what our aid policy should be," and determine "how we can bring Americans out of there."

"Now that is our objective," he stressed. "To bring Americans home, permit the South Vietnamese to maintain themselves as a free and independent country." After asking, "Are we going to give up in South Vietnam?" he answered, "The most important program, of course, is our national security, but I don't want the United States to have to put troops there."

If there was ever a year when he owed Jackie a lavish Christmas gift, it was this one, when she had lost a child and agreed to campaign in Texas. He decided on a fur coverlet and collected samples in the Oval Office. None struck him as good enough, and before leaving Thursday for New York he called a family friend and gave her carte blanche to select a fur, provided it arrived before Christmas.

At 4:00 p.m. his helicopter landed at the point on the Mason-Dixon Line where the Delaware and Maryland border intersected a newly completed stretch of Interstate 95 that would make it possible to drive from Boston to Washington without encountering a traffic light. After the public works titan Robert Moses introduced him generously, and erroneously, as "the chief architect of our present highway system," he predicted that the Boston-to-Washington corridor would become "one gigantic urban center," and cut a blue-and-gray ribbon to open a road soon to become the John F. Kennedy Memorial Highway.

The previous week he had driven into Manhattan in a motorcade of limousines, police cruisers, and motorcycles. Sirens screamed, lights flashed, intersections were blocked, stoplights ignored, and traffic tied in knots. This week he stopped for lights and signs, arriving in the city "like an ordinary motorist," according to Salinger. Even so, his limousine was part of a procession of thirteen cars, many filled with police and Secret Service agents. A section of the East River Drive was under repair, and construction barrels blocked one of its lanes. As the traffic merged, a passenger car threatened to separate his limousine from the Secret Service follow-up car. When the driver ignored shouts from agents to let them pass, one had to point a rifle out the window. After pulling off the drive, Kennedy's car hit every crosstown red light. A city bus blocked his limousine from turning onto Madison Avenue, enabling a woman to dash into the street and take a flash photograph of him. A policeman told a reporter, "She might well have been an assassin."

A police official criticized him for taking "unnecessary risks." Salinger explained that he had not wanted to disrupt traffic. Cynics said that he had not wanted to subject potential voters to delays, and *Time* remarked caustically that he had been "zeroing in on the 'safe-motorists' vote." But winning a few more votes in a state already securely in his column had to be a minor concern. He had probably dispensed with the motorcade because, like the renovations to Jackie's hospital room, it offended his egalitarian sensibilities, and he believed that these fast-moving, police-escorted motorcades only widened the distance between himself and the public.

Once he arrived at the Carlyle Hotel, he was safe, or at least safer. An Otis elevator engineer had been stationed in a shed on the roof to repair any malfunction that might trap him between floors, and a Secret Service detail had inspected and sealed his penthouse suite. But when he left to attend a party at the apartment of his sister and brother-in-law Jean and Stephen Smith, he slipped out a side door with his Secret Service detail, leaving a large police detail waiting in the lobby.

Stevenson was at the party, and face to face with the president he decided to warn him about Dallas. Oleg Cassini, who overheard their conversation, took Kennedy aside and asked, "Why do you go? Your own people are saying you should not." He stared back wordlessly and shrugged.

Before leaving the next morning for the Americana Hotel to address the yearly AFL-CIO convention, he met with Henry Luce, who also had a suite at the Carlyle. Luce had founded *Time* and *Life*, the nation's most influential magazines. Although the flattering photographs in *Life* had advanced Kennedy's career more than scores of complimentary and serious-minded articles, he believed that *Time* was biased against his administration. He complained to Luce that his magazine was making nit-picking criticisms. "What about the state of the world, Mr. Luce?" he asked, challenging him to fault his handling of the important issues. After thinking for a few moments, Luce conceded, "I think we are doing pretty good." During lunch afterward with his White House correspondent, Hugh Sidey, he admitted that the president had been right: his magazine *had* been nit-picking.

In his speech to the AFL-CIO, Kennedy enumerated his successes and challenged the nit-pickers to dismiss them. He had doubled the nuclear weapons in the U.S. strategic forces, he said, and "with that strength we work for peace." He had presided over the peaceful desegregation of thousands of schools, restaurants, and lunch counters. The average factory worker was taking home ten dollars more a week than when he was inaugurated. The stock market had hit record highs, "although we only get credit when it goes down." A robust economy was not enough, he said, unless it contributed "to the fullest extent possible" to ways "to improve our schools, to rebuild our cities, to counsel our young, to assure our health, and to care for our aged and infirm." He conceded that as long as the unemployment rate remained at 5.5 percent, "this issue of economic security, of jobs, is the basic issue facing the United States in 1963." He declared that his tax cut would be the surest remedy for unemployment, and the best guarantee that the nation would continue "sailing . . . on the winds of the longest and strongest peacetime expansion in the history of the United States." He called equal rights important, adding, "But no one gains from a full-employment program if there is no employment to be had; no one gains by being admitted to a lunch counter if he has no money to spend; no one gains from attending a better school if he doesn't have a job after graduation."

He described those opposing his programs to ameliorate youth unemployment, provide jobs training, give aid to depressed areas, and meet other public needs as "powerful and articulate," and criticized them for "campaigning on a platform of so-called individual initiative," adding, "They talk loudly of deficits and socialism, but they do not have a single job-creating program of their own, and they oppose the efforts we are making." After calling his job-creating programs too urgent to be postponed, he recounted a story about Marshal Hubert Lyautey, the first French resident-general of Morocco, who had asked his gardener to plant a tree only to have the man respond, "Why plant it? It won't flower for a hundred years." Lyautey had replied, "Plant it this afternoon!"

When he finished, a young Irish nanny vaulted over a press table at the front of the ballroom, wriggled free of policemen and Secret Service agents, and dashed toward him. He called everyone off and shook her hand. "Last night, I dreamed he took my hand," she said. "I just had to make that dream come true."

He was driven a few blocks to the Hilton, where he told delegates to the Catholic Youth Organization's national convention, "I come here today . . . because we expect something of you." He reminded them that they had an obligation to repay the nation for "all of the talents which society helped develop in you," and echoed the "ask not" passage of his inaugural address, saying, "So we ask the best of you. . . . I congratulate you on what you have done, and most of all I congratulate you on what you are going to do."

Ignoring the protests of his Secret Service detail and police detachment, he again dispensed with a motorcycle escort. When his limousine stopped near the Hilton for a red light, delegates to the youth conference encircled it, forcing the police to raise their clubs and wade into the crowd to free a path. At another red light, a nurse dashed in front of his car to catch a patient who had left something behind, prompting a police inspector to say, "As far as I'm concerned, he can walk into the city the next time he visits."

He flew to Palm Beach that afternoon with O'Donnell, Powers, Smathers, and Macdonald. When Smathers remarked offhandedly, "Everybody on the Hill says Bobby is trying to knock Johnson off the ticket," Kennedy's denial was so vehement that the comment had obviously struck a nerve. "George, I presume you have *some* intelligence," he said sarcastically. "I *love* this job, I love every second of it." Why then, he asked, would he risk it by picking a fight with Johnson that might guarantee him losing all of the Southern states? And if he dropped

Johnson now, when his protégé Bobby Baker was in the headlines, it would appear that *he* had some kind of involvement in the Baker scandal that he wanted to conceal. And if that happened, he predicted, "*Life* magazine would put twenty-seven pictures of these lovely-looking, buxom ladies running around with no clothes on, twenty-seven pictures of Bobby Baker and hoodlums and vending machines, and then the last picture would be of *me*. And it would say 'Mess in Washington under Kennedy Regime,'" and then 99 percent of Americans would conclude that *he* was running around with the girls. (He had forgotten or decided to overlook that Smathers had been a regular at Baker's Quorum Club, and had known many of these "buxom ladies.")

Lyndon Johnson, a likely source for the rumors that Bobby was scheming to replace him, dined that evening at Chandler's, a midtown Manhattan restaurant featuring a screen between its bar and dining room composed of glass squares holding portraits of every U.S. president. When he wandered over to examine them, Chandler's owner pointed to an empty square next to Kennedy's portrait and asked, "When will I put your picture on there?" Johnson's face darkened with rage and he said, "Never! You'll never see it."

While Kennedy was out of town, Bobby, speaking in confidence and with his approval, told Ambassador Dobrynin that he believed relations between their countries depended to a large extent on a good personal relationship and understanding between the president and Chairman Khrushchev, and that another summit meeting could provide an opportunity for the two leaders to "calmly sit and talk everything over."

Jackie spent the weekend at Wexford. On Friday, she entertained her friend Robin Douglas-Home, a jazz pianist and socialite whom she had met during her 1962 Italian holiday. He had not seen her for several months and was struck by how relaxed and composed she seemed. She said she had been encouraged by how much Jack had come to value Caroline and John, and that losing Patrick had strengthened their self-sufficiency as a family. She was determined to accompany him to Texas even though, she admitted, "I'll hate every minute of it." But if he wanted her along, that was what mattered. Douglas-Home believed that he had never seen her happier.

Jackie was more upbeat about Texas during a telephone conversation with Letitia Baldrige, a close friend from boarding school who had recently served as White House social secretary. "You won't believe it, but I'm going campaigning to Texas with Jack next week, and I'm going because I want to," she said. "I'm anxious to hit the campaign trail again. Did you ever expect to hear me say that, Tish?" Baldrige detected a "note of genuine happiness" in her voice, one contrasting sharply with how she had sounded after Patrick's death. "Now she was so exuberant," Baldrige recalled. "I suddenly knew that her marriage was going well."

Saturday, November 16

CAPE CANAVERAL AND PALM BEACH

The *Miami Herald* reporter Nixon Smiley wrote of Kennedy's visit to the Cape Canaveral Space Center, "You had the feeling the air was electrified from the time of the President's arrival until a moment after his departure." Smiley described his hair as being "back lighted by filtered sunshine" and "distinctly reddish," adding, "He wore a deeper tan than most of the men around him. He was a picture of health." Dr. Wernher von Braun, who had come to brief Kennedy on the rocket that would launch U.S. astronauts toward the moon, also found his tan impressive and called him "in the very best of health."

While standing outside the Saturn Control Center, the astronauts Gus Grissom and Gordon Cooper briefed Kennedy and von Braun on the long-duration flights they were taking to prepare themselves for a moon voyage. Inside the windowless blockhouse, where technicians manned the panels that would monitor and control the missile launches, Kennedy sat on a folding chair, surrounded by NASA officials and listening impatiently as Dr. George Mueller, the associate administrator for manned space flight, delivered a fifteen-minute lecture summarizing developments in the lunar program. Briefings that required him to sit passively as someone reeled off facts and figures drove Kennedy crazy. As Mueller droned on, running his pointer over charts and explaining NASA's organization, Kennedy began interrupting him with questions. The moment Mueller stopped, he jumped up, grabbed one of the scale-model missiles arranged on a table in front of him, and asked if it was a Redstone, the one that had launched Alan

Shepard and Grissom on their suborbital flights. After being told it was, he held it against a model of the Saturn V, von Braun's lunar-mission rocket, and asked if they were built to the same scale. The Redstone model was a foot high, the Saturn seven times that. When Mueller confirmed that they were, he exclaimed, "Amazing!" "Fantastic!" and "Gee, looks like we've come a long way." Robert Seamans, who headed NASA, believed this was the moment that Kennedy finally grasped the dimensions of the project he had launched. Von Braun found his boyish enthusiasm "deeply sincere and very charming."

Kennedy knew that his brother Joe had died while on a mission to obliterate bunkers on the French coastline that were being prepared as launching sites for the unmanned rockets that the Germans planned to fire at British cities, and he knew that von Braun, who had belonged to the Nazi Party, had engineered those rockets. He had mentioned this when they met in 1953 at a New York television studio while waiting to appear on a program announcing the nominations for *Time*'s Man of the Year. When von Braun later recounted their conversation, he spoke of Joe being killed "in an airplane accident that was closely related to the fledgling missile technology," a delicate way of framing his connection to the Kennedy family.

After emerging from the Saturn Control Center into the blinding sunshine, von Braun and Kennedy were driven to a launch pad where the skyscraper-high Saturn I rocket stood pointed at the heavens. Von Braun explained that when it was launched the next month, it would be more powerful and would carry a heavier payload than anything the Soviet Union had shot into space.

After staring at it for several moments, Kennedy said, "Now, this will be the largest payload that man has ever put in orbit. Is that right?" After von Braun again assured him that it was, he said, "That is very, very significant."

While briefing Kennedy at the Marshall Space Flight Center in Huntsville the previous year, von Braun had noticed that he was a man who liked to evaluate things on the basis of what he could see and touch, so he was not surprised when Kennedy suddenly strode toward the Saturn I rocket, not stopping until he stood directly underneath it. He looked up and, rocking back and forth on the balls of his feet, said in a soft voice, "When this goes up we'll be ahead of the Russians. . . . When this goes up we'll be ahead of the Russians."

Sidey, who overheard this, had also been with him at a campaign stop in Oklahoma City in 1960 when he had told an audience, "I will take my television black and white. I want to be ahead of them [the Russians] in rocket thrust." And when he had been at the White House on April 14, 1961, two days after the Soviet cosmonaut Yuri Gagarin had become the first human to orbit the earth, Kennedy had invited him into the Cabinet Room so that he could listen to his advisers debate the wisdom of racing the Soviet Union to the moon. "What can we do now?" Kennedy had demanded. "Is there any place we can catch them?" The science adviser Jerome Wiesner and NASA's director, James Webb, argued that a manned lunar landing would not be as scientifically important as several less costly and dramatic ventures. NASA's chief scientist, Hugh Dryden, thought it might require an investment similar to the Manhattan Project, the government program that had developed the atomic bomb. Budget Director David Bell wondered if the nation could support such a huge expenditure. Sorensen was concerned that it would divert resources from social programs. But Kennedy cared more about beating the Russians to the moon. "If someone can just tell me how to catch up," he said. "Let's find somebody—anybody. I don't care if it's the janitor if he knows how." After the meeting ended inconclusively, Sidey stopped him at the door and asked what he had decided. "Wait here," he said, gesturing for Sorensen to follow him into the Oval Office. Several minutes later Sorensen emerged and said, "We are going to the moon."

Kennedy traveled by helicopter from the launch pad to a Navy vessel from which he would watch a submarine launch a Polaris missile. On the way he passed over Merritt Island, where construction was proceeding for the 87,000-acre Moonport. He looked down to see a thrilling incarnation of American power in the middle of the American Century, an undertaking as ambitious and historic as the Panama Canal and the Manhattan Project. Seamans pointed out the future launch pad and Vertical Assembly Building, where the Saturn missiles would be assembled and stored. Once completed, it would be the fourth-largest structure on earth, bigger than the Pentagon and taller than anything south of the Washington Monument.

The previous year, during a speech at Rice University, Kennedy had said, "We choose to go to the moon in this decade and do other things, not because they are easy, but because they are hard, because that goal will serve to organize and measure the best of our energies and skills." He had then compared the lunar mission to the exceptionalism of the founders of the Plymouth Bay Colony, quoting Governor William Bradford, who had said that "all great and honorable actions are accompanied with great difficulties, and must be . . . overcome with answerable courage." Here, rising on this sandy barrier island, was a twentieth-century incarnation of Bradford's "Shining City on a Hill" and his "answerable courage." Here, captured in brick and mortar, was the exploring spirit of Lewis and Clark. Here, too, was proof that, as Kennedy had proclaimed in his American University speech, "Man can be as big as he wants. No problem of human destiny is beyond human beings," as well as evidence that he was poised to marry the power of the presidency to the poetry of the stars.

The Polaris launch combined several things that Kennedy loved—the U.S. Navy, the ocean, and technological wizardry. But despite the handsome windbreaker that he received upon landing on the missile support ship and immediately put on (because it was not a hat), and the missile with "Beat Army" painted on its fuselage shooting dramatically from the water with a great swoosh and an explosion of orange flames, all he wanted to talk about during the flight back to the mainland was the space program. Referring to the Saturn I rocket, he asked Seamans, "Now, I'm not sure I have the facts straight on this. Will you tell me about it again?"

Seamans ran through the size of its payload and the magnitude of its liftoff thrust.

"What's the Soviet capability?" he asked.

Much less, Seamans said, only 15,000 pounds of usable payload and a thrust capacity of 800,000 pounds as compared with 1.5 million for the Saturn.

"That's very important," he said. "Now be sure the press understands this." He gave Seamans the name of a reporter he wanted him to brief, and as they parted he reminded him to stress that the United States was about to score an important victory over the Soviet Union. Seamans did as he was told, and a front-page article in the *New York Times* the next day reported that the president had been "enthralled" by the sight of the Saturn I missile, which was expected to make "space history" the following month by putting the United States ahead of the Soviet Union in the weight of payload sent into orbit.

Four days before leaving for Cape Canaveral, Kennedy had signed a directive instructing NASA's Webb "to assume personally the initiative and central responsibility within the Government for the development of a program of substantive cooperation with the Soviet Union in the field of outer space." The directive stipulated that discussions with the Soviets should include "cooperation in lunar landing programs," with a progress report to be on the president's desk by December 15. But now, having stood in the shadow of the Saturn rocket and flown over the Moonport, Kennedy's competitive spirit had been revived, and his emotional connection to the space program rekindled, leaving him once again determined to beat the Soviets to the moon.

Sunday, November 17—Monday, November 18

PALM BEACH, TAMPA, MIAMI

As they were driving to the West Palm Beach airport on Monday morning, Kennedy told Torby Macdonald that the weekend had been "really living," and one he would never forget. The weather had been perfect, windless sunny days followed by clear nights. On Saturday afternoon they had sat on the patio in swimsuits watching the Navy-Duke football game. He had bet on Navy and after winning had insisted that Powers and Macdonald fetch their wallets and pay up. On Saturday evening he sang "September Song" and talked endlessly about von Braun's prediction that the United States would beat the Russians to the moon. On Sunday they had gathered on the patio to watch the Bears play the Packers, and again he won the wager. The weekend reminded Macdonald of the months before the Second World War, "when there was nothing of moment on anybody's mind." The only jarring note came when he and Kennedy were swimming together and began discussing how they both feared being incapacitated by a stroke, as their fathers had been. Macdonald asked Kennedy how he would like to die. "Oh, a gun," he said. "You never know what's hit you. A gunshot is the perfect way."

While Kennedy was enjoying the weekend pleasures of the average middle-aged, middle-class American male, his programs and initiatives were moving forward.

During a speech at the New York Economic Club, McNamara announced that a major cut in defense spending was "in the works," calling it "a fundamental strategic shift . . . not just a temporary slash."

The Associated Press reported that "the withdrawal of 1000 U.S. servicemen from South Vietnam will start Dec. 3, Major General Charles J. Timmes announced today. The men are to depart by the end of the year, leaving about 15,500 troops in the country."

Secretary of Health, Education, and Welfare Anthony Celebrezze presented the administration's case for Medicare to the House Ways and Means Committee, describing it as "legislation to provide health care for the elderly under the Social Security program." It was necessary, he said, because "the best that private insurance has been able to do to solve the dilemma of high costs and low income is to offer either low-cost policies with inadequate protection or more adequate policies that are priced out of reach of most of the aged." The committee was not expected to vote on Medicare that year, but as the hearing progressed, the prospects for favorable action appeared to be improving.

Deputy Attorney General Nicholas Katzenbach announced that the administration was "hopeful" that the civil rights bill would reach the House floor by mid-December and be passed by Christmas. The *New York Times* editorialized that even if this timetable was not met, its postponement into 1964 "would not necessarily be fatal."

Walter Heller received a memorandum from Under Secretary of Agriculture Charles Murphy responding to his request to provide recommendations for "Widening Prosperity," the new title of the president's antipoverty program. Murphy wrote that because of the difficulty of "proposing any dramatic new legislative program to attack poverty in a time of tight budgetary restrictions," he suggested waiting to launch it until the fall of 1964.

Jim Bishop and Pierre Salinger happened to dine at the same Palm Beach restaurant on Saturday evening. Salinger told Bishop that Kennedy was eager to read his book. It struck Bishop as odd that he should be so insistent on seeing the manuscript but promised to rush it to the White House.

DURING HIS FLIGHT from West Palm Beach to Tampa on Monday morning, Kennedy stopped in the aisle to talk with Secret Service Agent Floyd Boring. Putting a hand on his shoulder, he said, "I have a feeling it's going to be a great day."

Agent Emory Roberts, who was also on Kennedy's Secret Service detachment, had received a call that morning from Agent Gerald Blaine, who was in Tampa preparing for the president's visit. Blaine had accompanied Kennedy on the previous summer's motorcades in Dublin and Rome, and after witnessing crowds in those cities breaking through police lines and engulfing Kennedy's limousine he was concerned it might happen in Tampa, where he would be riding in the longest motorcade of his presidency—a twenty-eight-mile drive from Al Lopez Field, the spring training home of the New York Yankees, through downtown to the Fort Homer Hesterly Armory. Blaine was also worried because Tampa had a large Cuban community with pro- and anti-Castro factions, and because a right-wing fanatic named Joseph Milteer had been recorded telling a police informant that the best way to kill the president would be "from an office building with a high-powered rifle." The Secret Service had tracked Milteer to Georgia and placed him under surveillance, but the threat had unsettled Blaine enough that he called Roberts to recommend that he and Boring station two agents on the steps flanking the trunk of the president's limousine. This would put them close enough to protect him from spectators dashing toward the car, and in a position where they could shield him from the kind of sniper threatened by Milteer.

Boring seized on his casual encounter with Kennedy on Air Force One to raise this sensitive subject. Taking a deep breath, he said, "Mr. President, we have a very long motorcade, so we're going to have to stick to a tight time schedule. Two people have made threats against your life and even though we have them in custody, you might want to keep your stops during the motorcade to a minimum."

Removing his hand from Boring's shoulder, Kennedy said, "Floyd, this is a political trip. If I don't mingle with the people, I couldn't get elected dog catcher." He was down the aisle before Boring could suggest positioning agents on the rear steps.

The Secret Service had not guarded candidates during the 1960 campaign, so Tampa would be the first time that it had protected Kennedy while he was in campaign mode. Not only would he be taking the longest motorcade of his presidency, but he would be making a record number of stops in a single day: arrival and departure ceremonies at MacDill Air Force Base, a visit to the military's Strike Command headquarters, lunch at the officers' club at the base, a speech at Al Lopez Field to commemorate the fiftieth anniversary of the first flight from Tampa to St. Petersburg, another speech to members of the Florida Chamber of Commerce at the armory, and another to the United Steelworkers union at a downtown hotel. Blaine and the agents preparing for the visit had screened the reporters who would be covering him and the dignitaries who would be welcoming, dining, and sharing platforms with him. They had flown his black Lincoln Continental from Washington the night before and would guard it until he climbed inside. They had ordered policemen stationed on overpasses on his route and on catwalks inside the armory, and told the motorcycle policemen to drive straight ahead and run down unauthorized individuals approaching his limousine. They had put agents in the kitchen of the officers' club who would choose at random which tray of food would be sent to his table, and posted an agent outside the home of a man overheard boasting that the Ku Klux Klan had authorized him to assassinate the president. But they did not have the manpower to run background checks on everyone who would get close to him, nor could they be certain that one of the 25,000 people attending these events would not be armed, perhaps explaining why an off-duty St. Petersburg policeman was able to carry a pistol into the armory while agents were confiscating a Brownie box camera from a fourteen-year-old boy.

Evelyn Lincoln remembered Kennedy "glowing with good health and confidence" as he disembarked in Tampa. Reporters described him being "relaxed, healthy, and suntanned." (Since he had been in Florida for only two days, a sun lamp had to have accounted for his deep tan.) He wore three different outfits in Tampa. He arrived in a gray suit, white shirt, and blue tie with a small gold stripe, but when he spoke to the Chamber of Commerce at the armory three hours later, he was dressed in a midnight-blue suit with a solid dark blue tie and a white shirt with French cuffs anchored by cufflinks, clothes he presumably considered more suitable for an audience of conservative businessmen. By the time he left for Miami he had changed again. Perhaps wearing clean clothes and fresh shirts every few hours was something that, like a tan, made him feel good.

He was smiling and relaxed as his motorcade departed Al Lopez Field, and he struck his Secret Service driver, Bill Greer, as excited by how well the trip was going. The Tampa police chief drove the lead car, with Agent Blaine sitting next to him in the front seat. Greer drove the presidential limousine. Boring sat next to him while Agents Lawton and Zbaril stood on the rear steps. There were buttons, banners, and crowds pushing against police barriers. Girls screamed and women leaped into the air, just as they had in 1960. When the crowds thickened, Greer slowed down and Lawton and Zbaril jumped off the rear steps and jogged alongside. When he accelerated, they remounted and Kennedy noticed them for the first time. He leaned forward and, speaking into Boring's ear so he could be heard over the roar of the motorcycles, said, "Floyd, have the Ivy League charlatans drop back to the follow-up car."

Boring was surprised that he had allowed the agents to ride on the steps for so long. He relayed the message verbatim over the walkie-talkie to Blaine, who was also surprised because Kennedy usually made his wishes known at the beginning of a motorcade. He was unfamiliar with the word "charlatan" and jotted it down so he could check its meaning. Kennedy had cultivated a closer relationship with the agents than most presidents, and probably meant the comment as an affectionate put-down. Most *did* in fact dress like Ivy Leaguers. But for a president who was trying to be more Irish than Harvard, Ivy Leaguers, even if they were charlatans, reminded the public of his own Ivy League background.

"It's excessive, Floyd," he told Boring when they arrived at the armory, "and it's giving the wrong impression. . . . Tell them to stay on the follow-up car. We've got an election coming up. The whole point is for me to be accessible to the people."

The tension between the agents' desire to minimize his interactions with the public and his desire to maximize them was apparent all day. After arriving at MacDill Air Force Base, he had unsettled the Secret Service by climbing in one door of his limousine and out the other in order to greet some military wives and children who had been confined to a parking lot. After eating lunch at the MacDill officers' club he insisted on speaking with the black waiters, who grabbed towels and wiped their hands before shaking his. He delayed his departure from Tampa so he could talk with each of the thirty-three motorcycle policemen who had escorted his motorcade. "As he shook our hands he looked us in the eye and said each of our names," one recalled. "It was thrilling. I didn't wash my hands for a week."

The lead editorial in Tuesday's *Tampa Tribune* confirmed the wisdom of his tanning, shirt-changing, hand-shaking, and accessibility. The editors wrote, "The Democrats' main selling points next year, it appears, will be Peace, Prosperity, and Personality (Mr. Kennedy's)." After describing him as "a bright-eyed relaxed young man" who had charmed Tampa by "distributing cheer with an expert hand," they complimented him for offering "a smile and a handshake for all within reaching distance, [and] a cordial wave for the crowds along the motorcade route," and concluded that his performance had illustrated the problem Republicans faced in 1964, noting, "Sunshine, as reflected from peace, prosperity, and personality, is a tough product to compete against." The editorial could only have reinforced his determination to follow the same script in Texas.

He witnessed the power of his "Personality" firsthand while answering questions from members of the Florida Chamber of Commerce at the Fort Homer Hesterly Armory. Most of the questions were timid and respectful, along the lines of "Why didn't you bring Caroline?" and "How will the recent wheat deal with Russia affect our economy?" Finally, someone asked why he was pushing civil rights "so vigorously."

Lunch counters, hotels, theaters, pools, and other public accommodations in Tampa remained segregated. The state's congressional delegation, including his friend George Smathers, opposed the civil rights bill, and if you could have polled the armory audience, most would have probably accused him of pushing integration too fast. But instead of filibustering the question or offering platitudes and generalities, he reaffirmed the practical and moral underpinnings of the controversial public accommodations section of his bill, defending it as necessary to guarantee "domestic tranquility," and reminding the audience that treating black Americans "as I would like to be treated, and as you would like to be treated" was in line with the Golden Rule. He concluded, "No country has ever faced a more difficult problem than attempting to bring [up] ten percent of the population of a different color, educate them, give them a chance for a fair life. That is my objective and I think it is the objective of the United States as I have always understood it."

The white businessmen and their wives gave this statement the loudest and most prolonged applause of the afternoon. Decades later, a *St. Petersburg Times* reporter interviewed members of that audience and concluded that they had been "mesmerized," and that "no one really heard what he said—only how he said it." An attorney's wife who had arrived a skeptic, because she felt Kennedy was "not sensitive to the problems of the South," changed her mind after seeing him. "He was so young and handsome . . . ," she recalled, "a knight in shining armor."

He told the crowd greeting him at the Miami airport that he agreed with Woodrow Wilson's statement that "a political party is of no use unless it is serving a great national purpose." At the Inter-American Press Association banquet at the Americana Hotel, he ended his prepared speech with a signal to Castro that he was prepared for a secret dialogue. It echoed what he had told Jean Daniel on October 24. He praised the initial Cuban revolution as a genuine uprising "against the tyranny and corruption of the past." After accusing Castro of betraying it, he said:

> It is important to restate what now divides Cuba from my country and from other countries of this hemisphere. It is the fact that a small band of conspirators has stripped the Cuban people of their freedom and handed over the independence and sovereignty of the Cuban nation to forces beyond the hemisphere. They have made Cuba a victim of foreign imperialism . . . a weapon in an effort dictated by external powers to subvert other American republics. *This, and this alone, divides us. As long as this is true, nothing is possible. Without it, everything is possible* [emphasis added]. Once this barrier is removed, we will be ready and anxious to work with the Cuban people in pursuit of those progressive goals which a few short years ago stirred their hopes and the sympathy of many people throughout the hemisphere.

Here again was his message for Castro: better relations with the United States did not require that he renounce socialism or even communism, only that he detach himself from Moscow and cease attempts to export communism to other nations in the hemisphere.

During the flight back to Washington he told Smathers, "God, I hate to go out to Texas." He added that he had "a terrible feeling about going." His "terrible feeling" was that the feud between Vice President Johnson and Texas senator Ralph Yarborough would sabotage the trip. "Look how screwed up it's going to be," he said. "You've got Lyndon, who is insisting that Jackie ride with him [in motorcades]. You've got Ralph Yarborough, who hates Lyndon and Johnson doesn't want Yarborough with him. . . . They're all prima donnas of the biggest order, and they're all insisting that they ride either with me or with Jackie. The law says the vice president can't ride with the president. . . . I just wish to hell I didn't have to go. Can't you think of some emergency we could have?"

He told Powers, "Thank God nobody wanted to kill me today!" He made this kind of comment so often that Powers usually shrugged it off. This time, he added that if anyone tried to kill him with a high-powered rifle outfitted with a telescopic sight, he would do it during a motorcade, when there would be so much noise and commotion that no one would be able to point and say, "It came from that window!"

Tuesday, November 19

WASHINGTON

Lincoln remembered Tuesday as a day when "there was no hurry, no tension, no hustle" and Kennedy was memorably relaxed. After noticing that O'Donnell and Powers were absent, he asked her, "Where are those clowns?" Exhausted after Florida, she explained. "We were on that trip too," he said, "but we are here, aren't we, Mrs. Lincoln?"

He sat in a rocking chair in her office between meetings, his head resting against its back, one leg across a knee, speaking slowly and pensively as he rocked. He talked about his encouraging reception in Florida, why he had refused police protection in New York, the wonderful photographs of John in *Look*, and how the Bobby Baker scandal might affect his reelection campaign.

"You know, if I am reelected in '64," he said. "I am going to spend more and more time toward making government service an honorable career." He considered it absurd that in the Space Age someone who had become chairman of a congressional committee because of his longevity could tie up a bill and prevent it reaching the House floor for a vote. In his second term, he said, "I am going to advocate changing some of the outmoded rules and regulations in Congress, such as the seniority rule," adding, "To do this I will need as a running mate in '64 a man who believes as I do." As if thinking out loud, he continued, "I am going to Texas because I have made a commitment. I can't patch up those warring factions. This is for them to do, but I will go because I have told them I would. And it is too early to make an announcement about another running mate—that will perhaps wait until the convention."

"Who *is* your choice of a running mate?" Lincoln asked.

Staring straight ahead, he said without hesitation, "At this time I am thinking about Governor Terry Sanford of North Carolina. But it will not be Lyndon." Sanford was a logical choice. Kennedy was impressed with his economic and antipoverty programs, and he represented the enlightened "New South" that the president needed to court in 1964.

Lincoln had not seen Johnson in the Oval Office for almost a month and had already suspected that the president was considering replacing him. Sanford would later say that although he and Kennedy had never discussed the vice presidency, he did not doubt that the conversation had occurred as Lincoln had reported it. He knew that the president had become exasperated with Johnson, but thought his comments might have been "one of those things that you say . . . just to get it off your chest."

Johnson's close relationship with Bobby Baker, and the likelihood that he would be tarred by the unfolding scandal, was reason enough for Kennedy to consider replacing him. He had also become increasingly worried about the prospect of a Johnson presidency, telling Jackie several times, "Oh, God, can you ever imagine what would happen to the country if Lyndon was president?" In 1964, Sorensen would ask Jackie to comment on a draft manuscript of his book about her husband's administration. Her markings deleted or modified every complimentary reference to Johnson. Where Sorensen had written that Kennedy had "learned from Lyndon Johnson," she noted, "I don't think he learned anything about campaigning from Lyndon Johnson—because Johnson's style always embarrassed him." She criticized Sorensen's statement that the two men had enjoyed "a deep mutual respect," writing, "I think you overstate this a bit—from JFK's side," then crossed out the entire sentence. She told Sorensen that his "glowing references" to Johnson did not "reflect President Kennedy's thinking," adding, "You must know—as well or better than I—his steadily diminishing opinion of him then. As his term progressed, he grew more and more concerned about what would happen if LBJ ever became president. He was truly frightened at the prospect."

AT A 10:00 A.M. CEREMONY in the Rose Garden the president of the National Poultry and Egg Board and the president of the National Turkey

Foundation presented Kennedy with a fifty-five-pound turkey. The Poultry Board president ceremoniously removed the gargantuan beast from his cage and introduced him as "Tom, one of our finer specimens." A sign dangling around the creature's neck said, "Good Eating, Mr. President." Flashbulbs exploded and children from the White House school screamed, "He's a real turkey!" As Tom gobbled and shook his brilliant red wattles, the president said, "On behalf of Mrs. Kennedy and the children, I want to tell you how pleased we are and how grateful. This is a great occasion for the American people. This is really an even sacred occasion." Eisenhower had eaten his ceremonial turkeys, reason enough for Kennedy to spare Tom, but he also disliked killing animals and had not forgotten the appalling hunting expedition at Johnson's ranch. He decided to spare Tom, saying in a mock-serious tone of voice, "It would be a shame, a terrible shame to interrupt a great line like Tom's. We'll just keep him."

The U.S. ambassador to Ghana, William Mahoney, who had arrived early for a 10:30 meeting only to be dragged outside by Kennedy to witness the festivities, remembered the moment as "priceless." Back in the Oval Office, Kennedy asked after Mahoney's infant daughter. She had recently been born in a Ghanaian hospital and given the middle name Fitzgerald. Mahoney claimed that although his mother's maiden name was Fitzgerald, they really had Kennedy in mind. He laughed and said, "Oh, come off it." But Mahoney insisted she had been named for him, and could see he was touched.

Mahoney complained that he was tired of approaching President Kwame Nkrumah before the beginning of every General Assembly session to request that Ghana vote against admitting Communist China to the United Nations. Kennedy replied that he was hoping to improve relations with Peking during his second term. To that end, Assistant Secretary of State for Far Eastern Affairs Roger Hilsman would be delivering an address about U.S.-Sino relations next month that would "open the door a little bit." He showed Mahoney a draft of Hilsman's speech. It called for improving relations with the Chinese on the same terms that he was offering Castro—cease all attempts to export revolution and communism to third-world countries—and concluded, "We do not know what changes may occur in the attitudes of future Chinese leaders, but if I may paraphrase a classic canon of our past, we pursue today towards Communist China a policy of the Open Door: We are determined to keep the door open to the possibility of change, and not to slam it shut against any development which might advance our national good, serve the free world and benefit the people of China." His intention to change U.S. China policy was not a secret. He had told Marie Ridder that it was on his agenda for his second term, and Dean Rusk said they often discussed it, and he thought Kennedy would have reached out to the Chinese in 1965.

He asked Mahoney, who had managed his campaign in Arizona in 1960, if he would help him again next year, when his likely opponent would be Mahoney's fellow Arizonan Barry Goldwater. The news of Goldwater's ascendency had not reached Mahoney in Africa, and he was stunned. "You know, Mr. President, you've got to give the opposition credit for having some sense. Just a little sense," he said. "And they're not, they're just not that stupid."

"Well, that's the word that's out, Bill. God, wouldn't that be a delight."

"It's too good to be true."

Mahoney had represented the NAACP in Arizona during the 1940s, winning several important school desegregation victories. He had missed Goldwater's rise in the polls but had been following the civil rights bill. Referring to Kennedy's June 11 civil rights speech, he said, "I just want to tell you that I'm just proud as hell of you."

He laughed and said, "You know, I'm kind of proud of myself."

He rose from his rocking chair and picked up an article titled "JFK Could Lose" that would appear in the next edition of Look. After putting on his glasses (the first time Mahoney could remember him wearing them), he read portions out loud. It reported the results of a poll taken among residents of Silver Lake, a pivotal Iowa township that had voted for the winning candidate in seventeen consecutive presidential elections since 1896. Kennedy had beaten Nixon there by seventeen votes, but Look was reporting that twenty-nine of the voters supporting him in 1960 now intended to vote for Goldwater, while only fourteen of the Nixon voters were switching to him. "The outcome of the poll does not appear to reflect positive Goldwater strength so much as certain dissatisfactions with Kennedy," the reporter concluded, "particularly over the Negro civil rights demonstrations." It was a surprising statement given that Silver Lake was in a county of fifteen thousand people with only two black residents.

Continuing to read out loud, Kennedy quoted a farmer who had supported him in 1960 but now opposed him and had told Look, "I know the Negroes are here, but by God I think we're giving them too much rope. It won't be long before they'll be running a Negro for president." A farmer who still supported him had said, "So far as letting them go to the same schools and things, I think they would be better off to have their own schools and they would have a lot less trouble." Another man said, "I think some Communists are behind this personally," and another, "I think Kennedy is too lenient with them damn niggers."

"What do you think of that?" he asked Mahoney.

He called it shocking and said, "Look, there's only one way to go."

"You're telling me. And that's where we're going."

Mahoney sensed that despite the bravado, Kennedy found the article unsettling. As they parted, he mentioned his forthcoming trip to Texas and the feud among Johnson, Yarborough, and Connally. At least Jackie was accompanying him, he said, adding, "She's going all the way with me in '64."

ATTWOOD CALLED BUNDY'S ASSISTANT Gordon Chase on Tuesday morning to report that at 2:00 a.m. Lisa Howard had reached Castro's confidant Rene Vallejo and put Attwood on the phone. (Attwood would learn later that Castro had been eavesdropping on an extension.) Vallejo had repeated Castro's invitation to travel to Cuba to open negotiations, promising secrecy and tight security. Attwood replied that the White House wanted any preliminary talks preceding face-to-face negotiations to occur at the United Nations. Vallejo said he was unable to travel to New York, but would instruct Cuba's UN representative, Carlos Lechuga, to discuss an agenda. Chase wrote in a memorandum of his conversation with Attwood, "The ball is now in Castro's court. As soon as Lechuga calls Bill to set up an appointment for the discussion of an agenda, Bill will get in touch with us." Bundy called Attwood back later on Tuesday to tell him that the president had decided that once he and Lechuga had agreed upon an agenda, he wanted to see him personally in order to decide what to tell Castro.

In Havana on Tuesday, Castro told Jean Daniel, "He [Kennedy] still has the possibility of becoming, in the eyes of history, the greatest president of the United States, the leader who may at last understand that there can be coexistence between capitalists and socialists. . . . I know, for example, that for Khrushchev, Kennedy is a man you can talk with. I have gotten this impression from all my conversations with Khrushchev. Other leaders have assured me that to obtain this goal [coexistence] we must first await his reelection." After praising

Kennedy for having "come to understand many things over the past few months," he added, "If you see him again, you can tell him that I'm willing to declare Goldwater my friend if that will guarantee [his] reelection."

Like Kennedy, who was pursuing a two-track strategy of seeking to negotiate with Castro while trying to overthrow him, Castro had his own double strategy. While encouraging clandestine talks with Attwood, he continued his attempts to subvert other Latin American governments. On the same day that Attwood summarized his conversation with Vallejo for Chase, Richard Helms, deputy director of plans at the CIA, was showing Bobby Kennedy a Belgian-made submachine gun the Agency had filched from a shipment that Cuban operatives were preparing to land on the coast of Venezuela. The arms were destined for a group plotting to disrupt that nation's elections and foment a coup against President Romulo Betancourt. The gun's Cuban army markings and serial number had been scraped away, but CIA technicians had applied acid to the barrel that restored them so they could be photographed before fading again. The gun and photographs were hard evidence of Cuban-sponsored subversion that violated the post-missile-crisis agreement between the United States and the Soviet Union. After seeing the pictures, Bobby called the White House to arrange an immediate meeting between Helms and the president.

Kennedy studied the photographs that Helms had spread across the Oval Office coffee table and asked how the Cubans had managed to land such a large cache of weapons on a Venezuelan beach. After he examined the submachine gun and slid it back into the canvas bag that Helms had used to carry it into the White House, Helms said, "I'm sure glad the Secret Service didn't catch us bringing this gun in here." Kennedy grinned, shook his head, and said, "Yes, it gives me a feeling of confidence."

He held a final briefing on Tuesday with Dean Rusk and Michael Forrestal before their departure for Honolulu and Tokyo. Rusk would cross paths in Honolulu with Lodge, who was returning to Washington to have lunch with Kennedy on November 24. From Honolulu, Rusk and Forrestal would fly to Tokyo with other administration officials to confer with the Japanese cabinet and prepare the ground for the president and First Lady's trip to the Far East in January. After Rusk left, Kennedy told Forrestal that he thought the odds of the United States winning the war in Vietnam were about a hundred to one. "When you come back, I want you to come and see me, because we have to start to plan for what we are going to do now, in South Vietnam," he said. "I want to start a complete and very profound review of how we got into this country; what we thought we were doing; and what we now think we can do. I even want to think about whether or not we should be there."

He had also mentioned a major Vietnam policy review to Senator Wayne Morse of Oregon, an early critic of U.S. involvement in the conflict, when Morse came to the White House in November to confer about the administration's education bill. "Wayne, I want you to know you're absolutely right in your criticism of my Vietnam policy," he had said. "Keep this in mind, I'm in the midst of an intensive study which substantiates your position on Vietnam. When I'm finished, I want you to give me half a day and analyze it point by point."

Heller came into the Oval Office late Tuesday afternoon to brief him on the antipoverty program. Federal agencies were embracing the program, he said, but wanted reassurance that the president was firmly behind it. Kennedy's reply showed that he had taken Scammon's analysis of the rising importance of middle-class suburban voters to heart. "I'm still very much in favor of doing something on the poverty theme if we can get a good program," he said, "but I also think it's important to make clear that we're doing something for the middle-income man in the suburbs, et cetera. But the two are not at all inconsistent with one another. So go right ahead with your work on it."

Lewis Weinstein, a distinguished Boston attorney who had supported Kennedy since his first campaign in 1946, stopped in the Oval Office for a brief conversation after attending a meeting of the President's Committee on Equal Opportunity in Housing. He reported that he was about to take office as chairman of the Conference of Presidents of Major Jewish Organizations, and asked if Kennedy would sponsor a conference with Jewish leaders to discuss the oppression of Jews in the Soviet Union. After he pointed out that no president since Theodore Roosevelt had championed Russian Jews, Kennedy said, "Well, here's one President who's ready to do something," and promised to hold the conference after his return from Texas. He called Weinstein the next day to apologize for not giving him more time and to promise to send him a new photograph. It "shows my battle scars and wrinkles," he said, adding, "I'm not the skinny kid you once knew. In the picture I'm looking upward, watching eternity."

When Salinger came to say good-bye before leaving for Honolulu, Kennedy looked up from a stack of papers, removed his glasses, and said with an air of fatigue, "I wish I weren't going to Texas." That morning Salinger had received a letter from a woman in Dallas saying, "Don't let the President come down here. I'm worried about him. I think something terrible will happen to him." He decided not to mention the letter, because he knew Kennedy would dismiss it, just as he had the other warnings. But Lincoln had no qualms about relaying her husband's premonitions to him. Before going home that evening she told him that for days Abe had been telling her that he had a bad feeling about the trip, and wished the president were not going.

"If they are going to get me," he said, "they will get me even in church."

Wednesday, November 20

WASHINGTON

During their weekly White House breakfast meeting with Kennedy, the Democratic congressional leaders expressed reservations about his decision to visit Dallas, given what had happened to Stevenson. When House Majority Whip Hale Boggs cautioned that he was going into "quite a hornet's nest," he replied, "Well, that always creates interesting crowds." His mind was wandering, and he drew doodles of sailboats, writing above them "20th anniversary," and "August," perhaps references to August 1963, the twentieth anniversary of the sinking of *PT 109*, or to August 1964, the twentieth anniversary of his brother's death.

He would be away for most of the next twelve days, first in Texas, then in Hyannis Port for Thanksgiving. He spent some of Wednesday attending to personal business. He complained to Dr. Burkley about a case of jock itch, signed a lease to rent Brambletyde next July, asked Lincoln to check on the forecast for Texas so Jackie would pack the right clothes, and told Turnure to make sure that Jackie had a hairstyle that could withstand the wind while she was riding in an open limousine. Turnure suggested a shorter motorcade, or putting the bubble top over the car. "Take a forty-five-minute drive around Washington with Dave Powers," he said. "See what you look like when you come back."

He read a carbon copy of Jim Bishop's *A Day in the Life of President Kennedy* as soon as it arrived. Bishop never revised, so this was his first and only draft, written in less than three weeks and padded with dull descriptions of the

White House furniture and biographies of Kennedy's staff and cabinet. Among his revelations were that the president liked a grilled cheese sandwich and consommé for lunch, kept the pool heated to ninety degrees and did the breaststroke so he could swim and talk (Bishop had not wondered why he had turned the customarily solitary activity of swimming into a group event), and treated time "as though he has been told he has a week to live."

Kennedy approved the manuscript without asking for a single revision. Jackie was more sensitive, or read it more closely, and requested sixty minor changes. Bishop agreed to all but one, refusing to cut Dave Powers's remark that his family called him the president's "other wife." Bishop included some observations in his memoirs that had escaped inclusion in A Day in the Life. "A bit of old-fashioned Boston peeked through his habits," he wrote. "He sat on the same cushion of the same settee every night. He lit a big cigar and poured a cold beer. Then . . . [he] would ask Mrs. Kennedy to play the same music: a recording of Camelot. He was in a pleasant rut: same cigar, same beer, same music, same cushion."

Kennedy's last meeting was a late-afternoon conference with Roger Hilsman and Undersecretary of State U. Alexis Johnson, prompted by a communication from Cambodia's Prince Sihanouk requesting that the United States cut off aid to his nation. They showed him a draft of a proposed reply that he considered too harsh. He added some words of friendship and reconciliation, leading Johnson to reflect, "He was always seeking to conciliate; he was always seeking to understand other people and what their motives were. He could never quite accept the fact that other people would not always return his good will."

Before greeting the seven hundred guests attending the annual White House Judicial Reception, he hosted a reception upstairs for the Supreme Court justices and their wives. He remained seated, rocking in his chair, a hand under his chin as he scrutinized the justices. Sixty-five-year-old Associate Justice William O. Douglas had just married twenty-three-year-old law student Joan Carol Martin, and this was her first visit to the White House. Like de Kooning, who had been surprised to find Kennedy "incandescent, golden, and bigger than life," Joan Douglas noticed that "he was not black and white, as he had seemed to be in pictures," but was "vibrant and glowing. . . . [and] an outdoorsman, like my husband." De Kooning had been captivated by the notion of this "gallant, intelligent, handsome man leading the country and the world." Joan Douglas thought he had taken "all the formaldehyde out of [the] government," becoming "a noble figure moving through the pages of history."

He and Jackie descended a red-carpeted stairway to the reception. There was no receiving line, so his cabinet, members of the federal judiciary, and Justice Department employees surrounded them as they moved between rooms while the Marine band played tunes from *My Fair Lady* and *Camelot*. Treasury Secretary Dillon tracked him down in the East Room to say good-bye before leaving for the Far East with Rusk and Salinger. "You're going off to Japan," Kennedy said. "I've got to go to Texas. I wish we could trade places." Dillon thought he was "in wonderful form" and "looked great." The Supreme Court justices also remarked on his high spirits to Chief Justice Earl Warren. But Ethel Kennedy thought he seemed withdrawn and preoccupied. Either she had detected something the others had missed, or he was in high spirits *and* worried about Vietnam, Bobby Baker, and the feuding Texas Democrats, and she and the Supreme Court justices were noticing the same "extraordinary variety of expressions" that had mesmerized de Kooning.

Bobby Kennedy spent almost forty-five minutes at the reception talking to Jackie about Texas and asking if she was certain she had recovered sufficiently from Patrick's death to endure the strain of campaigning. November 20 was his thirty-eighth birthday, and Ethel threw a party for him at Hickory Hill after the Judicial Reception. Bobby told one of his guests that he had misgivings about Texas, saying flatly, "I don't want him to go." He asked O'Donnell if he had seen the letter from Byron Skelton urging the president to skip Dallas. O'Donnell said he had decided not to show it to him since if he suggested removing an important city like that from the itinerary because Skelton was nervous, he would have thought he had lost his mind.

Sometime that evening Jean Daniel delivered Kennedy's message to Fidel Castro. After making Daniel repeat Kennedy's criticism of the Batista regime three times, Castro said, "I believe Kennedy is sincere. I also believe that today the expression of this sincerity could have political significance." After condemning the Bay of Pigs and the U.S. blockade, he continued, "But I feel he inherited a difficult situation. . . . I also think he is a realist: he is now registering that it is impossible to simply wave a wand and cause us, and the explosive situation throughout Latin America, to disappear." Showing that he understood the thrust of Kennedy's message, he said, "All the same, at a time when the United

States is selling wheat to the Russians, Canada is trading with China . . . why should it be impossible to make the Americans understand that socialism leads, not to hostility toward them, but to coexistence? Why am I not Tito or Sekou Toure?"

Kennedy skipped his brother's party because he wanted Jackie to be rested for Texas. They dined alone at the White House, and she read him a letter from her mother urging her to "have a wonderful time in Texas!" In return, he showed her a tongue-in-cheek letter he had received from her sister. Lee had written that whenever Jackie went on trips she always received beautiful presents, mentioning that while Onassis had given Jackie an expensive gift after the cruise, she had received only "3 dinky bracelets that Caroline wouldn't wear to her own birthday party."

He asked Jackie what she was packing. Referring to the November 22 luncheon at the Dallas Trade Mart, he said, "There are going to be all these rich Republican women at that lunch, wearing mink coats and diamond bracelets, and you've got to look as marvelous as any of them. Be simple—show these Texans what good taste really is." She held up some dresses and outfits, and they chose a pink suit with a navy-blue collar and a matching pink pillbox hat for Dallas.

After dinner he received a call from George Ball, who had just returned from Paris and wanted to brief him on U.S. and Common Market relations. He told Ball that he planned to return from Texas on Saturday evening so he could have lunch the next day with Ambassador Lodge, and suggested that he come to Wexford on Sunday evening. They could prepare for his meeting with Chancellor Erhard of West Germany the next Monday, and it would give him an opportunity to show Ball around his new house.

Thursday, November 21

WASHINGTON, SAN ANTONIO, HOUSTON, FORT WORTH

Kennedy was edgy on Thursday morning, probably worried that the feuding Texas Democrats would wreck the trip and Jackie would be so miserable that she would refuse to campaign next year. As soon as he arrived at the Oval Office he asked Lincoln to check the forecast for San Antonio and Houston. The day before, the Navy had promised cool weather, and Jackie had packed woolen suits. Lincoln reported that today the Air Force was predicting that Texas would be warmer than normal. He swore and called the naval office responsible for the forecast and bawled out the hapless sailor who answered. He fumed some more after learning that Jackie's bags had already gone to the plane. "Hot. *Hot*," he complained to Lincoln. "Jackie's clothes are all packed and they're the *wrong* clothes."

He met briefly with Charles Darlington and Thomas Estes, his ambassadors to Gabon and Upper Volta. As they left, Darlington noticed him putting a hand on his back before straightening up, a gesture he recognized because he also suffered from back pain. But sometime that morning Kennedy would also tell O'Donnell, "I feel great. My back feels better than it has in years."

Because of the cool and drizzly weather, Nanny Maud Shaw was opposed to letting John ride the helicopter to Andrews with his parents. Kennedy overruled her and dressed the boy in a peaked yellow sou'wester that made him resemble a tiny fisherman. Caroline put on her favorite clothes to say good-bye, and she and Shaw waved from the roof.

As Kennedy and his son were walking to the Marine Corps helicopter, an aide handed him a letter from McGeorge Bundy requesting a two-week vacation in January. He grinned and scrawled across the bottom, "Fine. I think it's time I left myself." Hale Boggs, who had called Dallas a "hornet's nest," was passing the White House as the helicopter lifted off. He jumped out of his car and waved, even though he knew no one could see him. Kennedy spent the short flight teasing his son and kicking his foot until he shouted, "Don't, Daddy!" When John learned that he was returning to the White House he burst into tears.

Kennedy tucked a file card into the bathroom mirror of his compartment on Air Force One containing the statistics he had asked Powers to collect. They showed that whereas he had won Texas by only 46,223 votes in 1960, Lyndon Johnson, who had been running for senator as well as vice president, had beaten his Republican opponent by 138,693 votes, and the Democratic governor of Texas, Price Daniel, had won by a margin of 1,124,972 votes. He planned to cite these numbers to remind Texas Democrats that too many party members had voted Republican for the top of the ticket and to shame them into a greater effort on his behalf in 1964.

The enmity between Senator Yarborough and the more conservative party establishment led by Governor Connally and supported by Vice President Johnson was real, but the notion that Kennedy could resolve it by visiting Texas for a few days was preposterous. Johnson and Yarborough lived in Washington, and if that had been Kennedy's only goal he could have easily invited them to the Oval Office for peace talks. His principal reasons for going remained the same as when he had proposed the trip the previous year: to raise money; energize the party; demonstrate that he could appeal to the oil men, executives, and rednecks composing its conservative wing; and improve his chances of winning Texas by the kind of margins Johnson and Governor Daniels had enjoyed in 1960. To reach out to conservative Democrats, he was speaking that evening at a dinner in Houston honoring Congressman Albert Thomas that would be attended by the city's business community. The next day, there would be a Chamber of Commerce breakfast in Fort Worth, a luncheon at the Dallas Trade Mart, and a fundraising dinner in Austin at which Johnson planned to introduce him by saying, "And thank God, Mr. President, that you came out of Dallas alive!"

The trip would end with a weekend at Johnson's ranch that he was dreading. During the flight he told Powers and O'Donnell, "You two guys aren't running out on me and leaving me stranded with poor Jackie at Lyndon's ranch. If I've got to hang around all day Saturday, wearing one of those big cowboy hats, you've got to be there, too." They both declined, saying that they had promised their families to be home by Saturday.

He poked his head into Jackie's compartment as she was brushing her hair and said, "Oh, Jackie, just thought I'd check to see if you were all right." She was beginning to find his constant concern with her happiness tiresome. "Yes, Jack, I'm fine," she said, the irritation in her voice apparent. "Now will you just go away."

He strolled down the aisle to where the reporters were sitting. He was smoking a small cigar and had to parry questions about whether or not it was Cuban. (It was.) A reporter asked him about Goldwater and he joked, "I don't think Barry is going to have time for a presidential campaign, though. He's too busy dismantling the federal government."

To reduce the risk of Jackie's becoming tired, he had insisted that their schedule should be relatively light and had refused a request from Congressman Henry Gonzalez, one of his strongest allies in the state, to visit a San Antonio high school that Gonzalez had arranged to have renamed in his honor. Gonzalez now took him aside on Air Force One to complain that he was spending only two hours in San Antonio, even though he was more popular there than in the other cities on his itinerary. After Gonzalez pressed him to change his mind and stop at the new John F. Kennedy school, he promised to return sometime that winter to dedicate it.

For months Gonzalez had been complaining to him about the dangers faced by U.S. advisers posted to South Vietnam. His godson, Miguel Jr., was a helicopter cargo master and despite being an "adviser" had flown more than three hundred combat missions. After coming under hostile fire and being forced to grab a rifle from a South Vietnamese soldier to shoot back, he had begged Gonzalez to send him a pistol. Gonzalez had related the story to Kennedy and asked how he could deny soldiers like his godson the means of defending themselves. Kennedy probably had Miguel Jr. in mind when he had shouted to McNamara, as he was preparing to announce the withdrawal of a thousand advisers by the end of the year, "and tell them that means the helicopter pilots, too." Before returning to his compartment, Kennedy turned to Gonzalez and said, "Oh, and by the way, Henry, I've already ordered . . . all the helicopters to be out of Vietnam by the end of the year."

Teenagers filling the observation deck of the San Antonio airport screamed "Jackie!" She waved as the president strode to a chain-link fence and shook hundreds of outstretched hands to the consternation of his Secret Service agents, who were finding it impossible to enforce the rule that the hands of anyone approaching him should be visible and empty. Gonzalez had been standing in a San Antonio crowd like this one when a man shoved a .38 into his stomach and pulled the trigger. The gun had misfired, but he still suffered flashbacks. He had one as Kennedy was shaking hands, telling a companion that it would be easy for someone in the crowd to kill him, and recalling a recent conversation with Congressman Wilbur Mills of Arkansas, during which Mills had snarled, "That damn princeling, silver spoon in his mouth, what the hell does he know about Texas?"

When Kennedy campaigned in San Antonio in 1960, sixty thousand spectators had lined the route of his motorcade. Today, more than twice that number had turned out. He heard shouts of "Viva Kennedy," saw hundreds of schoolchildren cheering and waving flags, and brushed showers of confetti off his hair and shoulders. Spectators broke through police barricades when he stopped to shake hands with some secretaries standing outside an office building, prompting a reporter for the *San Antonio Express* to observe that "despite the conglomeration of Secret Service agents on hand, it's appalling to note how simple it would be to approach a president."

He kept a close eye on Jackie. When she began appearing apprehensive, he tried to distract her by suggesting that they make a game of counting the "jumpers" and "leapers" in the crowd, but there were so many they soon abandoned it. The wind was strong and the motorcade sped through some of its twenty-six-mile route, messing up her hair. Seeking shelter from the wind, she asked Governor Connally, who was sitting next to his wife, Nellie, on the jump seats, if they could trade places. Kennedy immediately made them switch back. The back bench was higher than the jump seats, and anyone sitting there was more visible.

There were some sour notes. Demonstrators from the NAACP held signs proclaiming, "Rights Not Favors" and "Mr. President, You Are in a Segregated City." A man jumped from the sidewalk and gave him an energetic thumbs-down. An American Legion post had hired a skywriting plane to spell out "Cuba?"—a reminder that he had still not dislodged Castro from power. A constable on traffic duty overheard a man in a stopped car telling another that the president would not "make it out of the city alive," but drove off before he could stop them. The Secret Service failed to keep a mental patient dressed as a priest and carrying a black bag from taking a front-row seat for the ceremony at the Brooks Aerospace Medical Center, where the president was dedicating a medical library and laboratories.

Senator Yarborough refused to ride in the motorcade with Lyndon and Lady Bird and climbed into the third car with Henry Gonzalez, a departure from protocol that would dominate the following day's front pages. It was payback for Connally's failure to invite him to a reception for the president at the governor's mansion the next evening, and for not seating him at the head table at the fundraising dinner. Asked by a reporter to comment on these snubs, he said, "Governor Connally is so terribly uneducated governmentally, how would you expect anything else?"

Kennedy gave no hint to the crowd at Brooks that he had ever harbored doubts about the lunar mission. His speech demonstrated how quickly he could change his mind, and how much personal experience—in this instance, his visit to Cape Canaveral—could sway him. He told them that Americans stood "on the edge of a great new era characterized by achievement and by challenge" that called for "pathfinders and pioneers." He recounted having seen the Saturn rocket booster that would soon launch "the largest payload that any country in the world has ever sent into space." He reaffirmed his commitment to the space race, saying, "I think the United States should be a leader. A country as rich and powerful as this . . . should be second to none." He said that when the Saturn rocket was launched in December, "I hope the United States will be ahead. And I am for it." He closed with a poetic image, recounting how as boys the Irish writer Frank O'Connor and his friends would take off their hats and toss them over orchard walls that appeared too high to climb. Once their hats were on the other side, they had to follow them. "This nation has tossed its cap over the wall of space," he said, "and we have no choice but to follow it. . . . With the help and support of all Americans, we will climb this wall with safety and speed, and we shall then explore the wonders on the other side."

Five minutes later he stood in a laboratory at Brooks, peering through the porthole of an oxygen chamber similar to the one at Children's Hospital. Four airmen had been inside since November 3, living like lunar astronauts at a simulated altitude of 27,500 feet and breathing 100 percent pure oxygen. He put on a headset to speak with them, the same way he had communicated with Patrick's doctors. After wishing them good luck, he asked the scientist in charge of the experiment if space medicine might lead to improvements in oxygen chambers for premature infants. Before leaving Brooks, he invited Astronaut Gordon Cooper to accompany him to Dallas, saying that he could use having a "space hero" along on that leg of the trip. Cooper declined, explaining that he had to be at Cape Canaveral the following day for some important tests. Had he gone, he would have ridden in the president's limousine, sitting in the backseat between Jack and Jackie.

Kennedy was jubilant during the flight to Houston, twirling in his swivel chair and asking if the reception would be as good as in San Antonio. Fearing that the crowds in Houston might be sparse, he had decided against a formal motorcade. Fewer people did turn out than in San Antonio, but they were equally enthusiastic. He asked Powers to estimate their number. "For you? About as many as turned out the last time you were here," Powers said. "But a hundred thousand more today for Jackie." Kennedy beamed. Looking at his wife, he said, "Jackie is my greatest asset." As they pulled into the Rice Hotel, Powers noticed him giving her an adoring look.

The hotel had stocked their suite with caviar, champagne, and Heineken beer. Before they could enjoy it, Johnson arrived for a meeting and Jackie disappeared into the bedroom. Two weeks before, Johnson had told his friend Horace Busby that when he was with Kennedy in Austin on the evening of November 22, he planned to inform him that he had decided against running for vice president in 1964 and would instead return to Texas to run a newspaper. "You be the editor and I'll be the publisher," he had said to Busby. "You'll let me write at least one column a week and we are going to run all the interests out of Texas." Busby knew that he had been trying to buy a newspaper, but did not think he was serious, and that like any "star performer" he just needed to be flattered and cajoled.

His meeting with Kennedy was so acrimonious that Jackie could hear them shouting from the next room. Kennedy was angry because he believed that Johnson could have made peace between the warring factions in Texas. He had complained to Bobby earlier that Johnson was "a son of a bitch" because he would not "lift a finger" to settle the Yarborough-Connally feud. Nothing had happened that day to change his opinion. After Johnson stormed out of the suite, Kennedy told Jackie, "That's just Lyndon. He's in trouble." He did not explain if he was in trouble with *him,* or because of the Bobby Baker investigation, or because he could not control Yarborough and Connally.

Jackie admitted disliking Connally. "I just can't bear him sitting there saying all these great things about himself," she said. "And he seems to be needling *you* all day."

"For heaven's sakes, don't get a thing on him," he said. He pointed out that if everyone on the trip ended up hating one another, "nobody will ride with anybody."

He doodled on a sheet of hotel stationery, drawing a sailboat heeling slightly in the wind. He put a diamond-shaped figure above it, perhaps one of the kites he and John had flown off the back of the *Honey Fitz* the previous summer. The doodle was unusual because there was not a single word on the page. Most of his scribblings communicated impatience and boredom. This one was evocative and serene.

He and Jackie dined in their suite with the publisher of the *Houston Chronicle.* A poll commissioned by the paper showed Kennedy losing Texas to Goldwater by about 100,000 votes if the election were held that day. He told Kennedy that as a courtesy he would not be publishing it until he left town. Kennedy was impressed that the poll showed Connally running ahead of him, and Yarborough winning by the largest margin of all.

The atmosphere was more cordial when Lyndon and Lady Bird came into their suite after supper. When Lady Bird asked what he would like to do at their ranch on Saturday he told her that he wanted to ride, a request that must have surprised Jackie since he was allergic to horses and never rode in Virginia. But he was serious enough to order riding breeches sent overnight from the White House. Perhaps he was rewarding her for coming to Texas by doing something that he knew would please her.

David Broder would write in the next day's *Evening Star,* "Mrs. Kennedy, on her first official excursion outside Washington since her husband's election, unleashed her dazzling smile, her demure charm and her dashing wardrobe on the obviously impressed citizenry of San Antonio, Houston, and Fort Worth." Jackie also counted the day as a success. As her private secretary Mary Gallagher was brushing her hair, she said, "Gosh, Mary, you've been such a great help. You'll just have to plan to do a lot of campaigning next year."

Before driving to the Houston Coliseum for the testimonial dinner honoring Congressman Albert Thomas, the Kennedys stopped in the hotel ballroom to address a meeting of the League of United Latin American Citizens. He introduced her by saying, "In order that my words will be even clearer, I am going to ask my wife to say a few words to you also." She delivered some well-practiced sentences in Spanish, beginning, "I am very happy to be with you and part of the noble Spanish tradition which has contributed so much to Texas." There were cheers and shouts of "*Olé!*" Lady Bird thought the president looked "beguiled," and Powers noticed them exchanging another loving look.

Jack Valenti, one of Johnson's aides, had helped organize the testimonial dinner and was crouched below the stage when Kennedy delivered his speech. From this vantage point he could see his hands shaking as he spoke. It was not a minor tremor but a violent shaking, and Valenti was amazed that someone who appeared so relaxed when he spoke extemporaneously could find it so daunting to deliver a prepared speech. Nerves may have caused him to flub a line and say that the United States was about to fire "the largest payroll" into space. He quickly corrected himself, saying "payload into space." Then, demonstrating how quickly his mind worked, he quipped, "It will be the largest payroll too. And who should know better than Houston. We put a little of it right in here."

He and Jackie arrived in Fort Worth shortly after eleven that night and checked into a small three-room suite at the Texas Hotel that the Secret Service had chosen because it had only one entrance. Mary Gallagher should have preceded them so she could unpack Jackie's suitcase and lay out her nightclothes, but she had taken the wrong motorcade car and arrived late. Kennedy chewed her out for a slip-up that, like the erroneous weather report, he considered a threat to Jackie's happiness and her willingness to campaign the next year.

They could not sleep in the same bed because the special hard mattress that he brought on trips covered only half of the king-sized box spring and the hotel had neglected to provide a single mattress for Jackie. She was so exhausted that instead of calling housekeeping, she decided to sleep alone in the small bedroom. They embraced and he said, "You were great today." She went next door and laid out the pink suit and pillbox hat she would wear the following day.

Friday, November 22

FORT WORTH AND DALLAS

Kennedy woke to hear George Thomas knocking gently on his bedroom door. He said, "Okay," his signal that Jackie had slept in a different room and Thomas could come in, pull the curtains, draw his bath, and drop off the morning papers.

He shaved, bathed, and put on his back brace—pulling straps, fastening buckles, and wrapping a long Ace bandage in a figure-eight pattern around the brace and his thighs that left him sitting up ramrod straight on his bed. Then he slipped on the white shirt with narrow stripes that he had ordered from Pierre Cardin in Paris after admiring it on Ambassador Alphand.

His bedroom did not face the parking lot where he would be speaking at 8:00 a.m., so he tiptoed into Jackie's room and looked down. Several thousand people had already gathered in the half-light in raincoats and under umbrellas. "Gosh, just look at the crowds down there!" he exclaimed. "Isn't that terrific?" When Larry O'Brien arrived to discuss how to persuade Yarborough to ride with Johnson in today's motorcades, he led him to the window and said, "Just look at the platform. With all those buildings around it the Secret Service couldn't stop someone who really wanted to get you."

He showed O'Brien the front page of the *Dallas Morning News*. A banner headline proclaimed "Storm of Political Controversy Swirls Around Kennedy on Visit." A headline farther down the page said "Yarborough Snubs LBJ." "Christ, I come all the way down here to make a few speeches—and this is what appears on the front page," he said, adding in a harsh voice, "I don't care if you have to throw Yarborough into the car with Lyndon. Get him in there."

He flipped through the newspapers and found a more encouraging article in the *Chicago Sun-Times*. It reported, "Some Texans, in taking account of the tangled Texas political situation, have begun to think that Mrs. Jacqueline Kennedy may turn the balance and win her husband the state's electoral votes."

He asked Dave Powers if he had seen the crowd downstairs. "And weren't the crowds great in San Antonio and Houston," he added. "And you were right, they loved Jackie."

He had been told to expect 2,500 people at the early morning rally. Twice that number cheered as he mounted the flatbed truck serving as a platform. He disliked overcoats as much as hats and shook off the Secret Service agent offering him a raincoat. He shouted, "There are no faint hearts in Fort Worth!" and the crowd roared. The rally had been scheduled early because many in the audience would be union members who had to punch time clocks. He looked down to see clerks and housewives, men in work clothes, and nurses and waitresses in uniforms—a crowd like the one in Boston that had prompted him to say, "These are my kind of people."

He made a joke of Jackie's absence, saying, "Mrs. Kennedy is organizing herself. It takes longer, but, of course, she looks better than we do when she does it."

He praised the defense industries that employed many of them and promised his commitment to "a defense system second to none." He spoke about space, another field where he would not accept second place, announcing that "next month the United States will fire the largest booster in the history of the world, putting us ahead of the Soviet Union in that area for the first time in our history." Achievements like these, he said, depended "upon the willingness of the citizens of the United States to assume burdens of citizenship." He concluded, "Here in this rain, in Fort Worth . . . we are going forward!"

The audiences in Billings and Salt Lake City had proved that he had anticipated their weariness with the cold war. The cheers and applause in Fort Worth confirmed that he understood that working-class Americans hungered for a noble cause. As he left for the Chamber of Commerce breakfast in the Hotel Texas ballroom, he told Henry Brandon of the London *Times*, "Things are going much better than I had expected."

As Jackie walked into the ballroom, the businessmen and their wives leaped to their feet. Some stood on chairs, cheering and filling the room with deafening whistles. Kennedy said, "Two years ago, I introduced myself in Paris by saying that I was the man who had accompanied Mrs. Kennedy to Paris. I am getting somewhat that sensation as I travel around Texas." The head of the Chamber of Commerce gave Jackie a pair of boots, and presented him with a ten-gallon hat. "We couldn't let you leave without providing you some protection against the rain," he said. Someone shouted, "Put it on!" He smiled, waved it in the air, and said, "I'll put it on in the White House on Monday. If you come up, you'll have a chance to see it there."

Jackie was so delighted by her reception that she told O'Brien, "I'm going to be making a lot of these trips next year." Back in their suite she said, "Oh, Jack, campaigning is so easy when you're president. I'll go anywhere with you this year."

"How about California in the next two weeks?"

"I'll be there."

"Did you hear *that*?" he asked O'Donnell, who had just walked into the room.

He opened the *Dallas Morning News* and saw a full-page advertisement placed by a right-wing group calling itself the "American Fact-Finding Committee." It was bordered in black like an obituary, headlined "Welcome Mr. Kennedy to Dallas," and listed twelve charges against him framed as questions, among them: "Why have you scrapped the Monroe Doctrine in favor of the 'Spirit of Moscow'?" "Why did you host, salute and entertain Tito . . . ?" and "Why has Gus Hall, head of the U.S. Communist Party, praised almost every one of your policies . . . ?"

In 1961, the publisher of the *Morning News,* Ted Dealey, had come to the White House for a conference and accused Kennedy and his appointees of being "weak sisters," telling him to his face, "We need a man on horseback to lead this country, and many people in the Southwest think that you are riding Caroline's tricycle." Kennedy fired back that the difference between them was that "I was elected president of this country and you were not and I have the responsibility for the lives of 180 million Americans, which you have not," adding, "I'm just as tough as you are . . . and I didn't get elected president by lying down." He answered Dealey again in a speech he gave several weeks later. Knowing that Dealey had not fought in World War II, he said that he had observed that men tend to like the idea of war until they have tasted it, and speaking of people on the fringes of society (like Dealey) who looked for scapegoats and simple solutions, he said, "They call for a 'man on horseback' because they do not trust the people. . . . They equate the Democratic part with the welfare state, the welfare state with socialism, socialism with communism." The solution, he said, was to "let our patriotism be reflected in the creation of confidence in one another, rather than in crusades of suspicion."

He handed the *Dallas Morning News* to Jackie, open to the nasty advertisement. "Oh, you know, we're heading into nut country today," he said. "But, Jackie, if somebody wanted to shoot me from a window with a rifle, nobody can stop it, so why worry about it?"

Some residents of "nut country" had woken this morning to find a flyer on their doorstep with two photographs of Kennedy, straight on and in profile. They resembled police mug shots and announced that he was "Wanted for Treason." He was accused of "betraying the Constitution," "turning the sovereignty of the U.S. over to the Communist controlled United Nations," giving "support and encouragement to the Communist inspired racial riots," and appointing "anti-Christians to Federal office."

Pacing around the room as he spoke, he said, "You know, last night would have been a hell of a night to assassinate a president. I mean it. There was the rain and the night, and we were all getting jostled. Suppose a man had a pistol in a briefcase." (At this, he pantomimed someone pulling out a gun and pointed his index finger at the wall, jerking his thumb to simulate a trigger.) He continued, "Then he could have dropped the gun and the briefcase and melted away in the crowd." The performance was more Walter Mitty than Hitchcock, probably an attempt to put Jackie at ease by making fun of the advertisement.

He and Jackie had been in the suite for almost twelve hours but only now did they notice that they had been surrounded by original works of art, including paintings by Monet, Picasso, Dufy, and Van Gogh. They had also overlooked a catalog on the coffee table titled "An Art Exhibition for the President and Mrs. John F. Kennedy." It listed the titles and provenance of the artworks and explained that they were on loan from local collectors and museums. The Kennedys had arrived late and exhausted and had been busy that morning, but it was still odd that a president who had made the arts a signature issue and a First Lady who had studied art history had failed to recognize that, for example, Dufy's whimsical *Bassin de Deauville*, with its gaily colored sailboats zipping across a harbor, was an original and not a print. "Isn't this sweet, Jack," she said. "They've just stripped their whole museum of all their treasures to brighten up this dingy hotel suite." The wife of a Fort Worth publishing executive had organized the show, and he could have easily written her a note after returning to Washington. Instead, he grabbed a telephone book, looked up her number, and called. After they spoke, he handed the phone to Jackie, who said, "They're going to have a dreadful time getting me out of here with all these wonderful works of art."

His last visitor, Lyndon Johnson, had brought his sister and brother-in-law to shake his hand. "You can be sure of one thing, Lyndon," he said in front of these witnesses. "We're going to carry two states next year—Massachusetts and Texas. We're going to carry at least those two states."

"We going to carry a lot more than those two," Johnson promised.

His use of the word "we" had to have caught Johnson's attention. Perhaps Kennedy had changed his mind about replacing him on the ticket after his encouraging reception in San Antonio, Houston, and Fort Worth, but it is also possible that the "we" was an uncalculated expression of his momentary exuberance.

Before leaving, he disappeared into his bedroom and changed his wardrobe, putting on a blue-striped shirt, a solid blue silk tie, and a newly pressed gray-and-blue lightweight suit. While he was gone, Secret Service Agent Roy Kellerman told O'Donnell that there was a chance of rain forecast for Dallas and asked if they should put the bubble top on the Lincoln Continental limousine taking the president from Love Field to the Dallas Trade Mart. Jackie liked the top because it protected her hair from the wind, but Kennedy loathed it, once telling a friend, "They put me in a bubble top thing and I can't get to the people. . . . I belong to them and they belong to me." Knowing how he felt, O'Donnell told Kellerman to leave it off unless it was raining.

Only thirty miles separated Fort Worth and Dallas. It made no practical sense for Kennedy to fly between them, but it made political sense, because newsmen could film him being greeted at Love Field. During the few minutes that he was airborne he changed into his third clean shirt of the day, told Representative Olin Teague of Texas that he would go to Cape Canaveral in December to watch the Saturn launch because he thought the space program "needed a boost," wrote some last-minute ideas to include in his speech at the Trade Mart, scribbling, "Equal choice / not any reflection / back—govt reform / we are going forward," and summoned Connally and Yarborough into his cabin, where in three minutes he strong-armed Connally into inviting Yarborough to the reception in Austin and seating him at the head table. As Connally left his cabin he muttered, "How can anyone say no to that man?"

During the flight his Air Force aide Godfrey McHugh overheard O'Brien and O'Donnell telling members of his Secret Service detachment, "Please, when we go to Dallas, don't sit like you always do in the front seat of the car [the presidential limousine] because we want to give him full exposure. He will win them by his smile. . . . We want him to be seen. It's enough to have two Secret Service men without having a third body in front." The agents were not happy with the request, but they complied nevertheless.

When he landed at Love Field in 1961, no one had greeted him except the chief of police. Today he looked out the window, saw several thousand supporters and a line of dignitaries, and told O'Donnell, "This trip is turning out to be terrific. Here we are in Dallas, and it looks like everything in Texas is going to be fine for us." As he and Jackie waited in the aisle for the door to open, Powers said, "You two look like Mr. and Mrs. America," and reminded them that he should wave to those on the right hand side of the car while she waved to the left, because "If both of you ever looked at the same voter at the same time, it would be too much for him!"

The weather had turned on a dime: gray and drizzly when they left Fort Worth, sunny and warm when they landed in Dallas. Abandoning protocol, Jackie disembarked first. They may have lined up this way in the aisle, but it is also possible he decided that she should precede him because after yesterday he knew that she would draw the loudest cheers. Intentional or not, it symbolized a slight shift in their marital balance of power.

A reporter watching her emerge from Air Force One compared the bright sunlight hitting her pink suit to "a blow between the eyes." This was the first time that most at Love Field had seen her and the president in color outside of some magazine photographs. It was an electrifying moment, like the one in *The Wizard of Oz* when a black-and-white Kansas becomes a dazzling, Technicolor Oz. A Dallas woman said she was amazed at his coloring, "because I had only seen him previously on black-and-white TV. He was very fair, almost pink, and his hair was almost blond in the sunlight." A television correspondent exclaimed, "I can see his suntan all the way from here!"

Instead of climbing into his limousine, he headed for the crowd lining the airport fence. A local television reporter shouted, "He's broken away from the program and is shaking hands with the crowd." The Texas journalist Ronnie Dugger wrote in his notebook, "Kennedy is showing he is not afraid." Jackie followed him to the fence and also began shaking hands. It was the first time that the *New York Times* reporter Tom Wicker could remember her working an airport crowd.

Sorensen's observation that different parts of Kennedy were seen by many people but no one saw them all was correct. But if you assembled those parts of him that were visible at various times and places to his friends and staff, and to people like those greeting him in the brilliant sunshine at Love Field, you not only had Laura Bergquist's "fascinating human animal" but someone who had also managed to convey his kindness, humor, intelligence, and humanity to those who knew him only from what they read in a newspaper or saw on a television screen or from behind an airport fence.

His friends knew a man who was kind and gregarious, delighted in children, venerated courage, paid excessive attention to ceremony and his appearance, possessed an irreverent sense of humor, and was a secret romantic, yet was also what Sidey called "a serious man on a serious mission." They knew a man who had brought his competitive spirit to the greatest contest of all—that with other presidents for a favorable verdict from the high court of history. They knew a man who was chronically impatient with anyone or anything that bored him, had a chip on his shoulder about the WASP establishment, lied easily and often about his health and sex life, and could be too cautious politically but too reckless when it came to driving, extramarital affairs, and exposing himself to crowds such as the one greeting him at Love Field. Because of his passion for secrecy and his practice of compartmentalizing his life, few among his friends and aides knew all of this, but they knew enough to know that his courage and mendacity, generosity and sudden rages, idealism and cunning, had made him a very complicated yet appealing human being. And because he had succeeded in communicating some of this to the American people, they sensed that despite his wealth and education, he was not only like them but also genuinely liked them, and really *did* prefer the workers in the kitchen to the WASPs in the dining room, the middle-class Americans greeting him at Love Field to the businessmen awaiting him at the Trade Mart.

A local broadcaster called his welcome at Love Field "completely overwhelming," but not everyone was friendly. Some high school students hissed, and a man held up a sign proclaiming, "You're a traiter [sic]." Another sign said, "Help JFK Stamp Out Democracy." A large placard announced, "Mr. President, because of your socialist tendencies and because of your surrender to communism, I hold you in complete contempt."

As Jackie was climbing into the limousine, a reporter asked how she liked campaigning. "It's wonderful," she gushed. "It's wonderful." As they were pulling away, Kennedy noticed a boy in a Scout uniform. They locked eyes, and he gave the boy a mischievous wink.

THE SITE OF THE LUNCHEON had determined the route of his motorcade. Connally had wanted him to speak to an invitation-only event at the Trade Mart, but Jerry Bruno, who was advancing the trip, feared it would be too much a rich man's affair and proposed a larger and less-exclusive gathering at the Women's Building at the State Fairgrounds. Bruno thought Connally opposed holding it there because the ceiling was too low to accommodate a two-tiered head table, and he wanted to seat himself on the top tier while relegating opponents like Yarborough to the bottom. Connally finally put his foot down, insisting that the president could not come to Dallas unless he spoke at the Trade Mart, and the White House capitulated. Had Kennedy driven from Love Field to the fairgrounds, he would have taken a different route through Dealey Plaza, traveling at a higher rate of speed. But because he was heading to the Trade Mart, he would have to make a sharp right turn off Main Street onto Houston Street, then drive a block before slowing down for a sharp left onto Elm Street that was almost a hairpin, leaving him traveling around ten miles per hour as he passed the Texas School Book Depository.

His motorcade was configured like the ones in Tampa and San Antonio. At its center were three vehicles: the lead car, a white Ford with no markings driven by the Dallas police chief, Jesse Curry, with Sheriff Bill Decker and two Secret Service agents riding as passengers, then the president's limousine, a Lincoln Continental driven by Secret Service Agent Bill Greer with Agent Roy Kellerman in the passenger seat, Governor and Mrs. Connally on the jump seats, and the president and First Lady sitting on the rear seat. A contingent of Secret Service agents rode in the third car. Kennedy's limousine had running boards but he discouraged agents from standing on them. Sometimes he permitted them to stand on the two steps flanking the trunk, but in Dallas, as in Tampa, he had vetoed this.

Aside from the fact that the spectators were more numerous and welcoming than anyone had anticipated, there was nothing unusual or memorable about the first thirty-five minutes of the motorcade. Had he ridden in dozens more like it during the campaign, Connally might have forgotten that as they passed the balcony of a ramshackle house he saw a lone man standing on a balcony with a "Kennedy Go Home!" sign, and that after noticing it the president had said, "I see them everywhere I go. I bet that's a nice guy." Yarborough might not have remembered thinking, as he stared up at the tall office buildings lining Main Street, "What if someone throws a flower pot down on top of Mrs. Kennedy or the President?" Nor would John and Nellie Connally have recalled that the president asked Jackie to remove her sunglasses because he thought they made her appear too removed and inaccessible, or that the glare was so blinding that Jackie had absentmindedly put them on twice more before finally burying them in her pocketbook. Nor would it have been remembered that the president and First Lady could raise the volume of the cheering simply by waving, or that he had stopped to greet some children holding up a sign saying, "Mr. President, Please Stop and Shake Our Hands," or that a teenaged boy had darted into the street and pointed a camera at him before a Secret Service agent tackled him, or that as he waved he kept murmuring, "Thank you, thank you, thank you." No one could hear him, but he presumably felt that, like writing a sympathy note to the mother of a severely burned child moments before his own child died, it was something he ought to do.

His route took him along Main Street and through the heart of downtown Dallas. The Secret Service did not check the upper floors of buildings unless they had received specific threats, so people stood on rooftops and hung out open windows, cheering and tossing confetti. Spectators were ten to fifteen thick on the sidewalks. In places they had spilled into the street, slowing the motorcade to a crawl and prompting Greer to keep far to the left in order to leave the greatest possible distance between the crowd and the right hand side of the limousine, where the president was sitting.

Where Main Street flowed into Dealey Plaza the crowds thinned and his limousine slowed to make two turns, first the ninety-degree right onto Houston

Street, then a block later the even sharper left onto Elm Street past the seven-story School Book Depository. From here, Elm headed down a gentle incline to the Stemmons Freeway and a triple underpass. Jackie, who was perspiring in her pink wool suit, saw it and thought, "How pleasant that cool tunnel will be." Nellie Connally turned around from her jump seat and said to Kennedy, "You sure can't say that Dallas doesn't love you!" Their eyes met, his smile widened, and he said, "No, you can't."

The photographer Cecil Stoughton was riding seven cars back. He heard some loud bangs and imagined a cowboy in a ten-gallon hat standing on a rooftop, firing his six-shooter into the air to welcome the president to Dallas.

Kennedy was waving as the first bullet entered his upper back and exited his throat. It missed his vital organs and was a survivable wound. His hands flew up to his throat and his expression went blank. Nellie Connally remembered his eyes being "full of surprise," and Agent Kellerman thought he said, "My God, I'm hit." His back brace kept him upright, an immovable target. Another bullet smashed into the rear of his head and Jackie cried out, "They've killed my husband! I have his brains in my hand."

AFTER DALLAS

Jackie wept first, and from her and from Dallas a tidal wave of tears rolled across the nation and around the world. In New York, there was a murmur and then a rising wail as the news jumped between tables at a midtown restaurant. Advertising men in tailored suits hurried into St. Patrick's Cathedral and fell onto their knees. Outside, drivers hunched over steering wheels, sobbing as dashboard radios broadcast the news. A crowd gathered at the Magnavox showroom on Fifth Avenue, watching on television sets piled two stories high as Walter Cronkite choked back tears before announcing that the president was dead. Chorus girls rehearsing for an evening television show at the Ed Sullivan Theater on Broadway kicked in unison, arms linked around waists as tears streamed down their cheeks.

In Washington, a rookie police officer wept as he lowered the flag on the Capitol dome to half mast and looked down to see that drivers had abandoned their cars and stood in the street, staring up at the flag and crying. In his Senate office, Senator Hubert Humphrey, who had challenged Kennedy for the 1960 nomination, put his head in his arms and wept for thirty minutes. Senator Fulbright jumped up from his table at the F Street Club, threw down his napkin, and shouted, "God damn it! I told him not to go to Dallas." Adlai Stevenson exclaimed, "That Dallas! Why, why didn't I insist that he not go there?" Medgar Evers's widow thought, "I knew it! I knew it!" She had never believed that someone like him—someone like her husband—would be allowed to live. In Chicago, Mayor Richard Daley burst into tears while lunching with his cronies, and across the Pacific in the Solomon Islands, one of the natives who had helped rescue Kennedy sat in his garden, staring at his photograph and crying. At Harvard, a girl wept on the steps of the Widener Library and a boy hit a tree in time to a tolling church bell. When the captain of a transatlantic jet heard that the Jackie's brother-in-law Stanislaus Radziwill was aboard, he left the cockpit, sat down beside him, and burst into tears. When Rusk announced his death over the public address system of the plane carrying cabinet members to Japan, there was an anguished cry as passengers clapped their hands over their faces. President Truman cried so much when he called on Jackie before the funeral that he had to be put to bed in the White House. A poem by the columnist Art Buchwald began each line, "We weep for," and concluded, "We weep because there is nothing else we can do." The cartoonist Bill Mauldin drew the statue of Abraham Lincoln at the Lincoln Memorial, sitting with his head in his hands. A twelve-year-old girl in Oregon who had shaken his hand and shaken her own into a glass jar to "save" his germs, emptied the jar into a shoe box, covered it with a small American flag, and wept as she buried it in her backyard. November 22 would be the first time many children saw an adult cry, and after hearing the news from sobbing teachers they went home to find their mothers in tears. A girl remembered her mother doing the ironing as she watched television, her tears sizzling as they hit the hot iron.

Not everyone mourned. Some white Southerners celebrated, and a wire service story reported schoolchildren in Texas cheering. Schlesinger was appalled by Stevenson's reaction, writing in his diary that on the night of November 22, Stevenson had walked into the White House "smiling and chipper as if nothing had happened," and had been the same way later that evening during a gathering at Averell Harriman's. After discussing Stevenson's demeanor with others, he wrote, "We agree, I think, that we have practically never heard Stevenson make a generous remark about Kennedy," and called his behavior something that it would "take a long time to forgive."

Algeria declared a week of official mourning, and the Nicaraguans held a state funeral. Peasants in the Yucatán slashed a clearing and planted a memorial garden; Liberian woodcutters fashioned a giant wooden carving of his head; and Portuguese men wore black ties and armbands, as if mourning a relative. Thousands of Poles rushed into the Warsaw cathedral following a requiem Mass and kissed an American flag covering a symbolic bier. The CIA reported that "Cuban reaction to the President's killing and the aftermath have reflected more sensitivity and apprehension than any regime in the world," and that Soviet leaders had been "as profoundly moved and shocked by the slaying of President Kennedy as were leaders of America's closest allies." Soviet interest in maintaining the atmosphere of détente created by the nuclear test ban treaty was demonstrated by the appointment of First Deputy Premier Anastas Mikoyan, the most powerful Soviet official after Khrushchev, to represent the USSR at President Kennedy's funeral. Khrushchev instructed his wife to write Jackie a personal note, an unprecedented gesture for a Soviet leader that his son believed was meant to stress "the sincerity and personal nature of his sympathy." The woman narrating a documentary about him on Soviet state television broke down, and tears filled Gromyko's eyes as he left the residence of the American ambassador. Yevgeny Yevtushenko was reading his poetry in a Moscow hall when he noticed audience members whispering and their faces taking on a tragic expression as if, he said, "that person had just lost a mother or father or brother." Years later, Yevtushenko would tell the actor Kirk Douglas, "People cried in the street. . . . They sensed that, in him [Kennedy], there might be a chance for our two countries to get together."

Sir Laurence Olivier interrupted a performance at the Old Vic and asked the audience to stand while the orchestra played "The Star-Spangled Banner." An Englishman told an American friend, "There has never been anything like it here since Trafalgar, and the news of Nelson's death reached London, and men cried in the streets." Big Ben tolled every minute for an hour, lights dimmed in Piccadilly Circus, and Prime Minister Alec Douglas-Home reported that distraught British teenagers were "openly crying in the street." Danes carried bouquets to the American embassy and left behind a six-foot-high wall of flowers. Sixty thousand West Berliners held an impromptu torchlight procession and gathered in the square where Kennedy had said "*Ich bein ein Berliner.*" Workmen in Nice laid down their tools and wept, and at the dedication of the Avenue du President Kennedy, the president of the Paris city council said, "Never, perhaps, has the death of a foreign chief of state so profoundly moved every Frenchman and every Parisian." President Charles de Gaulle told a friend, "I am stunned. They are crying all over France. It is as if he were a Frenchman, a member of their own family." As the French statesman Jean Monnet walked to Arlington in Kennedy's funeral procession, he told Walt Rostow that the French had reacted so emotionally because "he [Kennedy] reestablished the credibility of American strength and vitality after the Eisenhower years—and then showed in 1963 [that] he would use that power compassionately, and for peace." This, Monnet said, had "touched the life of every family in France."

A postman in a Connecticut suburb reported housewives on his route speaking about Kennedy's death "as if they had lost a son or daughter." A Detroit housewife said, "I feel as if a member of my family had died, I really do." Future president Jimmy Carter cried for the first time since his father had died, and McGeorge Bundy admitted that he had mourned Kennedy more than his own father, who had died in October. Roswell Gilpatric believed he was so shattered because "I felt about him as I've never felt about another man in my life." The columnist Joe Alsop said, "I had never known I loved the president," and believed that nothing had ever moved him more, "not even the death of my own father." In a condolence letter stained by tears, David Ormsby-Gore wrote Jackie, "I mourn him as though he were my own brother."

When Elaine de Kooning heard the news, she was working on her favorite portrait. It showed him wearing a sweatshirt, sailing pants, and sneakers, and squinting in the sunlight, looking just as he had that first day in Palm Beach. "The assassin dropped my brush," she said. "I was traumatized. I had identified painting with painting Kennedy. For a full year, I couldn't paint at all." Later, she explained, "I felt that I had lost a brother or a lover. . . . I can't believe the gunshots obliterated that brain, that personality. I was crushed. It was a personal loss."

A poll conducted within a week of his assassination by the National Opinion Research Center at the University of Chicago reported that 53 percent of Americans, ninety million people, had shed tears during the four days between his death and funeral. Blacks and Northerners were most likely to have wept, but even one in three Southern whites admitted crying. A majority of Americans said his assassination had been a "unique event" in their lives, more traumatic than Pearl Harbor or President Franklin Roosevelt's sudden death. Seventy-nine percent reported mourning him like "someone very close and dear."

Because Americans felt they knew him almost as well as someone sitting across the breakfast table, they wanted more than a distant grave. Once their tears had dried, or before, they began naming roads and bridges, tunnels, highways, and buildings for him, creating a grief-stricken empire of asphalt, mortar, brick, and bronze so extensive that if you extinguished every light on earth except those illuminating something named for him, astronauts launched from the Kennedy Space Center would have seen a web of lights stretching across

Europe and North America, and others scattered through Africa and Asia—and if proposals to stamp "Land of Kennedy" on every Massachusetts license plate, or to rename West Virginia "Kennedyiana" had been approved, they would have seen even more.

George Orwell believed it was impossible to "prove" that William Shakespeare had been a great author, writing, "There is no test of literary merit except survival, which is in itself an index of majority opinion." By that standard, Kennedy was a great president.

A grieving nation installed plaques marking where he had slept, lived, campaigned, ate, and prayed, creating an instant biography in bronze. There were markers at the Hitching Post Inn in Cheyenne and at the Carpenter Hotel in Manchester, where he had slept, and at the U.S. Post Office on State Line Avenue in Texarkana, where he had delivered a campaign speech with one foot planted in Texas and the other in Arkansas. A plaque showed where he stood while giving a 1962 address in Independence Hall, and others marked the building at the University of Michigan where he proposed the Peace Corps, and the booth at the Union Oyster House in Boston where he sat on Sunday mornings, reading newspapers and eating chowder.

Fifty years later, millions of people a day still cross Kennedy bridges in Niamey, Vienna, Liège, Mumbai, Bonn, Minnesota, North Dakota, Pennsylvania, Ohio, and Kentucky, and drive down Kennedy boulevards, avenues, drives, expressways, causeways, and highways in Chicago, Maryland, Antibes, Tampa, Jersey City, San Francisco, Montreal, Key West, Waterville, Luxembourg, Humboldt, Curaçao, Casablanca, and Corpus Christi, to name a few. They play in Kennedy memorial playgrounds and parks; swim in Kennedy pools; stroll through Kennedy squares, plazas, and platzes in Providence, Utica, Bonn, Berlin, Iowa City, Atlantic City, Antwerp, Detroit, Seattle, and Syracuse; and pass Kennedy sculptures, fountains, busts, and memorial flagpoles. Students attend more than a hundred John F. Kennedy elementary, middle, and high schools in the United States. Their parents attend meetings in Kennedy Democratic clubs and union halls; belong to a Kennedy American Legion or Kennedy Knights of Columbus post; send letters from Kennedy post offices; conduct business in Kennedy civic centers; arrive or depart from Kennedy airports in New York and Ashland; attend concerts in Kennedy auditoriums; sail on Kennedy ferries, tugboats, and lifeboats; and play at golf courses, exercise in recreation centers, live in nursing homes or public housing developments, or are patients at hospitals carrying his name.

There are forty Kennedy schools in Argentina, and his name is on a boys' club in Uganda; a recreational center in Copenhagen; the largest sport center in Italy; a memorial park in Miraflores, Peru; an island in an ornamental lake in Melbourne; a youth center in the Ivory Coast; and three high schools, a college dining room, and a secondary school in Kenya. You can shop in the Kennedy Mall in Dubuque, and study at the John F. Kennedy School of Government at Harvard. Every Saturday before Thanksgiving, thousands of competitors run between Boonsboro and Williamsport, Maryland, in the JFK Fifty Mile Marathon. Teams from around the world enter the JFK Field Hockey Tournament in Virginia Beach, sailors compete in the John F. Kennedy Memorial Regatta at the U.S. Naval Academy in Annapolis, and long-distance swimmers race in the PT109 Memorial Swim, held in the Solomon Islands on the anniversary of the day that he swam to tiny Plum Pudding Island, since renamed "Kennedy Island."

You can wander through the John F. Kennedy Peace Forest in Jerusalem, navigate the Kennedy Passage in Alaska, hike through the Mojave to the JFK Mountain profile, admire the Kennedy Rose in Stirling Forest Gardens, watch birds in the Kennedy Wildlife Sanctuary in Oyster Bay, climb Mount Kennedy in the Yukon or Kennedy Peak in the Dolomites, worship at a church in Parma whose cornerstone contains an urn filled with the earth from his grave, and study in the John F. Kennedy Library in Addis Ababa, and then drive an hour and drink beer with prostitutes at the J. F. Kennedy bar in Wolkite—or at least you could have a few years ago. You can visit the Kennedy Memorial at Runnymede, an acre of English ground that Parliament transferred to the United States, and look up from underneath the American scarlet oak, planted here because every November it weeps its red leaves onto the seven-ton black Portland stone commemorating him, and see planes leaving Heathrow for John F. Kennedy International Airport.

James MacGregor Burns called the memorials and grief "something that goes beyond rational calculation." Burns had been the only author to write an authorized Kennedy biography. Kennedy had expected a book like his acclaimed *Roosevelt: The Lion and the Fox*, and gave him access to his Senate files and submitted to hours of interviews. His 1960 biography was admiring but suggested that Kennedy lacked moral passion, listening too much to his intellect and too little to his heart.* Faced with explaining why a man he had criticized for lacking passion had excited such passionate grief, Burns said, "Was it a fabrication? Was it that he was handsome, and his wife and kids—one statesmen who had cute kids? You don't find that many." He concluded that it had to be "something that transcends all this."

The transcendent reason was that Kennedy was being mourned for his promise as well as for his accomplishments, a promise that had become increasingly evident during his last hundred days. This is why Albert Schweitzer praised him as a man "who could have been the savior of the world," William Attwood believed the next five years of his presidency would have "ushered in a kind of American renaissance at home and abroad," Ted Sorensen called his death "an incalculable loss of the future," the diplomat Chip Bohlen thought that when he was killed and Johnson sworn in, it represented "the future giving way to the present or the past," and the Israeli statesman Abba Eban, after defining tragedy as "the difference between what is and what might have been," called his assassination "one of the most authentically tragic events in the history of nations."

"What might have been" is speculation, but what Kennedy intended to do is not.

David Ormsby-Gore wrote in his condolence letter to Jackie, "He had great things to do and would have done them." Anyone wishing to wager against him doing these great things, and becoming a great president, should consider what he had already done.

He had been determined to see combat and demonstrate his courage during the war despite his poor health. After failing his military physicals, he had followed a strict regimen of physical conditioning and been accepted by the Navy, then pulled strings to be transferred from Intelligence to PT boats, and through willpower, courage, physical stamina, and luck had survived the sinking of *PT 109* and been decorated for heroism. He had run for Congress at the age of twenty-nine, and despite being gravely ill he had beaten more seasoned opponents. He had challenged Lodge for the Senate in 1952, and confounded the professionals by beating him decisively in a year when Republicans handily won the

---

* Burns admitted in 1965 that he might have underestimated him. In fact, he had written a remarkably accurate portrait of him in 1959, and his second thoughts indicated how much Kennedy had changed.

White House and Eisenhower carried Massachusetts. He had been determined to win a Pulitzer Prize, and he had. He had told Margaret Coit that he would become president, and seven years later, despite his youth and religion, he had done that, too. He had wanted to deliver the greatest speech by a president since the Gettysburg Address, and his inaugural address had been just that.

He had told Henry Brandon that to win the presidency he had to be a cold warrior, but to win a second term he had to be seen as searching for a peaceful end to the cold war. Days before leaving for Dallas he told Averell Harriman that he planned to make improved relations with the Soviet Union and a comprehensive test ban treaty, one including underground testing, the "principal thrust" of his second term. He also intended to travel to Moscow for a summit meeting with Khrushchev; launch a secret dialogue with Castro; explore the possibility of establishing a relationship with China; withdraw a thousand advisers from Vietnam by the end of 1963 and remove more during 1964; settle the cold war; end the threat of a nuclear war; launch an attack on poverty; pass his tax cut, civil rights, and immigration bills; preside over the most robust, full-employment economy in American history; and continue marrying poetry to power and inspiring the young.

What he intended to do is easier to discern than *why* he intended to do it. His remark during his dispute with the American Legion that "more often than not, the right thing to do is the right thing politically" shows that he realized that morality and political success were not exclusive, but raises the question of how much he wanted to accomplish these things because he considered them moral imperatives, or because they had engaged his emotions, or because he saw them as hurdles he needed to jump if he was to be judged a great man. Emotions, morals, and ambition were so tightly woven in him that unbraiding them would have been difficult enough had he served two terms, written his own memoirs, and been the subject of books by advisers like Schlesinger and Sorensen that were not composed under the shadow of Dallas. What *is* clear is that just as ambition and realpolitik had characterized his congressional career and early White House years, morality and emotion tempered his ambitions during his last hundred days.

Nor is it speculation to contrast what he intended to do with what happened.

Lincoln noted in her diary on November 23 that "Bobby asked me to take all of the tapes (telephone and recordings of cabinet room meetings) home for safe keeping"—presumably to prevent them from falling into Johnson's hands. Bobby kept their existence secret from Sorensen and Schlesinger, who were both writing accounts of the administration, and gave them to the Kennedy Library. Kennedy never had the chance to write his memoirs and plead his case before the high court of history, but it is inconceivable that someone who admired history and the written word as much as he did, had dictated the most moving and memorable passages in his inaugural address, and had won a Pulitzer Prize would not have written one of the most literate, honest, and engrossing presidential memoirs of all time.

Johnson asked Kennedy's aides to stay on but forbade them to wear their *PT 109* tie clasps in the White House. Many of those who had been closest to Kennedy resigned in 1964, including O'Donnell, Powers, Schlesinger, Salinger, Sorensen, and Bobby. Most of his foreign policy team, including Rusk, McNamara, and Bundy, stayed on. Johnson kept Hoover at the FBI beyond retirement age and urged him and Richard Katzenbach, who had replaced Robert Kennedy as attorney general, to reopen the sex angle of the Bobby Baker scandal, perhaps hoping it might blacken his predecessor's reputation. The *Evening Star* reported in March 1965 that Rometsch had asked the State Department for permission to return to the United States so she could marry "a staff member of an important congressional committee" (presumably La Verne Duffy), and had admitted belonging to two Communist youth organizations before moving to West Germany. The paper also reported that Republicans on the Senate Rules Committee wanted to explore the party-girl aspects of the Baker case, and that one of Baker's girls was claiming that her clients had included "some members of the executive branch."

Congress passed Kennedy's immigration bill, the Immigration and Nationality Act of 1965. It made immigration easier for residents of the Far East and Asian Subcontinent, and with the exception of the Civil Rights Act has probably done more to transform American society than any legislation in the last half century.

The "Great Society," Johnson's domestic legislative program, was largely a compendium of Kennedy's bills and initiatives. Medicare had been gaining traction before Dallas, and according to a *New York Times* editorial published on November 22, "The most forgotten of all the great forgotten issues of 1963, medical care for the aged, is finally getting a modicum of attention on Capitol Hill" and "the chances for sound action have been improved by the recommendations of a 12-member private advisory group." Johnson pushed Kennedy's tax-cut bill through Congress, but Kennedy had been on track to achieve this. The House had approved his bill in September, and when Bradlee needled him about not getting it passed before the end of the year, he had said, "God, what does it matter, Ben? We're going to get the tax bill. It's going to come in February. O.K., it's not this year but it's two months later." On November 23, Walter Heller asked Johnson if he wanted him to continue pursuing the antipoverty program that Kennedy had planned to launch in 1964. Johnson said yes, but suggested calling it "The War on Poverty." After Johnson escalated U.S. participation in the Vietnam War in 1965 without raising taxes, Heller resigned in protest from the Council of Economic Advisers.

Kennedy had persuaded Halleck and Dirksen to support his civil rights bill, and the House Judiciary Committee had reported out a strengthened bill including a provision prohibiting racial discrimination in employment. Congress enacted the Civil Rights Act in July 1964. Kennedy would have succeeded in getting a civil rights bill through Congress, but perhaps not until after the election. On the one-year anniversary of Dallas, *Look* magazine published an article by the reporter Richard Wilson titled, "What Happened to the Kennedy Program." Wilson interviewed Democratic and Republican congressional leaders and found them unanimous in concluding, that the Kennedy program "would have been adopted had he lived, just as it was adopted when he was dead." Senate Majority Leader Mansfield said, "The assassination made no real difference. Adoption of the tax bill and civil rights bill might have taken a little longer, but they would have been adopted." Senate Minority Leader Dirksen said, "The program was on its way before November 22, 1963. Its time had come." According to House Majority Leader Carl Albert, "The pressure behind this program had become so great that it would have been adopted in essentially the same form whether Kennedy lived or died," and House Minority Leader Halleck said, "The assassination made no difference. The program was already made." They had to have known that their opinions would upset the notoriously touchy Johnson, but they made them anyway. There was no political gain in voicing them and considerable risk, since all four men would have to work with Johnson during the next four years, making their statements all the more impressive and credible.

Goldwater lost to Johnson in a landslide, running so poorly that almost forty conservative GOP House members lost their seats. Kennedy would have won a resounding victory, too, although with fewer votes in the South, and he would not have benefited from the assassination factor. But like Johnson, he would have had a liberal majority in Congress that would have made it easier to pass his legislative agenda.

First Deputy Premier Anastas Mikoyan led the official Soviet delegation to Kennedy's funeral. Jackie took his hand and said, "Tell Mr. Khrushchev from me that my husband and Mr. Khrushchev would have brought peace to the world by working together. Now, Mr. Khrushchev will have to do it alone," a comment that speaks volumes about her low regard for Johnson. Ambassador Dobrynin believed that if Kennedy had lived, relations between the United States and the Soviet Union would have improved after a second summit between Kennedy and Khrushchev, because "Khrushchev did not want a repetition of the painful and damaging 1961 meeting in Vienna."

Jean Daniel had been with Castro when they were interrupted by news of the assassination. A stunned Castro said, "This is bad news. This is a serious matter, an extremely serious matter. There is the end of your mission of peace." On November 25, Chase sent Bundy a memorandum about what he called "Bill Attwood's Cuban exercise," writing that "the events of November 22 would appear to make accommodation with Castro an even more doubtful issue than it was." He continued, "While I think that President Kennedy could have accommodated with Castro and gotten away with it with a minimum of domestic heat, I'm not sure about President Johnson." When Lechuga ran into Attwood in the UN Delegates' Lounge on December 2, he informed him that he had received a letter from Cuba (Castro himself had written it) authorizing him to discuss a specific agenda for secret talks. In a memorandum to Bundy, Chase said that Attwood did not know if the letter had been written before or after November 22, but added, "In any event, Lechuga has apparently received no stop order since the assassination. One might assume, therefore, that the assassination has not changed Castro's mind about talking to the U.S." He reported that Attwood thought the new administration should listen to what Castro was proposing, and that "it would be very interesting to know what is in the letter."

During a December 19 National Security Council meeting on the Cuban situation, Bundy described the recent contacts with Castro, and said that the initiative had been on Castro's part "and we are essentially faced with a decision as to whether or not we are prepared to listen to what Castro has to say." President Johnson decided not to listen. Chase wrote in a memorandum that his reaction to continuing the talks was "somewhere between lukewarm and cool." In January, Chase told Attwood that Johnson would not be pursuing the opening to Castro in an election year.

Bobby Kennedy sent a memorandum to Dean Rusk in early December 1963 urging him to rescind the regulations prohibiting U.S. citizens from traveling to Cuba. He argued that the travel ban, which had been imposed by Eisenhower in the final days of his presidency, was "inconsistent with traditional American liberties" and lifting it would be "more consistent with our views as a free society and would contrast with such things as the Berlin Wall and Communist controls on such travel." His proposal was vetoed at a State Department meeting that he was not invited to attend.

Johnson met with Lodge on November 24 and, instead of discussing a timetable for the phased withdrawal of U.S. advisers, told him, "I am not going to lose Vietnam. I am not going to be the president who saw Southeast Asia go the way China went." Two days later, he approved a National Security Memorandum containing just the sort of language that Mansfield had cautioned Kennedy against using. It stated, "It remains the central object of the United States in South Vietnam to assist the people and Government of that country to win their contest against the externally directed and supported Communist conspiracy." Although it also said that the "objectives" of the withdrawal of U.S. military personnel remained, no U.S. advisers were withdrawn before the end of the year.

On November 22 there had been 16,300 advisers in Vietnam, but no combat units. During the U.S. involvement in the conflict under the Eisenhower and Kennedy administrations, 78 U.S. servicemen had been killed in action. After Johnson had been in office for a year there were more than 23,300 advisers in the country and 225 had been killed. By December 1965, after Johnson had escalated the war and sent U.S. combat units into battle, there were 185,000 U.S. troops in Vietnam and almost 1,600 American dead. By the end of 1967, U.S. forces numbered 485,000 with almost 16,000 killed.

Clark Clifford had advised both Kennedy and Johnson and served as Johnson's secretary of defense during his last year in office. He later wrote, "On the basis of personal intuition and a knowledge of both men, I believe that because of profound differences in personality and style, Kennedy would have taken a different path [on Vietnam] in his second term." Elaborating on what this path would have been, he added, "I believe Kennedy would have initiated a search for either a negotiated settlement or a phased withdrawal."

Robert McNamara wrote in his memoirs that Kennedy's comments to Huntley and Brinkley on September 9, 1963, had been an aberration and that "the great preponderance of President Kennedy's remarks—both before and after this interview, in public and in private—was that, in the end, the South Vietnamese must carry the war themselves; the United States could not do it for them." Walter Cronkite, whose interview had elicited one of these public remarks, wrote, "I have always believed that had he [Kennedy] lived, he would have withdrawn those advisors from Vietnam." Senator Wayne Morse, who frequently butted heads with Kennedy over Vietnam, said, "He'd seen the error of his ways. I'm satisfied that if he'd lived another year we'd have been out of Vietnam." In his 1970 oral history, the former deputy secretary of defense Roswell Gilpatric said, "Based on my exposure to the President's views over that nearly three-year period, I felt he was looking for an opportunity to pull back, and it would have been very hard to persuade him to reverse course." He admitted that it was impossible to know for sure what Kennedy would have done, but said, "my view is consistent with everything he did do and said before his death," adding, "he would have been very reluctant to involve ourselves to the extent that the country did after Johnson took over." John Connally wrote in his autobiography, "My guess is that Jack Kennedy would have withdrawn American troops from Vietnam shortly into his second term. . . . He was less charmed by the generals than Johnson and less susceptible to their pressures. I believe he had already concluded that the war was unwinnable."

Walt Rostow served in both administrations, first as an adviser to Kennedy in the White House, then in the State Department, and finally as Johnson's national security adviser. He was an unwavering hawk on Vietnam who had pushed for a more robust American commitment to both presidents. While riding a ski lift in Aspen with Marie Ridder, he said, "I'm doing better with Johnson because Kennedy wouldn't listen to me about Vietnam."

McGeorge Bundy served as Johnson's national security adviser for two years and supported his escalation of the war. In an oral history archived in the LBJ Library, he said that he believed Kennedy "would have been freer to cut loose" from Vietnam after the 1964 election because he would not have had to face the electorate again, whereas until March 1968, Johnson had been planning to seek a second term. He said about Kennedy, "I don't think he would ever have wanted to have the ground war become our war," dismissed as "total baloney" the argument that Kennedy and Johnson would have pursued the same policy in Vietnam because they were both advised by himself, Rusk, and McNamara, and said the three of them understood they were working for different presidents, who were making their own decisions. In 1993, Schlesinger wrote in his diary that Bundy had told him that "on reflection he did not think that JFK would ever have sent U.S. ground forces into the Vietnam War." Bundy believed that Johnson's decision to escalate the war was grounded in his character. He pointed out that Johnson had also been more hawkish than Kennedy during the Berlin and Cuban missile crises, calling him "temperamentally sort of always more 'one more regiment' than Kennedy."

The military analyst Daniel Ellsberg, who would leak the Pentagon Papers to the *New York Times* in 1971, ran into Bobby Kennedy at a Washington party in 1967 and asked him why his brother had sent only advisers when the Taylor-Rostow report was so emphatic that ground combat forces were necessary. Bobby skirted the question of what his brother would have done had he lived. "But I do know what he *intended*," he said. "All I can say is that he was absolutely determined not to send ground units." When they continued the conversation later in Bobby's office, Ellsberg asked if JFK would have accepted a defeat in Vietnam. "We would have fuzzed it up," Bobby said. "Would have gotten a government in that asked us out or that would have negotiated with the other side. We would have handled it like Laos." But why was JFK so averse to combat units? Ellsberg asked. "What made him so smart?" Bobby slammed his hand down on his desk and said, "Because *we were there!*" He slammed it down again and, with his face contorted in anger and pain, added, "We were there in 1951. We saw what was happening to the French. *We saw it.* My brother was determined, determined, never to let that happen to us."

JACKIE REMAINED DRY-EYED in public, and her composure and stoicism captured even hearts hardened to her husband. She maintained her self-control as she and Caroline knelt before his casket in the Senate rotunda, and as she stood on the steps of St. Matthew's Cathedral while John offered his father's casket the salute she had helped him practice at Wexford. She refused to cry while packing to leave the White House, even as her staff wept around her. "Now is not the time to cry, Provie," she told her maid. "We will cry later when we're alone." Later that winter, a nun giving religious instruction to a class of children that included Caroline told them about a woman in the Bible who had cried until her heart broke. Caroline interrupted to say in a sad little voice, "I know a lady who cries a lot." When the nun ignored her, she persisted, saying, "I know a lady who cries all the time." When the woman finally asked who was crying so much, she said, "My mommy." In the spring of 1964, Jackie told Father Richard McSorley, the Jesuit priest and academic who had become her informal confessor, "I had worked so hard at the marriage. I had made an effort and succeeded and he had really come to love me and to congratulate me on what I did for him. And, then, just when we had it all settled, I had the rug pulled out from under me."

She asked West to install a plaque over the mantel of the Lincoln bedroom stating, "In this room lived John Fitzgerald Kennedy and his wife Jacqueline Kennedy, during the two years, ten months, and two days he was President of the United States: January 20, 1961–November 22, 1963." It sat below one saying, "In this room Abraham Lincoln slept during his occupancy of the White House as Presidency of the United States: March 4, 1861–April 13, 1865." She believed that like Lincoln, her husband had been martyred because he had tried to end the injustices borne by black Americans, and that he would not have gone to Texas when he did had his approval rating not dropped following the introduction of his civil rights bill. After Nixon won the 1968 election, due largely to the Republican strategy of appealing to anti-civil-rights sentiment in the Southern states through coded statements about "states' rights," he ordered the plaque removed.

Before leaving the White House, Jackie sat alone in the Cabinet Room with West. Staring at him intently, she whispered, "Mr. West, will you be my friend for life?" Left speechless by this request, he nodded his assent. That summer she told Stan Tretick, whom she had battled for years over photographs of Caroline and John, "Oh, Stanley, remember how all the time in the White House I used to hate you so much? And now we are such good friends." In the month following Dallas she spent several weekends at Wexford with Ben and Tony Bradlee. They all found it impossible to talk about anything except Kennedy and the assassination. Bradlee remembered the weekends demonstrating that "the three of us had very little in common without the essential fourth." A reminder of her last weekend with her husband surfaced after her death in 1994, when the Kennedy Library received some of his clothes that she had stored. In the pocket of a pair of his trousers, the archivists found the sugar cubes she had given him to feed Leprechaun during their last weekend together at Wexford. She had either been unwilling to go through his pockets or could not bear to throw the cubes away.

After buying several of Elaine de Kooning's drawings and paintings of her husband from a gallery, she went to de Kooning's studio to see the others. She arrived, according to de Kooning, with an attitude of "Well, here I am and I can have what I want." She liked two charcoal drawings of him sitting on the patio at Palm Beach. In both, he wore dark glasses and had thrown a leg over the arm of a chair so that his crotch was framed in the center of the picture. De Kooning told her she was saving those two for herself. Upset at being rebuffed, Jackie said, "Well, they make him look like a fag on the Riviera." De Kooning replied, "They look good to me," and decided not to sell her any of her other Kennedy portraits and drawings.

In the fall of 1964, Jackie invited Henry Brandon to her new Fifth Avenue apartment. She had just moved in, and a maid led Brandon through unfinished rooms cluttered with packing boxes to a library overlooking Central Park. He had spent most of the preceding year in Moscow, so this would be the first time he had seen her since the funeral. She was paler and more ethereal than he remembered, with a more austere beauty. Speaking in a muffled voice, as if in a trance, she said, "I often wake up at night suddenly, and then I look for Jack next to me . . . and he is not there. . . . I wonder whether I am going to see him after death?" She kept returning to his place in history, saying, "Bobby tried to console me by suggesting that if Jack had been shot after the Bay of Pigs, he would have looked like the worst president."

It did not strike Brandon as much of a consolation, but for Jackie and Bobby, who knew how consumed Kennedy had been with the verdict of history, it was comforting to know that at least he had not been killed before he could witness the ratification of his test ban treaty, advance his tax cut and civil rights bill, demonstrate the kind of president he would have been, show her the marriage they might have had, and marry the poetry of his speeches to the power of the presidency—in other words, before his last hundred days.

ACKNOWLEDGMENTS

I found the extensive oral history collections at the Kennedy Library in Boston, and the Johnson Library in Austin, to be crucial resources, not least because many of those who knew Kennedy best have recently died, and their oral history interviews offer particularly detailed and poignant memories of their last encounters and conversations with Kennedy. I was also granted access to two lengthy oral histories that had been previously closed to researchers, those of Kennedy's close friends Paul Fay and Lem Billings (the Fay oral history has since been opened to the public). I would like to thank Robert F. Kennedy, Jr., for giving me access to the Billings history, and to Paul Fay's son for allowing me to read his father's oral history. In September 2011, the Kennedy Library released Jackie Kennedy's oral history, and in 2012, it released the last of Kennedy's Oval Office tapes. Both made it much easier to reconstruct his thoughts and conversations during his last hundred days. Arthur Schlesinger's extensive journals, published in 2007, were also an important resource. His published journals, however, represented only about 15 percent of the whole, and his other entries, available in the manuscript room of the New York Public Library, proved to be invaluable.

Several authors—most notably Sally Bedell Smith, Richard Reeves, Barbara Leaming, and Robert Dallek—interviewed many key Kennedy figures in the final years of their lives, and the material in their books that is based on their interviews is an oral history in its own right, and I am sure I will not be the last author to be in their debt. Ralph Martin's A Hero for Our Times (1983) and Seeds of Destruction (1995), both based on extensive interviews with people who knew Kennedy intimately and have since died, are also cited often in my chapter notes. Two former Secret Service agents, Clint Hill and Gerald Blaine, have recently written memoirs, both with the author Lisa McCubbin, that were important sources for my accounts of Kennedy's trips to Tampa and Texas. John Logsdon's *John F. Kennedy and the Race to the Moon* provided important insights into JFK's proposal for a joint lunar mission. Dallek's and Giglio's books contain groundbreaking analysis of Kennedy's health, as does Susan Schwartz's informative biography of Dr. Hans Kraus. I am also grateful to Dr. Heidi Kimberly for reviewing JFK's medical records with me, and explaining in detail his various illnesses and complaints. For Kennedy's Vietnam policy I relied on the FRUS material, and books by Rust, Newman, Jones, and Porter, as well as the primary material and analysis found in *Vietnam If Kennedy Had Lived* by Blight, Lang, and Welch. I found Porter's argument that Kennedy was using the optimistic Pentagon reports and the 1963 Taylor-McNamara mission to justify withdrawing U.S. advisers convincing and supported by the cables and anecdotal evidence. *The Kennedys: America's Emerald Kings* by Thomas Maier was particularly perceptive about the importance of JFK's Irish heritage, and Maier was the first author to reveal the poignant conversations between Jackie and Father McSorley in 1964. In instances where Kennedy's inaugural address influenced his decisions and approach to an issue, I relied on material from my previous book about the speech, *Ask Not*.

At the Kennedy Library, Stephen Plotkin and Sharon Kelly were, as usual, wonderfully accommodating and helpful, as was Laurie Austin in the audiovisual department. I consulted the Laura Bergquist Papers at Boston University and the Margaret Coit Papers at the University of North Carolina at Greensboro, and would like to thank the librarians at both institutions. I am also grateful to Sally Bedell Smith for suggesting that I consult William Manchester's papers (cited in the notes as "Death of a President"), and to the librarians at the Wesleyan Library manuscript collection for making them available.

Four interviews in particular were especially illuminating, and I would like to thank Ben Bradlee, Harris Wofford, Marie Ridder, and Lee White. For my earlier book about JFK's inaugural address, *Ask Not*, I also spoke with Ted Sorensen, Hugh Sidey, Arthur Schlesinger, Paul Fay, Oleg Cassini, Deirdre Henderson, and Charlie Bartlett, among many others, and I have used some material from those interviews in this book as well. Nancy Dutton has provided me with invaluable counsel and encouragement during the writing of this book and my previous one about Robert Kennedy's 1968 campaign.

I am grateful to Thad and Sarah Beal, and Harry Spence and Robin Ely, for their hospitality and friendship during my frequent trips to Boston. Every winter, Sandy,

Stephanie, Lily, and Isobel Carden have welcomed me into their family and home in Florida, and some of my best work has been done while sitting on their pleasant terrace. I am also indebted to George Whitney for hosting me in Florida and Massachusetts, and reminding me that not everyone shares my fascination with JFK. My wife, Antonia, again came to my rescue with some fast word processing and eagle-eyed editing, and my daughters, Phoebe, Edwina, and Sophie, gracefully endured three more years of hearing about the Kennedys. Ben Weir tracked down a copy of Irene Galitzine's book while spending a junior-year semester in Italy and translated it. He also gave my manuscript a careful and insightful read, proving himself to be a much better editor than any twenty-two-year-old has a right to be. I was sorry to lose Nick Trautwein when he moved from Penguin Press to *The New Yorker,* but fortunate to be handed over to Ginny Smith, who has been everything an author could want in an editor: sure-footed, enthusiastic, and nurturing. Her able assistant Kaitlyn Flynn has flawlessly handled the many tasks involved in turning my manuscript into a book. I am also grateful to Stefan McGrath and Josephine Greywoode at Allen Lane, my British publisher, for their encouragement and perceptive comments. While this book was being written, the Robbins Office was staffed by a talented and skillful group of professionals that included Karen Close, Katie Hutt, Ian King, Arielle Asher, Rachelle Bergstein, Micah Hauser, and Louise Quayle. I have dedicated the book to my agents Kathy Robbins and David Halpern, with gratitude for their wisdom and enthusiasm over the years.

NOTES

Abbreviations

ES: *Washington Evening Star*
FRUS: Foreign Relations of the United States
JFKL: John F. Kennedy Library
JFKLOH: John F. Kennedy Library Oral History Collection
JFKPP: John F. Kennedy Personal Papers
JFKPOF: John F. Kennedy Presidential Office Files
LBJLOH: Lyndon B. Johnson Library Oral History Collection
LOC: Library of Congress
NYPL: New York Public Library
NYT: *New York Times*
WP: *Washington Post*

December 31, 1962

ix "What makes journalism so fascinating": Bradlee (*Conversations*), p.12.
ix "a stunning resemblance": "Shining a Light on the Other de Kooning," *NYT,* November 21, 1993.
ix "gray, sculptural": Slivka, p. 201.
x watching as he nervously riffled through papers: Ibid.
x Caroline . . . with her own easel: Lincoln Papers, Box 6, January 3, 1963 Diary entry, JFKL.
x "Is this pose all right?": Munro, p. 256.
x She was intrigued: Slivka, p. 202.
x She told friends: Hall, p. 230.
xi He was larger than life and smaller: Ibid., p. 229.
xi After running out of space: Bledsoe, p. 33.
xi "heavily forested interior": Persico, p. 96. Sherwood admitted, "I could never really understand what was going on in Roosevelt's heavily forested interior."
xi "a shrinking from ostentation or display": Gullion, JFKLOH.
xi Laura Bergquist of *Look*: Bergquist (Knebel), JFKLOH.

xi "different parts of his life": Sorensen (*Counselor*), p. 102.

xii "the remote and private air": Norman Mailer, "Superman Comes to the Supermarket," *Esquire,* November 1960.

xii "No one ever knew John Kennedy": Reeves, p. 19.

xii "very introverted man": Strober, p. 51.

xii "a simple man": Rose Kennedy Papers, Box 82, JFKL.

xii "a romantic": Ibid.

xii "to reveal yourself is difficult": Ibid.

xii He took French lessons: Hirsh, JFKLOH.

xii He sent a friend abroad: Hersh, pp. 431–33.

xii asked a neighbor: Martin (*Hero*), p. 499.

xiii "that of the man who is always making": "President Kennedy and Other Intellectuals," *The American Scholar,* Fall 1961.

xiii "Can't you get it into your head": Von Post, p. 103.

xiii Mailer wondered: "Superman Comes to the Supermarket," *Esquire,* November 1960.

xiii Bergquist detected a vulnerability: Martin (*Seeds*), p. 371.

xiii While attempting to seduce: Coit, JFKLOH.

WEDNESDAY, AUGUST 7–SATURDAY, AUGUST 10

3 "It was involuntary": Adler, p. 53.

3 when he looked up from his papers: "John F. Kennedy and PT 109," JFKL Web site.

3 "In 'forty-three, they went to sea": Anthony (*Kennedy White House*), p. 239.

4 All of which may explain why: Bradlee, author interview.

4 He called Travell before flying: Travell, p. 421.

4 "the happiest time of his administration": Guthman and Shulman, p. 384.

4 "We'll never have another day": Beschloss (*Crisis Years*), p. 608.

4 the three happiest days: Turbidy, JFKLOH.

4 "the greatest weekend": Powers Papers, box 9 (interview with Vanocur), JFKL.

4 "bursting with vigor": Travell, p. 442.

5 "All we are getting here still": Maier, p. 442.

5 "I don't understand how you can get such a big kick": Fay, p. 58.

5 "It's time for Father and Son": Ibid., p. 232.

5 "John, aren't you lucky": Ibid., p. 243.

5 "Soon you'll have three": Lincoln (*My Twelve*), p. 282.

5 When Kennedy failed to appear for an excursion: Fay, JFKLOH; Sally Bedell Smith, p. 390.

5 "I'd known a lot of attractive women": Fay, p. 183.

5 After returning to Washington: Powers Papers, Box 9 (Vanocur interview), JFKL.

5 "could not bear to be alone": Ibid.

5 During the summer of 1963 they often sat together: O'Donnell and Powers, p. 375; Powers Papers, Box 9 (Vanocur interview), JFKL.

6 "a remarkably intensive but productive period": Sorensen (*Counselor*), p. 328.

6 "many President Kennedys": Taylor, JFKLOH.

6 "If they think they're going to get me": Fay, JFKLOH.

6 He told his best friend: Billings, JFKLOH.

6 "Why would anyone write a book": Abel, JFKLOH.

7 "an extremely hesitant person": *NYT,* October 31, 1993.

7 "no enemies to the right": Kraft, p. 6.

7 "he finally realized that the decision": Martin (*Hero*), p. 446.

8 "You mean there might be radioactive": Ibid., p. 443.

8 commencement address at American University: JFKL Web site.

8 "one of the greatest state papers": Sorensen (*Kennedy*), p. 733.

8 **Soviet leader Nikita Khrushchev praised it:** Manchester (*Remembering*), p. 206

8 **"strongest civil rights speech made by any president":** Farmer, JFKLOH.

8 **June 11, 1963, civil rights speech:** JFKL Web site.

8 **"Can you believe that white man":** Sorensen (*Counselor*), p. 282.

8 **"eloquent, passionate":** King, JFKLOH.

9 **"sailed with the wind":** John F. Kennedy (*Profiles*), p. 19. Sorensen made substantial contributions to the book. Kennedy was most involved in writing the introductory and concluding chapters, and this sentence, with its nautical reference, sounds more like him than like Sorensen.

9 **After the test ban treaty was initialed:** Sorensen (*Kennedy*), p. 745.

9 **After a Gallup poll reported:** Sorensen (*Counselor*), p. 284.

9 **"Great historical events":** Ibid.; *NYT*, November 22, 1988.

9 **"There comes a time":** Hodges, JFKLOH.

9 **"I may lose the next election":** Taylor Branch, p. 839.

10 **"a new spirit of hopefulness":** Cousins, p. 9.

10 **"Nothing is more powerful than an individual":** Norman Cousins, "The Improbable Triumvirate," *Saturday Review,* October 30, 1970.

10 **"Kennedy could bring bravery":** Burns, p. 281.

10 **Frost had presented him with a signed:** Parini, p. 415; Clarke, p. 215 (afterword in revised edition, 2011).

10 **"Be more Irish than Harvard":** Clarke, p. 215 (afterword in revised edition, 2011).

10 **1961 speech at University of Washington:** JFKL Web site.

10 **During the Cuban missile crisis:** Ibid.

11 **He sat silently during the flight:** Tuckerman and Turnure, JFKLOH.

11 **Another passenger remembered:** Ibid.

11 **"I'm never there when she needs me":** O'Donnell and Powers, p. 233.

11 **While he was cruising:** Martin (*Hero*), p. 106.

11 **"You'd better haul":** Ibid.

11 **But when she gave birth to Caroline:** Doris Kearns Goodwin, p. 793.

11 **He boasted of her being:** Billings, JFKLOH.

11 **Before flying to Otis:** Martin (*Hero*), pp. 464–65.

12 **Hospital personnel described him:** *Newsweek,* August 19, 1963; *Boston Globe,* August 8, 1963.

12 **He pulled aside:** *Portland Press Herald* (Maine), November 21, 2003.

12 **"Nothing must happen to Patrick":** Auchincloss, JFKLOH.

12 **A jubilant crowd:** *Boston Globe,* August 8, 1963.

13 **Before returning to Children's Hospital:** Sorensen (*Kennedy*), p. 367.

13 **She was so encouraged:** Gallagher, p. 288.

13 **"This is the kind of thing":** Auchincloss, JFKLOH.

13 **Her mother believed:** Ibid.

13 **Upon returning to the Ritz:** Lincoln (*My Twelve*), p. 295.

13 **After a full minute of silence he wrote:** *Boston Traveler,* August 13, 1963.

13 **Weeks later, an accountant:** Lincoln (*My Twelve*), p. 295.

14 **His father attended Mass:** Doris Kearns Goodwin, p. 312.

14 **While serving in the Pacific:** Story related by Kathleen McCarthy, a great-niece of Joe and Rose Kennedy, to the *St. Petersburg Times,* November 11, 1999.

14 **While staying with Paul Fay:** Joan (Fay) Bernstein, author interview.

14 **While rushing to grab a quick lunch:** Baldrige (Hollensteiner), JFKLOH.

14 **He studied photographs:** Tuckerman, JFKLOH.

14 **One brutally cold:** Halle, JFKLOH.

15 **"deeply concerned with other people's feelings":** George W. Ball, "Kennedy Up Close," *New York Review of Books,* February 3, 1994.

15 **David Ormsby-Gore, who made his acquaintance:** Lord Harlech (Ormsby-Gore), JFKLOH.

15 **These attributes had helped him win:** Halle, JFKLOH.

15 **"someone who understands what courage is":** Wofford, p. 31.

15 Sorensen described Kennedy: Sorensen (*Counselor*), p. 109.

15 A friend who knew the truth: Martin (*Seeds*), p 321.

16 Powers lay down: O'Donnell and Powers, p. 376.

16 Neither could recall him ever retiring: Billings, JFKLOH.

16 He never raised the subject with Sorensen: Sorensen (*Counselor*), p. 164.

16 "I'd better keep my nose clean": Cassini, p. 323.

16 During his first congressional campaign: O'Donnell and Powers, p. 70; Dalton, JFKLOH.

16 He was sensitive about being the first Catholic: O'Donnell and Powers, p. 405.

16 While recuperating in Palm Beach: JFKPP, Box 40, JFKL.

16 A tense 1961 summit: Lincoln (*My Twelve*), pp. 229–30.

17 That fall, after the Berlin crisis: Sidey, p. 214.

17 He saw a severely burned: O'Donnell and Powers, p. 377.

17 "He put up quite a fight": Ibid.

17 he ducked into a boiler room: Salinger (*With Kennedy*), p. 101.

17 After returning to his room: O'Donnell and Powers, p. 377.

17 His eyes were red: *Boston Record-American*, August 10, 1963; *Boston Globe*, August 9, 1963 (evening edition).

17 As he described Patrick's death: Anthony (*Kennedy White House*), p. 234.

17 Lincoln called Patrick's death: Lincoln (*My Twelve*), p. 296.

17 Sorensen thought: Sorensen (*Kennedy*), p. 367.

17 Jackie said, "He felt the loss": Bergquist and Tretick, p. 120.

17 "There'll be no crying in this house": Edward Kennedy, p. 41.

18 Ormsby-Gore detected: Ormsby-Gore (Lord Harlech), JFKLOH.

18 In *Pilgrim's Way*: Sorensen (*Kennedy*), p. 14.

18 His first words to the crew: Hamilton, p. 599.

18 But the bravado ended: Ibid., p. 606.

18 While delivering a Veterans Day address: McNeely, JFKLOH.

18 At a Memorial Day event: JFKPP, Box 40, JFKL.

18 Moments after his inauguration: Jacqueline Kennedy, p. 153.

18 After John's birth Ireland's ambassador: Kiernan, JFKLOH.

18 During the Cuban missile crisis: Pitts, p. 236.

18 after the Bay of Pigs: Jacqueline Kennedy, p. 185.

19 He cried again while discussing the Bay of Pigs: Leaming (*Mrs. Kennedy*), pp. 94, 96; Anthony (*As We Remember*), p. 179.

19 Kennedy asked Judge Francis Morrissey: Morrissey, JFKLOH.

19 Kennedy wept throughout: Cushing, JFKLOH.

19 "Come on, dear Jack": Ibid.

19 As Cushing spoke at the grave: Manchester (*Death*), p. 8.; *Look*, November 19, 1964.

19 Seeing him bent over the grave: Manchester (*Death*), p. 37.

19 Back at Otis, he wept: Jacqueline Kennedy, pp. 185–86; Leaming (*Mrs. Kennedy*), p. 299; Anthony (*Kennedy White House*), p. 234; Manchester (*Death*), p. 8.

19 His reference to "the work we have to do": Auchincloss, JFKLOH.

MONDAY, AUGUST 12

20 harebrained and ultimately unsuccessful: Edward Kennedy (*True Compass*), p. 86.

20 The White House announced that the president was missing: *NYT*, August 13, 1963.

20 "shadowboxing in a match": Collier and Horowitz, p. 146.

20 The headmaster of Choate: Parmet (*Jack*), p. 136.

21 "an oasis of stability": Edward Kennedy (*True Compass*), p. 63.

21 "Good morning, Mr. President": Speech by Edward Kennedy to Democratic National Convention, August 15, 2000.

21 so they could play flashlight tag: Edward Kennedy (*True Compass*), p. 34.

22 Cousins provided a list: Cousins, pp. 128–36.

22 Notes he scribbled on the way to Otis and in the Ritz: JFKPP, Box 12, JFKL.

23 JFK telephone call to Mansfield on August 12: Presidential Recordings, transcript of dictabelt 25B.2, August 12, 1963, JFKL.

23 Meeting with Dirksen in 1961: Baker, p. 98.

23 Rusk concerned that his office was bugged: Schoenbaum, p. 280.

23 "You bugging, Hoover?": Bishop (*Confession*), p. 383.

23 JFK ordered microphones installed: Bouck, JFKLOH.

24 "I don't want to hear your bad words": *NYT*, December 26, 1994.

24 Secret Service agents swept through the Oval Office: Bishop (*A Day*), pp. 5–6.

24 JFK took King into the Rose Garden: Branch, p. 837.

24 King concluded that JFK was worried about surveillance in the White House: Schlesinger (*Robert Kennedy*), p. 258. After his meeting with the President, King, referring to the fact that he and JFK had held their discussion outside, told his aide Andrew Young, "The President is afraid of Hoover himself. . . . I guess Hoover must be buggin' him too."

25 "I would like for you to surrender": Baker, pp. 97–99.

26 Conversation between JFK and RFK: Ibid.

26 Dirksen wrote Eisenhower a carefully worded letter: Beschloss (*Crisis*), p. 635.

26 "Forgive your enemies": Adler and Folsom, p. 194.

27 "a very real, a very earthy": Knebel, JFKLOH.

27 "Kennedy doesn't pay": McCarthy, p. 123.

27 he slighted his own family: Ibid., p. 124.

27 He had resisted his father's demand: Clifford, pp. 336–39.

27 "a positive force for public good": Edward Kennedy (*Words Jack Loved*), JFKL.

28 "He may be a fine politician": Ridder, author interview.

28 "nothing more than a bright ribbon": *NYT*, January 18, 1962.

28 Dirksen had issued a statement: Neil MacNeil, p. 219.

28 Eisenhower had also been critical: *Time*, August 9, 1963.

29 Kennedy remained pessimistic: Cousins, pp. 128–29.

29 "militant activated atheism": Hulsey, p. 178.

29 "His nose counts": *WP*, October 13, 1963.

29 Kennedy replied, "Maybe not": Baker, p. 98.

30 July 25 telephone call between JFK and Katzenbach: Presidential Telephone Records, 23D.5, July 25, 1963, JFKL.

30 he finally filled in his blank checks: Baker, pp. 98–99.

30 "emotionally more wrapped up": Bohlen, JFKLOH.

30 Seaborg believed treaty was "like a religion": Strober and Strober, p. 260.

30 On July 31, he told Seaborg: Presidential Recordings, tape 103/A39, JFKL.

30 His decision proved: Adler and Folsom, p. 57.

30 "Ike said I had coin in his bank" and subsequent conversation: Baker, pp. 98–99.

31 about the "tactics" of the IRS: Beschloss (*Crisis*), p. 636.

31 he called an attractive Hungarian émigrée: Sally Bedell Smith, p. 380, pp. 395–96.

31 Mimi Beardsley watched him reading condolence letters, one after another: Alford, p. 120.

31 She believed, she wrote later: Ibid., p. 125.

TUESDAY, AUGUST 13

32 On Tuesday morning Kennedy complained: JFKPP, box 48 (medical files), JFKL.

32 "We should stress the fact": Ibid.

32 he was "suffering terribly": Hamilton, pp. 110–11.

32 **a dietary regimen:** JFKPP, Box 58 (medical files), JFKL.

33 **loved fish chowder:** Gallagher, p. 40.

33 **"with gallantry and no perceptible loss":** Michael O'Brien, p. 764.

33 **"a word of self-pity":** *NYT,* November 17, 2002.

33 **"In retrospect, it is amazing":** Sorensen (*Counselor*), p. 106.

33 **"There is always inequity":** JFK press conference #28, March 21, 1962, JFKL Web site.

33 **His physicians, however, knew a man:** "The Medical Ordeals of JFK," Robert Dallek, *The Atlantic,* December 1962; "The Medical Afflictions of President John F. Kennedy," *White House Studies,* volume 6, number 4, 2006.

34 **He swallowed a pharmacopoeia of capsules:** JFKPP, Box 47 (medical files), JFKL.

34 **"It's best if you don't":** Travell, p. 312.

34 **During a taped January 5, 1960, interview:** Transcript of January 5, 1960, discussion among Bradlee, Cannon, and Kennedy, JFKL.

34 **It called his health "excellent":** JFKPP, Box 58 (medical files), JFKL.

35 **first postelection press conference:** *NYT,* November 11, 1960.

35 **A month after Cohen and Travell:** *NYT,* May 3, 1973.

35 **His search for a quick fix:** Ibid., December 4, 1972.

36 **"You cannot be permitted to receive therapy":** JFKPP, Box 58 (medical), JFKL.

36 **"a potential threat to your well-being":** Leamer, p. 545.

36 **Cohen unburdened himself:** JFKPP, Box 58 (medical), JFKL.

37 **Kraus's pioneering studies:** Schwartz, pp. 121–24.

37 **Burkley and Cohen threatened to go to the president:** Burkley, JFKLOH; Schwartz, p. 176.

37 **When Kraus examined Kennedy:** Schwartz, p. 178.

37 **"You will be a cripple soon":** Ibid., pp. 177–79.

37 **Kraus flew to Washington:** JFKPP, Box 47 (medical), JFKL; Kraus Papers, Box 1, JFKL.

37 **"a definite increase of strength":** Kraus Papers, Box 1, JFKL.

37 **"in a not too distant future":** Ibid.

37 **"a very long step":** JFKPP, Box 47 (medical), JFKL.

37 **Kennedy asked Ken O'Donnell to fire Travell:** JFKPP, Box 58 (medical), JFKL.

38 **"I hate to use the word blackmail":** Ibid.

38 **Kennedy's back improved:** Schwartz, pp. 192–93.

38 **"I wish I could have known you":** Anthony (*Kennedy White House*), p. 253.

38 **James Joyce had taught Kraus English:** Schwartz, p. 7.

38 **"I know, Doctor, you've come a long way":** Ibid., p. 187.

39 **Kraus returned to his office:** Ibid., p. 188.

39 **Kraus considered Kennedy cured:** Ibid., p. 197.

39 **"I wish I had more good times":** Jacqueline Kennedy, p. 21.

Wednesday, August 14

40 **When Kennedy arrived:** Hennessey-Donovan, JFKLOH.

40 **Hennessey was a cheerful:** Ibid.; Edward Kennedy (*True Compass*), p. 45; Hennessey-Donovan, "Bringing Up the Kennedys," *Good Housekeeping,* August 1961.

40 **he was paying her tuition:** Ibid.; Hennessey-Donovan, JFKLOH.

41 **"There are ninety-six thousand":** Hennessey-Donovan, JFKLOH.

41 **Jackie presented the hospital staff:** *Boston Globe,* August 15, 1963.

41 **"You've been so wonderful to me":** Pottker, p. 194.

41 **The improvements had been as modest:** Travel, JFKLOH.

41 **he read about the renovations in the** *Washington Post:* WP, July 25, 1963.

41 **He telephoned:** Presidential Recordings, "Furniture at Otis Air Force Base," cassette G, July 25, 1963, JFKL.

41 he called: Ibid.
42 "To think that big blockhead": Fay, JFKLOH.
42 "the nice people of Boston": Pottker, p. 138.
42 "Money is never to be squandered": Rose Fitzgerald Kennedy, p. 118.
42 He did not give his children bicycles: Edward Kennedy (*True Compass*), p. 70; I have also relied on Beran's discussion of Joe Kennedy's determination to emulate the old-money values of the Boston Brahmins.
42 "It's all right to struggle": Ibid., p. 94.
43 the duke "does have great integrity": John F. Kennedy (*Prelude*), p. 14.
43 His legal residence in Boston: Morrissey, JFKLOH; Lincoln (*My Twelve*), p. 75.
43 offering fashion tips to friends: Fay, p. 48, 177.
43 "I hope to make this house": Halle, JFKLOH.
43 "You've got great taste": Ibid.
43 He later gave his friend Joe Alsop: Joseph Alsop, JFKLOH.
43 He bought monogrammed handkerchiefs: Fay, JFKLOH.
43 "like a rich man's plane": Bergquist and Tretick p. 123; Tretick, JFKLOH.
44 "Are you out of your mind?": Fay, JFKLOH; Fay, pp. 246–47.
44 In the Navy, he had preferred: Renehan, p. 243.
44 "receptive to everybody": Hamilton, pp. 512–13; Renehan, p. 231.
44 "He is a terribly cold man": Schlesinger (*Thousand*), p. 18.
44 "and then getting into his government limousine": Fay, JFKLOH.
44 "Of course, they'd be so great": Jacqueline Kennedy, p. 66.
44 U. E. Baughman, who headed the Secret Service: Baughman, p. 256.
44 Deirdre Henderson, who served: Henderson, author interview.
45 "I was taken into the kitchen": John F. Kennedy, "A Dictated Letter (Circa 1959) to Jacqueline Kennedy on Weekend in Rhode Island," audio-visual collection, JFKL.
45 "These are the kind of people": Manchester (*Remembering*), p. 18.
45 "a plain, inexpensive casket": Lawrence O'Brien, p. 161.
45 "Kiss her again": Laura Bergquist Papers, Box 20, Boston University Library.
45 "like a couple of kids": *Boston Globe*, August 15, 1963.
45 An old friend who saw the resulting photograph: Leaming, p. 301; photograph of them holding hands, *WP*, August 15, 1963, and *NYT*, August 15, 1963.
45 "a small gesture": Hill, p. 248.
45 "extremely close and affectionate": Anthony (*As We*), p. 193.

THURSDAY, AUGUST 15

49 Eisenhower began honoring: *NYT*, August 16, 1963.
49 he had sent Senator Fulbright: Hulsey, p. 179.
49 Lodge told Clifton: Lodge, JFKLOH.
50 he received a condescending letter: William J. Miller, p. 336.
50 "American security must always be considered": Ibid., p. 337.
50 Bobby warned him that in about six months: Guthman and Shulman, p. 301.
50 Sorensen . . . joked that he hoped he was being sent to North Vietnam: Sorensen (*Counselor*), p. 357; Sorensen, JFKLOH.
50 "instinct for magnanimity": Schlesinger (*Thousand Days*), p. 989.
50 "involving a leading Republican": Ibid.
50 "The idea of getting Lodge mixed up": O'Donnell and Powers, p. 16.
51 It had started when Lodge's grandfather: Doris Kearns Goodwin, pp. 100–103.
51 "I didn't want them to go through": McCarthy, p. 22.
51 "I'm afraid that they feel": Fay, p. 165.

52 The Irish ambassador . . . Thomas Kiernan: Kiernan, JFKLOH.

52 "Do you know it is impossible": Fay, p. 124.

52 He told the columnist Betty Beale: Beale, p. 67.

52 "the world should be made": Talbot, JFKLOH.

52 "It won't go over with the WASPs": Bradlee (*Conversations*), p. 68.

52 "nursed an Irish distaste": O'Donnell and Powers, p. 16.

52 "That's the last Nixon will see": Ibid.

52 "I think a fair regard": Guthman and Shulman, p. 401.

53 "a most loyal and devoted friend": Lodge, p. 22.

53 "the only man I have ever met": Ibid., p. 21.

53 "I never want to see": Hilty, p. 30; Maier, p. 137.

53 "He is a total politician": Halberstam (*Quagmire*), p. 154.

53 "In becoming a Republican": "Modernize the GOP," *Atlantic Monthly*, March 1950.

53 He had introduced a bill: Lodge, pp. 68–69.

53 "rich man's club": "Modernize the GOP," *Atlantic Monthly*, March 1950.

54 "loft a pass, swap a joke": *NYT*, November 22, 1988.

54 "That in twenty years": Reeves, p. 254.

55 Topping told him: Topping, pp. 151–57.

55 Bobby wrote in his diary: RFK Pre-administration Personal Folders, Box 24, JFKL. Bobby also described the trip in his oral history for the JFK Library (Guthman and Shulman, pp. 436–39).

55 "the desperate attempt": *Meet the Press*, December 2, 1951.

55 "a white man's war": Martin (*Hero*), p. 438.

57 "If we permit Laos to fall": McNamara memorandum, JFKPOF, Box 29a, JFKL.

57 "There he sat, telling me": O'Donnell and Powers, p. 244.

57 The chiefs warned that if the Chinese: Hilsman, p. 147.

57 "Since he couldn't think": Schlesinger (*Kennedy*), p. 338.

57 "Do you understand?": Porter, p. 146.

57 "his knowledge of the French problem": Taylor, JFKLOH.

58 "When I sat there and looked": Fay, JFKLOH.

58 "God, I hope you've been enjoying": Ibid.

59 Kennedy told John Kenneth Galbraith: Galbraith (*A Life*), p. 383.

59 He told Rusk: Rusk, pp. 240–41.

60 "Dave, how would you like this to be said": O'Donnell and Powers, p. 14.

60 MacArthur told him: JFKPOF, Box 30, JFKL; Guthman and Shulman, p. 354.

60 "a hell of an impression": Martin (*Seeds*), p. 444.

60 "Well, now, you gentlemen": Schlesinger (*Robert Kennedy*), p. 704; Taylor, RFK Oral History Collection, JFKL.

60 After returning from a fact-finding mission: FRUS, 1961–1963, Volume I, Vietnam, 1961, Document 228.

60 "instinctively against the introduction": Blight, Lang, and Welch, p. 56.

60 "when and if the U.S. military recommend it": FRUS, 1961–1963, Volume I, Vietnam, 1961, Document 253.

61 "I don't recall anyone who was strongly": Schlesinger (*Robert Kennedy*), p. 704; Taylor, RFK Oral History Collection, JFKL.

61 "I want you to hear this": Fay, JFKLOH; Paul Fay Forum, June 15, 2003, JFKL.

62 "We can see the light": Oberdorfer, p. 190.

62 "with a feeling of depression": Ibid., p. 192.

62 "Seven years and billions": FRUS, 1961–1963, Volume II, Vietnam, 1962, Document 330.

62 "This is not what my advisors": Oberdorfer, p. 194.

62 "I got angry at Mike": Ibid.

63 In a special "eyes only" annex: Hilsman, pp. 465–66.

63 an assessment from Edmund Gullion: Hilsman, JFKLOH.

63 **"Keep it down"**: Ibid.

64 **"We don't have a prayer"**: Thompson (*Kennedy*), p. 16.

64 **"to seize upon any favorable"**: Report of a memorandum written by McGeorge Bundy's aide Michael Forrestal, *NYT*, December 5, 1998.

64 **"sucked into Vietnam little by little"**: Brandon (*Anatomy*), p. 30.

64 **In the spring of 1963, he told Mansfield**: O'Donnell and Powers, p. 16.

64 **"In 1965, I'll become"**: Ibid.

64 **[footnote] Mansfield confirmed O'Donnell's**: Blight, Lang, and Welch, p. 136.

64 **Kennedy could point to the Pentagon's optimistic reports**: Porter, p. 166. Porter makes a convincing case that Kennedy seized upon the overly optimistic reports from the Pentagon to justify reducing the U.S. commitment to South Vietnam.

64 **"Barring greatly increased resupply"**: Rust, pp. 90–91.

65 **Kennedy activated the hidden Oval Office microphone**: Recording of Kennedy-Lodge conversation, Tape 104/A40, JFKL.

65 **"when he was bored"**: Dickerson, p. 63.

65 **he filled a page with doodles**: JFKPP, Box 43, JFKL.

66 **"I suppose these are the worst press relations"**: Lodge, JFKLOH.

67 **"Are you getting any lately?"**: Dickerson, p. 67.

67 **"How's your romance going?"**: Bergquist Papers, Box 20, Boston University Library.

67 **"Who does he sleep with?"**: Ibid.

67 **"cool, brainy, blunt"**: Ibid.

67 **"a very swinging sexual animal"**: Ibid.

FRIDAY, AUGUST 16–SUNDAY, AUGUST 18

68 **"It's my daddy's turn!"**: Meyers, p. 207. This account was given to Meyers by Kennedy's military aide Major General Chester V. Clifton. Clifton does not date the story of Caroline and JFK at the candy store, but given its placement in the book, it happened during the summer of 1963, after Patrick's death, most likely when JFK arrived on Friday, August 16.

68 **"What You Don't Know About Kennedy"**: Fletcher Knebel, "What You Don't Know About Kennedy," *Look*, January 17, 1961.

69 **"I would describe Jack as rather like me"**: Fletcher Knebel Papers, Boston University Library, also cited in Sally Bedell Smith, pp. 7–8.

69 **"I'd say Jack didn't want to reveal"**: Rose Kennedy Papers, Box 82, JFKL.

69 **"strangely remote"**: Gallagher, p. 159,

69 **"something quite remote"**: Mailer, p. 44.

69 **"the subtle smile"**: *Newsweek*, January 27, 1961.

69 **"a smile that had nothing public"**: *Reporter,* February 16, 1961.

69 **"have a hard time getting to the bottom"**: Bergquist and Tretick, p. 179.

69 **"A penny for your thoughts"**: Martin (*Seeds*), p. 72.

69 **"a bright young woman"**: Anthony (*As We Remember*), p. 60.

69 **praised her "brilliant imagination"**: Ibid., p. 49.

70 **an iron will**: West, p. 195.

70 **"Look, Frank. Just smile"**: Taraborelli, pp. 25–26.

70 **"tremendous awareness"**: Anthony (*As We Remember*), p. 110.

70 **"The trouble with you, Jack"**: Adler (*The Eloquent*), pp. 37–38.

70 **"Where is this great Irish wit"**: Martin (*Seeds*), p. 322.

70 **"Jackie is superb in her personal life"**: Ridder, author interview.

70 **"Don't ask Jack mean questions"**: Dickerson, p. 65.

70 **"never allowing intimacies"**: Clifford, p. 304.

70 **"You have to believe that he loves"**: Ridder, author interview.

71 **"Fitzgerald breasts":** Bradlee (*Conversations*), p. 29.
71 **During a campaign trip to Oregon:** Lubin, pp. 78–79. Lubin pointed out the similarities between the Hopper painting and the Lowe photograph, placing them side by side in his book.
71 **"the two most isolated":** Andersen, p. 1.
71 **"See that smile on her face?":** Martin (*Hero*), p. 472.
71 **"Maybe now I'm getting through to him":** Leaming, p. 303.
72 **he read at meals, in the bathtub:** Jacqueline Kennedy, p. 41.
72 **When he returned that weekend, she reciprocated:** *NYT,* August 17, 1963.

MONDAY, AUGUST 19–TUESDAY, AUGUST 20

75 **Senator Mansfield handed him a three-page memorandum:** JFKPOF, digital locator 060-008, JFKL Web site; Mansfield Papers, series XXII, Box 103, Folder 14, Mansfield Papers, University of Montana.
76 **August 20 press conference:** *NYT,* August 21, 1963; JFKL Web site.
77 **"tragic mistake":** *Boston Globe,* August 21, 1963.
77 **"There's no doubt that any man":** Presidential Recordings, transcript of dictabelt 25B.5, 26C.1, August 23, 1963, JFKL.

WEDNESDAY, AUGUST 21–FRIDAY, AUGUST 23

78 **he received an early morning call:** Transcript in Ball Personal Papers, Box 9, JFKL.
79 **"eager young ladies":** Baker, p. 47.
79 **Her FBI file described her:** Rometsch FOIA (Freedom of Information Act) FBI file, available online and at the FBI.
79 **"illicit relations with highly":** Ibid.
79 **According to Evans's memorandum:** Ibid.
79 **"You've got to be careful":** Evan Thomas, p. 255.
80 **"high-level sex contacts":** Rometsch FOIA-FBI file.
80 **"Of course, no mention will be made":** Ibid.
80 **[footnote] After the fall of the Berlin Wall:** Koehler, pp. 250–51.
81 **"It is hard to overstate":** Leaming, p. 268.
81 **While editing a draft:** Katie Louchheim Papers, Box 78, LOC.
81 **If someone disparaged Profumo:** Spalding, JFKLOH.
81 **"He thought this was not at all the way":** Berlin, JFKLOH.
81 **Bobby decided it was too dangerous:** Beschloss (*Crisis*), p. 616.
81 **one of the most egregious instances of a womanizing:** The most perceptive and succinct analysis of JFK's womanizing can be found in Mark J. White's essay "Behind Closed Doors: The Private Life of a Public Man," pp. 256–76 in Mark J. White's *Kennedy: The New Frontier Revisited.* Another excellent summary can be found in Hagood's *Presidential Sex.*
82 **his need for a secret life:** Sally Bedell Smith, p. 153.
82 **"You've got to live every day":** Smathers, JFKLOH.
82 **"I've got this slow-motion cancer":** Martin (*Hero*), p. 49.
82 **He confided in Clare Boothe Luce:** Beale, p. 76.
82 **he suffered punishing headaches:** Strober and Strober, p. 78.
82 **being circumcised at the age of twenty-one:** Hamilton, p. 219.
82 **finding his father in flagrante:** Madsen, pp. 240–41.
82 **The fact that Kennedy's sexuality remained so unchanged:** Mark J.White, p. 259. White has a particularly insightful discussion of Kennedy's sexuality.
82 **"an adolescent in terms":** Strober and Strober, p. 56.
82 **"an immature relationship with girls":** Billings, JFKLOH.
82 **"seemed to relish sharing the details":** Baker, p. 78.

82 "part of him still seemed to be": Alford, p. 65.
82 "a little boy who wouldn't": Storm, p. 158.
83 "a real compulsion": Leaming, p. 60.
83 Charlie Bartlett, who had introduced: Pitts, p. 143.
83 "because I was thirty-seven years old": McMillan, author interview.
83 "absolutely no guilty conscience": Beaton, p. 301.
83 "to keep the White House white": Sally Bedell Smith, p. 156.
83 showing a keen interest in polygamy: Cassini, p. 324.
84 letters, diary, and testimony of Margaret Coit: Coit Papers, University of North Carolina at Greensboro; Coit, JFKLOH.
86 On August 21, he was still shifting gears: JFKPP, Box 12, JFKL.
87 "Personal Conduct in High Office": *ES*, August 21, 1963.

SATURDAY, AUGUST 24–SUNDAY, AUGUST 25

88 Jackie loved their rented house . . . rooms measured: Gallagher, p. 292.
88 The White House press office: *NYT*, August 25, 1963.
88 "having had the foresight": *ES*, August 25, 1963.
88 spoke of the house being "full of sadness": Martin (*Hero*), p. 467.
88 "Look at what the Pope said": Ibid.
89 "I wish you would tell him": Schlesinger (*Journals*), p. 201.
89 [footnote] "I *know* there is much joy": JFKPP, Box 43, JFKL.
89 "She hung on to him and he held her": Sally Bedell Smith, p. 396.
89 "Maybe he thought you were a waiter": Douglas Home, JFKLOH.
89 "Does the ambitious Greek tycoon": Evans, p. 194.
90 "Whatever you do in Greece": Hill, p. 250.
90 Michael Forrestal called to ask Kennedy: Rust, pp. 114–15.
90 Cable 243: FRUS, 1961–1963, Volume III, Vietnam, January–August 1963, Document 281.
90 Kennedy asked if he could delay making a decision: Rust, p. 114.
90 Hilsman and Harriman found Undersecretary Ball . . . on a golf course: Ball, LBJLOH.
91 Ball called Kennedy: Ball, pp. 371–72.
91 "ran counter to the grain of American principles": Ibid., p. 371.
91 Kennedy asked the White House photographer: Van Buren, p. 74.
92 he received Lodge's response: FRUS, 1961–1963, Volume III, Vietnam, January–August 1963, Document 285.

MONDAY, AUGUST 26–TUESDAY, AUGUST 27

93 "I think we should give priority": Manchester (*Remembering*), p. 204.
93 "It is important that he be corrected": Cousins, pp. 24–25.
94 "a lonesome figure": Ibid., p. 110.
94 "In closing, I want again to send my warm personal wishes": FRUS, 1961–1963, Volume VI, Kennedy-Khrushchev Exchanges, Document 95.
94 "One of the ironic things": Cousins, pp. 113–14.
94 "The President is in a grave situation": Nikita Khrushchev, pp. 497–98.
95 "Obviously, this is Khrushchev's own version": Ibid., p. 498.
95 Dobrynin's account in his memoirs: Dobrynin, p. 90.
95 Knebel got the idea: *NYT*, February 28, 1993.
95 Knebel also found inspiration: Reston, pp. 208–9.
95 a top-secret memorandum proposing Operation Northwoods: George Washington University, National Security Archive.
96 After receiving a summary: FRUS, 1961–1963, Volume X, Cuba 1962–1963, Document 314.

97 **After finishing the book:** Bergquist and Tretick, p. 15.

97 **During a discussion:** Fay, pp. 189–90.

97 **"I just don't see":** Zelikow and May, pp. 113–17.

97 **"Can you imagine LeMay saying":** O'Donnell and Powers, p. 318.

98 **"the President is not sure that":** Nikita Khrushchev, pp. 497–98.

98 **"the greatest defeat in our history":** Cowley, p. 259.

98 **"The military are mad":** Schlesinger, unpublished diary, NYPL.

98 **"The first advice I'm going to give":** Bradlee (*Conversations*), p. 122.

98 **A year later McNamara informed:** Presidential Recordings, Tape 118/A57, JFKL.

98 **"Do you intend to make a movie":** Douglas, p. 349.

98 **"as a warning to the Republic":** Schlesinger (*Robert Kennedy*), p. 450.

98 **"as a warning to the generals":** Talbot, p. 148.

99 **"if there were a third Bay of Pigs":** Fay, p. 190.

99 **ran a full-page advertisement:** *ES,* August 20, 1963.

99 **"Rebellion in the Air Force?":** *The New Republic,* Raymond Sentier, September 28, 1963.

99 **"damned everywhere as a Communist appeaser":** O'Donnell and Powers, p. 16.

100 **"The time has come when he who is successful":** Sergei Khrushchev, p. 674.

100 **"some absolutely unusual things":** Ibid.

100 **"You plan hundreds of targets":** Ibid., p. 675.

100 **Khrushchev also recommended scaling back the conventional army:** Ibid.

100 **"Availing myself of the return":** FRUS, 1961–1963, Volume VI, Kennedy-Khrushchev Exchanges, Document 115.

101 **Thompson's official memorandum:** FRUS, 1961–1963, Volume V, Soviet Union, Document 350.

101 **omits some of Kennedy's playful banter:** Dobrynin, pp. 105–6; Presidential Recordings, Tape 107/A43, JFKL.

102 **"certain aspects of the exploration of space":** Interview with Senator John Kennedy, *Bulletin of the Atomic Scientists,* November 1960.

103 **"Dramatic achievements in space":** Logsdon, pp. 104–7; McNamara-Webb memorandum, JFKL Web site.

103 **Kennedy had promised Americans a "New Frontier":** JFK acceptance speech to the 1960 Democratic National Convention, delivered at the Los Angeles Memorial Coliseum on July 15, 1960.

103 **"I believe that this nation should commit itself":** JFK speech to joint session of Congress, full text on JFKL Web site.

103 **"We set sail on this new sea":** Rice University speech, full text on JFKL Web site.

103 **"All right—why not?":** Sorensen (*Kennedy*), p. 544.

104 **"a very heavy burden":** JFK press conferences, JFKL Web site.

104 **During a November 1962:** Presidential Recordings, Tape 60, November 16, 1962, JFKL.

104 **July 20, 1963, press conference:** Transcripts of JFK press conferences on JFKL Web site.

105 **"appeared to be looking for an agreement":** FRUS, 1961–1963, Volume V, Soviet Union, Document 351.

105 **"Soviet propaganda has shown unusual restraint":** *NYT,* August 28, 1963.

105 **The meeting was among the most contentious:** Presidential Recordings, Tape 107/A42, Tape 108/A43, JFKL.

106 **"an egregious 'end run'":** Taylor, p. 292.

106 **"we began to lose":** Forrestal, LBJLOH.

WEDNESDAY, AUGUST 28

107 **"massive, militant, and monumental sit-in demonstration":** *NYT,* June 12, 1963.

107 **"We want success in Congress":** Wilkins, p. 291.

107 **"They're going to come down here":** Raywid, JFKLOH.

107 "They [the marchers] are going to express": July 17, 1963, press conference, JFKL Web site.

108 "Oh, Bruce, I wish I were out there": Bruce, p. 97.

108 a natural "instinct" for the medium: Hersh, p. 224.

108 "We wouldn't have had a prayer": Salinger, p. 54.

108 Kennedy had ordered: Traphes Bryant, pp. 17, 43.

108 "Jesus Christ, that's a terrific speech": Lee White, author interview.

109 "I have a dream": Ibid.; *NYT*, August 29, 2963.

109 "relief written all over his face": Wilkins, p. 293.

109 "a superb job of making your case": Ibid.

109 "the education of JFK on the race question": Roy Wilkins, JFKLOH.

109 King had a similar take on his evolution: King, JFKLOH.

110 the "joys and hardships" of being black: Roy Wilkins, JFKLOH.

110 His black valet George Taylor protested: Taylor, JFKLOH.

110 "That's not acceptable": Richard Goodwin, p. 4.

110 "Oh, I see, the back of the bus for Catholics": Recollecting JFK Forum, October 22, 2003, JFKL.

110 "What the hell. That's a decent thing to do": Branch, p. 362.

111 "I'm not going to just play at this business": Thompson, p. 52.

111 "an offering of a cactus bouquet": *NYT,* May 11, 1963.

111 King criticized him for vacillating: Bergquist and Tretick, p. 26.

111 spoke of "two Kennedys": King, JFKLOH.

111 had made him "sick": Schlesinger (*Journals*), p. 189.

111 "Lincoln had real agonizing moments": King, JFKLOH.

112 "We are confronted primarily": text of civil rights speech on JFKL Web site.

112 "Sometimes you look at what": *Newsweek,* July 8, 1963.

112 the "morality of integration" ... "the most eloquent, passionate, and unequivocal plea": King, JFKLOH.

112 Kennedy invited his widow and children: Martin (*Hero*), pp. 254–55.

112 "I don't understand the South": Schlesinger (*Thousand Days*), p. 966.

112 "to look into your hearts": JFK statement to Congress on submission of his civil rights bill, JFKL Web site.

113 "a complete blueprint for a totalitarian state": Gentile, p. 34.

113 "the destruction of the United States": Ibid.

113 "Well, if we're going down": Manchester (*Remembering*), p. 241.

113 "considerable anxiety over the President's civil rights speech": Schlesinger (*Journals*), p. 199.

113 "widespread and intense panic in the suburbs": Ibid.

113 A survey of non-Southern whites: Stewart Alsop and Oliver Quayle, "What Northerners Really Think of Negroes," *Saturday Evening Post,* September 7, 1963.

113 As soon as Kennedy learned: Wilkins, JFKLOH.

114 Speaking first, Wilkins said: Rosenberg and Karabell, pp. 131–40; Presidential Recordings, Tape 108/A43, JFKL.

114 his doodles showed: JFKPP, Box 12, JFKL.

THURSDAY, AUGUST 29–SATURDAY, AUGUST 31

117 "When we move to eliminate a government": Presidential Recordings, Tape 107/ A42, JFKL.

117 "You're not worth firing": Rust, p. 119.

117 "what they feel their prospects are for success": Presidential Recordings, Tape 107/A42, JFKL.

117 "Ah, do we cut our losses in such a way": Ibid.

117 On Wednesday, the CIA station chief: FRUS 1961–1963, Volume III, Vietnam, January–August 1963, Document 299.

118 "As of now there are no signs": Ibid., Document 297.

118 "our knowledge of composition of coup group": Ibid., Document 306.

118 "Situation here has reached point of no return": Ibid., Document 307.

118 "I don't think we ought to take the view": Presidential Recordings, Tape 107/A42, JFKL.

118 Harriman yelled, "Shut up!": Weintel and Bartlett, p. 87.

118 "This shit has got to stop!": Bird, p. 254; Reeves, p. 567.

118 "My God! My government's coming apart": Guthman and Shulman, p. 397.

118 "We are launched on a course": FRUS 1961–1963, Volume IV, Vietnam, August–December 1963, Document 12.

119 He told Lodge, "We will do": Ibid., Document 18.

119 "I wouldn't be surprised": WP, August 31, 1963.

119 Lincoln had left a message on his bed: JFKPP, Box 12, JFKL.

120 He gave in, calling Roosevelt: Sally Bedell Smith, p. 397.

120 "I don't want to read anything in the papers": Fay, p. 211.

120 He diagnosed a muscle sprain: JFKPP, Box 46, JFKL.

120 Kraus arrived on August 31: Schwartz, p. 198.

121 "I have just learned that you cut your vacation": Ibid.

121 "the enclosed envelope should be opened": FRUS 1961–1963, Volume IV, Vietnam, August–December 1963, Document 18, footnote 1.

121 Lodge's reply was curt: Ibid., footnote 2.

SUNDAY, SEPTEMBER 1

125 cruised to Martha's Vineyard to collect Styron: Styron wrote two accounts of his cruise with JFK that differ primarily in the dates he ascribes to it. I have relied on the Esquire article because it was published thirteen years closer to the event described. The articles are: (1) "The Short Classy Voyage of JFK," Esquire, December 1983; (2) "Havanas in Camelot," Vanity Fair, July 1996.

126 "the sex appeal of a movie hero": "The President and Other Intellectuals," The American Scholar, October 1961.

126 "slick, cool, and empty": Schlesinger (Thousand), p. 744.

126 "We wined him and dined him": Ibid.

126 "wistful need for more confident learning": Kazin, p. 253.

127 In 1961, he had become so exercised: Schlesinger (Thousand), p. 718.

127 After some one-sided articles: Sorensen Papers, Box 37, JFKL.

127 He and Ben Bradlee had been friends: Bradlee (Conversations), p. 114.

127 "at some future date": January 9, 1960, speech to the Massachusetts State Legislature, JFKL Web site.

127 "Those bastards, they're always there": Bradlee (Conversations), p. 128.

127 "the breath-taking talents": John F. Kennedy (Profiles), p. 221.

128 "his precise and persistent concern with the figure": Schlesinger (Journals), p. 107.

128 her famous post-Dallas "Camelot interview": Theodore White Papers, JFKL.

128 his goal was "greatness": Collier and Horowitz, p. 263.

129 "go for the top": Sidey introduction to Kennedy's diaries (Prelude), p. xvi.

129 "the romantic conviction that he was astride": Ibid., p. xxii.

129 sensed an "unknown quality": Bohlen, JFKLOH.

129 During a White House dinner: Berlin, JFKLOH.

129 When he discovered that Bradlee: Bradlee (Conversations), p. 153.

129 [footnote]: "I thought you might find this": Bundy Papers, Box 34, JFKL.

130 "Look at that damn interview": Manuscript for Paul Fay's book, The Pleasure of His Company, Fay Papers, JFKL. Fay cut this conversation from his final manuscript, probably to avoid distressing Schlesinger.

130 kept the current issue of History Today: Gallagher, p. 115.

130 When he heard that the Princeton: Hersh, p. 255; Rostow, JFKLOH; Collier and Horowitz, p. 289.
130 "This is a man determined": Hersh, p. 255. (Account is based on Hersh's 1996 interview with Donald.)
130 He asked Sorensen to study the Gettysburg Address: Sorensen (*Kennedy*), p. 240.
130 "There has never been a more formidable": Sidey (*John F. Kennedy*), p. 218.
130 "Courage is rightly esteemed": Reeves. p. 668n.
131 "This is a book about": John F. Kennedy (*Profiles*), p. 1.
131 Kay Halle never forgot: Halle, JFKLOH.
131 "Just listen to this": Dalton, JFKLOH.
131 While he was in Florida: Fay, p. 149.
131 "who is willing and able to summon his national constituency": JFK speech to National Press Club, January 14, 1960.
131 "dictators ride to and fro": From Churchill's speech to the House of Commons following the 1938 Munich pact.
132 engage in some in historical stage-managing: Clarke, pp. 99–101.
132 When Bradlee and Cannon asked: tape at JFKL.
132 "That's the trouble, Arthur": Rowe, JFKLOH.
132 the Sunday *New York Times Magazine*: "Our Presidents: A Rating by 75 Historians," *NYT*, July 29, 1962.
133 "At first I thought it was too bad": Schlesinger (*Journals*), p. 162.
133 "For years Eisenhower has gone along": Ibid., p. 178.
133 "These were the great years": The Speeches of John F. Kennedy: Presidential Campaign of 1960—Final Report of the Committee on Commerce, United States Senate, p. 193.
134 Before ordering a ban: Brinkley, p. 151.
134 "Of all the world's leaders": "The Short Classy Voyage of JFK," *Esquire*, December 1963; "Havanas in Camelot," *Vanity Fair*, July 1996.
134 "bright and persistent interrogation": Ibid.
134 "My God! They'd have my hide": Ibid.

Monday, September 2

135 "to plant a statement": Description of the Cronkite-Salinger conversations preceding the interview, Cronkite, pp. 246–47.
135 Cronkite was still smarting: Cronkite, pp. 185–88; Cronkite, JFKLOH.
136 He began by asking: JFKPOF (speech files), Box 46, JFKL.
137 "He both threatened and reassured Diem": *NYT*, September 4, 1963.
137 "effectively pulled the rug out from under Diem": Cronkite, p. 247.
138 His last appointment was a conference: Fay, pp. 1–5; Fay, JFKLOH.
138 Like most White House aides: Smathers, JFKLOH.
138 "a very insecure, sensitive man": Dallek (*Flawed Giant*), p. 10.
138 "That man can't run this committee": Guthman and Shulman, p. 153.
138 "We're all going to forget": Duke, JFKLOH.
138 He had invited Johnson to opening day: Rowe, LBJLOH.
138 "worse than drafting a state document": Thomas (*Dateline*), p. 22.
138 "That will never be a sport": Beschloss (*Crisis*), p. 666.
138 "The three most overrated things": Woods, p. 376.
139 "It's not very noble to watch": Bradlee (*Conversations*), p. 194.
139 "I think I'm the antithesis of": Cannon and Bradlee interview, JFKL.
139 "Nobody cares whether I come": Fay, p. 3.
139 "I cannot stand Johnson's damn long face": Woods, p. 382.
139 "an insufferable bastard": Reedy, p. 130.

139 **He spoke of withdrawing from the ticket:** Lincoln (*Kennedy and Johnson*), p. 196; Woods (*LBJ*), p. 414.
139 **He claimed that the Kennedy inner circle had convened a secret meeting:** Henggeler, p. 64.
139 **an "almost spectral" presence:** Schlesinger (*Robert Kennedy*), p. 622.
139 **His aide Harry C. McPherson, Jr., was appalled:** McPherson (Interview I), LBJLOH.
140 **"obvious depression":** Reedy, p. 127.
140 **"I think it would be a good idea":** Fay, pp. 3–6; Fay, JFKLOH.
140 **Although Kennedy had gutted his speech:** Bartlett, LBJLOH.
141 **The Scandinavian trip:** Reedy, pp. 25–26.

TUESDAY, SEPTEMBER 3–FRIDAY, SEPTEMBER 6

142 **The official diary of Kennedy's engagements:** JFKL Web site.
142 **he filled two pages with doodles:** JFKPP, Box 12, JFKL.
142 **Many of his doodles:** Greenburg, pp. 136–57.
142 **"I don't understand all this":** Ibid., p. 144.
143 **"something out of Ian Fleming":** *NYT*, September 4, 1963.
143 **Roger Hilsman attended a meeting:** FRUS, 1961–1963, Volume IV, Vietnam, August–December 1963, Document 63.
143 **Kennedy missed most of Friday's:** Ibid., Document 66.
144 **"a symptom of the state the U.S. government was in":** Mecklin, p. 206.
144 **Lincoln affixed a memorandum:** JFKPP, Box 12, JFKL.
144 **a recent memorandum from the pollster Louis Harris:** JFKPOF, Box 30, JFKL.
144 **"dismiss him as a second rate figure":** JFKPP, Box 12, JFKL.
145 **Lincoln noted that he was experiencing "discomfort":** Lincoln Papers, Box 6, JFKL.
145 **"Dr. McDonald came":** Ibid.
145 **Kennedy fussed over the trappings of his presidency:** Stoughton, pp. 59–60; Day, p. 141.
146 **pored over the guest lists:** Baldrige, JFKLOH.
146 **no one dared leave a heel print:** Powers, JFKLOH.
146 **He oversaw the placement:** Baldrige, JFKLOH.
146 **Much of what King Zaher:** Stoughton, pp. 59–60; *NYT*, September 29, 1963; see also "Entertaining in the White House" on JFKL Web site—excerpt from *Entertaining in the White House* by Marie Smith, Acropolis Books, Washington, D.C., 1967.
146 **"as pleased as a small child":** Bradlee (*Conversations*), p. 82.
147 **Kennedy had recently noticed:** Stoughton, p. 60.

SATURDAY, SEPTEMBER 7–SUNDAY, SEPTEMBER 8

148 **"I think it would be good for Jackie":** Turkerman and Turnure, JFKLOH.
148 **he made a humorous show:** Sally Bedell Smith, p. 398.
148 **"she did it":** Ibid.
148 **"How do you think Lyndon would be":** Bartlett, JFKLOH; Bartlett, LBJLOH.
148 **Bartlett knew that:** Bartlett, JFKLOH.
148 **"He could have shot you, Charlie":** Manchester (*Death*), p. 35.
149 **"Brother, they could have gotten me":** Martin (*Hero*), p. 474.
149 **"What do you think of the rule":** Travell, pp. 361–63.
149 **"My wife will have a pension":** Ibid.
149 **"I guess that is one of the least desirable":** Fay, pp. 113–14.
149 **"What would you have done":** O'Donnell and Powers, p. 19.
149 **During a game of charades in Palm Beach:** Merriman Smith, p. 229.
149 **"Did you ever stop and think":** Martin (*Seeds*), p. 449.

149 "Boy! Aren't we targets?": Stein, p. 291.

150 "Crowds don't threaten me": Louchheim, p. 149.

150 "I will not live in fear": Travell, pp. 364–65.

150 "If this plane goes down": Sorensen (Counselor), p. 248.

150 "Well, probably neither you nor I": Lawrence, JFKLOH.

150 "I firmly expect this commitment to be kept": Richard Lewis, p. 504.

150 "Well, if anyone's going to shoot me": Jacqueline Kennedy, p. 251.

150 "Get it away from here!": Spalding, JFKLOH.

151 His sensitivity to the narrow margins: Rostow, JFKLOH.

151 On Saturday evening: Dallas, pp. 228–29.

152 "more than any other man except my husband": Pottker, p. 155; Andersen, p. 116.

152 "loyal to the extreme": Dallas, p. 221.

152 "He's pretty good, Daddy": Ibid., p. 226.

152 "I think it is the Second Most Important Man": Collier and Horowitz, p. 289.

153 "We don't want any losers": Rose Kennedy, p. 143.

153 "It was all due to my father": Schlesinger (Journals), p. 150.

153 "I'm not going to listen": Thompson, p. 13.

153 "This is my rocker": Dallas, p. 207.

153 Joe Kennedy's birthday party continued: Ibid., pp. 228–29; Rose Kennedy, pp. 414–15.

153 "He did it so well": Sally Bedell Smith, p. 399.

154 "Happy Birthday, Dad": Dallas, p. 229.

154 "too young to write my memoirs": Bartlett, JFKLOH: MacNeil, p. 153.

154 "because it would be good for Jackie": Ibid.

154 "then nobody will want to talk to me": Ibid.

154 "What are you going to do, Jack?": Ibid.

154 He once told Paul Fay: Fay, p. 260; Fay, JFKLOH.

154 [footnote] "I didn't have the feeling from this conversation": Bartlett, LBJLOH; Martin (Seeds), p. 473.

MONDAY, SEPTEMBER 9

155 Kennedy appointed John Gronouski: NYT, September 11, 1963.

155 "Kennedy Building for '64": ES, September 11, 1963.

156 no single issue troubled him: Ira Mehlman, "John F. Kennedy and Immigration Reform," The Social Contract, Summer 1991; Thomas Maier, "A Legacy of Diversity," Newsday, November 20, 2003; and Maier, pp. 424–27.

156 [footnote] Typical were his dogged efforts: Gallagher, pp. 10–11, 27–29.

157 "The idea of the 'melting pot'": Kennedy (Nation), p. 35.

157 "strong orientation of an indefensible": Ibid., p. 45.

157 "The famous words of Emma Lazarus": Ibid.

157 "the principle of equality and human dignity to which our nation subscribes": Ibid., p. ix.

158 "I don't think that would be helpful": Transcript of JFK interview with Huntley-Brinkley, JFKPOF, Box 46, JFKL.

158 "What do you think about cutting taxes": Ibid.

158 "I think they should shoot everyone": Lincoln Papers, Box 6, JFKL.

158 He met with Mansfield: Presidential Recordings, Tape 108/A44, JFKL.

159 "an exercise in political assassination": NYT, September 8, 1963.

159 During their meeting, Senator Jackson: Presidential Recordings, Tape 109/A44, JFKL.

160 "The treaty is being so chewed up": Schlesinger, unpublished journals, September 16, 1963, NYPL.

160 "lead to a real turning point": FRUS, 1961–1963, Volume V, Soviet Union, Document 355 (editorial note).

160 "The President wishes Mr. Khrushchev to know": Department of State, Presidential Correspondence, Lot 77 D 163.

TUESDAY, SEPTEMBER 10–THURSDAY, SEPTEMBER 12

161 At a National Security Council meeting: Presidential Recordings, Tape 109/A44, JFKL; Hilsman, pp. 502–3; Strober and Strober, p. 433.

162 Kennedy attended a luncheon meeting of the Business Committee for Tax Reduction: Remarks at National Conference of the Business Committee for Tax Reduction, JFKL Web site.

162 Lincoln noted in her diary: Lincoln Papers, Box 6, JFKL.

162 On that occasion he had poured: New Yorker, August 7, 2000.

163 He had left his second gift: Lincoln Papers, Box 6, JFKL.

163 Kennedy had "fallen in love" with one: Artful Tom: A Memoir, chapter 24, www.artnet.com.

164 "the best humored briefing breakfast": Heller Papers, Kennedy/Johnson files, Box 6, JFKL.

165 a declassified summary: "Did the U.S. Military Plan a Nuclear First Strike for 1963," The American Prospect, number 19, Fall 1994.

165 "And we call ourselves the human race" and Rusk's comments on the 1961 briefing: Rusk, pp. 246–47.

165 In their 1993 article: "Did the U.S. Military Plan a Nuclear First Strike for 1963?" The American Prospect, Number 19, Fall 1994.

165 McNamara made a similar observation in 2003: Recollecting JFK Forum, 2003, JFKL.

166 A summary that the Pentagon provided: FRUS, 1961–1963, Volume VIII, National Security Policy, Document 141.

166 "JFK Press Talk": Boston Globe, September 13, 1963.

166 "more nearly an instrument of Presidential power": Tom Wicker, "Q's and A's About the Press Conference," NYT Magazine, September 8, 1963.

167 Thursday briefing: Transcript, JFKL Web site.

168 he offered his own "thank you": Ibid.; NYT, September 13, 1963.

168 "I saw your picture in the paper": Lincoln Papers, Box 6, JFKL.

THURSDAY, SEPTEMBER 12–SUNDAY, SEPTEMBER 15

169 "a little toe dance": Bradlee (Conversations), p. 205.

169 "Boy, he learns fast": Ibid., p. 206.

169 As he disembarked: Ibid.

169 As he entered the house: Ibid., pp. 205–12; Auchincloss, JFKLOH.

170 Twelve hundred guests: NYT, September 13, 1953.

170 compared them to "fine art books": West, p. 270.

170 "Now, you can only keep one": Anthony (As We Remember), p. 194.

170 "Got to steer her away": Bradlee (Conversations), p. 207.

170 "It was the simplest thing": Jacqueline Kennedy, p. 142.

171 Now he gave her: Leaming, p. 312.

171 She reciprocated with: Gallagher, p. 290.

171 She would write Charlie Bartlett: Sally Bedell Smith, p. 400.

171 "You two really are our best friends": Bradlee (Conversations), p. 208.

171 "You know, you're my only friend": Gallagher, pp. 243–44.

171 Jackie was not a keen golfer: ES, September 15, 1963.

171 A home movie: Audio-Visual Collection, JFKL.

172 He sent a cable to Lyndon Johnson: JFKPOF, Box 30, JFKL.

172 He decided to split the next summer: Pottker, p. 197.

172 "All around me I see ponies": Martin (*Hero*), p. 427.

172 Still, it had great waters: Auchincloss, JFKLOH

172 "Jackie here always wanted to be a nun": Bradlee (*Conversations*), p. 212.

172 His phone logs: Lincoln, Box 5, JFKL.

173 but the notes he made: JFKPP, Box 12, JFKL.

MONDAY, SEPTEMBER 16–SUNDAY, SEPTEMBER 22

174 "outrage and grief": *WP*, September 17, 1963

174 The result was a *New York Times* story: *NYT*, September 18, 1963.

175 On Tuesday morning he asked: Presidential Recordings, Tape 111/A46, JFKL; FRUS, 1961–1963, Volume V, Soviet Union, Document 355.

175 But he did say that: Presidential Recordings, Tape 111/A46, JFKL.

176 approved an "eyes-only personal" cable to Lodge: FRUS, 1961–1963, Volume IV, Vietnam, August–December 1963, Document 125.

176 Lodge was not fooled: Ibid., Document 126.

176 "that their experiences there and Lodge": Schlesinger, unpublished diaries, September 21, 1963, NYPL.

176 "Unless you do certain things": Porter, p. 174.

176 "would make possible a termination": Ibid.

177 "If further deterioration of the political situation": Taylor, p. 298.

177 "a good orthodox economist": Heller, JFKLOH; see also interview with Heller in *NYT*, June 21, 1987.

177 Director of the Budget Kermit Gordon: Gordon, JFKLOH.

177 "a first-rate intellect": Seaborg (*Adventures*), p. 182.

178 "All right, I've got the idea": Rostow, JFKLOH.

178 "If you're running for reelection": Presidential Recordings, Tape 66, JFKL.

178 "This woman kicks me": Heller, JFKLOH.

179 JFK address to the nation on his tax-cut bill: JFKL Web site; JFKPOF, Box 46, JFKL.

179 Nevertheless, in response: *NYT*, September 21, 1963.

179 Senator Fulbright called: Heller, JFKLOH.

179 "In a presidential campaign": White (*History*), p. 498.

179 "a touching little call": Heller, JFKLOH.

179 Heller had complained to Louchheim: Louchhiem papers, Box 78, LOC.

180 she had sometimes noticed a "chilly aloofness": Ibid.

180 "How warmly he greets 'pals' ": Ibid.

180 "unspoken but very powerful affection": Rostow, JFKLOH.

180 "Never in my time in public life": Ibid.

180 "evidence of the impressively cool": Schlesinger (*Journals*), pp. 77–78.

180 describing him as "warm, funny, quick": Ibid., p. 80.

180 "in a state of civil disorder": Presidential Recordings, Tape 111/A46–112/A47; Rosenberg and Karabell, pp. 143–49.

181 Bobby's first choice: Blaik, JFKLOH.

181 "an instrument for social evolution": *Jet*, October 10, 1963.

181 The black journalist Simeon Booker: Ibid.

181 Dr. King opened the White House meeting: Presidential Recordings, Tape 111/A46–112/A47; Rosenberg and Karabell, pp. 143–49.

182 "the kind of federal concern needed": *NYT*, September 20, 1963.

182 two men in a station wagon: *WP*, September 20, 1963.

182 He told the UN General Assembly: *NYT*, September 21, 1963.

183 "It must last": *WP*, September 21, 1963.

183 Before Kennedy left: Attwood (*Twilight*), p. 258.

183 **a memorandum he had received:** FRUS, 1961–1963, Volume XI, Cuban Missile Crisis and Aftermath, Document 367.
184 **"Unfortunately, the CIA is still in charge":** Attwood (*Twilight*), p. 259.
184 **said he was "adventuresome enough":** Ibid.
184 **Stevenson briefed the president:** Ibid.
184 **his twelve favorite books:** JFKL Web site.
184 **he was attempting to write his own Bond-style thriller:** Martin (*Hero*), p. 501; Martin (*Seeds*), pp. 449–50.
185 **While cruising on the Honey Fitz:** Fay, JFKLOH.
185 **"stretched prone on the long pier":** Associated Press story published on September 21, 1963; UPI story in *NYT*, September 21, 1963.
185 **"Look desperate, like you heard shots":** Blaine, pp. 130–31.
185 **While he was down, Knudsen said:** *NYT*, August 14, 1983.
185 **some kind of "premonition":** Ibid.
185 **He was so furious with Cormier and Merriman:** Martin (*Seeds*), pp. 449–50.
185 **Two weeks later:** Ibid., p. 450.

Monday, September 23
187 **Monday was one of the busiest days:** *NYT*, September 22, 1963.
187 **recent events in Vietnam had "raised serious questions":** FRUS, 1961–1963, Volume IV, Vietnam, August–December 1963, Document 142.
187 **let whatever cutbacks occurred "speak for themselves":** Ibid., Document 143.
187 **"work out a time schedule":** Ibid.
187 **"the need for reform and change":** Ibid.
187 **"The only thing that really counts for us":** Schlesinger, unpublished diaries, October 2, 1963, NYPL.
188 **[footnote] "still trying too hard to get a national consensus":** Ibid.
188 **believed the mission would be "a disaster":** FRUS, 1961–1963, Volume IV, Vietnam, August–December 1963, Document 124.
188 **Hilsman wrote a "Top Secret; Personal and Private":** Ibid., Document 144.
188 **Kennedy met with Bobby and Burke Marshall:** Presidential Recordings, Tape 112/A47, JFKL.
189 **William Hamilton, an aide:** Presidential Recordings, Tape 12/A47–113/A48, JFKL; Rosenberg and Karabell, pp. 149–73.
190 **"firmly, deeply dedicated to the principle of segregation":** *WP*, September 24, 1963.
190 **He asked the ABC correspondent:** FRUS, 1961–1963, Volume XI, Cuban Missile Crisis and Aftermath, Document 374.
191 **she informed the CIA:** George Washington University, National Security Files, May 1, 1963, memorandum from Helms to McCone.
191 **Richard Helms wrote in a memorandum:** Ibid.
191 **During what he called:** FRUS, 1961–1963, Volume XI, Cuban Missile Crisis and Aftermath, Document 275.
191 **When Kennedy heard:** George Washington University, National Security Files, March 4, 1963 memorandum by Gordon Chase.
192 **Donovan returned in April:** FRUS, 1961–1963, Volume XI, Cuban Missile Crisis and Aftermath, Document 310.
192 **Kennedy expressed more interest:** Ibid., Document 315.
192 **Attwood met with Lechuga:** Ibid., Document 374.
192 **Bobby told Attwood he was concerned:** Ibid.
192 **Three days later, Attwood ran into Lechuga at the UN:** Ibid.

TUESDAY, SEPTEMBER 24–MONDAY, SEPTEMBER 30

193 "The next time I watch": Sander Vanocur, "Kennedy's Voyage of Discovery," *Harper's Magazine,* April 1964.

193 mocking him as "Johnny Appleseed": Sidey, p. 350.

193 "I want the crowds": Bruno, p. 15.

194 Vanocur thought he seemed happier: Vanocur, "Kennedy's Voyage of Discovery," *Harper's Magazine,* April 1964.

194 admitted to feeling a "little rivalry": Sally Bedell Smith, p. 411.

194 While speaking of his administration's: JFKPOF (speech files), Box 46, JFKL.

194 After finishing, he turned: Cliff, JFKLOH.

194 "one of the worst reporters could remember": Vanocur, "Kennedy's Voyage of Discovery," *Harper's Magazine,* April 1964.

195 "The message that he brought": *Newsweek,* October 7, 1963.

195 "unresponsive and restless": Bruno, p. 25.

195 "the center of action": Sorensen (*Legacy*), p. 38.

195 "just crazy about planes": ES, September 26, 1963.

195 JFK speech at Billings: JFKPOF (speech files), Box 46, JFKL.

196 Lisagor noticed a look of total surprise: Press Panel (Lisagor), JFKLOH.

196 "Well, I think I know how you ladies": O'Donnell and Powers, pp. 54–55; Bishop (*A Day*), p. 35.

196 "A politician is a communicating": Rostow, JFKLOH.

196 The students listening to him speak: U.S. Senate Subcommittee of the Subcommittee on Communications, *The Speeches, Remarks, Press Conferences and Statements of Senator John F. Kennedy, August 1, 1960, through November 7, 1960.* Washington, D.C.: U.S. Government Printing Office, 1961.

197 he had "inadvertently, intuitively": Richard Goodwin, p. 120.

197 Great leaders drew vitality: Schlesinger (*Journals*), p. 92.

197 "I am confident that when the role": JFKPOF (speech files), Box 46, JFKL.

197 On the flight to Jackson Hole: Udall, JFKLOH.

197 He scribbled down some ideas and facts: JFKPP, Box 12, JFKL.

198 "I've got to take the black one": Thompson, p. 9.

198 he wanted to visit Mike Mansfield's father: Bruno, p. 17.

198 "Would you thank him for me?": Ibid.

198 "I wonder how many majority leaders": O'Donnell and Powers, p. 379.

198 Instead of reading his prepared speech: JFKPOF (speech files), Box 46, JFKL.

199 "it may well be that man recognizes": Ibid.

199 Yet the largest and most enthusiastic crowd: *NYT,* September 27, 30, 1963.

199 JFK speech at Salt Lake City: JFKPOF (speech files), Box 46, JFKL.

200 JFK 1960 speech in Salt Lake City: U.S. Senate Subcommittee of the Subcommittee on Communications, *The Speeches, Remarks, Press Conferences and Statements of Senator John F. Kennedy, August 1, 1960, through November 7, 1960.* Washington, D.C.: U.S. Government Printing Office, 1961.

200 "That was a great speech": Press Panel (Lisagor), JFKLOH.

200 admitted feeling the same way: Ibid.

200 "If JFK had any doubts": Vanocur, "Kennedy's Voyage of Discovery," *Harper's Magazine,* April 1964.

200 "I never know when I press these": *NYT,* September 28, 1963.

200 He arrived at the lodge: Stoughton and Clifton, p. 125.

200 "the Blue Hills of Boston": *NYT,* September 28, 1963.

200 "I do not think that these trips": *Newsweek,* October 7, 1963.

201 "The leadership of the American Legion": O'Donnell and Powers, p. 74.

201 "more often than not, the right thing": Ibid., p. 75.

201 **Asked what issue:** *Issues and Answers* transcript, ABC, September 29, 1963.

201 **"It's because they really like you":** Bruno, p. 26.

201 **"Jerry, he is very, very happy":** Ibid.

201 **"Thank God, he got out of the state":** Oberdorfer, p. 203.

201 **Kennedy drafted a press release:** JFKPP, Box 12, JFKL.

202 **he edited the release:** Ibid.

202 **"possible some people will join":** *WP*, October 1, 1963.

202 **Kennedy scribbled the kind of to-do list:** JFKPP, Box 12, JFKL.

202 **"I think there's something ominous":** Schlesinger (*Journals*), p. 200.

202 **Kennedy generously praised Schlesinger's Salt Lake City speech:** Schlesinger, unpublished journals, October 2, 1963, NYPL.

202 **Kennedy objected to its stipulation . . . "What if I'm no longer president?":** Ibid.

Tuesday, October 1–Sunday, October 6

205 **"What are you trying to do?":** Gallagher, p. 295.

205 **"he gently guided her ahead":** *WP*, October 2, 1963.

205 **"a man whose place in history":** *NYT*, October 2, 1963.

206 **"I am overcome":** *WP*, October 2, 1963.

206 **"See, Jack, he brought it to me!":** Ibid.

206 **"I was wondering why":** Ibid.

206 **Jackie left postcards for her children:** Martin (*Hero*), p. 469.

206 **and gave Evelyn Lincoln a letter:** JFKPP, Box 12, JFKL.

206 **General Krulak had overseen the drafting:** Newman, p. 401.

206 **"All through the Saigon briefings and in the field":** William Bundy Papers, unpublished manuscript, JFKL; also cited in Newman, p. 402.

206 **McNamara and Taylor's affirmed in their report:** FRUS, 1961–1963, Volume IV, August–December 1963, Document 167.

207 **An earlier draft of their report:** Sullivan, JFKLOH; Jones, p. 379; Schlesinger (*Robert Kennedy*), p. 716.

207 **As soon as Kennedy noticed the omission:** Schlesinger (*Robert Kennedy*), p. 716.

207 **When they returned:** Presidential Recordings, Tape 114/49, JFKL; transcript in Blight, Lang, and Welch, pp. 99–103.

208 **He protested when McGeorge and Bill Bundy:** Cooper, pp. 215–16.

208 **"Look, I'm under instructions":** Ibid., p. 216.

208 **"Reports of disagreements do not help":** FRUS, 1961–1963, Volume IV, August–December 1963. Document 169; Presidential Recordings, Tape 114/49, JFKL.

208 **"set it in concrete":** McNamara, p. 80.

208 **"And tell them that means":** O'Donnell and Powers, p. 17.

208 **"the military program in South Viet Nam":** While House Press Release, reported in *NYT*, October 3, 1963.

209 **"was part of a plan the President asked him to develop":** Gilpatric, JFKLOH.

209 **"Many, many were opposed to approving a plan":** McNamara made this statement while being interviewed by Anthony Lewis on NPR, October 22, 2003. The transcript is cited by James K. Galbraith in "Kennedy, Vietnam and Iraq," Salon.com, November 22, 2003.

209 **Jackie had been careful not to spoil:** Branch and Callaway, p. 233.

209 **Kennedy asked his driver:** Lincoln (*My Twelve*), p. 299.

209 **Kennedy played with him:** Bradlee (*Conversations*), p. 192; Shaw, JFKLOH.

209 **"I'm having the best time of my life":** Halle, JFKLOH.

210 **Two years earlier, Fulbright:** Woods, pp. 266–67.

210 **Fulbright urged Kennedy to skip Dallas:** Manchester (*Death*), p. 39.

210 **"Box Score for '64":** *Time*, October 4, 1963.

211 "Did you read that *Time* magazine yet?": Presidential Recordings, Tape 114/A49, JFKL.
211 "any one of a thousand": Fulbright, JFKLOH.
212 promised not to become "Kennedy's errand boy": Manchester (*Death*), p. 22.
212 Connally went to the Capitol: Ibid.
212 "How about those fund-raising affairs in Texas, John?": Connally, pp. 171–73; Reston, pp. 246–47.
212 Kennedy met with his Vietnam advisers again on Saturday: Presidential Recordings, Tape 114/A50, JFKL.
213 "urgent covert effort": FRUS, 1961–1963, Volume IV, August–December 1963, Document 182.
213 "directed that no formal announcement be made": Presidential Recordings, Tape, 114/A50, JFKL; FRUS, 1961–1963, Volume IV, August–December 1963, Document 179.
213 "Our decision to remove a thousand U.S. advisors": Ibid.
213 "if you put a hat on a Kennedy": Doris Kearns Goodwin, p. 718.
213 "You remind me of my Vietnam advisors": Louchheim Papers, Box 78, LOC.

MONDAY, OCTOBER 7

214 Kennedy signed the instruments: WP, October 8, 1063; ES, October 7, 1963; NYT, October 8, 1963.
214 "no single accomplishment in the White House": Sorensen, p. 740.
215 "the deepest satisfaction of his three years": O'Donnell and Powers, p. 380.
215 "It doesn't matter about you and me": John F. Kennedy (*Prelude*), introduction by Hugh Sidey, p. xxxiii.
215 "Dave, if we were only thinking of ourselves": O'Donnell and Powers, p. 325.
215 "I'd rather my children": Alford, p. 94.
215 "That's what they tell me": Time, November 12, 2001.
215 "We have begun the process": NYT, October 5, 1963.
215 "the beginning of the end": NYT, October 2, 1963; NYT (editorial), October 3, 1963.
216 "I firmly believe that as much as I was shaped": Renehan, p. 2.
216 "men tend to like the idea of war": Chattanooga Times, November 4, 1961.
216 "all war is stupid": "Warrior for Peace," David Talbot, Time, June 21, 2007.
216 "War will exist until that distant day": John F. Kennedy quotations, JFKL Web site.
216 "This war here is a dirty business": Hamilton, pp. 614–18.
216 "He said we were a 'fine looking crowd'": Ibid., pp. 561–62.
217 "the terrific discrepancy between people at home": Maier, p. 169.
217 He told a friend that his brother's death: Renehan, p. 2.
217 "The world organization that will come out": John F. Kennedy (*Prelude*), p. 86.
217 "any man who has risked his life": Hamilton, pp. 700–701.
217 Fifteen years later, he told Sidey: John F. Kennedy (*Prelude*), Sidey introduction, p. xxv.
217 "If I had to single out one element": Ibid., p. xxix.
217 "You know, there are only two pacifists": Strober and Strober, pp. 67–68.
218 "My boss has abandoned me": Baker, p. 180.
218 "Somehow I got it into my head": Ibid.
218 Three days later, Williams declared: WP, October 10, 1963.
219 "Bobby, Lyndon and I just want you to know": Baker, p. 182
219 "petrified that he'd be dragged down": Ibid.
219 "Bobby, my brother is fond of you": Ibid., p. 183.

TUESDAY, OCTOBER 8–SUNDAY, OCTOBER 13

220 "What have we got today?": Heller Papers, Box 6, JFKL.
220 the *Look* photographer Stanley Tretick: Tretick, JFKLOH.

220 "journalistic thieves": Bergquist Papers, Box 20, Boston University Library.

220 "Well, I didn't say that": Tretick, JFKLOH.

220 "We'd better get this out of the way": Ibid.

220 "the mood of the boy": Ibid.

221 "the six o'clock comedy hour": Heller Papers, Box 6, JFKL.

221 "a major foreign policy mistake": WP, October 11, 1963.

221 "the worst political mistake": Beschloss (Crisis), p. 644.

221 Kennedy opened the press conference: Transcript at JFKL Web site.

221 "President Nudges": NYT, October 10, 1963.

221 "Give me good old Barry": Fay, p. 259.

221 "No vice whatsoever": Ibid.

222 "God, I'd like to be able to do": David Bell, JFKLOH.

222 "Keep your seat, Barry": Baker, p. 143.

222 "I'm a great big wolf": Halle, JFKLOH.

222 Caroline walked into the room: Bergquist Papers, Box 20, Boston University Library.

222 "You know, I've been taking care of": Halle, JFKLOH.

222 "a sight to gladden the eye": Bergquist Papers, Box 20, Boston University Library.

222 "What do you think of him?": Tretick, JFKLOH; Bergquist and Tretick, p. 125.

222 He struck Tretick: Ibid.

222 "joyous, funny, mutually fascinated": Tretick, JFKLOH; Bergquist Papers, Box 20, Boston University Library.

222 "a hell of a picture": Tretick, JFKLOH.

222 Churchill was already four sheets: Bergquist Papers, Box 20, Boston University Library.

223 "Oh no! No! No! No!": Bergquist and Tretick, p. 126.

223 They were there when John stood outside: Ibid., p. 128.

223 "I'm cute! I'm cute!": Ibid., p. 127.

223 Bergquist claimed she was not: Bergquist, JFKLOH.

223 she always saved her best jokes for him: Martin (Seeds), p. 294.

223 "a somber, sobering quality": Bergquist, JFKLOH; Bergquist and Tretick, p. 31.

223 something "remote and tragic": Bergquist Papers, Box 20, Boston University Library.

223 "Oh, you caught that": Ibid.; Bergquist, JFKLOH; Bergquist Papers, Box 20, Boston University Library.

223 "subject to moods": NYT, October 14, 1963.

223 "a very serious preoccupied": Bergquist Papers, Box 20, Boston University Library.

224 He weighed himself: Powers, JFKLOH.

224 He had recently complained to Fay: Fay, JFKLOH.

224 He should have been more concerned: JFK Personal Papers, Box 48, JFKL.

224 Jackie's secretary Mary Gallagher: Gallagher, pp. 268–69.

224 during the campaign he had ordered Lincoln: Lincoln (My Twelve), p. 113.

224 "look so handsome at these parties": Hamilton, pp. 358–59.

224 "Why don't we go out on to the terrace": Gromyko, p. 181.

225 "Could we go for a ride": Ibid., p. 137.

225 "I don't deny": Ibid., p. 177.

225 "The fact is, there are two groups": Ibid., pp. 181–82.

225 His caution was a good example: Strober and Strober, p. 43.

226 "I don't want you to get discouraged": Presidential Recordings, Tape 115/A51, JFKL; FRUS, 1961–1963, Volume V, Soviet Union, Document 363.

226 As they were talking, one of Kennedy's children: Presidential Recordings, Tape 115/A51, JFKL.

226 A reporter meeting the usually dour Gromyko: WP, October 11, 1963.

226 "eager to maintain a show": Ibid.

227 "to develop further the success": FRUS, 1961–1963, Kennedy-Khrushchev Exchanges, Document 118.

227 "I am convinced then": Beschloss (*Crisis*), pp. 662–63.

227 The State Department never sent it: Ibid., p. 663.

227 Earl Blaik and Kenneth Royall followed Gromyko: Blaik, JFKLOH; *Newsweek*, October 28, 1963; *Time*, October 4, 1963.

228 American women were by comparison "not glamorous": JFKPP, Box 40, JFKL.

228 "Thank you very much, Mr. President": Tree, JFKLOH.

228 "Madam, you are raising": Ibid.

228 "I never know whether women": Ibid.

228 "If they are politicians, they don't care": Louchheim Papers, Box 78, Library of Congress.

228 "I don't know how to treat women": Tree, JFKLOH.

228 "just thought of themselves": Ibid.

228 "quite uneasy with women": Ibid.

228 Nancy Dickerson had a similar take: Dickerson, pp. 63–64.

229 "Let's get women off the weather beat": Ibid.

229 Jackie encouraged: Jacqueline Kennedy, pp. 305–6.

229 "Look, I may not be the best-looking": Graham, pp. 290–91.

229 Assistant Secretary of Labor Esther Peterson: Peterson, JFKLOH.

229 "Gentlemen, we are here to talk about": *WP*, October 11, 1963.

229 praising their report as "very useful": Ibid.

230 Bergquist asked if he had seen the recent photograph of the Nixons: Bergquist and Tretick, p. 129.

230 "What are you doing tonight?": Schlesinger (*Journals*), p. 201.

230 "My name is Polly Parrot": Bergquist and Tretick, pp. 129–30.

230 Kennedy obtained copies of the photographs: Tretick, JFKLOH; Bergquist Papers, Box 20, Boston University Library; Bergquist and Tretick, p. 130.

231 "No, Jack. I guess it's your year": Bergquist Papers, Box 20, Boston University Library.

231 A *Newsweek* article titled: *Newsweek*, October 28, 1963.

231 Other articles reported: *ES*, October 11, 1963; *NYT*, October 8, 1963.

231 "all-night parties in foreign lands": *WP*, October 15, 1963.

231 "the lavish hospitality of a man": Martin (*Hero*), p. 470.

231 Communication proved difficult: *NYT*, October 12, 1963.

231 "You're a good swimmer, Jackie": Pottker, p. 196.

231 "inexplicably fascinating and beautiful": Galitzine, p. 157.

231 During the cruise she noticed: Ibid., p. 169.

231 "I loved you from the first moment": Bradford, p. 258.

232 "I think that I am lucky to miss you": William Manchester Papers (*Death of a President*), Box 43, Wesleyan University.

232 She shopped in the bazaars: *NYT*, October 15, 1963.

232 "a Parisian style to suit her personality": *WP*, October 15, 1963.

Monday, October 14–Friday, October 18

233 Articles that morning: *NYT* and *WP*, October 14, 1963.

233 A Gallup poll released that weekend: *WP*, October 13, 1963.

233 There was better news in a second Harris poll: *WP*, October 14, 1963.

234 "the most widely disliked Democratic President": *Newsweek*, October 28, 1963.

234 Writing about the impasse in the *New York Times*: *NYT*, October 14, 1963.

234 Bobby Kennedy testified: *NYT*, October, 16, 1963; *NYT*, October 18, 1963,

234 "politics in its purest definition": *NYT*, October 20, 1963.

234 "There always comes a time": Ibid.

234 reported an "improved climate": *NYT,* October 16, 1963.

234 A spokesman for the Washington NAACP: Bryant, p. 449.

235 Kennedy's back had continued bothering him: Schwartz, p. 204.

235 "I was melancholy after the death": *WP,* November 13, 1963. Maier first revealed the details of McSorley's counseling sessions with Jackie, see Maier, pp. 467–75.

235 Before, Kiernan said: Kiernan, JFKLOH.

235 Back at the White House, he shoved: Manchester (*Death*), p. 55.

235 Jackie was willing to indulge his affection: Kiernan, JFKLOH.

236 Kiernan sensed that the Irish were "getting her down": Ibid.

236 Kennedy's insistence that the three days: Tubridy, JFKLOH.

236 "like a desert queen she sat before": *WP,* October 16, 1963.

236 Eunice had bought a recording: LeMass, JFKLOH.

236 such sadness so plainly visible: Reed, JFKLOH; Sally Bedell Smith, pp. 415–16.

237 "To the disgrace of every living American": *WP,* October 18, 1963.

237 Kennedy attempted to make: Reeves, pp. 631–32.

237 leading Kennedy to complain: Louchheim Papers, Box 78, LOC.

237 "Look, I asked for your opinion": Duke, JFKLOH.

237 Jackie called before leaving Morocco: Jacqueline Kennedy, p. 292.

237 "No, no, you mustn't be like that": Ibid.

237 During a short layover: *NYT,* October 18, 1963.

237 Caroline carried a clay bird's nest: *WP,* October 18, 1963.

238 Caroline recited a French sentence: Hirsh, JFKLOH.

238 "I'll never be away again": Anthony (*White House*), pp. 251–52.

238 "Yes, Virginia, there is a Santa Claus": Manchester (*Death*), p. 31.

238 Standing on a platform on the South Lawn: *WP,* October 19, 1963.

SATURDAY, OCTOBER 19–MONDAY, OCTOBER 21

239 JFK speech at the University of Maine: JFKL Web site.

239 Two hours later he walked into: *NYT,* October 20, 1963; *Boston Sunday Advertiser,* October 20, 1963; *Boston Globe,* October 20, 1963; Bilodeau, JFKLOH.

240 His own Harvard football career: Leamer, p. 102.

240 "I want to go to Patrick's grave": O'Donnell and Powers, p. 378.

240 He had designed Patrick's headstone: Lincoln (*My Twelve*), p. 298.

240 He had also brought: Michael O'Brien, p. 779.

240 "Patrick seems so alone here": O'Donnell and Powers, p. 39.

240 A waitress cried, "Oh, my God": *Boston Globe,* October 20, 1963.

240 His impromptu walk was another security headache: *Boston Sunday Advertiser,* October 20, 1963; *Boston Globe,* October 20, 1963.

241 He asked the family chauffeur: Martin (*Hero*), pp. 473–74.

241 During the afternoon he crossed the street to visit Larry Newman: Martin (*Hero*), p. 442; Larry G. Newman, "Jack Kennedy Was My Neighbor," *Parade,* November 22, 1964.

241 The weather was too cool: Martin (*Hero*), pp. 473–74; Dallas, pp. 4–5.

241 "Look who's here, Dad": Dallas, pp. 4–5.

241 "Mrs. Dallas, take good care of Dad": Ibid.

241 "He's the one who made all this possible": O'Donnell and Powers, p. 39.

MONDAY, OCTOBER 21

242 A front-page article: *NYT,* October 20, 1963.

242 Kennedy had witnessed poverty like this: Clarke, p. 88.

242 **he often referred to the "blight" of poverty:** In his opening statement at the first televised debate, Kennedy said, "I saw cases in West Virginia here in the United States, where children took home part of their school lunch in order to feed their families." JFK Pre-Presidential Papers, Box 914, JFKL.

243 **"Tax reduction alone is not enough":** 1963 State of the Union speech, JFKL Web site.

243 **Heller had sent him a memorandum:** Sorensen Papers, Box 31, JFKL.

243 **Heller admitted that although the tax cut:** Thompson (ed.), p. 156; Heller, p. 20.

243 **He gave Kennedy an economic:** Ibid.

243 **"Walter, first we're going to get your tax cut":** Ibid., p. 152.

243 **He told Heller during their meeting:** Heller Papers, JFK-Johnson files, Box 6, JFKL.

243 **Bishop arrived at the White House:** Bishop (*A Bishop's*), p. 379.

244 **"one never knew how much of the warmth":** Ibid., p. 381.

244 **Instead, Kennedy stuck out his hand and said:** Ibid., pp. 381–82.

244 **"grown closer":** Thomas, p. 34.

244 **"You could see now that he liked":** Martin (*Hero*), p. 471.

244 **"It took us a very long time":** Anthony (*As We Remember*), p. 189.

244 **"Oh, Mr. West, I've gotten myself into something":** West, pp. 272–73.

245 **"And you see, this is where":** Ibid.

TUESDAY, OCTOBER 22–FRIDAY, OCTOBER 25

246 **"packing his bags and leaving":** Lincoln Papers, Box 6, JFKL.

246 **During dinner with Jackie and the Bradlees:** Bradlee (*Conversations*), pp. 215–21.

247 **Schlesinger believed that he was:** Schlesinger, unpublished diaries, NYPL.

247 **When Kermit Gordon described:** Ibid.

247 **"Sure I will, Jack":** Manchester (*Death*), p. 9; William Manchester Papers (*Death of a President*), Box 43, Wesleyan Library.

247 **Evelyn Lincoln passed along a tidbit:** Lincoln Papers, Box 6, JFKL.

247 **"Don't you see how most of the people":** Bradlee (*Conversations*), pp. 223–24.

247 **Thomas had also revealed:** Ibid.

248 **Bishop interviewed Jackie:** Bishop (*A Bishop's*), p. 386.

248 **"We'll start with Baker":** *WP* and *NYT,* October 24, 1963.

248 **"an investigation of any possible conflicts":** *WP,* October 24, 1963.

248 **"Highly reliable source reports":** FRUS, 1961–1963, Volume IV, Vietnam, August–December 1963, Document 210.

248 **"in the contest with Viet Cong":** Ibid., Document 207.

248 **Kennedy decided to send his Harvard roommate:** Parmet (*JFK*), p. 335.

249 **During a two-hour conference with House leaders:** Presidential Recordings, Tape 116/ A52–117/ A53, JFKL.

249 **"way beyond anything you asked":** Ibid.

249 **"*We're* the goats":** Ibid.

249 **"The colored vote in my district":** Ibid.

249 **On Wednesday evening Kennedy invited the Bradlees:** Bradlee (*Conversations*), pp. 221–27.

250 **At a meeting on Thursday with Rusk, Taylor, and Gilpatric:** FRUS, 1961–1963, Volume IX, Foreign Economic Policy, Document 38.

250 **He took another step toward reducing cold war tensions:** Jean Daniel, "Unofficial Envoy," *New Republic,* December 14, 1963; Mahoney, p. 287.

251 **"He says we've been screwing them":** Galbraith (*Name-Dropping*), p. 105.

252 **On Thursday, Bishop announced:** Bishop (*A Bishop's*), pp. 386–87.

253 **"My feelings about assassination are identical":** Bishop (*The Day*), p. xi.

253 **Bishop thought he "seemed fascinated":** Bishop (*A Day*), p. ix.

253 **Kennedy woke Friday to front-page articles:** *NYT,* October 25, 1963; *WP,* October 25, 1963.

253 a law that made flying the United Nations flag a criminal offense: Wright, p. 39.
253 Stevenson had celebrated the new spirit: *NYT,* October 25, 1963; *WP,* October 25, 1963.
253 An angry crowd surrounded him: Ibid.
253 "We are patriots," she explained: *NYT,* October 26, 1963.
253 She later blamed: William Manchester Papers (*Death of a President*), Box 43, Wesleyan Library.
253 Kennedy asked Schlesinger to call Stevenson: Schlesinger (*Thousand*), pp. 1020–21.
253 "You know, there was something very ugly": Ibid.
254 a bomb threat delayed Tito's departure: Duke, JFKLOH.
254 As he and Duke were driving to the pier: Ibid.; Reeves, pp. 633–34.
254 Lodge reported that the generals: FRUS, 1961–1963, Volume IV, Vietnam, August–December 1963, Document 216.
254 "We are particularly concerned": Ibid., Document 217.
254 Kennedy doodled: JFKPP, Box 12, JFKL.
254 "a casual sort of grandeur": Cassini, p. 247.
254 Jackie finally invited him: Jacqueline Kennedy, p. 293.
254 She considered them "really not very nice": Ibid.
255 He told Alphand he was wearing the same shirt: Alphand, p. 409.
255 After dinner, he offered Alphand the same analysis: Alphand, JFKLOH.
255 Jackie told Alphand: Alphand, pp. 409–10.
255 He wrote in his diary: Beschloss (*Crisis Years*), p. 611.
255 The Roosevelts mentioned the attack: Ibid., p. 410.
255 The next day, she told the Secret Service agent: Hill, pp. 266–67.

SATURDAY, OCTOBER 26–SUNDAY, OCTOBER 27

256 Kennedy criticized the speech: Schlesinger (*Journals*), p. 202.
256 with an eye to including the "poetry and power": Schlesinger (*Thousand*), p. 1015.
256 He liked Schlesinger's version better: Schlesinger (*Journals*), p. 202.
257 "the first American president to give art": Troy, p. 96.
257 "The Arts in America": John F. Kennedy, "The Arts in America," *Look,* December 18, 1962.
257 "I don't think he liked music": Strober, p. 62.
257 "Your children live on streets": Bergquist and Tretick, p. 177.
257 Americans were "too liberal to fight": Stewart Udall, "Robert Frost's Last Adventure," *NYT Magazine,* June 11, 1972.
257 Kennedy was so furious: Ibid.
258 During the flight he reminded him: Reed, JFKLOH.
258 "Apparently he never did anything wrong": Schlesinger (*Journals*), p. 202.
258 "I really don't think too much": Reed, JFKLOH.
258 He added a preamble: Ibid.; Schlesinger unpublished diaries, NYPL. A draft of the speech with JFK's edits was published in the Amherst College magazine, *About Amherst,* Fall and Winter edition, 2003–2004. The notes that Kennedy wrote during the flight are on the JFKL Web site, and at JFKPOF, Box 47, JFKL.
258 JFK speech at the Amherst College cage: JFKL Web site.
260 "a thousand light years away": *New York Post,* October 28, 1963,
260 "He once said to me": JFKL Web site.
260 Before leaving, he told Kay Morrison: Stewart Udall, "Robert Frost's Last Adventure," *NYT Magazine,* June 11, 1972.
260 [footnote] "Robert had a serious operation": JFKPOF, Box 29A, JFKL.
260 Jim Reed had been with him: Reed, JFKLOH.
261 In an exclusive story appearing: *Des Moines Register,* October 26, 1963.
261 He mentioned the Baker scandal to Schlesinger: Schlesinger, unpublished diaries, NYPL.

261 his official schedule noted: JFK daily schedule, JFKL Web site.

261 Evelyn Lincoln's phone logs show: Lincoln Papers, Box 5, JFKL.

261 According to the FBI file: FBI memorandums, FBI FOIA (Freedom of Information Act) material at FBI archives or at paperlessarchives.com; see also Evan Thomas, pp. 263–67.

262 She knew he could not tolerate a sulker: Billings, JFKLOH.

262 then to almost $100,000: *NYT,* November 10, 1963.

263 "Can you imagine me ending up": Bartlett, JFKLOH.

263 "Why are we building": O'Donnell and Powers, p. 356.

263 She had a similar reaction: West, p. 237.

263 While driving with West to the warehouse: Ibid., p. 238.

263 "John detests the country": Galitzine, pp. 170–71.

263 He had arrived at the White House: Thayer, pp. 120–22.

263 "Oh, Mr. West, he's been a houseguest": West, p. 235.

264 He had made a pass when they were teenagers: Pitts, pp. 22–23.

264 Eunice called it: Michaelis, p. 175.

264 Billings claimed to know: Billings, JFKLOH.

264 "because it was brand new": Ibid.

264 There were not enough closets: JFK's complaints about Wexford are mentioned in Gallagher, p. 300; Leaming, p. 319.

265 Nor did Wexford impress: Galitzine, pp. 171–72.

265 Jackie was riding when Galitzine arrived: Ibid.

265 "You'll be so young": Ibid.

265 Then he took her for a drive: Ibid.

265 He maintained the easy banter: Ibid., pp. 172–73.

265 During his 1946 campaign, Jim Reed had noticed: Reed, JFKLOH.

265 As the film flickered: Galitzine, p. 173.

MONDAY, OCTOBER 28–THURSDAY, OCTOBER 31

266 "The President came in all excited": Lincoln Papers, Box 6, JFKL.

266 A note says, "Staff members conferred": JFK appointment book, JFKL Web site.

266 The reporter Dan Oberdorfer writes: Oberdorfer, p. 204.

266 Bobby was given the task of persuading Hoover: Guthman and Shulman, p. 278.

266 Hoover also noted that the president had asked him: FBI memorandums, FBI FOIA (Freedom of Information Act) material at FBI archives or at paperlessarchives.com; also see Evan Thomas, pp. 263–67.

266 Hoover suggested that since the FBI: Ibid.

267 Mansfield and Dirksen left no record: Oberdorfer, p. 205.

267 According to Hoover's memorandum: FBI memorandums, FBI FOIA material at FBI archives or at paperlessarchives.com; also see Evan Thomas, pp. 263–67.

267 Hoover told Bobby afterward: Ibid.

267 While Hoover was still in his office: Ibid.

267 "Had they not had that meeting": Oberdorfer, p. 205.

268 Kennan had sent him a handwritten letter: Kennan, p. 317.

268 "the American diplomat who did more": *NYT,* March 18, 2005.

268 He responded on October 28: Kennan, p. 318.

269 When the Illinois congressman Roland Libonati persisted: Presidential Recordings, Telephone Recordings, Transcripts, Dictabelt 28A2, JFKL.

269 "Do you think he will know who we are?": Lincoln (*My Twelve*), pp. 299–300.

269 He called his father: Stoughton and Clifton, p. 130.

269 Lincoln wrote in her diary: Lincoln Papers, Box 6, JFKL.

269 Kennedy scrawled "POVERTY": JFKPP, Box 12, JFKL.

270 "a notable political achievement": *NYT*, October 30, 1963.

270 the *Boston Globe* called it: *Boston Globe*, October 30, 1963.

270 An anonymous House Republican: *WP* (Richard Lyons column), October 31, 1963.

270 Kennedy called Halleck that afternoon: Presidential Recordings, Telephone Recordings, Transcripts, Dictabelt 28A3, JFKL.

270 Since he had told Lodge: FRUS, 1961–1963, Volume IV, Vietnam, January–August 1963, Document 1.

271 Kennedy recorded the October 29 meeting: Presidential Recordings, Tape 118/A54; Hilsman, pp. 518–19; FRUS, 1961–1963, Volume IV, Vietnam, August–December 1963, Document 226.

272 When the meeting reconvened: Presidential Recordings, Tape 118/A54; FRUS, 1961–1963, Volume IV, Vietnam, August–December 1963, Document 235.

272 He and Bundy had received a cable from Lodge: FRUS, 1961–1963, Volume IV, Vietnam, August–December 1963, Document 226.

272 In a reply from Bundy: Ibid., Document 236.

273 In his reply, Lodge called out Kennedy: Ibid., Document 242.

273 This was not good enough for Bundy and Kennedy: Ibid., Document 249.

273 On October 30, 1960, Kennedy had driven: *NYT*, October 31, 1960.

273 women hurled themselves: Dilworth, JFKLOH.

274 His motorcade had been well advertised: *NYT*, October 31, 1963; *Newsweek*, November 4, 1963; *WP*, October 31, 1963.

274 In August, a mob of jeering: *NYT*, August 31 and September 1, 1963.

274 One thousand heads of families: Ibid., September 3, 1963.

274 When Kennedy spoke in Convention Hall: Text of the speech in Sorensen Papers, Box 73, JFKL.

275 he told a joke that Lawrence would call: Lawrence, JFKLOH.

275 According to Larry Newman: Martin (*Hero*), p. 267.

275 "one of the things of the time": Taylor, JFKLOH.

275 The Washington attorney Clark Clifford: Clifford, p. 331.

276 "I really am not in a position to do": Fay, JFKLOH.

276 He told Hilsman, "What we're going to do": Strober and Strober, p. 270.

276 The following week, Kennedy gave Bradlee: Bradlee (*Conversations*), pp. 227–29.

Friday, November 1–Sunday, November 10

279 Bundy woke Kennedy just after 3:00 a.m.: Reeves, p. 644.

279 Three hours later, a CIA cable: FRUS, 1961–1963, Volume IV, Vietnam, August–December 1963, Document 256.

279 At an early morning White House staff meeting: Ibid., Document 263.

279 "I think we have to make it clear this is not": Presidential Recordings, Tape 118/A54, JFKL.

279 He jumped to his feet: Taylor, p. 301.

279 Schlesinger thought he looked: Schlesinger (*A Thousand*), p. 997.

279 Forrestal believed that the deaths: McNamara, p. 84.

279 Jackie noticed that he had: Jacqueline Kennedy, p. 304.

280 and would later tell Cardinal Spellman: Parmet (*The Presidency*), p. 335.

280 "We must bear a good deal of responsibility": McNamara interview on *JFK: A Presidency Revealed*, a History Channel documentary.

280 "She's responsible for the death": Fay, JFKLOH.

280 While Jackie was at Wexford: Leaming, p. 323.

280 By the time he reconvened his advisers: Presidential Recordings, Tape 118/A55, JFKL.

281 When he began dictating his first speech: Mary Davis, JFKLOH.

281 "the words rolling out of his mouth": Lincoln (*My Twelve*), pp. 131–32.

281 He dictated his announcement that he was running: Ibid., pp. 105–6.
281 and dictated passages for his inaugural address: Lincoln Papers, Box 2, JFKL; cited in Clarke, pp. 29–37.
281 On November 4, he dictated: Presidential Recordings, Tape 118/A55, JFKL; transcript on JFKL Web site.
282 He may have been atoning for his complicity: Claflin, p. 279.
283 In a covering letter, Skelton wrote: William Manchester Papers (*Death of a President*), Box 43, Wesleyan Library.
283 While reviewing foreign policy issues: Presidential Recordings, Tape 118/A55, JFKL.
283 On Tuesday, Attwood briefed Bundy and Chase: The developments that Attwood described in the briefing are summarized in his subsequent memorandum: FRUS, 1961–1963, Volume XI, Cuban Missile Crisis and Aftermath, Document 374.
283 Bundy and Chase asked Attwood to write a memorandum: Ibid.
283 Bundy added that the president was more interested: Attwood (*Twilight Struggle*), p. 261.
283 At a Tuesday White House meeting on Cuba: FRUS, 1961–1963, Volume XI, Cuban Missile Crisis and Aftermath, Document 373.
284 Kennedy was in an expansive mood: Bradlee (*Conversations*), pp. 227–35.
285 "You know, I have made up my mind": Ormsby-Gore, JFKLOH.
285 An article by Attwood: William Attwood, "We Face a New Kind of World," *Look*, November 5, 1963.
285 Kennedy liked the article so much: JFKPP, Box 43, JFKL.
285 He criticized congressmen who found it: JFK's "Remarks before the Protestant Council, November 8, 1963," JFKL Web site.
286 William Styron was surprised to see him: William Styron, "The Short Classy Voyage of JFK," *Esquire*, December 1983.
286 Salinger informed reporters: WP, November 7, 1963.
286 He arrived at Wexford early: Bradlee (*A Good Life*), pp. 255–57; Bradlee (*Conversations*), pp. 235–39; Stoughton and Clifton, pp. 99, 126, 139.
287 Stoughton also filmed: Audiovisual collection, JFKL.
287 She knelt down . . . to show him how to do it correctly: Blaine, p. 71.
287 "I guess we all go through that": Stoughton and Clifton, p. 174.
287 "The Saints today are the peacemakers": WP, November 11, 1963.
287 he was an outspoken civil rights advocate: "Civil Rights Movement in Middleburg, Virginia," Eugene Scheel, www.loudounhistory.org.
287 On November 10, Pereira gave him a Bible: Moon, p. 19.
287 Bill Walton confirmed her impression: Ridder, author interview.

MONDAY, NOVEMBER 11–TUESDAY, NOVEMBER 12

288 "many miracles": Hirsh, JFKLOH.
288 "I think he'll be lonely": Helen Thomas, p. 33.
288 "Okay. Time to salute Daddy": Blaine, p. 72.
288 "This is one of the really beautiful places": Reeves, p. 654.
288 "I suppose I'll have to go back to Boston": Thompson, p. 15.
289 he persuaded Hirsh to repeat it: Hirsh, JFKLOH.
289 Hirsh took Caroline on an excursion: Ibid.
289 "Well, I think it's time": Ibid.
289 whose facility with languages had left him somewhat jealous: Bradlee (*Conversations*), p. 95.
290 "I can assure you that this flag": Reeves, p. 445.
290 These strategies converged on November 12: FRUS, 1961–1963, Volume XI, Cuban Missile Crisis and Aftermath, Document 376.

291 **Bundy called Attwood to deliver a message from the president:** Ibid., Document 377.
291 **Attwood told Bundy he would ask:** Ibid.
291 **Kennedy convened:** Sorensen (*Counselor*), pp. 347–48; O'Donnell and Powers, pp. 386–87; Sidey (*John F. Kennedy*), pp. 351–52; Guthman and Shulman, pp. 390–92; Reeves, pp. 655–57; Presidential Recordings, transcript on JFKL Web site.
291 **Lincoln had noticed Johnson's name appearing less often:** Lincoln (*Kennedy and Johnson*), p. 161.
292 **Sorensen believed he had been excluded:** Sorensen (*Counselor*), p. 346
292 **Kennedy even raised the subject of his forthcoming:** O'Donnell and Powers, p. 386.
292 **McGeorge Bundy was even thinking ahead:** Jacqueline Kennedy, p. 130.
292 **"Goldwater doesn't have a prayer":** *Saturday Evening Post,* November 2, 1963.
293 **A recent Gallup poll:** *Boston Globe,* October 27, 1963.

WEDNESDAY, NOVEMBER 13

295 **Kennedy stopped at Lincoln's desk to chat:** Lincoln (*Kennedy and Johnson*), p. 200.
295 **Bryant had noticed an increase:** Bryant, pp. 65–66.
295 **Kennedy had dismissed the rumors:** Transcript of October 31 press conference, JFKL Web site.
295 **when Bartlett raised the possibility:** Sally Bedell Smith, p. 426.
295 **Lincoln was in a different category:** Kennedy had given Lincoln's home address to a mistress living in Europe, and she wrote him there several weeks after the inauguration. Lincoln Papers, Box 3, JFKLOH.
296 **After examining Kennedy on Wednesday:** JFKPP, Box 46, JFKL.
296 **Kennedy chaired an afternoon meeting:** Sorensen Papers, Box 37, JFKL; *NYT,* November 13, November 14, 1963; Gordon, JFKLOH.
296 **he and Jackie appeared together:** Shaw, p. 113. *WP, NYT,* and *ES,* November 14, 1963.
297 **"What would the people think":** Lincoln (*My Twelve*), pp. 302–3.
297 **Lincoln and Shaw took the children into the Rose Garden:** Ibid.
297 **A prime example was his treatment of Stevenson:** Cassini, pp. 325–26.
298 **he had persuaded Bradlee to participate:** Bradlee (*Conversations*), pp. 237–39.
298 **Kennedy had invited Garbo:** Pitts, pp. 205–6; Michaelis, pp. 177–78.
298 **Garbo became inebriated:** Details of the dinner are based on three Garbo biographies—Barry Paris, *Garbo*; Scott Reisfield, *Greta Garbo—Portraits from Her Private Collection*; Karen Swenson, *Greta Garbo: A Life Apart.*
298 **"He never gave *me*":** Ibid.

THURSDAY, NOVEMBER 14–FRIDAY, NOVEMBER 15

299 **Kennedy's sixty-fourth press conference:** Transcript at JFKL Web site.
299 **If there was ever a year when he owed Jackie:** Lincoln (*My Twelve*), p. 303.
299 **At 4:00 p.m. his helicopter landed:** *NYT,* November 15, 1963.
300 **The previous week he had driven:** *Boston Sunday Globe,* November 17, 1963; *NYT,* November 15, 1963; *ES,* November 15; *Time,* November 22, 1963; Blaine, pp. 26–27.
300 **A policeman told a reporter:** *Time,* November 22, 1963.
300 **A police official criticized him:** *NYT,* November 15, 1963.
300 **Salinger explained:** *NYT,* November 14, 1963.
300 **"zeroing in on the 'safe-motorists' vote":** *Time,* November 22, 1963.
300 **Once he arrived at the Carlyle Hotel:** O'Donnell and Powers, p. 387; *NYT,* November 15, 1963.
301 **Stevenson was at the party:** Cassini, p. 239.
301 **Oleg Cassini, who overheard:** Ibid.

301 he met with Henry Luce: William Manchester Papers (*Death of a President*), Box 43, Wesleyan Library.

301 In his speech to the AFL-CIO: JFKL Web site.

302 When he finished, a young Irish nanny: *Boston Globe,* November 16, 1963.

302 he told delegates to the Catholic Youth Organization's national convention: JFKL Web site.

302 Ignoring the protests of his Secret Service detail: *NYT,* November 16, 1963.

302 At another red light: Ibid.

302 When Smathers remarked offhandedly: O'Donnell and Powers, p. 5 ; .. Smathers, JFKLOH.

303 "When will I put your picture on there?": Bishop (*The Day*), p. 87.

303 While Kennedy was out of town: Dobrynin, pp. 110–11.

303 On Friday, she entertained her friend Robin Douglas-Home: Robin Douglas-Home, "New Humility," *News of the World,* March 12, 1967, cited by Sally Bedell Smith, p. 431, and Bradford, p. 261.

303 "You won't believe it": Baldrige, p. 208.

SATURDAY, NOVEMBER 16

305 "You had the feeling the air was electrified": *Miami Herald,* November 17, 1963.

305 "in the very best of health": Von Braun, JFKLOH.

305 Inside the windowless blockhouse: Ibid.; Seamans, p. 113.

306 "Amazing!" "Fantastic!": Von Braun, JFKLOH.

306 Robert Seamans, who headed NASA, believed: Seamans, p. 113.

306 He had mentioned this when they met in 1953: Von Braun, JFKLOH.

306 When von Braun later recounted their conversation: Ibid.

306 "Now, this will be the largest payload": Seamans, pp. 113–14.

306 While briefing Kennedy at the Marshall Space Flight Center: Von Braun, JFKLOH.

306 "When this goes up we'll be ahead": *Time,* July 25, 1994; William Manchester Papers (*Death of a President*), Box 43, Wesleyan Library.

306 "I will take my television black and white": JFK speech at Municipal Auditorium, Oklahoma City, November 3, 1963.

307 "What can we do now?": *Time,* July 25, 1994; Murray and Cox, pp. 78–79.

307 JFK speech at Rice University, September 12, 1962: JFKL Web site.

308 "Now, I'm not sure I have the facts straight on this": Seamans, p. 114.

308 Seamans did as he was told: *NYT,* November 17, 1963.

308 Four days before leaving: Logsdon, p. 193.

SUNDAY, NOVEMBER 17–MONDAY, NOVEMBER 18

310 the weekend had been "really living": Lincoln (*Kennedy and Johnson*), p. 203.

310 The weather had been perfect: O'Donnell and Powers, p. 388; Manchester (*Remembering*), p. 263.

310 The weekend reminded Macdonald: Beschloss (*Crisis*), p. 665.

310 Macdonald asked Kennedy: Collier and Horowitz, p. 310.

310 "a fundamental strategic shift": *NYT,* November 19, 1963.

311 "the withdrawal of 1000 U. S. servicemen": *NYT* and *WP,* November 16, 1963.

311 "legislation to provide health care": *NYT,* November 19, 1963.

311 the administration was "hopeful": Ibid., November 18, 1963.

311 Walter Heller received a memorandum: Sorensen Papers, Box 37, JFKL.

311 Jim Bishop and Pierre Salinger happened to dine: Bishop (*A Day*), p. x.

311 "I have a feeling it's going to be a great day": Blaine, p. 145.

311 Agent Emory Roberts . . . had received a call: Ibid., pp. 136–37.

312 The Secret Service had tracked Milteer: Bugliosi, pp. 1268–71.

312 "Mr. President, we have a very long motorcade": Blaine, pp. 145–46.

312 **"Floyd, this is a political trip":** Ibid.

312 **The Secret Service had not guarded:** *Tampa Tribune,* November 19, 1963.

313 **Evelyn Lincoln remembered Kennedy:** Lincoln (*My Twelve*), p. 303.

313 **Reporters described him being:** *Tampa Tribune,* November 19, 1963.

313 **He wore three different outfits:** Ibid.

313 **He was smiling and relaxed:** Ibid.

314 **"Floyd, have the Ivy League charlatans":** Blaine, p. 148.

314 **"It's excessive, Floyd":** Ibid., p. 149; *NYT,* November 24, 1964; Warren Commission, exhibit 1025.

314 **After arriving at MacDill:** *Tampa Tribune,* November 19, 1963.

314 **After eating lunch:** Ibid.

314 **He delayed his departure from Tampa:** Ibid.

314 **The lead editorial:** Ibid.

315 **He witnessed the power:** Ibid.; Armory speech, JFKL Web site.

315 **Decades later, a *St. Petersburg Times*:** *St. Petersburg Times,* November 11, 1999.

315 **He told the crowd greeting him:** *Miami Herald,* November 18, 1963.

315 **Speech to the Inter-American Press Association:** JFKL Web site.

316 **"God, I hate to go out to Texas":** Martin (*Seeds*), p. 451, based on an interview with Smathers.

316 **"Look how screwed up it's going to be":** Beschloss (*Crisis*), pp. 665-66.

316 **"Thank God nobody wanted to kill":** Martin (*Hero*), p. 477.

TUESDAY, NOVEMBER 19

317 **Lincoln remembered Tuesday:** Lincoln (*Kennedy and Johnson*), p. 203.

317 **He sat in a rocking chair:** Ibid., pp. 203-7; Lincoln Papers, Box 6, JFKL. Some authors have doubted that the conversation happened as Lincoln reported it in her 1968 book. Box 6 of her papers, however, contains the shorthand notes that she made on a White House memorandum pad as he spoke—conclusive proof that Kennedy told her that he was considering replacing Johnson.

318 **Sanford would later say:** Sanford, JFKLOH.

318 **"Oh, God, can you ever imagine":** Jacqueline Kennedy, p. 278.

318 **In 1964, Sorensen would ask Jackie:** Sorensen (*Counselor*), p. 249. `

318 **At a 10:00 a.m. ceremony in the Rose Garden:** *NYT* and *WP,* November 20, 1963.

319 **Back in the Oval Office:** Mahoney, JFKLOH; Mahoney, pp. 284-85.

319 **It called for improving relations:** Hilsman, p. 352.

320 **He had told Marie Ridder:** Ridder, author interview.

320 **Dean Rusk said they often discussed it:** Rusk, p. 283.

320 **"You know, Mr. President":** Mahoney, JFKLOH.

320 **"I just want to tell you":** Ibid.

320 **and picked up an article:** George Mills, "JFK Could Lose," *Look,* December 17, 1963 (printed and on sale before November 22, 1963).

321 **"What do you think of that?":** Mahoney, JFKLOH.

321 **Attwood called Bundy's assistant:** Attwood (*Twilight*), p. 262.

321 **Chase wrote in a memorandum:** National Security File, Country File, Cuba, Contact with Cuban Leaders, 5/63-4/65. The memorandum was dated November 19, 1963, headed "Approach to Castro," and filed under "Top Secret-Sensitive."

321 **Bundy called Attwood back later:** Attwood (*Twilight*), p. 262.

321 **Castro told Jean Daniel:** "When Castro Heard the News," *New Republic,* December 7, 1963.

322 **Kennedy studied the photographs:** Beschloss (*Crisis*), pp. 666-67.

322 **"I'm sure glad the Secret Service":** Helms, p. 227.

322 **He held a final briefing on Tuesday:** O'Donnell and Powers, p. 389.

322 "When you come back": NBC White Paper on Vietnam, December 1971, cited in Newman, pp. 426–27; Schlesinger (*Robert Kennedy*), p. 722. The Forrestal-Kennedy conversation is also recounted by Brandon (*Anatomy*), p. 30.

323 "Wayne, I want you to know": *Boston Globe*, June 24, 1973, cited by Schlesinger (*Robert Kennedy*), p. 722.

323 "I'm still very much in favor": Heller Papers, Box 6 (Kennedy-Johnson files), JFKL.

323 Lewis Weinstein, a distinguished: Lewis H. Weinstein, "John F. Kennedy: A Personal Memoir, 1946–1963," *American Jewish History* 75, September 1985.

323 He called Weinstein the next day: Ibid.

324 "I wish I weren't going": Salinger, p. 3.

324 "Don't let the President come": Ibid., p. 1.

324 But Lincoln had no qualms: Lincoln (*My Twelve*), p. 305.

324 "If they are going to get me": Ibid.

Wednesday, November 20

325 During their weekly White House breakfast meeting: Manchester (*Death*), p. 14.

325 His mind was wandering, and he drew doodles: JFKPP, Box 12, JFKL.

325 He complained to Dr. Burkley: JFKPP, Box 48 (medical), JFKL.

325 signed a lease: Manchester (*Death*), p. 14.

325 asked Lincoln to check on the forecast: Lincoln (*My Twelve*), p. 305.

325 told Turnure to make sure: Manchester (*Death*), p. 10.

326 "A bit of old-fashioned Boston": Bishop (*A Bishop's*), p. 386.

326 He added some words of friendship: U. Alexis Johnson, JFKLOH.

326 Joan Douglas noticed: William Manchester Papers (*Death of a President*), Box 43, Wesleyan Library.

327 "You're going off to Japan": Ibid.

327 Dillon thought he was "in wonderful form": Ibid.

327 The Supreme Court justices also remarked: Ibid., Box 44.

327 Ethel Kennedy thought he seemed withdrawn and preoccupied: Manchester (*Death*), p. 18.

327 Bobby Kennedy spent nearly forty-five minutes: Ibid., p. 619.

327 Bobby told one of his guests: William Manchester Papers (*Death of a President*), Box 43, Wesleyan Library.

327 He asked O'Donnell if he had seen: Mahoney, p. 288; Manchester (*Death*), p. 33.

327 O'Donnell said he had decided: O'Donnell and Powers, pp. 18–19; Manchester (*Death*), p. 34.

327 Jean Daniel delivered Kennedy's message: "When Castro Heard the News," *New Republic*, December 7, 1963.

328 she read him a letter from her mother: William Manchester Papers (*Death of a President*), Box 43, Wesleyan Library; Sally Bedell Smith, p. 435.

328 he showed her a tongue-in-cheek letter: Ibid.

328 "There are going to be all these rich": Manchester (*Death*), p. 10.

328 She held up some dresses and outfits: Ibid.

328 He received a call from George Ball: Ball, p. 310.

Thursday, November 21

329 Kennedy was edgy: Lincoln (*My Twelve*), p. 305.

329 As soon as he arrived at the Oval Office: Ibid., pp. 305–6.

329 He met briefly: Darlington, JFKLOH.

329 "I feel great. My back feels better": O'Donnell and Powers, p. 4.

329 Nanny Maud Shaw was opposed: Manchester (*Death*), p. 59.

329 she and Shaw waved from the roof: Shaw, p. 160.

330 He grinned and scrawled: Bundy Papers, Box 34, JFKL.

330 Hale Boggs . . . was passing the White House: Manchester (*Death*), p. 60.

330 spent the short flight teasing his son: Lincoln (*My Twelve*), p. 306.

330 When John learned: Manchester (*Death*), p. 63.

330 Kennedy tucked a file card: O'Donnell and Powers, p. 4.

330 Johnson planned to introduce him by saying: Wright, p. 47.

330 "You two guys aren't running out": O'Donnell and Powers, p. 20.

331 He poked his head into Jackie's compartment: Gallagher, p. 312.

331 "I don't think Barry is going to have time": Reston, pp. 262–63.

331 Gonzalez now took him aside on Air Force One: Ibid., p. 263.

331 "Oh, and by the way, Henry": Ibid.

332 Teenagers filling the observation deck: *San Antonio Express*, November 22, 1963.

332 Gonzalez had been standing: Reston, p. 265.

332 San Antonio in 1960 . . . motorcade: *San Antonio Express*, November 22, 1963.

332 "despite the conglomeration of Secret Service agents": Ibid.

332 He kept a close eye on Jackie: Manchester (*Death*), p. 75.

332 Seeking shelter from the wind: Reston, p. 266.

332 There were some sour notes: *San Antonio Express*, November 22, 1963.

332 A constable on traffic duty overheard: Ibid.

333 The Secret Service failed to keep a mental patient: Ibid.

333 Asked by a reporter to comment: *ES*, November 22, 1963.

333 JFK speech at Brooks: JFKL Web site.

333 Five minutes later he stood in a laboratory: O'Donnell and Powers, pp. 21–22.

334 Before leaving Brooks, he invited: Cooper, p. 179.

334 Kennedy was jubilant: John Connally, "Why Kennedy Went to Texas," *Life*, November 22, 1967.

334 He asked Powers to estimate: O'Donnell and Powers, p. 22: Powers Papers (Vanocur interview), Box 9, JFKL.

334 As they pulled into the Rice Hotel: William Manchester Papers (*Death of a President*), Box 43, Wesleyan Library.

334 Johnson had told his friend Horace Busby: Thompson, p. 253.

334 His meeting with Kennedy was so acrimonious: Manchester (*Death*), p. 82; Reston, pp. 269–70.

334 He had complained to Bobby earlier: Dallek (*Johnson*), p. 41.

334 After Johnson stormed out of the suite, Kennedy told Jackie: Manchester (*Death*), p. 82; Reston, pp. 269–70.

335 "I just can't bear him sitting there saying": Jacqueline Kennedy, LBJLOH.

335 He doodled on a sheet of hotel stationery: Greenberg, pp. 156–57.

335 He and Jackie dined in their suite: Reston, p. 268; Yarborough, JFKLOH.

335 The atmosphere was more cordial: Leaming (*Mrs. Kennedy*), p. 332.

335 "Mrs. Kennedy, on her first official": *ES*, November 22, 1963.

335 "Gosh, Mary, you've been such a great help": Gallagher, p. 314.

336 From this vantage point he could see: Valenti, JFKLOH.

336 Nerves may have caused him to flub: Houston speech transcript, JFKL Web site.

336 Kennedy chewed her out for a slip-up: Gallagher, pp. 316–17.

336 They could not sleep in the same bed: Leaming (*Mrs. Kennedy*), p. 333.

336 "You were great today": Manchester (*Death*), p. 87.

FRIDAY, NOVEMBER 22

337 Kennedy woke to hear: Bishop (*The Day*), p. 5.

337 Then he slipped on the white shirt: Manchester (*Death*), p. 112.

337 "Gosh, just look at the crowds": Gallagher, p. 318.

337 "Just look at the platform": Lawrence O'Brien, pp. 156–57.

337 He showed O'Brien the front page: *Dallas Morning News,* November 22, 1963.

337 "Christ, I come all the way down here": Gillon, p. 20.

338 "I don't care if you have to throw": Lawrence O'Brien, p. 156.

338 "Some Texans, in taking account": *Chicago Sun-Times,* November 22, 1963.

338 "And weren't the crowds great": Manchester (*Death*), p. 112.

338 Speech at the parking lot rally: JFKL Web site.

338 "These are my kind of people": Manchester (*Remembering*), p. 18.

338 "Things are going much better": Brandon (*Special*), p. 196.

339 Speech in Hotel Texas ballroom: JFKL Web site; film at Sixth Floor Museum, Dallas.

339 Back in their suite she said: Bergquist and Tretick, p. 172; O'Donnell and Powers, p. 24.

339 Ted Dealey, had come to the White House: Manchester (*Death*), pp. 48–49.

339 Kennedy fired back: Ibid.; *NYT,* November 5, 1961.

339 He answered Dealey again: Schlesinger (*Thousand*), p. 753.

340 "Oh, you know, we're heading": O'Donnell and Powers, p. 25; Manchester (*Death*), p. 121; *ES,* November 22, 1963.

340 Some residents of "nut country" had woken: Manchester (*Death*), p. 64.

340 "You know, last night": Ibid., p. 121.

340 He and Jackie had been in the suite: Ibid., pp. 120–21; Pottker, p. 213; William Manchester Papers (*Death of a President*), Box 43, Wesleyan Library.

340 "Isn't this sweet, Jack": Ibid.

341 Instead, he grabbed a telephone book: Ibid.

341 "You can be sure of one thing": Wicker, p. 158; Reston, p. 273.

341 Secret Service Agent Roy Kellerman told O'Donnell: O'Donnell and Powers, p. 25.

341 "They put me in a bubble top thing": Martin (*Seeds*), pp. 452–53.

341 he thought the space program "needed a boost": Logsdon, p. 218.

341 "Equal choice / not any reflection": JFKPP (addition 2005), Box 50, JFKL.

342 "How can anyone say no": O'Donnell and Powers, p. 26.

342 "Please, when we go to Dallas": McHugh, JFKLOH.

342 When he landed at Love Field in 1961: Manchester (*Death*), p. 47.

342 "This trip is turning out": O'Donnell and Powers, p. 26.

342 "You two look like Mr. and Mrs. America": Ibid.

342 A reporter watching her emerge: MacNeil, p. 187.

342 This was the first time that most at Love Field: Jerry Crow, OH, Sixth Floor Museum archives.

342 A Dallas woman said she was amazed: Van Buren, p. 74.

342 "I can see his suntan": Bugliosi, p. 27.

343 "He's broken away from the program": Film archives, Sixth Floor Museum.

343 The Texas journalist Ronnie Dugger: Manchester (*Death*), p. 131.

343 It was the first time: Lieberson, p. 222.

343 Sorensen's observation: Sorensen (*Counselor*), p. 102.

343 Laura Bergquist's "fascinating human animal": Bergquist Papers, Boston University Library.

343 what Sidey called "a serious man": John F. Kennedy (*Prelude*), p. xxii.

344 A local broadcaster called his welcome: Film archives, Sixth Floor Museum.

344 Some high school students: Manchester (*Death*), p. 128.

344 "You're a traiter": Ibid.

344 "Help JFK Stamp Out": Ibid.

344 "Mr. President, because of your": *ES,* November 23, 1963.

344 "It's wonderful": Roberts, JFKLOH; MacNeil, p. 186.

344 As they were pulling away, Kennedy noticed: Jerry Crow, OH, Sixth Floor Museum.

344 Connally had wanted him to speak: Bruno and Greenfield, pp. 89–92.

345 **Connally might have forgotten:** John Connally, "Why Kennedy Went to Texas," *Life,* November 22, 1967; testimony of John and Nellie Connally to House Select Committee on Assassinations (HSCA), available on National Archives Web site.

345 **Yarborough might not have remembered thinking:** Yarborough, JFKLOH.

345 **Nor would John and Nellie Connally have recalled:** Connally, "Why Kennedy Went to Texas," *Life,* November 22, 1967; testimony of John and Nellie Connally to HSCA, available on National Archives Web site.

345 **or that he had stopped to greet some children:** Ibid.

345 **or that a teenaged boy had darted:** Sixth Floor Museum archives.

345 **"Thank you, thank you":** Connally, "Why Kennedy Went to Texas," *Life,* November 22, 1967.

345 **they had spilled into the street:** Clint Hill, OH, Sixth Floor Museum.

346 **"How pleasant that cool tunnel":** Manchester (*Death*), p. 154.

346 **"You sure can't say that":** Nellie Connally and Herskowitz, p. 7; Manchester (*Death*), p. 154.

346 **"No, you can't":** Manchester (*Death*),p. 154.

346 **He heard some loud bangs:** Trask, p. 32.

346 **Nellie Connally remembered his eyes:** Nellie Connally and Herskowitz, p. 7.

346 **Agent Kellerman thought he said:** Manchester (*Death*), p. 157.

346 **His back brace kept him upright:** Dallek (*Unfinished*), p. 694; James Reston, Jr., "That 'Damned Girdle': The Hidden Factor That Might Have Killed Kennedy," *Los Angeles Times,* November 22, 2004.

346 **Jackie cried out:** Nellie Connally and Herskowitz, p. 8.

AFTER DALLAS

347 **Jackie wept first:** Semple, p. 27; Manchester (*Death*), p. 163.

347 **In New York, there was a murmur:** Fries and Wilson, p. 13.

347 **Reaction in New York City:** *NYT,* November 23, 1963.

347 **Chorus girls rehearsing:** Fries and Wilson, p. 162.

347 **a rookie police officer wept:** Van Buren, p. 9.

347 **In his Senate office, Senator Hubert Humphrey:** Fries and Wilson, p. 226.

347 **Senator Fulbright jumped up:** Fleming, pp. 23–24.

347 **"That Dallas!":** McKeever, p. 539.

347 **Medgar Evers's widow thought:** Fleming, p. 158.

347 **In Chicago, Mayor Richard Daley:** Semple, p. 83.

348 **in the Solomon Islands:** Hamilton, p. 602.

348 **At Harvard, a girl wept:** Salinger and Vanocur, p. 153.

348 **When the captain of a transatlantic jet:** Manchester (*Death*), p. 498.

348 **When Rusk announced:** Salinger, p. 8.

348 **President Truman cried so much:** Louchheim, p. 120.

348 **A poem by the columnist:** Ibid., p. 32.

348 **The cartoonist Bill Mauldin:** Ibid., p. 39.

348 **A twelve-year-old girl in Oregon:** Van Buren, p. 140.

348 **A girl remembered her mother:** Ibid., p. 48.

348 **schoolchildren in Texas cheering:** Bob Moser, "Welcome to Texas, Mr. Obama," *Texas Observer,* August 4, 2010.

348 **Schlesinger was appalled by Stevenson's reaction:** Schlesinger (*Journals*), p. 208.

348 **Algeria declared a week of official mourning:** Dear Abby, pp. 92–105.

348 **Thousands of Poles:** United States Information Agency, Box 2, JFKL.

349 **Khrushchev instructed his wife:** Sergei Khrushchev, p. 698.

349 **The woman narrating a documentary:** *NYT,* November 25, 1963.

349 **tears filled Gromyko's eyes:** Semple, p. 218.

349 **Yevgeny Yevtushenko was reading:** Stein, p. 198.

349 **"People cried in the street":** Douglas, p. 366; Manchester (*Death*), p. 557.

349 **Sir Laurence Olivier interrupted:** Manchester (*Death*), p. 497.

349 **"There has never been anything like it":** Joseph Alsop Papers, Box 19, folder 6, LOC.

349 **"openly crying in the street":** Manchester (*Death*), p. 498.

349 **Sixty thousand West Berliners:** Ibid.

349 **Workmen in Nice:** United States Information Agency, Box 2, JFKL.

349 **"Never, perhaps, has the death":** Manchester (*Death*), p. 498.

349 **"he [Kennedy] reestablished":** Walt Rostow, JFKLOH.

350 **A postman in a Connecticut:** Semple, p. 78.

350 **A Detroit housewife said:** Ibid., p. 383.

350 **Jimmy Carter cried:** Fleming, p. 104.

350 **McGeorge Bundy admitted:** Alsop, p. 512.

350 **Roswell Gilpatric believed:** Gilpatric, JFKLOH.

350 **The columnist Joe Alsop said:** Alsop, p. 511.

350 **In a condolence letter:** William Manchester Papers (*Death of a President*), Box 42, Wesleyan Library.

350 **When Elaine de Kooning:** Munro, p. 256.

350 **"The assassin dropped":** Ibid.

350 **"I felt that I had lost a brother":** Hall, p. 230.

350 **A poll conducted within a week:** Greenberg and Parker, pp. 149–77.

350 **a grief-stricken empire of asphalt:** A collection of descriptions, photographs, and documents pertaining to buildings, roads, and places named for John F. Kennedy is in the Steinberg Collection, available in the audiovisual department of the Kennedy Library.

351 **George Orwell believed it was impossible:** From Orwell's essay "Lear, Tolstoy and the Fool," in Sonia Orwell and Ian Angus (eds.), *The Collected Essays, Journalism and Letters of George Orwell, Volume 4: In Front of Your Nose.*

352 **James MacGregor Burns called the memorials:** Burns, JFKLOH.

352 **His 1960 biography was admiring but suggested:** Burns, pp. 276–81.

353 **"Was it a fabrication?":** Burns, JFKLOH.

353 **"who could have been the savior":** Salinger and Vanocur, p. 125.

353 **William Attwood believed the next five years:** William Attwood, "Twenty Years After Dallas," *Virginia Quarterly Review,* Autumn 1983.

353 **"an incalculable loss of the future":** Dallek (*Unfinished*), p. 631.

353 **"the future giving way to the present":** Jacqueline Kennedy, p. 318.

353 **"the difference between what is":** Salinger and Vanocur, p. 125.

353 **"He had great things to do":** William Manchester Papers (*Death of a President*), Box 42, Wesleyan Library.

354 **He had told Henry Brandon:** Brandon (*Special Relationships*), p. 200.

354 **he told Averell Harriman that he planned:** Seaborg (*Adventures*), p. 198.

354 **"more often than not":** O'Donnell and Powers, p. 75.

354 **Lincoln noted in her diary:** Lincoln Papers, Box 6, JFKL.

355 **Johnson kept Hoover at the FBI:** FOIA material, FBI archives.

355 **The *Evening Star* reported:** ES, March 28, 1965.

355 **"The most forgotten of all":** NYT, November 22, 1963.

356 **"God, what does it matter, Ben?":** Jacqueline Kennedy, p. 277.

356 **Walter Heller asked Johnson:** Look, November 23, 1964.

356 **"What Happened to the Kennedy Program":** Look, November 17, 1964.

357 **"Tell Mr. Khrushchev":** JFK: A Presidency Revealed, History Channel film.

357 **"Khrushchev did not want a repetition":** Taubman, p. 604.

357 **"This is bad news":** "When Castro Heard the News," *New Republic,* December 7, 1963.

357 **On November 25, Chase sent Bundy a memorandum:** FRUS, 1961–1963, Volume XI, Cuban Missile Crisis and Aftermath, Document 378.

357 **When Lechuga ran into Attwood:** Ibid., Document 382.

357 **Bundy described the recent contacts:** Ibid., Document 388.

358 **Chase wrote in a memorandum:** Ibid.

358 **In January, Chase told Attwood:** Attwood (*Twilight*), p. 263.

358 **Bobby Kennedy sent a memorandum to Dean Rusk:** *WP*, April 23, 2009.

358 **Johnson met with Lodge on November 24:** Douglass, p. 374.

358 **"It remains the central object of the United States":** National Security Action Memorandum 273, South Vietnam, November 26, 1963, FRUS, 1961–1963, Volume IV, Vietnam, August–December 1963, Document 331.

358 **"On the basis of personal intuition":** Clifford, p. 381.

359 **Robert McNamara wrote in his memoirs:** McNamara, p. 87.

359 **Walter Cronkite, whose interview had elicited:** Cronkite, p. 243.

359 **Senator Wayne Morse, who frequently butted:** *Boston Globe,* June 24, 1973,

359 **In his 1970 oral history:** Gilpatric, JFKLOH.

359 **John Connally wrote:** Connally, p. 358.

359 **While riding a ski lift in Aspen:** Ridder, author interview.

359 **In an oral history archived:** Bundy, LBJLOH.

360 **In 1993, Schlesinger wrote in his diary:** Schlesinger (*Journals*), p. 754.

360 **Bundy believed that:** Bundy, LBJLOH.

360 **The military analyst Daniel Ellsberg:** Ellsberg, pp. 195–96.

361 **"Now is not the time to cry, Provie":** *WP*, November 22, 1964.

361 **Later that winter, a nun:** Ibid.

361 **In the spring of 1964, Jackie told:** Maier, p. 475.

361 **She asked West to install:** West, p. 287; Bradford, p. 284.

361 **After Nixon won the 1968 election:** Mathews (*Kennedy & Nixon*), p. 276.

361 **"Mr. West, will you be my friend":** West, p. 279.

361 **That summer she told Stan Tretick:** Bradford, p. 149.

361 **Bradlee remembered the weekends demonstrating:** Bradlee (*Good Life*), p. 262.

361 **A reminder of her last weekend:** *NYT,* February 5, 2010.

362 **After buying several of Elaine de Kooning's drawings:** Hall, p. 230.

362 **In the fall of 1964, Jackie invited Henry Brandon:** Brandon (*Special Relationships*), p. 201.

362 **She kept returning to his place in history:** Ibid.

BIBLIOGRAPHY

Adler, Bill (ed.). *The Eloquent Jacqueline Kennedy Onassis: A Portrait in Her Own Words.* New York: William Morrow, 2004.

———. *The Kennedy Wit.* New York: Bantam, 1965.

———, and Tom Folsom (eds.). *The Uncommon Wisdom of JFK: A Portrait in His Own Words.* New York: Rugged Land, 2003.

Alfand, Hervé. *L'etonnement d'etre: Journal (1939–1973).* Paris: Fayard, 1977.

Alford, Mimi. *Once Upon a Secret: My Affair with President John F. Kennedy and Its Aftermath.* New York: Random House, 2012.

Alsop, Joseph, with Adam Platt. *"I've Seen the Best of It": Memoirs.* New York: Norton, 1992.

Andersen, Christopher. *Jack and Jackie: Portrait of an American Marriage.* New York: William Morrow, 1996.

Anthony, Carl Sferrazza. *As We Remember Her: Jacqueline Kennedy Onassis in the Words of Her Family and Friends.* New York: HarperCollins, 1997.

———. *The Kennedy White House: Family Life and Pictures, 1961–1963.* New York: Simon & Schuster, 2001.

Attwood, William. *The Reds and the Blacks: A Personal Adventure.* New York: Harper & Row, 1967.

———. *The Twilight Struggle: Tales of the Cold War.* New York: Harper & Row, 1987.

Ayres, Alex (ed.). *The Wit and Wisdom of John F. Kennedy: An A-to-Z Compendium in Quotations.* New York: Meridian, 1966.

Baker, Bobby, with Larry L. King. *Wheeling and Dealing: Confessions of a Capitol Hill Operator.* New York: Norton, 1978.

Baldrige, Letitia. *A Lady, First: My Life in the Kennedy White House and the American Embassies of Paris and Rome.* New York, Viking, 2001.

Ball, George W. *The Past Has Another Pattern: Memoirs.* New York: W. W. Norton, 1982.

Bartlett, Charles L., and Edward Weintal. *Facing the Brink: An Intimate Study of Crisis Diplomacy.* New York: Charles Scribner's Sons, 1967.

Baughman, U. E. *Secret Service Chief.* New York: Harper and Row, 1961.

Beale, Betty. *Power at Play: A Memoir of Parties, Politicians and the Presidents in My Bedroom.* Washington, D.C.: Regnery Gateway, 1993.

Beaton, Cecil. *Beaton in the Sixties: The Cecil Beaton Diaries as He Wrote Them, 1965–1969.* New York: Knopf, 2004.

Beran, Michael Knox. *Bobby Kennedy and the End of American Aristocracy.* New York: St. Martin's Press, 1998.

Bergquist, Laura, and Stanley Tretick. *A Very Special President.* New York: McGraw-Hill, 1965.

Beschloss, Michael R. *The Crisis Years: Kennedy and Khrushchev, 1960–1963.* New York: Edward Burlingame Books, HarperCollins, 1991.

———. *Presidential Courage: Brave Leaders and How They Changed America, 1789–1989.* New York: Simon and Schuster, 2007.

Bird, Kai. *The Color of Truth. McGeorge Bundy and William Bundy: Brothers in Arms.* New York: Simon & Schuster, 1998.

Bishop, Jim. *A Bishop's Confession.* Boston: Little, Brown, 1981.

———. *A Day in the Life of President Kennedy.* New York: Random House, 1964.

———. *The Day Kennedy Was Shot.* New York: Funk and Wagnalls, 1958.

Blaine, Gerald, with Lisa McCubbin. *The Kennedy Detail.* New York: Gallery Books.

Blair, Anne E. *Lodge in Vietnam: A Patriot Abroad.* New Haven: Yale University Press, 1995.

Bledsoe, Jane K. *E de K: Elaine de Kooning.* Athens: University of Georgia, Georgia Museum of Art, 1992.

Blight, James G., Janet M. Lang, and David A. Welch. *Vietnam If Kennedy Had Lived: Virtual JFK.* Lanham, Md.: Rowman & Littlefield, 2009.

Bowles, Chester. *Promises to Keep: My Years in Public Life 1941–1969.* New York: Harper & Row, 1971.

Bradford, Sarah. *America's Queen: The Life of Jacqueline Kennedy Onassis.* New York: Viking, 2000.

Bradlee, Benjamin C. *Conversations with Kennedy.* New York: Norton, 1975.

———. *A Good Life: Newspapering and Other Adventures.* New York: Simon and Schuster, 1995.

Branch, Shelly, and Sue Callaway. *What Would Jackie Do? An Inspired Guide to Distinctive Living.* New York: Gotham Books, 2006.

Branch, Taylor. *Parting the Waters: America in the King Years, 1954–1963.* New York: Simon and Schuster, 1988.

Brandon, Henry. *Anatomy of Error: The Secret History of the Vietnam War.* London: André Deutsch, 1970.

———. *Special Relationships: A Foreign Correspondent's Memoirs from Roosevelt to Reagan.* New York: Atheneum, 1988.

Brauer, Carl M. *John F. Kennedy and the Second Reconstruction.* New York: Columbia University Press, 1977.

Brinkley, David. *David Brinkley: 11 Presidents, 4 Wars, 22 Political Conventions, 1 Moon Landing, 3 Assassinations, 2,000 Weeks of News and Other Stuff on Television and 18 Years of Growing Up in North Carolina.* New York: Alfred A. Knopf, 1995.

Bruce, Preston. *From the Door of the White House.* New York: Lothrop, Lee & Shepard, 1984.

Bruno, Jerry, and Jeff Greenfield. *The Advance Man: An Offbeat Look at What Really Happens in Political Campaigns.* New York: William Morrow, 1971.

Bryant, Nick. *The Bystander: John F. Kennedy and the Struggle for Black Equality.* New York: Basic Books, 2006.

Bryant, Traphes, with Frances Spatz Leighton. *Dog Days at the White House: The Outrageous Memoirs of the Presidential Kennel Keeper.* New York: Macmillan, 1975.

Buck, Pearl S. *The Kennedy Women: A Personal Appraisal.* New York: Cowles, 1970.

Bugliosi, Vincent. *Reclaiming History: The Assassination of President John F. Kennedy.* New York: Norton, 2007.

Burleigh, Nina. *A Very Private Woman: The Life and Unsolved Murder of Presidential Mistress Mary Meyer.* New York: Bantam Books, 1998.

Burns, James MacGregor. *John Kennedy: A Political Profile.* New York: Harcourt, Brace, 1960.

Caro, Robert. *The Passage of Power: The Years of Lyndon Johnson.* New York: Knopf, 2012.

Cassini, Oleg. *In My Fashion: An Autobiography.* New York: Simon and Schuster, 1987.

Charlton, Michael, and Anthony Moncrieff. *Many Reasons Why: The American Involvement in Vietnam.* New York: Hill and Wang, 1978.

Chauncey, Jill Rachelle. *Elaine de Kooning: Negotiating the Masculinity of Abstract Expressionism.* Thesis submitted to the University of Kansas, 2006.

Claflin, Edward B. (ed.). *JFK Wants to Know: Memos from the President's Office, 1961–1963.* New York: William Morrow, 1991.

Clarke, Thurston. *Ask Not: The Inauguration of John F. Kennedy and the Speech That Changed America.* New York: Henry Holt, 2004. (Rev. ed. 2011.)

Clifford, Clark. *Counsel to the President.* New York: Random House, 1991.

Collier, Peter, and David Horowitz. *The Kennedys: An American Drama.* New York: Summit Books, 1984.

Connally, John, with Mickey Herskowitz. *In History's Shadow: An American Odyssey.* New York: Hyperion, 1993.

Connally, Nellie, and Mickey Herskowitz. *From Love Field: Our Final Hours with President John F. Kennedy.* New York: Rugged Land, 2003.

Cooper, Chester. *The Lost Crusade: America in Vietnam.* New York: Dodd, Mead, 1970.

Cooper, Gordon. *Leap of Faith: An Astronaut's Journey into the Unknown.* New York: HarperCollins, 2000.

Cousins, Norman. *The Improbable Triumvirate: An Asterisk to the History of a Hopeful Year, 1962–1963.* New York: W. W. Norton, 1972.

Cowley, Robert (ed.). *The Cold War: A Military History.* New York: Random House, 2006.

Cronkite, Walter. *A Reporter's Life.* New York: Alfred A. Knopf, 1996.

Cutler, John Henry. *Cardinal Cushing of Boston.* New York: Hawthorn Books, 1970.

Dallas, Rita, R.N., with Jeanira Ratcliffe. *The Kennedy Case: The Intimate Memoirs of the Head Nurse to Joseph P. Kennedy During the Last 8 Years of His Life.* New York: G. P. Putnam's Sons, 1973.

Dallek, Robert. *Flawed Giant: Lyndon Johnson and His Times, 1961–1973.* New York: Oxford University Press, 1998.

———. *An Unfinished Life: John F. Kennedy 1917–1963.* New York: Little, Brown, 2003.

Damore, Leo. *The Cape Cod Years of John Fitzgerald Kennedy.* New York: Four Walls Eight Windows, 1993.

Day, J. Edward. *My Appointed Rounds: 929 Days as Postmaster General.* New York: Holt, Rinehart and Winston, 1965.

Dickerson, Nancy. *Among Those Present: A Reporter's View of 25 Years in Washington.* New York: Random House, 1976.

Dobbs, Michael. *One Minute to Midnight: Kennedy, Khrushchev, and Castro on the Brink of Nuclear War.* New York: Random House, 2008.

Dobrynin, Anatoly. *In Confidence: Moscow's Ambassador to America's Six Cold War Presidents.* New York: Random House, 1995.

Donovan, Robert J. *PT 109: John F. Kennedy in World War II.* New York: McGraw-Hill, 1961.

Douglas, Kirk. *The Ragman's Son.* New York: Simon and Schuster, 1988.

Douglass, James W. *JFK and the Unspeakable: Why He Died and Why It Matters.* New York: Touchstone, 2010.

DuBois, Diana. *In Her Sister's Shadow: An Intimate Biography of Lee Radziwill.* Boston: Little, Brown, 1995.

Ellsberg, Daniel. *Secrets: A Memoir of Vietnam and the Pentagon Papers.* New York: Viking, 2002.

Evans, Peter. *Ari: The Life and Times of Aristotle Socrates Onassis.* New York: Summit Books, 1986.

Fay, Paul. *The Pleasure of His Company.* New York: Harper & Row, 1966.

Fleming, Dan B., Jr. . . . *Ask What You Can Do for Your Country: The Memory and Legacy of John F. Kennedy.* St. Petersburg, Fla.: Vandamere Press, 2002.

Fries, Chuck, and Irv Wilson, with Spencer Green. *"We'll Never Be Young Again": Remembering the Last Days of John F. Kennedy.* Los Angeles: Tallfellow Press, 2003.

Fuchs, Lawrence H. *John F. Kennedy and American Catholicism.* New York: Meredith Press, 1967.

Galbraith, John Kenneth. *A Life in Our Times: Memoirs.* Boston: Houghton Mifflin, 1981.

———. *Name-Dropping: From FDR On.* New York: Mariner Books, 2001.

Galitzine, Irene. *Dalla Russia All Russia: Memorie di Irene Galitzine racolte da Cinzia Tani.* Milan: Longanesi, 1996.

Gallagher, Mary Barelli. *My Life with Jacqueline Kennedy.* New York: David McKay, 1969.

Gentile, Thomas. *March on Washington: August 28, 1963.* Washington, D.C.: New Day Publications, 1983.

Ghaemi, Nassir. *A First-Rate Madness: Uncovering the Links Between Leadership and Mental Illness.* New York: Penguin Press, 2011.

Giglio, James. *The Presidency of John F. Kennedy.* Lawrence: University Press of Kansas.

Gillon, Steven M. *The Kennedy Assassination–24 Hours After; Lyndon B. Johnson's Pivotal First Day as President.* New York: Basic Books, 2009.

Goldstein, Gordon M. *Lessons in Disaster: McGeorge Bundy and the Path to War in Vietnam.* New York: Times Books, 2008.

Goodman, Jon (essayist). *The Kennedy Mystique: Creating Camelot.* Washington, D.C.: National Geographic, 2006.

Goodwin, Doris Kearns. *The Fitzgeralds and the Kennedys.* New York: Simon and Schuster, 1987.

Goodwin, Richard. *Remembering America: A Voice from the Sixties.* Boston: Little, Brown, 1988.

Graham, Katharine. *Personal History.* New York: Knopf, 1997.

Greenberg, Bradley S., and Edwin B. Parker. *The Kennedy Assassination and the American Public: Social Communication in Crisis.* Stanford, Calif.: Stanford University Press, 1965.

Greenberg, David. *Presidential Doodles: Two Centuries of Scribbles, Scratches, Squiggles & Scrawls from the Oval Office.* New York: Basic Books, 2006

Gromyko, Andrei. *Memoirs.* New York: Doubleday, 1990.

Guthman, Edwin O., and Jeffrey Shulman (eds.). *Robert Kennedy: In His Own Words.* New York: Bantam, 1988.

Hagood, Wesley O. *Presidential Sex: From the Founding Fathers to Bill Clinton.* Secaucus, N.J.: Citadel Press, 1995.

Halberstam, David. *The Best and the Brightest.* New York: Random House, 1969.

———. *The Making of a Quagmire: America and Vietnam During the Kennedy Era.* Rowman and Littlefield, 2007.

Hall, Lee. *Elaine & Bill: Portrait of a Marriage.* New York: HarperCollins, 1993.

Hamilton, Nigel. *JFK: Restless Youth.* New York: Random House, 1992.

Hansen, Drew D. *The Dream: Martin Luther King, Jr., and the Speech That Inspired a Nation.* New York: Ecco, 2003.

Harvey, Dodd L., and Linda C. Ciccoritti. *U.S.-Soviet Cooperation in Space.* Coral Gables, Fla.: University of Miami, Center for Advanced International Affairs, 1974.

Heller, Walter. *The New Dimensions of Political Economy.* Cambridge, Mass.: Harvard University Press, 1966.

Hellman, John. *The Kennedy Obsession: The American Myth of JFK.* New York: Columbia University Press, 1997.

Helms, Richard, with William Hood. *A Look over My Shoulder: A Life in the Central Intelligence Agency.* New York: Random House, 2003.

Henggeler, Paul R. *In His Steps: Lyndon Johnson and the Kennedy Mystique.* Chicago: Ivan R. Dee, 1991.

Hersh, Seymour M. *The Dark Side of Camelot.* New York: Little, Brown, 1997.

Hill, Clint, with Lisa McCubbin. *Mrs. Kennedy and Me.* New York: Gallery Books, 2012.

Hilsman, Robert. *To Move a Nation: The Politics of Foreign Policy in the Administration of John F. Kennedy.* Garden City, N.Y.: Doubleday, 1967.

Hilty, James W. *Robert Kennedy: Brother Protector.* Philadelphia: Temple University Press, 1997.

Hulsey, Bryon C. *Everett Dirksen and His President: How a Senate Giant Shaped American Politics.* Lawrence: University Press of Kansas, 2000.

Isserman, Maurice, and Michael Kazin. *America Divided: The Civil War of the 1960s.* New York: Oxford University Press, 2000.

Jacobs, Seth. *Cold War Mandarin: Ngo Dinh Diem and the Origins of America's War in Vietnam, 1950–1963.* Lanham, Md.: Rowman & Littlefield, 2006.

Jones, Howard. *Death of a Generation: How the Assassinations of Diem and JFK Prolonged the Vietnam War.* New York: Oxford University Press, 2003.

Katzenbach, Nicholas deB. *Some of It Was Fun: Working with RFK and LBJ.* New York: Norton, 2008.

Kazin, Alfred. *New York Jew.* New York: Knopf, 1978.

Kearns, Doris. *Lyndon Johnson & the American Dream.* New York: Harper & Row, 1976.

Kennan, George F. *Memoirs 1950–1963*, Volume II. Boston: Atlantic Monthly Press, 1983.

Kennedy, Edward M. *True Compass: A Memoir.* New York: Twelve, 2009.

———(ed.). *Words Jack Loved.* Privately published, 1976.

Kennedy, Jacqueline. *Historic Conversations on Life with John F. Kennedy.* New York: Hyperion, 2011.

Kennedy, John F. *"Let the Word Go Forth": The Speeches, Statements, and Writings of John F. Kennedy 1947–1963.* New York: Delacorte, 1988.

———. *A Nation of Immigrants.* New York: Harper & Row, 1964. (Originally published by Anti-Defamation League of B'nai B'rith.)

———. *Prelude to Leadership: The European Diary of John F. Kennedy, Summer 1945.* Washington, D.C.: Regnery, 1995.

———. *Profiles in Courage.* New York: Harper & Row, 1964 [memorial edition].

———. *The Strategy of Peace.* New York: Harper & Brothers, 1960.

Kennedy, Robert F. *Thirteen Days: A Memoir of the Cuban Missile Crisis.* New York: Norton, 1971.

Kennedy, Rose Fitzgerald. *Times to Remember.* Garden City, N.Y.: Doubleday, 1974.

Khrushchev, Nikita. *Khrushchev Remembers.* Boston: Little, Brown, 1970.

Khrushchev, Sergei N. *Nikita Khrushchev and the Creation of a Superpower.* University Park: Pennsylvania State University Press, 2001.

Klein, Edward. *All Too Human: The Love Story of Jack and Jackie Kennedy.* New York: Pocket Books, 1996.

Knebel, Fletcher, and Charles W. Bailey. *Seven Days in May.* New York: Harper & Row, 1962.

Koehler, John O. *Stasi: The Untold Story of the East German Secret Police.* New York: Westview Press, 2000.

Kraft, Joseph. *Profiles in Power: A Washington Insight.* New York: New American Library, 1966.

Langguth, A. J. *Our Vietnam: The War, 1954–1975.* New York: Simon and Schuster, 2002.

Lasky, Victor. *J.F.K.: The Man and the Myth.* New York, Macmillan, 1963.

Leamer, Laurence. *The Kennedy Men: 1901–1963.* New York: William Morrow, 2001.

Leaming, Barbara. *Mrs. Kennedy: The Missing History of the Kennedy Years.* New York: Free Press, 2001.

Lechuga, Carlos. *In the Eye of the Storm: Castro, Khrushchev, Kennedy and the Cuban Missile Crisis.* Melbourne, Australia: Ocean Press, 1995.

Lewis, John, with Michael D'Orso. *Walking with the Wind: A Memoir of the Movement.* San Diego: Harcourt Brace, 1998.

Lewis, Richard. *Appointment on the Moon: The Full Story of Americans in Space, from Explorer I to the Lunar Landing and Beyond.* New York: Viking, 1969.

Lieberson, Goddard (ed.). *John Fitzgerald Kennedy: As We Remember Him.* New York: Atheneum, 1965.

Lincoln, Evelyn. *Kennedy and Johnson.* New York: Holt, Rinehart, and Winston, 1968.

———. *My Twelve Years with John F. Kennedy.* New York: David McKay, 1965.

Lodge, Henry Cabot. *The Storm Has Many Eyes: A Personal Narrative.* New York: Norton, 1973.

Logsdon, John M. *John F. Kennedy and the Race to the Moon.* New York: Palgrave Macmillan, 2010.

Louchheim, Katie. *By the Political Sea.* Garden City, N.Y.: Doubleday, 1970.

Lowe, Jacques. *Remembering Jack: Intimate and Unseen Photographs of the Kennedys.* New York: Bullfinch Press, 2003.

———, and Wilfred Sheed. *The Kennedy Legacy: A Generation Later.* New York: VikingStudio Books, 1998.

Lubin, David M. *Shooting Kennedy: JFK and the Culture of Images.* Berkeley: University of California Press, 2003.

Mackenzie, G. Calvin, and Robert Weisbrot. *The Liberal Hour: Washington and the Politics of Change in the 1960s.* New York: Penguin Press, 2008.

MacNeil, Neil. *Dirksen: Portrait of a Public Man.* New York: World, 1970.

MacNeil, Robert (ed.). *The Way We Were: 1963, the Year Kennedy Was Shot.* New York: Carroll & Graf, 1988.

Madsen, Axel. *Gloria and Joe.* New York: Arbor House, 1988.

Mahoney, Richard. *Sons and Brothers: The Days of Jack and Bobby Kennedy.* New York: Arcade, 1999.

Maier, Thomas. *The Kennedys: America's Emerald Kings.* New York: Basic Books, 2003.

Mailer, Norman. *The Presidential Papers.* New York: Putnam's, 1963.

Manchester, William. *The Death of a President: November 20–November 25, 1963.* New York: Harper & Row, 1967.

——. *Remembering Kennedy: One Brief Shining Moment.* Boston: Little Brown, 1983.

Martin, Ralph G. *A Hero for Our Time: An Intimate Story of the Kennedy Years.* New York: Macmillan, 1983.

——. *Seeds of Destruction: Joe Kennedy and His Sons.* New York: G. P. Putnam's Sons, 1995.

Mathews, Chris. *Jack Kennedy: Elusive Hero.* New York: Simon and Schuster, 2011.

——. *Kennedy & Nixon: The Rivalry That Shaped Postwar America.* New York: Simon and Schuster, 1996.

McCarthy, Joe. *The Remarkable Kennedys.* New York: Dial Press, 1960.

McCollister, John C. *God and the Oval Office: The Religious Faith of Our 43 Presidents.* Nashville, Tenn.: W Publishing Group, 2005.

McKeever, Porter. *Adlai Stevenson: His Life and Legacy, A Biography.* New York: William Morrow, 1989.

McNamara, Robert S. *In Retrospect: The Tragedy and Lessons of Vietnam.* New York: Vintage Books, 1996.

Mecklin, John. *Mission in Torment: An Intimate Account of the U.S. Role in Vietnam.* Garden City, N.Y.: Doubleday, 1965.

Meyers, Joan Simpson. *John Fitzgerald Kennedy—As We Remember Him.* Philadelphia: Courage Books, 1965.

Michaelis, David. *The Best of Friends: Profiles of Extraordinary Friendships.* New York: William Morrow, 1983.

Miller, Merle. *Lyndon: An Oral Biography.* New York: G. P. Putnam's Sons, 1980.

Miller, William J. *Henry Cabot Lodge.* New York: James H. Heineman, 1967.

Milne, David. *America's Rasputin: Walt Rostow and the Vietnam War.* New York: Hill and Wang, 2008.

Mollenhoff, Clark M. *Despoilers of Democracy.* Garden City, N.Y.: Doubleday, 1965.

Moon, Vicky. *The Middleburg Mystique: A Peek Inside the Gates of Middleburg, Virginia.* Sterling, Va.: Capital Books, 2002.

Munro, Eleanor. *Originals: American Women Artists.* New York: Da Capo Press, 2000.

Murray, Charles, and Catherine Bly Cox. *Apollo: The Race to the Moon.* New York: Simon and Schuster, 1989.

Newman, John M. *JFK and Vietnam: Deception, Intrigue, and the Struggle for Power.* New York: Warner Books, 1992.

Oberdorfer, Dan. *Senator Mansfield: The Extraordinary Life of a Great American Statesman and Diplomat.* Washington, D.C.: Smithsonian Books, 2003.

O'Brien, Lawrence F. *No Final Victories: A Life in Politics from John F. Kennedy to Watergate.* Garden City, N.Y.: Doubleday, 1974.

O'Brien, Michael. *John F. Kennedy: A Biography.* New York: Thomas Dunne Books, St. Martin's Press, 2005.

O'Donnell, Kenneth P., and David F. Powers with Joe McCarthy. *Johnny, We Hardly Knew Ye: Memories of John Fitzgerald Kennedy.* Boston: Little, Brown, 1970.

Parini, Jay. *Robert Frost: A Life.* New York: Henry Holt, 1999.

Parmet, Herbert S. *Jack: The Struggles of John F. Kennedy.* New York: Dial Press, 1980.

———. *JFK: The Presidency of John F. Kennedy.* New York: Dial Press, 1983.

Persico, Joseph E. *Roosevelt's Secret War: FDR and World War II Espionage.* New York: Random House, 2002.

Pitts, David. *Jack and Lem: John F. Kennedy and Lem Billings—The Untold Story of an Extraordinary Friendship.* New York: Carroll & Graf, 2007.

Porter, Gareth. *Perils of Dominance: Imbalance of Power and the Road to War in Vietnam.* Berkeley: University of California Press, 2005.

Pottker, Jan. *Janet and Jackie: The Story of a Mother and Her Daughter, Jacqueline Kennedy Onassis.* New York: St. Martin's Press, 2001.

Prados, John (ed.). *The White House Tapes: Eavesdropping on the President.* New York: The New Press, 2003.

Reedy, George. *Lyndon Johnson: A Memoir.* New York: Andrews and McMeel, 1982.

Reeves, Richard. *President Kennedy: Profile of Power.* New York: Simon and Schuster, 1993.

Renehan, Edward J., Jr. *The Kennedys at War 1937–1945.* New York: Doubleday, 2002.

Reston, James, Jr. *The Lone Star: The Life of John Connally.* New York: Harper & Row, 1989

Rosenberg, Jonathan, and Zachary Karabell. *Kennedy, Johnson, and the Quest for Justice: The Civil Rights Tapes.* New York: Norton, 2003.

Rusk, Dean. *As I Saw It.* New York: Norton, 1990.

Russo, Gus, and Stephen Molton. *Brothers in Arms: The Kennedys, the Castros, and the Politics of Murder.* New York: Bloomsbury, 2008.

Rust, William J. *Kennedy in Vietnam: American Vietnam Policy, 1960–1963.* New York: Charles Scribner's Sons, 1985.

Salinger, Pierre. *With Kennedy.* Garden City, N.Y.: Doubleday, 1966.

———, and Sander Vanocur (eds.). *A Tribute to John F. Kennedy.* Chicago: Encyclopedia Britannica, 1964.

Schlesinger, Arthur M., Jr. *Journals: 1952–2000.* New York: Penguin Press, 2007.

———. *Journals: 1952–2000.* Unpublished diary entries at Schlesinger Papers, New York Public Library.

———. *Robert Kennedy and His Times.* New York: Random House, 1978.

———. *A Thousand Days: John F. Kennedy in the White House.* Boston: Houghton Mifflin, 1965.

Schoenbaum, Thomas J. *Waging War and Peace: Dean Rusk in the Truman, Kennedy and Johnson Years.* New York: Simon and Schuster, 1988.

Schwartz, Susan E. B. *Into the Unknown: The Remarkable Life of Hans Kraus.* New York: iUniverse, 2005.

Seaborg, Glenn T., with Eric Seaborg. *Adventures in the Atomic Age: From Watts to Washington.* New York: Farrar, Straus and Giroux, 2001.

———. *Kennedy, Khrushchev, and the Test Ban.* Berkeley: University of California Press, 1981.

Seamans, Robert C., Jr. *Aiming at Targets: The Autobiography of Robert C. Seamans Jr.* Washington, D.C.: NASA History Office, 1996.

Semple, Robert B., Jr. (ed.). *Four Days in November: The Original Coverage of the John F. Kennedy Assassination by the Staff of the New York Times.* New York: St. Martin's Press, 2003.

Shaw, Maud. *White House Nannie: My Years with Caroline and John Kennedy, Jr.* New York: New American Library, 1965.

Sidey, Hugh. *John F. Kennedy, President.* New York: Atheneum, 1964 (new edition).

Slivka, Rose. *Elaine de Kooning: The Spirit of Abstract Expressionism, Selected Writings.* New York: George Braziller, 1994.

Smith, Amanda (ed.). *Hostage to Fortune: The Letters of Joseph P. Kennedy.* New York: Viking, 2001.

Smith, Merriman. *Merriman Smith's Book of Presidents: A White House Memoir*. New York: W. W. Norton, 1972.

Smith, Sally Bedell. *Grace and Power: The Private World of the Kennedy White House*. New York: Random House, 2004.

Sorensen, Ted. *Counselor: A Life at the Edge of History*. New York: Harper, 2008.

———. *Kennedy*. New York: Harper and Row, 1965.

———. *The Kennedy Legacy*. New York: Macmillan, 1969.

Stein, Jean. *American Journey: The Times of Robert Kennedy*. New York: Harcourt Brace Jovanovich, 1970.

Steinberg, Neil. *Hatless Jack: The President, the Fedora, and the History of an American Style*. New York: Plume, 2004.

Storm, Tempest, with Bill Boyd. *The Lady Is a Vamp*. Atlanta: Peachtree Publishers, 1987.

Stoughton, Cecil, and Chester V. Clifton, narrated by Hugh Sidey. *The Memories: JFK, 1961–1963*. New York: Norton, 1973.

Strober, Gerald S., and Deborah H. Strober. *"Let Us Begin Anew": An Oral History of the Kennedy Residency*. New York: HarperCollins, 1993.

Talbot, David. *Brothers: The Hidden History of the Kennedy Years*. New York: Free Press, 2007.

Taraborelli, Randy. *Jackie Ethel Joan: Women of Camelot*. New York: Warner Books, 2000.

Taubman, William. *Khrushchev: The Man and His Era*. New York: Norton, 2003.

Taylor, General Maxwell D. *Swords and Plowshares: A Memoir*. New York: Norton, 1972.

Thayer, Mary Van Rensselaer. *Jacqueline Kennedy: The White House Years*. Boston: Little, Brown, 1967.

Thomas, Evan. *Robert Kennedy: His Life*. New York: Simon and Schuster, 2000.

Thomas, Helen. *Dateline: White House*. New York: Macmillan, 1975.

Thompson, Kenneth (ed.). *The Johnson Presidency: Twenty Intimate Perspectives of John F. Kennedy*. Lanham, Md.: University Press of America, 1986.

———. *The Kennedy Presidency: Seventeen Intimate Perspectives of John F. Kennedy*. Lanham, Md.: University Press of America, 1985.

Topping, Seymour. *On the Front Lines of the Cold War: An American Correspondent's Journal from the Chinese Civil War to the Cuban Missile Crisis and Vietnam*. Baton Rouge: Louisiana State University Press, 2010.

Trask, Richard B. *That Day in Dallas: Three Photographers Capture on Film the Day President Kennedy Died*. Danvers, Mass.: Yeoman Press, 1998.

Travell, Janet. *Office Hours: Day and Night—The Autobiography of Janet Travell, M.D.* New York: New American Library, 1968.

Troy, Tevi. *Intellectuals and the American Presidency: Philosophers, Jesters, or Technicians?* Lanham, Md.: Rowman and Littlefield, 2002.

Van Buren, Abigail. *Where Were You When President Kennedy Was Shot? Memories and Tributes to a Slain President as Told to Dear Abby*. Kansas City: Andrews and McMeel, 1993.

Van Natta, Don, Jr. *First off the Tee: Presidential Hackers, Duffers, and Cheaters from Taft to Bush*. New York: Public Affairs, 2003.

Von Post, Gunilla. *Love, Jack*. New York: Crown, 1997.

Warren Commission. *The Official Report of the President's Commission on the Assassination of President John F. Kennedy*. Stamford, Conn.: Longmeadow Press, 1993.

Weiner, Tim. *Legacy of Ashes: The History of the CIA*. New York: Doubleday, 2007.

Weintel, Edward, and Charles Bartlett. *Facing the Brink: An Intimate Study of Crisis Diplomacy*. New York: Charles Scribner's Sons, 1967.

West, J. B. *Upstairs at the White House: My Life with the First Ladies*. New York: Coward, McCann, & Geoghegan, 1973.

White, Jon Manchip. *Marshal of France: The Life and Times of Maurice de Saxe [1696–1750]*. Chicago: Rand McNally, 1962.

White, Lee. *Government for the People: Reflections of a White House Counsel to Presidents Kennedy and Johnson*. Lanham, Md.: Hamilton Books, 2008.

White, Mark J. (ed.). *Kennedy: The New Frontier Revisited*. New York: NYU Press, 1998.

White, Theodore H. *In Search of History: A Personal Adventure*. New York: Harper & Row, 1978.

———. *The Making of the President 1964*. New York: Atheneum, 1965.

Wicker, Tom. *JFK and LBJ: The Influence of Personality Upon Politics*. Chicago: Ivan R. Dee, 1991.

Wilkins, Roy. *Standing Fast: The Autobiography of Roy Wilkins*. New York: Viking, 1982

Wofford, Harris. *Of Kennedys and Kings: Making Sense of the Sixties*. New York: Farrar, Straus and Giroux, 1980.

Woods, Randall Bennett. *Fulbright: A Biography*. Cambridge, U.K.: Cambridge University Press, 1995.

———. *LBJ: Architect of American Ambition*. New York: Free Press, 2006.

Wright, Lawrence. *In the New World: Growing Up with America, 1960–1984*. New York: Knopf, 1988.

Zelikow, Philip, and Ernest May (eds.). *The Kennedy Tapes: Inside the White House During the Cuban Missile Crisis*. New York: Norton, 2001.

INDEX

ALLEN LANE
an imprint of
PENGUIN BOOKS

Recently Published

Justin Marozzi, *Baghdad: City of Peace, City of Blood*

Adam Tooze, *The Deluge: The Great War and the Remaking of Global Order 1916-1931*

John Micklethwait and Adrian Wooldridge, *The Fourth Revolution: The Global Race to Reinvent the State*

Steven D. Levitt and Stephen J. Dubner, *Think Like a Freak: How to Solve Problems, Win Fights and Be a Slightly Better Person*

Alexander Monro, *The Paper Trail: An Unexpected History of the World's Greatest Invention*

Jacob Soll, *The Reckoning: Financial Accountability and the Making and Breaking of Nations*

Gerd Gigerenzer, *Risk Savvy: How to Make Good Decisions*

James Lovelock, *A Rough Ride to the Future*

Michael Lewis, *Flash Boys*

Hans Ulrich Obrist, *Ways of Curating*

Mai Jia, *Decoded: A Novel*

Richard Mabey, *Dreams of the Good Life: The Life of Flora Thompson and the Creation of* Lark Rise to Candleford

Danny Dorling, *All That Is Solid: The Great Housing Disaster*

Leonard Susskind and Art Friedman, *Quantum Mechanics: The Theoretical Minimum*

Michio Kaku, *The Future of the Mind: The Scientific Quest to Understand, Enhance and Empower the Mind*

Nicholas Epley, *Mindwise: How we Understand what others Think, Believe, Feel and Want*

Geoff Dyer, *Contest of the Century: The New Era of Competition with China*

Yaron Matras, *I Met Lucky People: The Story of the Romani Gypsies*

Larry Siedentop, *Inventing the Individual: The Origins of Western Liberalism*

Dick Swaab, *We Are Our Brains: A Neurobiography of the Brain, from the Womb to Alzheimer's*

Max Tegmark, *Our Mathematical Universe: My Quest for the Ultimate Nature of Reality*

David Pilling, *Bending Adversity: Japan and the Art of Survival*

Hooman Majd, *The Ministry of Guidance Invites You to Not Stay: An American Family in Iran*

Roger Knight, *Britain Against Napoleon: The Organisation of Victory, 1793-1815*

Alan Greenspan, *The Map and the Territory: Risk, Human Nature and the Future of Forecasting*

Daniel Lieberman, *Story of the Human Body: Evolution, Health and Disease*

Malcolm Gladwell, *David and Goliath: Underdogs, Misfits and the Art of Battling Giants*

Paul Collier, *Exodus: Immigration and Multiculturalism in the 21st Century*

John Eliot Gardiner, *Music in the Castle of Heaven: Immigration and Multiculturalism in the 21st Century*

Catherine Merridale, *Red Fortress: The Secret Heart of Russia's History*

Ramachandra Guha, *Gandhi Before India*

Vic Gatrell, *The First Bohemians: Life and Art in London's Golden Age*

Richard Overy, *The Bombing War: Europe 1939-1945*